FESS PARKER:

TV'S FRONTIER HERO

BY WILLIAM R. CHEMERKA

Fess Parker: TV's Frontier Hero

Published in the USA by:

BearManor Media
P.O. Box 71426
Albany, Georgia 31708
www.BearManorMedia.com

ISBN-13: 978-1-59393-655-6 (alk. paper)

Book design and layout by Valerie Thompson.

TABLE OF CONTENTS

Dedication

To Lenny Hekel, my best friend in childhood, who played George Russel to my Davy Crockett many years ago.

ACKNOWLEDGMENTS

Many individuals made important contributions to this book. Thanks to my wife, Deborah Chemerka; Lenny Hekel; Dr. Bruce Winders, the Alamo's Historian and Curator; Tony "Skip" Malanowski; Sally Baker, Site Director of the Crockett Tavern Museum; Texas-Bob Reinhardt; Paul DeVito; Dr. Murray Weissmann; Mike Boldt; Pastor Rodriguez; Joseph Musso; Tom Beck; Ken Blankenship, Director of the Cherokee Museum; Mary Adamic and Maxine Hof at Disney Publishing Worldwide; the Hal Leonard Corporation; Trinh Dang, Associate Manager Clip Licensing, Twentieth Century Fox Television; Robert Foster; Gary Foreman; Tom Robbins of the National Park Service; Clavin Fisher; Wendy Fisher; Ray Herbeck, Jr.; The Alamo Society [www.alamosociety.org]; Mark Monica; Karen Dusik; Bev Friberg Cameron; Gert Petersen; Howard Bender; Inahlee Bauer; John Bourdage; McKee Andrus, Administrative Assistant, Registrars Office, the University of Texas at Austin; Donnie Adams; Alan Jerome Greenwood; the Bunny Platoon [www.bunnyplatoon.com]; William Groneman III; David Zucker; Robert Weil; John Farkis; Cynthia Levine; John Shearer; Karen Brown, Library Assistant, Local History Department, Chattanooga-Hamilton County Bicentennial Library; Gene and Regina Vincente; Don Vicaro; Lou Mongello; Ron Barzo; Tony Woolway, Chief Librarian of Media Wales; Dan Markovich; Judy Southwell; Anne English; John English; Mike Makras; the Daughters of the Republic of Texas Library; Sid Holmes, Director of the West Texas Music Hall of Fame;

John Bargiel; Valarie Pinter; and Phil Collins, who generously wrote this book's Introduction.

Particular help was offered by a number of talented performing artists and close friends of Fess Parker's. Thanks to Ed Ames, Jeanne Ames, Veronica Cartwright, Carol Toso, Darby Hinton, Cheryl Ladd, Robert Loggia, Audrey Loggia, Nolie Fishman, Lynda Ellenshaw Thompson, Harrison Ellenshaw, and Ron Ely, who was kind enough to write this book's Foreword.

Thanks also to Fess Parker's Texas friends who are among the most generous people I have ever met. They provided hours of detailed recollections and anecdotes which I could never have included in this book without their help. As such, a ten-gallon-hat salute to Phil Kendrick, Morgan Woodward, Jimmy Tittle, Bob Milstead, Harwell Barber, Dr. William E. King, Imogene Mensel Collins, Doris Bohannon Grosvenor, Carolyn Wright, Brad Thompson, and food entrepreneurs Tom and Lisa Perini of the Perini Ranch Steakhouse in Buffalo Gap, Texas.

Special thanks also to Art Henzell and Bob Andrews of Mullen & Henzell L.L.P., Bill Osterbauer, Richard E. Fogg, Dave Davis, Jed Steele, Dale Hampton, Dr. Donald Rhodes, Bill Powell, Max Evans, Mark Streeter of the *Savannah Morning News*, and *Daniel Boone* producer Barney Rosenzweig.

Leslie A. Wilson of Fess Parker Enterprises, who served as Fess' executive assistant, went to extraordinary lengths to provide me with important documents, photographs, and contact information. Her efforts are greatly appreciated. Thanks also to Sao Anash of Muse Management and Tara-Mae Ross, the Fess Parker Winery's Merchandising Manager.

Of course, Fess Parker's family played an essential role in this book. Marcy Parker, Eli Parker, Ashley Parker Snider, Kristopher Parker, and Tim Snider made invaluable contributions. They provided their full support to this volume and shared precious family moments that I was privileged to hear. I am indebted to them for so many things.

An above-and-beyond-the-call-of-duty salute goes to Charles S. Bargiel, Fess Parker's good friend and attorney. Chuck was instrumental to so many important parts of this book, especially those dealing with contracts, negotiations, legal proceedings, and real estate transactions. He also organized interview sessions with a number of people who are featured in this book. And Chuck's horse-trading skills are Parkeresque, to say the least. Thanks, CB!

And thanks to Ben Ohmart, Sandra Grabman, Valerie Thompson, Sarah DeSimone and the rest of the staff at BearManor Media for their support and guidance.

Of course, the words of Fess Parker were indispensable to this humble volume. My personal tape-recorded interviews and written notes with the "King of the Wild Frontier," which were compiled since my first meeting with him in 1987, were fundamental to the pages that follow. Besides our numerous phone calls, letters, and e-mails over the years, we crossed paths in California, Texas, New York, and Washington D.C. and on most occasions Fess Parker Wines were on hand. Thank you, Fess. Thanks for everything.

FOREWORD
BY RON ELY

At Fess' eightieth birthday party, a friend stood to give a toast in which he recited all the labels that applied to Fess. I borrow from Charles Bargiel here as he stated, "Fess is a father, husband, friend, businessman, actor, athlete, entrepreneur, son, winemaker, hotelier, singer, neighbor, benefactor, patriot, veteran, Texan," and on and on, giving voice to a list that seemed never ending. The audience that night was comprised of friends from the entire continuum of Fess' life. Charles Bargiel, himself, is one of those friends collected by Fess from his Santa Barbara days. In fact, he was the lawyer from a small local Santa Barbara firm that Fess chose to lead his fight against the powerful Twentieth Century Fox legal team in his lawsuit against them. This fact was a source of great pride to Fess in that he and his "small town lawyer" took the fight to the giant corporation. It was a fight that Fess and Chuck Bargiel won. Just to set the record straight here, Charles Bargiel may practice in Santa Barbara, but he can stand toe to toe with any big city legal force brought against him.

On that festive night we were all assembled in a huge tent erected for the occasion. It was impossible to be there and not feel some history around you—human history with a hundred different stories defining a friendship with a man that somehow linked us all together. I knew most of those people myself and from one end of the tent to the other I could name them and recall their relationship with Fess. It was an eclectic collection of childhood friends, college buddies, Navy pals, colleagues from the film or business world, and neighbors from Santa Barbara, Santa Ynez, and Los Angeles. I knew their stories with Fess and they knew mine. Fess liked to share his friendships and in so doing, he made them all stronger. That would be a good lesson for anyone to learn.

You will meet many of Fess' friends here in the pages of William Chemerka's fine account of Fess' life. What a life it was too, spanning more than eight decades, from the Great Depression to the great prosperity. Fess began his life in a small Texas town in Comanche County. That was one of many things we had in common as my family background traces back to that same county. Although we never investigated the possibility, we both felt there might be some ancestral connection between us. Both the Parkers and my grandparent's family moved on to other towns, eventually settling many miles apart but still within the boundaries of that great state. That was another thing we shared: a deep love and devotion to our home state of Texas.

We also shared the same values, dreams, and basic ambitions. As words like honor, courage, integrity, and courtesy seemed to lose their meaning in a society quickly losing its core, it was always nice to sit for a while with Fess and speak the same language. It would be almost impossible to summarize Fess in a few words, but perhaps it would suffice to say that he was a man of the West who was sentient to an earlier day.

Les Brown Jr. and his orchestra played at that birthday party, as he had done for Fess and his wife, Marcy, at other events. I am thinking especially of the reception for their daughter, Ashley, upon her marriage to Rodney Shull. Their events were always memorable, and of course, there was much about that reception to put into a memory box. I remember dancing with my pre-teen daughter that night, with Robert Mitchum pretending to cut in, much to my daughter's delight. As examples go, that one does a fair job of depicting the tone of casual formality that graced all their parties.

So it was with the eightieth birthday party. Oddly enough, I do not remember if I gave a toast that night or not. My guess would be that I did. I do, however, remember some of the others, in addition to Charles Bargiel, who got to their feet to speak or sing or in some cases do both. What was most remarkable to me on that evening was the commingling of recent and lifelong friendships at every table in that tent. It might have been on that night that I realized what made Fess so different from every other person I had ever known.

The one word that Charles Bargiel used, tucked in among all the others in describing Fess, that leapt out at me that night, was the word, "friend." There he was, on his eightieth birthday, surrounded by people from all walks of life who considered themselves, each and everyone, to be a friend of Fess Parker's.

It was easy to see how that could happen. He was very approachable. His demeanor was friendly and unthreatening. He was also a fan of other people who achieved greatly. He was without guile or pretense. His manner was humble and even with his size he was unimposing. He spoke in a slow, measured rhythm that was pure Texas. He never tried to be anything else or speak in a manner that was not bred into him.

Although he had developed some sophistication in the world of food and wine, his pleasures were simple ones. His successes were gained with grit and determination, and often in spite of the road-blocks others put before him. He did not flaunt his achievements in any visible way. He also did not harbor resentment for those who had opposed him, although he was very aware of their identities. He preferred low-mileage used cars to new cars, and his automobile of choice was a Mercedes. All of which we discussed over countless meals and cups of coffee over the years.

Fess was a proud man. He had a right to be. He had a history of great success that was not limited to business or career. He and Marcy had a marriage that spanned more than five decades. He had two children, Eli and Ashley, who had become successful adults, themselves raising children that were all moving in the right direction. He had grandchildren, a great-grandchild and Godchildren to whom he was always attentive and mindful. He had an array of accomplishments that were as diverse as his friendships. He could sing and play a guitar just as easily as he could saddle and ride a horse. He loved words and reading, and was intent on learning everything he could about everything right up until his final days. He sought to engage people at their core, at that place that was most comfortable for them and in that way learn about them. He could discuss historical events as easily as he could speak of current affairs. His mind was always alive and ready to hear an interesting story.

Fess was not a big laugher. He was a smiler. I do not believe I ever heard a guffaw or a belly laugh out of Fess in all the years I knew him. He was more a chuckler, or chortler when he was greatly amused. That is not to say he did not have a sense of humor. He did. He loved to hear funny stories and he loved to tell them as well. I believe that Fess made a conscious choice at some early stage in his life to keep a lid on all his reactive emotions. He did not express his anger outwardly. In fact, I am sure that most people who knew him would say that they never saw him angry. I have seen him go through some things that would have had others raging to the heavens, but that was not Fess' way. He managed tough situations with great calm and reasonableness, and as a result usually achieved satisfactory solutions.

I saw him on the last afternoon of his life. My three children, his Godchildren, and my wife, Valerie, and I sat with him and Marcy for two hours or more simply talking and telling meaningless stories. His eyes were bright and alert and there were glimpses of the same Fess that would meet me for lunch and a beer at the Dutch Gardens or the Red Barn or the coffee shop at his hotel. It really did not matter where, but those were times when we would share some of our deeper thoughts with each other, knowing that they would never be spoken to another soul. As we left on that last afternoon we all shook his hand, said we loved him, and kept our emotions intact until we could get to the car and out of view. The last to shake his hand was my son, Cameron, who shared a special bond with Fess. I watched from the door as Fess held Cameron's hand for a prolonged moment as if he were trying to convey something to him—to impart something that was beyond words.

There is so much to be learned from Fess' life and the way he lived it. I am thankful to Bill Chemerka for compiling this history of my friend and brother. It is comforting to have these pages to remind me of so many of the tiny facets of what was such a huge presence in my life. I will miss Fess—do miss Fess—more than I ever imagined. There is no question his passing has left a void in my life just as it has in the lives of his family and other close friends. These pages might help those who did not know him to understand the great loss to those of us who did.

RON ELY

INTRODUCTION
BY PHIL COLLINS

To try to put into words the effect Fess Parker had on me and my life is impossible really. He somehow ignited a passion in me that lives on to this day: my life long fascination with the Alamo, its heroes and stories.

Like many other boys in the 1950s, his portrayal of Davy Crockett gave us the inspiration to *be* Davy Crockett. While other kids played football, we were putting on our coonskin hats and rifles, and getting ready to take on a bear or an Indian brave—to say nothing of his very cool fringed jacket and trousers.

Throughout the years of meeting fellow Alamo enthusiasts and historians, nearly all of them cite him and the Walt Disney series in the 50s as pivotal to their love of Texas history.

My youngest child, Mathew, is six years old, and is totally smitten with the film, just as I was. It's incredible that this American story—with all its tall tales—can bridge an ocean and somehow bond so many people.

Of course, I didn't realize way back then at my young age that other kids knew about this Davy Crockett guy. I thought this secret was all mine. As the years rolled by I learned that presents at Christmas that year consisted of 75 percent Davy Crockett items. That's a lot of coonskin hats.

Of course, when I refer to Davy Crockett I'm really referring to Fess Parker—they was the same person. His velvet voice worked perfectly for the part, and maybe worked against him getting other roles. He was so identified with that character. Even if that frustrated him as an actor, it must have warmed his heart to see the affection from so many people over the years that had grown up with him in that role.

The two films made from the weekly series by Walt Disney—*Davy Crockett, King of the Wild Frontier* and *Davy Crockett and the River Pirates*—were made in an age of innocence now long gone. That's why I'm so pleased that my son can watch them time and time again and still get the same amount of pleasure from them. They still have that magic.

Bill Chemerka has done a splendid job tracing the life of Fess Parker with lively anecdotes and warm memories.

God bless Fess Parker; he symbolized an era for kids like me all over the world.

PHIL COLLINS

AUTHOR'S INTRODUCTION

WEDNESDAY. DECEMBER 15, 1954
SEVEN-THIRTY P.M.
ABC-TV'S *DISNEYLAND*

The program opened with its familiar Tinker Bell tour of Disneyland's four themed lands: Fantasyland, Tomorrowland, Adventureland, and Frontierland.

Walt Disney appeared on the screen and proclaimed: "Characteristic of American folklore that most of our favorite legends and fables are based on the lives of real men—like Davy Crockett of Tennessee." Then lively illustrations depicting moments in Crockett's life followed—augmented with a few key lyrical lines from a song that would eventually be called "The Ballad of Davy Crockett." And then Disney appeared again, holding a rustic-looking journal. He said, "And now, from Davy's own journal, the first of three stories: The Indian War."

Fess Parker's *Davy Crockett* character was about to enter the homes and the public consciousness of the country; as a matter of fact, the lives of millions of kids around the world were about to change. And for some, like this writer, the change would be forever.

The first episode of the trilogy, "Davy Crockett: Indian Fighter," wasn't a complete surprise. Fess Parker had been introduced to TV audiences in a short segment on *Disneyland's* debut program on October 27. Dressed as the famous Tennessee pioneer, he sang some verses from "The Ballad of Davy Crockett" as Director Norman Foster and a film crew looked on. But that program was merely a teaser of what was to come. The complete episode, "Davy Crockett, Indian Fighter," had finally arrived—in glorious black and white.

The episode began with an illustration of a young frontier boy, and then a song began, a song that would soon pervade backyards, elementary school playgrounds, and radio station playlists: "Born on mountain top in Tennessee/Greenest state in the land of the free…." At the conclusion of the brief animated introduction, the production shifted to live action as the camera depicted three men on horseback riding up to a rustic frontier cabin. One was playing a guitar and singing. Viewers soon learned the mounted musician's name: George Russel. The character, played by veteran performer Buddy Ebsen, playfully scolded Davy Crockett to get his "britches out here." Out from the cabin's doorway walked Fess Parker as *Davy Crockett.* Popular culture was about to experience an historic phenomenon that even Walt Disney never anticipated. And there was something very unique about what Crockett wore on his head: a coonskin cap.

That was then.

Thirty-three years later, I met Fess Parker for the first time. He had flown to San Antonio, Texas from his home in California to attend a meeting of the Alamo Foundation, an organization that was attempting to improve the Alamo experience for those visiting the famous Shrine of Texas Liberty. A friend, Gary Foreman, who was assisting the group, invited me along for the ride to the airport to pick up Fess. I had met Gary the year before in San Antonio during the Texas Sesquicentennial's Alamo re-enactment ceremony on Alamo Plaza. As grown men we were still playing Davy Crockett at the Alamo. Now it was time to *meet* Davy Crockett.

Fess came strolling into the luggage claim area. I expected him to be wearing buckskins and, of course, a coonskin cap; however, he was wearing jeans, a light blue seersucker sports jacket, and carrying a tennis racket. It was a mild culture shock. After all, where was his iconic headgear? And where was his trusty rifle, "Old Betsy?" Fortunately, he was wearing cowboy boots, a kind of acknowledgement to his roots. After all, Fess was a native Texan. The boots, though, made him even taller than his 6'5"—some say 6'6"—frame. I stood 6' 2," but he still towered over me in so many ways.

During the weekend, Fess found time for me to conduct an interview with him. I planned to publish it in *The Alamo Journal*, the official publication of the Alamo Society. We sat down in his top-floor suite at the Emily Morgan Hotel and I promptly started to ask him questions about his most famous portrayal on screen. I quickly discovered he was much like his *Davy Crockett* character: confident, unflustered, soft-spoken, rugged, and witty. Above all, he was friendly. And there was a quality of humility about him that generated trust and respect. It didn't take long to realize that my childhood hero was a man of integrity, charm, grace, and strength.

Obviously, during the previous thirty years he had been asked many of the same questions about Davy Crockett that I posed to him, but he answered them as if they had never been asked before. Interestingly enough, he was more interested in me than my questions. But that was the manner in which he interacted with everyone; it was simply the way he was brought up. If people were going to invest their time with him, he wanted to make sure that the investment returned dividends. He gave me so much information that I realized I couldn't include the entire interview in a single issue of *The Alamo Journal*; I had to do it in two. "The Fess Parker Interview, Part One" appeared in issue #57 of *The Alamo Journal* in September 1987. "Part Two" followed in the November issue.

I informed Fess that Walt Disney's *Davy Crockett* inspired me as a youngster; in fact, history became my favorite subject in junior and senior high school. Years later Uncle Sam linked me with a Crockett-like figure. As fate would have it, my basic training unit, the Third Training Regiment at Fort Dix in 1966, was named "The Pioneers," and featured a man wearing a coonskin cap in its logo. I later become a history major in college and after graduation became a high school history teacher. I particularly enjoyed teaching about frontier America and regularly showed selections from *Davy Crockett, King of the Wild Frontier*—in 16mm film, videocassette and DVD formats—in my U.S. History I classes nearly every year. Fess seemed very interested in my teaching career, which had just marked its 15th year (an additional fifteen years would follow). Little did I imagine that one day Fess would acknowledge my classroom efforts in a few memorable ways.

Midway through the interview, he gave me the phone number of Tom Blackburn, the talented man who wrote the *Davy Crockett* screenplay and the lyrics to "The Ballad of Davy Crockett." He thought that Blackburn could provide additional details that he failed to mention. At the end of the interview, he gave me his business card and wrote an extra phone number on it in case I needed to ask some follow-up questions. I kept asking him questions for the next twenty-three years. And over that time, Fess Parker became a friend.

Excerpts from my periodic in-person and phone conversations with Fess were printed regularly in *The Alamo Journal* until 2003, when I started a new quarterly: *The Crockett Chronicle*, which was dedicated to the life and legend of David Crockett. Each issue featured a "Talkin' With Fess" interview section. He answered questions from me and fellow readers about seemingly everything anyone would ever want to know about *Davy Crockett, King of the Wild Frontier.* Occasionally, he commented about the winery he started in Los Olivos, California in 1989. Twenty-five years after the Crockett Craze, Fess had become the "King of the Wine Frontier."

I continued publishing the "Talkin' With Fess" column until Fess' death in 2010.

However, there was much that I never published. I thought that one day it might make an interesting read for those who still maintained fond recollections of toy flintlocks, coonskin caps, and TV's most memorable frontier hero.

I had offered to write Fess' biography for him years ago but he told me that he wasn't particularly interested. He just didn't think himself worthy of a book exclusively dedicated to him. His humility was noteworthy. But I kept on reminding him every few years. I even suggested that I would be happy to assist him in writing his own life story. "Thank you for the reminder in regard to my autobiography," he wrote on February 26, 1998. "Although your offer is very generous, I have concluded that I am not prepared to do one at this time. I do believe I've got another twenty years to think about it!"

Later, I later asked him if I could lead an effort to have him represented with a star on the Hollywood Walk of Fame. He said that he wasn't interested in that either. "I don't like the idea of people walking over me all day long," he said with a chuckle. That was Fess.

Of course, Fess spent most of his professional coonskin cap-wearing years as the title character in *Daniel Boone*, the NBC-TV series that ran from 1964–1970. He also made numerous appearances as other characters in various television productions and motion pictures. His entertainment career was unique and so was his life away from the cameras.

This humble volume not only traces a special man's life but includes behind-the-scenes looks at the making of Walt Disney's *Davy Crockett* and the *Daniel Boone* TV series, an examination of the Davy Crockett Craze and "The Ballad of Davy Crockett," and an exploration of some relatively unknown Fess Parker projects.

I hope you enjoy this journey down memory lane, but be forewarned: it's a dangerous path filled with bears, Creek warriors, rough-neck frontiersmen, aggressive politicians, Santa Anna's soldiers, and government bureaucrats.

No need to worry, though. *Fess Parker, TV's Frontier Hero* is close by.

WILLIAM R. CHEMERKA
JUNE 2011

CHAPTER I
GROWING UP IN TEXAS

Fort Worth, Texas literally began as a fort in 1849. But it quickly developed into a town when it became a stop along the famous Chisholm Trail, the historic cattle-drive route. However, the negative impact of the Civil War, Reconstruction, and the Depression of 1873 was so great that citizens abandoned Fort Worth by the droves. Fewer than 7,000 people resided in the community in 1880, but when the Texas & Pacific Railway passed through the town it began another economic revival. By the turn of the twentieth century over 25,000 resided in Fort Worth. Years later, Fess E. Parker (born October 15, 1900) and his wife, Ricksy (born April 23, 1898), became part of the Fort Worth community. Their only child was born in Fort Worth, Texas on August 16, 1924.

"My father and mother had both graduated from a junior college called Meridian and they both taught school in different places," explained Fess. "They got married and my dad got a job in the bank in Fort Worth. My mother took care of the domestic side. And then I was born. Three months later, we moved to San Angelo, Texas, where my dad took a job as an accountant in a wholesale grocery organization."

San Angelo, like Fort Worth, began as a frontier outpost in 1867, and developed steadily over the years. Its population reached 10,000 residents by 1910. San Angelo was a relatively small urban area—Dallas and San Antonio's populations, for example, both topped 90,000 at the time—but Fess considered it a "city." In San Angelo, Fess' father worked in such diverse private and public sector jobs as bookkeeper, salesman, animal-feed store operator, hotel clerk, local tax assessor, and county supervisor, among other jobs. His mother,

Ricksy McKnight McFarland—who was better known as Mackie—continued to be a homemaker.

Fess was actually born as F. E. Parker, Junior.

"My father went as F. E. Parker," said Fess, who acknowledged that as a youngster no one called him by his real name. "Growing up, my grandparents called me June Bug or Bug; my friends called me Parkie or Junior. When I got to high school I said, 'What is my name?' And my dad said, 'F period, E period, junior.' I said 'No!' I'm going to use Fess."

Fess believed that his father had been named after a member of Congress.

"My grandmother told me that she admired Senator Simeon Fess from Illinois," he explained. "So she named her son, my father, after him." However, Simeon Fess didn't become a U.S. Senator until 1923, a year before Fess was born. The Ohio Republican had served earlier in the U.S. House of Representatives from 1913 to 1923, and had been President of Antioch College from 1907 to 1917. So it is doubtful that the senator's name was a household word in the Parker family in time to influence the naming of Fess' father. Nevertheless, the Simeon Fess connection became part of Parker Family lore.

Fess wasn't satisfied with only a first and last name. He wanted a complete identity, one with a middle name, so he searched a book of names for something appropriate for the letter E.

"I found Elisha," said Fess. "Fess Elisha Parker. That's rhythmic! I used it for the first time in high school."

The Parkers lived in single-story wood-frame house located on a San Angelo sub-division street corner. "It was at 2314 Dallas," noted Fess. "They bought it. I think it cost $2,700. It was a little two-bedroom house: living room, dining room and kitchen."

With a gas stove, a washing machine and an ice-box, Mackie Parker kept the Parker home running. "The ice man brought forty or fifty pounds of ice at a time," said Fess. "I'd have cereal for breakfast during the school week and maybe bacon and eggs on the weekend."

The Parker's washing machine had a family connection.

"It was a Maytag washing machine because my uncle sold them," explained Fess. "My uncle, William J. Zickler, was my mother's sister's husband."

Fess recalled that his mother hung the clothes and bed linens on rope lines in the backyard near the detached two-car garage which featured a room where an African-American maid resided for several years. When unadorned, the clotheslines caused many a spill when Fess and his neighborhood friends got tangled up in them as they played.

Fess spent his elementary years at the Stephen F. Austin grade school in San Angelo which was located several hundred yards away from his house. He walked to school carrying his books and his lunch. His mother usually prepared a peanut butter sandwich which she placed a brown paper bag. It wasn't much of a noon-time meal but Fess never complained.

The school's student body numbered about 125 students. "Grades one to five," stated Fess, who enjoyed reading adventure books, pulp westerns, assorted dime novels, and *Texas History Movies*, a cartoon history of the Lone Star State. "I thought I read better than most."

But his behavior wasn't better than most.

"I was always getting into trouble, mostly for talking," admitted Fess. "One punishment was with a paddle, the other one was to take a gallon bucket and pick up the rocks on the school grounds. I would be assigned three buckets or six buckets depending on the infraction."

A second round of discipline awaited him at home.

"I'd get it at home," chuckled Fess. "If I got a paddling at school my dad assumed another one wouldn't hurt. He used a belt. He was pretty good at it."

Fess expected appropriate punishment after one particular dangerous adventure with his father's car.

"It was on a Sunday afternoon and nothing was going on so I was sitting around and fooling with the car seeing if I could make it go," declared Fess. "I remember going out when I was about six years old, and I got in it and stood on the starter and I drove it around the block. So I took a little trip." However, no one noticed that he and the car were missing during the short joyride. Fess escaped punishment.

On most Sundays, Fess attended the local Methodist Church with his parents or grandparents. He attended the church's Sunday

A young Fess Parker in Texas.
Photo courtesy of the Parker Family.

school and later joined the rest of his family for the regular service. But he confessed that Sunday services weren't particularly enjoyable.

"Ah, the main service—of which I thought would go on forever," said Fess. "Oh, man, I'd get so hungry."

At Sunday school, Fess recalled kissing his first girl.

"Coming out of Sunday school, I kissed a girl—can't remember her name right now," said Fess, who was around eight or nine years old at the time. "We had just finished the class and were walking down the hall and emotions got the best of me, and I gave her a little peck on the cheek."

He remembered three other female elementary-school classmates.

"There were several attractive little girls in my class: Evelyn Tyler, Helen Marie Wooford, and Bonnie Lou Zickler," remarked Fess.

After school, Fess played with friends, especially his best friend, Archie Joe Thurmond. "He was just a nice kid and I enjoyed his company," said Fess. "I guess he enjoyed mine. We were close friends for a long time." Fess was also good friends with his next-door neighbors, Dale and Ralph Chase. When his friends weren't around Fess enjoyed playing as if he were a frontier hunter stalking wild game. Since he and father never went hunting, his backyard expeditions were the creations of his imagination. He acknowledged that as an only child it was easy for him to assume the role of an independent backwoodsman. But he admitted that he stayed close to home when he played by himself. "I played mostly in trees and down in the sand."

On some weekends he went fishing with his father in nearby rivers and local lakes. "He liked to fish but I didn't like it," remarked Fess. "We always stayed too long. I got thirsty."

He also spent some of his free time as a member of the Cub Scouts.

"I thought the uniform was neat," said Fess, who later joined the Boy Scouts but eventually dropped out. "I got stymied at the First Class level."

When the school year ended, young Fess spent summers at his grandparents' farms. His maternal grandmother, Molly Bostick Allen, and his grandfather, W. J. Allen, had a ranch in Erath County, Texas; his paternal grandmother, Corabelle Lightfoot Parker, and his grandfather, Otis Lycurgus Parker, who was born in Arkansas, had a ranch in Comanche County, south of DeLeon, Texas. Interestingly, the DeLeon City Cemetery was the final resting place of Cyrus Campbell, a blacksmith who is credited for making the leg irons which were placed on Mexican General Antonio López de Santa Anna following the Battle of San Jacinto in 1836. Little did Fess know that the Mexican commander would one day play a role in his life. However, W. J. Allen died leaving his wife, Molly, to run the farm on her own.

Fess spent his first summer with his grandparents in 1930.

"They were farmers and ranchers," said Fess. "I did what I was big enough to do." He picked crops, carried drinking water to those working in the fields, and later worked a plow with its team of mules. "I rode horses but I didn't milk cows!" he stated.

He found a friend in Brad Thompson, who lived at a neighboring ranch. "My family only lived about a quarter of a mile away from his grandparent's place so we just got to know each other as kids," said Thompson. "Fess had a bicycle and I had a horse, and we would trade off: I would ride his bicycle and he would take a ride on my horse. We all had the same friends, like J. B. and Weldon McConnell and Bullet East. On Sundays, we all went skinny dipping in the Allen stock tank, the place where the livestock drank their water. Bullet East was the fastest one of all of us; in fact, he could take his clothes off while running and still beat us all into the tank. Now, Fess was the big tall kid. He talked slow, just like he did in the movies later on. He was an impressive young man: good-looking, mannerly, and easy to talk to. He never forced a conversation on anyone. I enjoyed his company."

Fess described the Allen home as a "typical wooden farmhouse with a big screened-in porch and four bedrooms." His grandmother grew peaches, pears, cotton, peanuts, watermelon and corn, and raised livestock.

"She was everything because my grandfather had passed away," said Fess. "She was a very strong, self reliant, not-to-be-fooled kind of lady. She had no electricity. Being a city boy I got a little nervous when it got dark. And all the food was cooked on a wood stove. The outhouse was about seventy-five or a hundred yards away from the house."

Despite the lack of modern conveniences, Fess considered his late grandfather, W. J. Allen, successful. "He was a farmer or rancher as such," noted Fess. "There was oil in the neighborhood and he bought land. As a result, he had enough to buy all of his children a farm and send them to college."

Still, the Great Depression of the 1930s was a difficult time. Tens of thousands of businesses closed, unemployment was high, and expectations were low. "People worked for a dollar a day and the hours were from sun up to sundown," said Fess.

Fess' paternal grandparents also had no electrical power.

"There were no lights," remarked Fess. "We didn't even have lamps. People just kind of found their way into bed after dark." Fess' bed was usually the back porch's floor. Prior to retiring each night, family members would entertain each other by exchanging stories. Fess remembered one told to him by grandfather, Otis.

"Some of the local boys were stealing his watermelons," explained Fess. "So he decided to lay and wait for them. And, sure enough, two or three of them showed up. He jumped up and yelled at them, and they took off and he took off after them. And he chased them. Finally, he found a place where he figured that they would have to come back through and wherever they went they were gonna come back that way. So he just sat down and waited. Sure enough, here they came. He spooked them again and they took off."

However, years later, Grandpa Otis pointed out to Fess that those same boys served honorably in World War I.

"The boys went off to war and came back," said Fess. "And my grandfather was down at the train to meet them. They were glad to see him there at that circumstance."

Fess appreciated that his grandfather was able to excuse the youthful indiscretions of the young men who later went on to serve their country. He realized that his grandfather was a forgiving man. And Fess believed his grandfather's character was passed on to his father, and eventually to him. "There are things you learn from your folks," he remarked.

The grandparents' farms were also the places where periodic family gatherings took place. Although he was an only child, Fess had plenty of aunts, uncles and cousins. "My mother, Mackie, was one of eight children," said Fess. "Her twin, Mack, died at birth. I only remember Jewel, Esther, Lester, Tommy, and John. They were all married and had families. My father had one younger brother, John."

Fess' uncle, John, was a unique man.

"He had a proclivity for getting married and unmarried," laughed Fess. "He was married and divorced a couple of times. He was a guy who could have been anything, and he had a great personality."

And he made an impression on his nephew.

"I thought he was King Kong," remarked Fess. "He took me around while he looked at cattle and bought and sold cattle. He was a horse trader, really. He bought and sold livestock. What he had to work with was really interesting. He had a little pickup—I don't know whether it was a Ford or a Chevrolet—and a trailer. And he started driving throughout the countryside and wherever he went he noted whether there was a cow or a calf, some livestock that he possibly could acquire and then resell. It was fun. I enjoyed riding with him in the pickup."

More unconventional than his father and a bit more adventurous, Uncle John Parker used his personality to consummate trades. He relied primarily on a hand shake and his word to seal agreements, and he kept all of his promises and obligations.

"I probably took something from him," acknowledged Fess, who would later devote much of his post-Hollywood career in the real estate business.

In 1932, Fess' father ran for office.

"I was eight years old and he won the political position of tax assessor," he recalled. "He was a pretty good speech maker. He had a big political rally on the lawn of the courthouse which I thought was the most magnificent building I had ever seen."

Fess' father ran for re-election in 1934, but lost in a close contest that may have involved a fraudulent vote count. However, he didn't challenge the returns. Nevertheless, he was out of work. "Of course, it was the Depression," said Fess. "He had different jobs. He worked in a filling station, he washed cars. He often admonished me. He said, 'You don't want to do this. You keep going to school.'"

The senior Parker also told Fess to appreciate and respect private property. Borrowing something from someone outside the family was discouraged, but if someone else loaned an item to the Parkers it had to be returned to the lender in the same condition. Call it a Parker Family law.

Fess promptly broke the law.

He had borrowed a small outboard motor and used it to propel him and a few friends in an old boat on Lake Nasworthy, a reservoir that was located several miles southwest of San Angelo. But the poor excuse of a boat sprang leaks and sank. His buddies swam to shore

Fess Parker at eleven years old.
Photo courtesy of the Parker Family.

but Fess, aware of his father's law about borrowing things, immediately retrieved the motor from the bottom of the lake.

Fess appreciated his father's advice.

"He was a good guy doing the best he could in a bad time," said Fess. "Basically, my dad was a good father." Fess stated that the occasional disciplinary belt whacks he received from his father were not excessive. "He was not abusive in any way. He was always supportive."

Fess Parker earns his junior high football letter.
Photo courtesy of the Parker Family.

The Parkers sold their house and moved a few years later.

"We ended up in Dallas for the Texas Centennial," said Fess. "And then we came back to San Angelo in '37 or '38, and then my dad ran for office and won again. He was well liked and probably could have done more political efforts. But he just worked because he wanted to get me through college."

Fess' father was demanding at times. He wanted his son to follow in his athletic footsteps and play football. "He was about six-foot two-and-a-half," said Fess. "He was a good athlete; he played baseball and football in junior college." Fess played end on his junior high school team, but his team didn't exclusively compete against other junior high school teams: they sometimes scrimmaged against the San Angelo High School squad. "I got knocked out for the first time," noted Fess, who played both offense and defense. "I saw this knee coming up and I was out."

His father also wanted him to play an instrument. Fess agreed and decided to play the piano, but ended up playing trumpet. "My dad put it in my hands," remarked Fess. "He felt that a piano player was more on the effeminate side." However, the junior high school band needed someone big enough to carry another instrument. "They needed a tuba player." Fess managed the rare tasks of playing in the football game and playing the tuba during the halftime break. "And I had to load that damn thing in the back of the car every night."

Despite his dislike for the trumpet and tuba, Fess enjoyed listening to popular music. "I enjoyed music, and music has been an unusual thing in my life," he said. "As a boy growing up in Texas, I participated in singing patriotic songs with my grade school chums. I later became familiar with songs performed by W. Lee O'Daniel's Light Crust Doughboys, and Bob Wills and the Texas Playboys. And by the 1940s, like everyone else, I was well aware of 'Deep in the Heart of Texas.'"

When he wasn't playing football, Fess worked in a grocery store. "I stuffed groceries and sometimes I carried the bags to the shoppers' cars," he said. "I made a little money."

Despite a few disciplinary paddle whacks from the principal, Fess enjoyed his junior high years. "I really liked junior high," he noted. "I liked the classes."

Fess Parker, #93, standing in the back row of the San Angelo Bobcats team photo.
Photo courtesy of the Parker Family.

Fess thought that playing on his junior high school football team would be enough to satisfy his father's wishes but the senior Parker wanted him to play at San Angelo High School.

Reluctantly, Fess went out for the football team.

"I wasn't all that thrilled about football," said Fess. "I was fourteen years old and I was six-foot three and one hundred-seventy pounds. I wasn't ready to play football with guys who were eighteen or nineteen." Added pressure came from his father who attended many of the team's daily practices. Nevertheless, Fess persevered and made the squad as the San Angelo Bobcats' second-string right end. And when he wasn't on the football field, he kept on playing the tuba.

Outside of school, Fess dated and frequently went to the movies. San Angelo had three movie houses at the time: the Texas, the Paramount, and the Royal. "The Texas was the only one with a balcony," he noted. Like many of boys his age, Fess said that he was particularly fond of Western films and serials.

He also joined Citizens' Military Camp, a U.S. military summer training program created by the National Defense Act of 1920. The program carried no obligation of full-time service but it provided an incentive for some to enlist in the U. S. Army. "I spent time on the rifle range and learned the basics of military life," explained Fess. "You were supposed to be eighteen but I went at sixteen. I ended up at Camp Bullis outside of San Antonio. It was hotter than hell. We lived in tents and those tents got awfully hot."

Another summer adventure was a car trip Fess took with two older friends and their mother to Philadelphia in 1940. "It was quite an eye opener to see Arkansas and Tennessee and so forth; I had never been out of Texas," replied Fess, who had saved nearly $40 to finance his journey. "I had my sixteenth birthday along the way. It was interesting because everything was minimal—the highways were minimal; the motels cost about two or three dollars a night."

During his junior year, he bought his own car.

"I had this 1921 Model T roadster, classic Ford black," said Fess. "It only cost forty dollars. I sold my bicycle and borrowed twenty bucks from the bank. My dad co-signed the loan." Fess paid back the loan by working in the grocery store and a filling station.

"At six-foot-six in the open Model T, he was well known going down the street," said Phil Kendrick, a high school friend who was two years younger than Fess. "As tall as he was, sittin' up high, a good lookin' guy, of course, in that Model T, well the girls were definitely attracted to him."

"That was some car," said Dallas Perkins, a friend from Abilene. "You could seat two people comfortably in it but you could squeeze a few more in it if you had to. But it had old leaf springs, no shock absorbers."

"Who can forget that car of his?" said Jimmy Tittle, who attended Abilene High School when he first met Fess. "It was something."

Fess spent too much time in his car and with his friends. His school work suffered. "I was a very poor student, I didn't make very good grades," admitted Fess. Despite his less-than-satisfactory academic performance he still maintained his insatiable thirst for reading. "I'd rather do what I wanted to do which was just read," he said. "I preferred picking a book and reading it. I'd read at home, I'd read everywhere. The genre that was most appealing to me was

Fess Parker with his beloved Model T.
PHOTO COURTESY OF THE PARKER FAMILY.

the adventure stories, some of which were built on actual historical events."

Fess was graduated from high school in 1942, six months after the United States entered World War II. In the autumn, he enrolled in Texas A. & M. While there a production company was shooting a film about the Aggie Corps but Fess didn't appear in it. The film, *We've Never Been Licked*, was eventually released on August 30, 1943. A promotional poster stated that the film was "inspired by the fighting sons of Texas A. & M."

Fess didn't stay at Texas A.& M. for long; he joined the U.S. Navy.

"It was July 1943,"stated Fess. He was interested in flying but was too tall to be a pilot. He was subsequently sent to Camp Pendleton, California where he was trained as a field radio operator. The training wasn't particularly demanding but he appreciated learning a new skill and he enjoyed the camaraderie of the other young men who came from all over the country. A number of his fellow sailors enjoyed going to bars while on liberty. Fess reluctantly tagged along. "I tried to drink but I didn't care for it," said Fess, who avoided smoking as well. "I puffed on a few but that was it."

Fess Parker in the U. S. Navy, 1944.
PHOTO COURTESY OF THE PARKER FAMILY.

Following training and a service period, he was assigned to a quartermaster's supply warehouse. Fess was also stationed for a brief time at San Bruno, California, and while on furlough he visited his parents in Abilene. Later he served on a shallow-draft mine sweeper, *YMS334*, commanded by Captain Paul Rafferty, during operations near Hawaii and the Philippines. "It was a unique opportunity for me coming from Texas," explained Fess, who achieved the rank of Seaman First Class. "Except for the mines, we saw no combat." The native Texan never got seasick but he bumped his head a number of times. "I was a little tall for the overheads," he noted.

While on a stateside pass, Fess visited the Hollywood set of *State Fair*, a film starring Jean Crain, Dana Andrews, and Dick Haymes that was released in August of 1945. He enjoyed watching the Twentieth Century Fox musical during production; as a matter of fact, Fess found the film-making business interesting but he was still contemplating a post-military career in law.

He left the service on April 29, 1946. Fess arrived back in the United States on a troop ship. "We were coming into San Francisco harbor and I looked up at the bridge and we hit the bridge!" exclaimed Fess. "I don't know how much damage was done." However, the ship survived and Fess disembarked. He was eventually sent cross country to Lido Beach, Long Island where he was discharged. Before heading home he went to Broadway and quickly forgot about being a lawyer. The lights of the Great White Way and his recollections of visiting the *State Fair* set altered his career selection. "I decided that I wanted to be an actor," he said. "I just felt that I'd like to do that." But he was unable to secure a single interview or audition.

Fess went back to Texas—his parents had moved to 1716 Durham Avenue in Brownwood—and enrolled in Hardin-Simmons University in Abilene where he spent much of his free time hanging around with friends. He also spent time at his grandparents' farms where he performed various chores.

One of the first things he did upon arriving home was to spruce up his Model T. "I had it all painted gray with red spokes and a red leatherette interior," explained Fess, who considered it more than an automotive upgrade. The classic car was the key to all of his social activities in and around Abilene.

"The drugstore in Abilene, the Clinic Pharmacy, became a high school and college hangout," said Kendrick. "It was four-story building that housed doctors and dentists, and on its ground floor was a pharmacy-drugstore. It was a typical drugstore with a soda fountain that served sodas and sandwiches. It was kind of a gathering place.

Fess Parker on the Allen farm windmill.
PHOTO COURTESY OF THE PARKER FAMILY.

If you wanted to see your friends you'd go there, especially on the weekends. Sometimes we would sit on the curb and listen to the music that came from a car. Somebody always had their car there with the music on."

Double dating was particularly popular in Abilene.

"Fess dated Shirley Gaskill and I dated Gene Ray Bates, a friend of Fess.'" said Imogene Mensel Collins, who was a senior at Abilene High School at the time. "We would go over to Fess' house and play bridge. Fess and Gene would give me lessons because I was new to the game. Fess' mother would always bring us iced tea."

"You just didn't go out with one guy all the time," said Doris Bonhannon Grosvenor, a classmate of Collins. "I went out with Fess on four or five dates. He was awfully nice, he was wonderful. Everybody just adored him. He came to pick me up not in his Model T but in his daddy's red car. His father worked for the beverage control commission and he had this car with all these spotlights on it. It was quite something."

Fess' mother always told him to be polite and considerate with the girls he took out. And she reminded him to be considerate and courteous with the girls that he didn't date.

"My sister was tall," said Dallas Perkins, another one of Fess' friends. "She used to say that she was five-foot twelve when asked. But if Fess was ever around he would always try and stand next to her so that no one noticed her height. He was very thoughtful. That's the way he was. He was friendly, nice, and just plain pleasant to everybody in my family."

Despite his consideration for others, Fess was always up for a practical joke and he teamed up with Perkins for a prank.

"Fess backed up his Model T near the doors of a drugstore that was located on south 12th and Butternut where I was working behind the counter, jerking sodas," said William E. King, one of Fess' friends from Abilene who attended Hardin-Simmons. "Fess was with Dallas. Now, Fess had separate spark and gas levers next to his steering wheel on his car that he could manipulate and cause the car to backfire. Dallas steps up near the entrance of the drugstore and yells out, 'I will teach you to fiddle with my wife!' Fess started the car and then all of a sudden we heard, Bam! Bam! Bam! Everybody thought it was gunshots. People jumped out of the booths and off their stools and went right to the floor. I didn't know who was outside so I ducked down behind the counter; I didn't want to get shot. The man who owned the place, George Shahan, was in the back and he nearly had a heart attack! I later learned that Dallas jumped back in Fess' car and they took off. If George Shahan had a gun he would have shot both of them."

The car-backfire incident notwithstanding, King held Fess in the highest regard. "He was a great friend," said King. "He was a friendly guy. I had government classes with him."

Another incident with his car resulted in tragedy.

While he was in Abilene in 1946, Fess took his girlfriend at the time for a drive in his old Ford Model T but was hit in the rear by a drunk driver. "He bumped me in the rear and I turned around and looked and he bumped me again," stated Fess. "He pulled up alongside me and said, 'Why don't you get over, you stupid son of a bitch.'" Fess followed the man home and confronted him. "He had a knife out." The man stabbed Fess in his neck from his left ear to his jaw. "He broke the blade on my jaw bone. I had about twenty some odd veins severed." Fess recalled that his girlfriend was "paralyzed" in shock. Surprisingly, Fess forced the man to drive him to the hospital. "In his car!" exclaimed Fess.

Fess was covered in blood when he arrived at the hospital.

"They got the blood stopped and tried to piece him together as well as they could," said Morgan Woodward, another friend who later heard about the altercation. "It was not exactly the best plastic surgery job in the world."

Fess believed that if charges were filed against the assailant they wouldn't hold because the altercation took place on the attacker's property. "Nothing more ensued," said Fess. However, Fess did consider another course. "Fess said that he thought about killing the guy," remarked Woodward.

"He had a long scar on his neck," explained Grosvenor. "It was bad."

"I remember going to the hospital to see him," said Collins. "They put two beds together to make him more comfortable."

"I saw the scar on Fess," noted King. "He told me, 'I nearly got killed.'"

Fess' face was numb for about a year. "I would horrify my dates," said Fess in an interview published in *The Alcalde*, a University of Texas alumni publication, in 2003. "We'd go get something to eat, and I'd be chewing my lip and blood would be flowing down, and I wouldn't even know it. That cleared up."

In interviews later in life, it was mentioned that his injury required him to cease playing football on the college level. But he never played football after high school. "Fess was always asked if he played," stated Kendrick. "It seems to me he told reporters he intended to play but he suffered a life-threatening injury when he was cut with the knife. I really think he was big enough but he never gave playing football in college a thought. He was having too much fun with the college social life."

A noticeable chin scar originated years before the knife incident.

"As I recall I was playing with one of my schoolmates and we were playing a game where you catch the other guy and tap his hands," declared Fess. "I was around twelve or fourteen. My shoes were off and I slipped on the floor and cut my chin. I went to a doctor and he sewed me up."

Fess and Kendrick took separate higher education paths.

"After the war, he went to Hardin-Simmons and I went to Abilene Christian, so we didn't see much of each other," said Kendrick. "Strangely as it seems, we both decided to go to the University of Texas in the fall of '47. Neither one of us knew that the other one was gonna be there. We were all coming back from the service, trying to figure out what we were going to do."

Initially, Parker forgot about his brief Broadway escapade and once again focused on the law as a career.

"I went to Hardin-Simmons University for a couple of semesters and later entered law school at the University of Texas in Austin," said Fess, who soon realized that law was not a career choice. "I didn't give it much effort and my grades were quite poor." He withdrew from classes during the spring semester of 1948 but returned in the summer.

"He tried law but that was too much studying for him," laughed Kendrick. "If it was easy, he wanted to major in it. He heard that the Russian teacher didn't get many students and that the school was going to eliminate his position." Kendrick explained that the

Fess Parker contemplates his future after returning from World War II.
Photo courtesy of the Parker Family.

professor planned to maintain his classroom enrollment numbers and save his job by recruiting students in a unique way. "He was giving everybody an A," proclaimed Kendrick. "Fess said, 'I need an A.'" And Fess soon added Russian to his course work.

Fess became aware of Kendrick's non-academic interest: singing and acting.

"I had participated in Denton College's summer program of debate tournaments and plays," explained Kendrick. "The senior Stacy Keach was the director of our play. Fess came to see the play that I was in. He was very interested—I guess more interested than I ever dreamed because I really didn't know that he had a secret desire to do something like that."

Besides their friendship, Fess and Kendrick eventually became fraternity brothers.

"I joined a fraternity, Pi Kappa Alpha," said Fess.

"Our fraternity house was four blocks from the university," said Kendrick. "It was a big old house, built in the 1880s. But it only had room for twelve guys. Fess didn't live there; he lived with various fraternity brothers in various apartments. But nearly all of us ate lunch and dinner at the fraternity house. 'Granny' ran the kitchen. It was a great fraternity." Fess and his frat brothers also enjoyed attending dances and parties at the Driskill Hotel in Austin.

"I met Fess I the fall of 1947," said Bob Milstead. "A year later as fraternity brothers we shared a garage apartment. Each side had a room with two twin beds, a closet and a bath. I remember that we didn't eat too well back then because we didn't have any money. But his folks would sometimes come to Austin with sacks of groceries. Mrs. Parker would cook for us and we would eat and eat. She was a saint; she was so good. The next semester we got a real apartment with more space. We brought in Dodo McQueen as an additional roommate."

Pi Kappa Alpha was known for its collective voices.

"We were a singing fraternity," said Kendrick. "We had a lot of fraternity songs and we would sing two or three of them at lunch. We were usually serenaded by the sororities around ten o'clock at night. All the girls had to be in by 10:30. It was a great fraternity life."

Fess quickly realized that singing was a way to make an impression on the sorority girls.

"But Fess really couldn't sing very well," noted Kendrick, who sang tenor or whatever vocal part was needed at the time. "He couldn't stay on key in a harmony group. He wanted me to help him so I practiced with him and he really enjoyed it. He sang well; he did a very good job. He had a good voice and learned to stay on key."

Fess confidently joined the fraternity choir. "And I sang second tenor in the University Sing-Song competition between fraternities," remarked Fess, who made a noticeable contribution to the singing group. "We went from never having placed in the competition to either winning or coming in second place," said Kendrick.

Fess maintained a high profile with the coeds.

"He always had a college girlfriend," stated Kendrick. "Always."

Fess also improved his dancing skills.

"He was a decent dancer but he wasn't outstanding," remarked Kendrick, who later joined Fess in a tap dance class. "But he went out with a girl who was a dancer. He went out with her for about two years. I thought he was going to marry her but he wasn't ready to get married. Fess had this burning desire to be an actor and a singer."

But not all his friends were aware of his yearning to act.

"We had conversations all the time but he never mentioned that he wanted to be an actor," said Harwell Barber, a classmate of Fess' at Hardin-Simmons who lived in Abilene. "But he was a very jovial fellow, a very nice person. He always had a kind word to say and I never really saw him mad. He kept that personality all his life."

Fess turned a prank-like gift into a career-opening opportunity.

He was going with a girl named Priscilla Kern—he called her Prissy," explained Kendrick. "For his birthday, as a joke, she went down to the pawn shop and bought a real cheap guitar. It was intended as a joke but he learned how to play that guitar. That's how he ended up being able to play the guitar when he went on his interview for the *Davy Crockett* job."

Despite his height, Fess preferred his coeds on the short side.

"Fess liked cute little women and Priscilla Kern was a cute little girl," said Woodward, who joined the fraternity in 1948 after transferring from North Texas Agricultural College. "In fact, my girlfriend was Priscilla's roommate. They shared a nice apartment."

Besides his interest in girls, Fess enjoyed having fun—sometimes at the expense of others.

"He loved to play practical jokes," laughed Kendrick. "How we stayed friends, I'll never know. He was always pulling something on me that was outrageous. He dreamed up one on one of our fraternity brothers. It was typical of Fess. He would totally plan and plot something and follow through but have other people do it. He could talk me into anything. We were going to summer school the summer before senior year to get our grade point averages up and make sure we'd graduate."

"Fess and I were neither on the honor roll," added Woodward.

During that summer, Kendrick explained that Fess created a practical joke on a romantically-challenged student who was led to believe that he was secretly admired by a coed. Fess asked Prissy to phone the guy and tell him sweet nothings. "She told him that her heart went pitter patter every time she saw him," said Kendrick. "She really had him going. Finally, she said it was time for them to meet. The guy showed up at the apartment but when Prissy opened the door he saw Fess, his friends, and their dates there. He was red-faced, he was embarrassed. He really felt like a fool." But the student was good natured and never held a grudge against Fess or his friends.

Practical jokes, notwithstanding, Fess never participated in the frequently-painful, fraternity initiation ceremonies. "My brother had been SMC—president—of Pi Kappa Alpha," explained Woodward. "Fess was already a member and I was invited to pledge. But Fess never took part in any kind of ritual, and they could be torture. Fess was a friendly guy and I appreciated that."

One day, Fess approached Kendrick with a life-changing question.

"He said, 'Phil, how do you get in one of these plays?'" said Kendrick. "I said that you go out there and you try out."

And Fess did.

"There was a student-produced musical, *Time Staggers On*," noted Kendrick. "He showed up a got a part."

But a small part, a very small part.

"He had no lines," laughed Kendrick. "He just stood there and a girl sang a serious love song."

Fess was pleased that he was part of the production but frustrated that he had nothing to do on stage. He didn't expect to get a leading role but he didn't anticipate being nothing more than human furniture. Fess asked Kendrick for advice.

"He asked me what he could do with his hands," remarked Kendrick. "He said that he felt awkward just standing there. But I told him to *just stand there.*"

Fess wasn't satisfied with his good friend's answer. Prior to the dress rehearsal he came up with an idea that he hoped would break his mannequin-like role. Fess told Kendrick that he planned to pull a yo-yo out of his pocket during the song. "I told him to forget it," stated Kendrick, who later was pleased to see that Fess didn't include the impromptu yo-yo act during the final dress rehearsal.

The actual performance, though, was another matter.

"During the actual show he breaks out a yo-yo right in the middle of her song!" chuckled Kendrick. "There wasn't a peep in the audience. They couldn't understand what was going on; nobody knew how to react. He thought he would get a rip-roaring laugh. Afterwards, the girl was in tears; she was mortified! I never mentioned the incident again until I brought it up to him about a year or two before he died. He told me that it was terribly embarrassing."

Fess had another uncomfortable moment on stage while at the University of Texas.

"Fess was in a show called *Texas Tower Time*," said Woodward. "It was a variety show with lots of people in it. He was dressed as Roman in a toga. He had no lines or a song to sing. He was just one of the Romans. He was sitting stage center and he forgot to close his legs. He was sitting with his legs wide open. He got the biggest laugh of the evening. Fess finally caught on and quickly closed his legs. The house just exploded in laughter!"

"Yes, sir, I remember that performance," laughed Milstead. "I actually thought he was playing Mars, the Roman god, in *Time Staggers On*."

In any event, Fess received laughter—something at least—from an audience based upon what he did on stage. In a way, it was intoxicating. But like singing, he lacked dramatic training and experience. He decided to make up for lost time by concentrating on the efforts of every college performer in a campus production. He observed actors, chorus members, musical soloists, and even guest lecturers. Fess made mental notes of everything because he had his sights on the movie-making capital of the world.

"Of course, later when he told me had plans to go to Hollywood I told him he was crazy," said Kendrick. "But he could focus better than anybody that I'd ever known. When he decided on something he really worked at it."

Fess remained busy when not in class. He worked at odd jobs and attended concerts.

"I had the good fortune to hear a concert by Burl Ives, who inspired me to learn American folk songs," said Fess. "I also helped book engagements for a dance band. And I was a water ski instructor on Lake Austin during the day and a janitor at night at a state employment office. I was busy but I made some money, too."

Kendrick recalled that Fess was more than just a "ski instructor."

"He and a friend, Dodo McQueen, became the Daring Devils on Water Skis on Lake Austin," stated Kendrick. "They advertised and handed out circulars. They made some money, too!"

The friendship between Fess and Kendrick grew.

"I believe Phil may have been the closest friend Fess ever had," said Woodward. "Fess was like Reagan: both very popular but with very few close friends—I mean confessors. But I don't believe Fess confessed to anybody." Woodward became another good friend. Woodward served in World War II in the Army Air Corps. Discharged on December 5, 1945, Woodward, like Fess, was a bit older than the other college freshmen.

Fess' enrollment in the Russian class would earn him extra credit that went beyond an A grade or a Dean's List roster.

His professor, Dr. Arthur Coleman, was an acquaintance of veteran film actor Adolph Monjeau, who had earned a Best Actor Oscar™ nomination for his performance as Walter Burns in the 1931 motion picture, *The Front Page*. "Monjeau was coming to town to narrate *Peter and the Wolf*," explained Fess. "Well, Professor Coleman asked me to pick him up and drive him around since I had a car. I agreed. I picked him up at the train station and took him to the hotel. He had to refresh himself. And then I picked up Professor Coleman and took both of them to the fraternity house for dinner."

Despite his celebrity, Parker thought that the actor was quite convivial.

"We just hit it off conversationally," said Fess. "He was very pleasant. Of course, I was interested in motion pictures but I never approached him about it directly. But just as he was about to leave town, he asked if I was interested in working in motion pictures. I told him that I was and he said that I could look him up if I ever went to Hollywood. He had given me his phone number."

On June 3, 1950, Fess received a B. A. degree in history from the University of Texas' School of Arts and Sciences. "After I graduated in 1950, I left home for Hollywood," he said.

The move to California was more than risky: it was seemingly foolish. It wasn't as if Fess had a resume filled with leading roles in major college productions. He didn't. He sang in a fraternity choir and flipped an unscripted yo-yo on stage. That was it.

But he was determined.

Before he left Texas, Fess promised that he would give himself three years to make it in the movie business. "I figured that three years was more than enough time," Fess pointed out. "If that didn't work out, I would leave and do something else. Anything but law."

In the summer of 1950, Fess arrived in Hollywood.

"As I recall, he hitchhiked out to Los Angeles," said Kendrick.

But Tinseltown was a different place from the one that Fess has visited during the final year of World War II. The new competitive medium, television, threatened motion picture box office revenue. And a 1948 Supreme Court ruling against the big studios' monopoly on film production and distribution made its first impact when Howard Hughes broke up RKO studios into two separate entities on December 31, 1949. Old Hollywood was changing.

However, those were seemingly small concerns for Fess as he settled in at an inexpensive Hollywood apartment he shared on Argyle Street not far from the famous Pantages Theater, the venue where the Oscar™ ceremonies were held from 1949 through 1959. He applied for unemployment insurance which helped with his expenses and later moved into a Laurel Canyon room that had no kitchen. "I had a hot plate," noted Fess. "And the shower was outside. It cost $30 a month." Fess paid the rent by using his unemployment checks and taking such odd jobs as taking the evening inventory in a women's lingerie shop. "I usually had two or three sources of income," said Fess. "It was difficult for my parents. My dad told me that he didn't think anything would come of it."

Back in Texas, everyone had doubts about his move to Hollywood. His father was particularly concerned that his son's acting pursuits weren't practical but Fess' mother was optimistic. Mackie believed in her son's dreams.

"Monjeau was true to his word and I met him and his son, Peter, and his wife at a Sunday brunch at his house," stated Fess. "He told me to give him a call next week and said he would introduce me to his agent." Fess appreciated the gesture. "The difficulty in those days was obtaining an agent."

Monjeau introduced Fess to his agent, Bert Allenberg, who also represented Clark Gable. "He said that my name, Fess, could be somewhat of a problem," explained Fess. "One of his associates agreed and suggested I use another name. In any event, I visited several studios and talked to various people involved with new talent but nothing came out of those meetings."

Fess still managed to secure voice-over work on *Harvey*, the fanciful Jimmy Stewart comedy. Principal photography had been completed on the Universal-International motion picture on June 6, 1950, but post-production continued. The studio needed a number of looping sessions in which better-quality dialogue replaced some less-than-satisfactory portions of the original audio track. In a scene in which Jimmy Stewart's character describes his oversized rabbit-friend to Nana Bryant's Mrs. Hazel Chumley, the actress turns to her chauffer, Leslie, played by William Val, and asks, "Leslie, did he say pooka?" Fess provided Val's response: "Yes, M'am. That's what the man said." *Harvey* was released on October 13, 1950.

The uncredited voice-over work in *Harvey* was the only film he worked on during his first year in Hollywood. Though somewhat disappointed, Fess decided to utilize his time and his G.I. Bill benefits by enrolling in graduate school at the University of Southern California. "I was pursuing a Masters degree in the history of the theatre," said Fess. "And I spent two semesters there."

Fess, to be sure, selected USC for something more than academics.

"Cecil B. DeMille's brother was the head of the drama department as USC," said Kendrick. "He thought that if he got to know him he might be introduced to Cecil B. DeMille. He was always analyzing things out about how he could benefit from doing this rather than that."

Fess Parker at the beginning of his acting career.
Photo courtesy of the Parker Family.

Fess was never introduced to the legendary director but another introduction proved fruitful. He was introduced to William Hammerstein who was casting a national touring company for *Mr. Roberts*, the World War II naval dramatic comedy starring Henry Fonda which won the 1948 Tony Award for Best Play. Fess and a few fellow USC drama students got the parts as crew members in the ensemble. *Mr. Roberts* began its West Coast run in San Francisco.

During his summer tour at $32 a week, Fess took every opportunity to talk to fellow cast members about the business of acting. Without any background in show business, he asked numerous questions and paid careful attention to the professionals. "I was fortunate that Henry Fonda gave me of his time," said Fess. "I also observed how the leads—Lee Van Cleef, Jack Klugman and others—handled themselves both on and off stage. I learned a lot from that."

Fess managed to secure representation with Wynn Rocamora. It was good to have an agent but Fess found it difficult to dress properly for auditions. "It was a challenge to keep your meager wardrobe presentable," he said. Rocamora arranged an audition for Fess in the bio-pic, *The Will Rogers Story*, but the film's casting director, Bill Tinsman, suggested instead that he audition for the lead in *The Winning Team*, a film about baseball great Grover Cleveland Alexander. Alexander was a superb National League pitcher who won 373 games but battled alcoholism and epileptic-like seizures throughout his career. It was a challenging role. Fess was given the script to read but the studio decided to give the role to an established actor. "It was Ronald Reagan," laughed Fess.

Fess managed to secure a small part in *Untamed Frontier,* a Universal-International western which starred Joseph Cotton, Shelley Winters and Scott Brady. The film was released during the summer of 1952, and Fess earned his first screen credit as Clem McCloud.

During the filming of *Untamed Frontier*, Cotton was injured. While the production was on hold, Fess secured work as Cousin Ben, an uncredited role in Universal-International's *No Room for the Groom*. The Douglas Sirk-directed romantic comedy, which starred Tony Curtis and Piper Laurie, completed production quickly enough to open months before *Untamed Frontier.* About 13 ½ minutes into *No Room for the Groom*, Fess appears on the big screen for the first time. Towering over everyone and dressed bucolically in jeans and a long-sleeve shirt, Fess ambles into the kitchen of Tony Curtis' character, Alvah Morrell, who just so happens to own a winery. "Good evening,'" says Fess as he slaps Lillian Bronson's Aunt Elsa character on the shoulder. "Try the grapes," Fess suggests to Lynne Hunter's Cousin Betty. "They're grown here." After Aunt Elsa introduces Cousin Ben to Piper Laurie's Lee Kingshead character, Fess says, "Hello, Cousin Lee," and promptly slaps a shoulder greeting on her before exiting the kitchen with Cousin Betty and a bowl of grapes. Fess appears in several more scenes and has a few more lines. He seemed comfortable on camera and his rural-flavored comedic characterization was surprisingly effective.

Though surprised, his friends back home were delighted that Fess was working in the film business. One friend in particular viewed Fess' new status as one which could generate unique social dividends: Phil Kendrick. Fess invited his friend to California with the promise of arranging a date for him with a Hollywood starlet. "I'd be out there within a week after hearing that," said Kendrick. "Of course, I never met any starlets. He didn't want to share his starlets; that's what I finally figured out." The only Hollywood personalities Kendrick ever saw were the ones he noticed on the Saturday unemployment line. "It was a good way to see actors," he laughed.

Fess followed his first films with the part of Jim Randolph, a Confederate sergeant, in the 1952 western *Springfield Rifle*, which starred Hollywood legend Gary Cooper. Fess was pleased to work with Cooper whose impressive *High Noon* had been released several months earlier.

"He was a guy who I respected because of the way he approached his craft," explained Fess. "He was a quiet guy, conservative. One day while on location in Lone Pine, California, I was in a room with three other guys from the film. Gary Cooper walked in and asked if anybody wanted to go with him into town to get a milkshake. I got right up and said, 'I'll go!' I thought it was not only great to get off the set but it was even better to be in the company of Gary Cooper. Of course, I thought that he was joking when he said 'milkshake.' I thought that was his way of saying 'whiskey' or 'beer' or something else. Well, we got to town. We went to a drugstore

Fess Parker on the set of *Springfield Rifle*.
PHOTO COURTESY OF THE PARKER FAMILY.

and had the milkshakes. A milkshake! But we had no conversation while we were there. When we got finished, we drove back to the set."

Fess embraced Cooper's restrained but confident acting style. He appreciated the natural understated manner in which Cooper portrayed a character and internalized it. In Cooper's films, Cooper essentially played himself, and Fess would do it the same way in the years that followed.

Once his scenes in the film were completed, Fess returned to his California apartment and looked for work. Securing acting jobs on a regular basis was more difficult than Fess had imagined.

Morgan Woodward spent time in the service during the Korean War before returning to the United States in 1953. "I landed in Long Beach from Japan," said Woodward. "So I called Fess immediately when I got off the ship." He assumed that his friend was firmly established in Hollywood but that was not the case. Woodward discovered that Fess was indeed a struggling actor. He learned that during the most difficult times between roles Fess didn't have enough money for rent and sometimes found shelter under porches. Fess even resorted to dinners of canned spaghetti and mustard. Woodward wanted to return home to Texas as soon as possible but Fess had other ideas.

"He encouraged me to come out and stay," said Woodward. "I think he wanted me to share his misery. I didn't come out until about a year and a half later, at his behest."

Fess carried on. He auditioned and sought acting jobs wherever he could find them. He was cast as shell-shocked Marine vet in a United States Navy Training Film titled *Combat Psychiatry: The Division Psychiatrist.* The 1954 Cascade Pictures of California production (MN 7499B), which was filmed at Camp Pendleton, identified and explained the problems that some Korean War veterans faced upon their return to the United States. The on-screen report on Fess' character read: "Shaken bad by explosion which killed a buddy—Would not give up weapon—Hard charger before." Fess' appearance in the film was hardly a significant resume entry, but it was work.

His prospects started to improve. Fess managed to secure parts on several television dramas including *Dragnet, Annie Oakley, My Little Margie, Tales of the Century*, and *Death Valley Days* where he appeared with Nancy Hale in an episode titled "The Kickapoo Run." He also teamed up with actress Laraine Day in *White Collar*, an unsold TV pilot. He was making progress in the acting field but not as fast he liked.

Marcella Rinehart, an attractive singer who performed at the Zebra Room in the Townehouse Hotel on Wilshire Boulevard in Los Angeles, stopped at Fess' apartment complex one afternoon, looking for a friend but found her future husband.

Rinehart, who was born in Cedar Rapids, Iowa in 1928, enjoyed singing at an early age. After she was graduated from high school she secured her first professional engagement. "I went to Davenport, Iowa and worked at a little club on the Mississippi River," she said. "Later I sang at the Broadmoor Hotel in Colorado Springs and then at the Brown Palace in Denver. I was a blues and ballad girl."

Fess Parker in an early promotional head shot.
PHOTO COURTESY OF THE PARKER FAMILY.

By the early 1950s she was in Los Angeles performing at the Ambassador Hotel and other venues. Starting in 1953, Marcy, as she was called by her family and friends, performed five nights a week from nine until midnight in the Zebra Room with the Frankie Ortega Trio. "I think I was getting a hundred dollars a week," she said.

Marcy recalled when she and Fess first crossed paths.

"I actually met Fess in May—I believe it was May 5, 1954—at his apartment's swimming pool at Peyton Hall on Hollywood Boulevard in Hollywood," said Marcy. "I lived at 7764 Hollywood Boulevard, only about four blocks away. I had a girlfriend, Betty Richardson, who was living below him and I had gone over to be with her but she hadn't gotten home as yet. I was laying on a chaise lounge next to the pool. I went into the pool for a swim. Fess was already in the pool. I was swimming along and he swam up next to me and started talking. We had a few conversations and he asked me where I was working. Well, the next night that I sang in the Zebra Room, he was there. And he was coming to the Zebra Room repeatedly. We started seeing each other but we weren't a couple. I was going out with a Norwegian architect at the time."

Fess frequently visited Marcy at the Zebra Room with his friends. "He had a lot of nice friends," said Marcy. "He was particularly close with his Texas friends." When they were alone on dates they frequented inexpensive Hollywood restaurants. But most of the time he dined at Marcy's apartment. "He enjoyed my cooking," she added.

Fess also wanted Kendrick to give the entertainment business another try since his talented fraternity brother had an impressive performance resume from college; in fact, Kendrick worked his way through college as a radio announcer. Kendrick agreed and spent part of the 1954 summer with Fess. Kendrick enrolled at USC and arrived in a new 1954 Buick convertible. "White with black leather interior," beamed Kendrick. "It was *the* car to go to Hollywood in."

At the time, Fess was rooming with John Lupton and John Rice, an old friend from San Angelo. "I had a cot at the foot of Fess' bed," said Kendrick, who had another motive for his West Coast move: an attractive girlfriend, Carolyn Wright, 17, from Abilene Christian had transferred to nearby Pepperdine University. Kendrick was so impressed by Wright's looks that he wanted Fess to meet the girl. "She was strikingly beautiful," noted Kendrick. "I gave Fess her phone number and told Fess I would appreciate it if he would show her around Hollywood."

Fess eventually saw Wright and was quickly taken by her looks.

"He not only showed her around Hollywood but fell in love with her," said Kendrick. "I knew they were seeing each other but I had no idea they were romantically involved. She wrote me regularly and told me how much fun she was having with Fess and his group of friends."

When Kendrick arrived at Fess' apartment he noticed a change in his friend's demeanor. "He was very sullen," explained Kendrick. "It looked to me like he was depressed. And finally I asked him what was wrong. He said, 'I've fallen in love with Carolyn. I've never been this much in love with anybody.'"

At first, Kendrick thought he was listening to an apology.

"Fess told me that he had proposed to her and that she said, 'No!'" exclaimed Kendrick. "Fess had feelings for her but the girl did not share his level of romantic interest. I believe she led him along. He was under the impression I might be proposing to Carolyn when I arrived. We compared notes and realized the 'blond bombshell' had misled us both."

Marcy wasn't concerned about Fess' infatuation; in fact, she took it all in stride. The four of them, along with other friends, had even socialized and gone out together. "They were much older than me so it was never going to get serious," said Wright. "I was only seventeen. I was only in California because I wanted to go there but my dad wouldn't allow it until I attended at least one semester at Abilene Christian. I did, and then I was off to California. But Fess was just not meant for me."

However, she never told Fess about her lack of romantic feelings for him until his proposal. Fess remained heartbroken—and a bit angry.

"He told me that we needed to teach this Carolyn a lesson," said Kendrick.

Fess, the prankster, quickly devised a plan that would end the relationship in grand style—and on his terms. The two friends agreed that they would each deliver a phony proposal of marriage to her on the same night, Fess for the second time. "Fess said, 'Let's go get some engagement rings at Woolworths,'" remarked Kendrick. "I went along with it." They purchased some cheap rings at the department store and prepared their next step.

One evening, they all went out the Zebra Room where Marcy was performing. When they had a moment alone on the dance floor, Kendrick pressed the ring in Wright's hand and delivered his phony proposal. "Minutes later, Fess gets up and does the same thing," stated Kendrick. Fess told Wright that he knew about his friend's proposal and wanted her to reconsider his own. "Fess told her, 'It's time you decided. I want an answer.' She didn't return to the table. She went to the restroom. Marcy noticed this from the stage; she knew what was going on."

It was an immature move on the part of Fess and his friend but it achieved its goal.

"I was appalled by what they did," said Wright. "I went into the bathroom and cried. Marcy came in and she kind of helped me out. I thought they both were serious. I didn't know it was a joke until some time later." Wright thought the best response to the dual proposals was a swift exit from the club.

"We never saw her again," said Kendrick.

But Marcy's Norwegian boyfriend soon found out about Fess.

"Her fiancé, the architect, didn't take it too well," said Kendrick. "One night he came by his apartment. I was home; they were all out." He knocked on the door and started to yell: 'I'm lookin' for Marcella Rinehart!' I told him that she wasn't here. Then he yelled again: 'Where's Fess Parker?' I told him that he wasn't here either. After a while he left." And soon thereafter the Norwegian side of the romantic triangle was missing.

Fess took another trip back to Texas and was greeted with some flattering local press coverage from the *Abilene Reporter News* which described him as a potential husband: "Attention, tall West Texas babes with a bare finger on the left hand, don't amble—scramble, hop or fly, ride a pogo stick or something—but don't let him get away. The Him is icy-green-eyed Fess Parker, who towers six feet something into the ozone."

The article also featured a photograph of Fess with two his University of Texas classmates: Phil Kendrick and Joe Bob Jay.

"That was a fun time," said Kendrick."

The last production that Fess worked in before meeting Walt Disney was *City Detective*, the TV drama that starred Rod Cameron as Lieutenant Bart Grant. Fess appeared as a character named Tony in an episode that eventually aired on March 15, 1955. It was another small credit that he added to his resume. But it was a film that he worked on earlier that provided him with the break of a lifetime.

CHAPTER 2
FROM "THEM!" TO DAVY CROCKETT

Walt Disney's *Davy Crockett* almost didn't happen.

In 1954, Disney was considering a number of frontier characters, like Daniel Boone and Johnny Appleseed, to be featured in *Disneyland*, his new weekly ABC-TV program. The selected character would be an integral part of Frontierland, one of the television show's segments and one of the proposed "lands" scheduled to be a part of the new Disneyland theme park in Anaheim, California.

"I've always wanted to do American history," said Disney in an April 1955 *Newsweek* article. "I'm not really telling history, though, I'm telling about people."

However, frontier hero Davy Crockett emerged as Disney's "people" story because the Tennessean's illustrious life was filled with "tall tales and true from the legendary past."

Crockett was born on August 17, 1786, and grew up in the pioneer backwoods. He fought during the Creek Indian War of 1813–14, but later defended Native American rights while serving in the U.S. House of Representatives. While in Congress and on the campaign trail he delivered lively political speeches, demonstrated flintlock rifle skills at public shooting matches, and honestly represented the poor frontier families of his district. During his lifetime, he was celebrated with books, songs, plays, portraits, newspaper articles, and almanacs. After serving three terms in the U.S. House of Representatives, Crockett journeyed to Texas where he joined the revolution against the dictatorship of General Antonio López de Santa Anna. Crockett, 49, fought and died at the Battle of the Alamo on March 6, 1836.

Surprisingly, Walt Disney had been interested in creating a Davy Crockett production a decade earlier. According to a Los Angeles County Museum of Arts guide book that accompanied a 1990 Thomas Hart Benton exhibition, the famous artist was asked by the Disney organization in 1946 to "create a cartoon operetta based on the life of Davy Crockett, but he found it impossible to create anything satisfying within the constraints the studio imposed." Benton's fluid style, perhaps, was a bit too abstract for the detailed images that Disney embraced. As a result, the Benton-Disney project never materialized. However, Benton later created studio art for the 1954 film *The Kentuckian*, which starred Burt Lancaster as a buckskin-wearing frontiersman.

In mid-1954, Disney searched for someone to play the title role of *Davy Crockett* but he didn't want a name actor who would overshadow the character. He wanted a solid performer who could portray a classic frontier hero with honor, courage, and humor—and someone who could appeal to both youngsters and adults.

Buddy Ebsen, who had been the dancing model in Disney's "Project Little Man," the embryonic forerunner of Audio-Animatronics, was one of the actors considered to portray Crockett. Ebsen, 46, was a veteran character actor, singer, and dancer who had shared the motion picture screen with such stars as Shirley Temple, Judy Garland, and Gregory Peck. "He was a talent," said Fess. "He performed in vaudeville, film, television, and on Broadway. He danced and wrote songs. I think they had also considered Sterling Hayden, Ronald Reagan and some others for the role."

A leading candidate for the role was James Arness, who had appeared as *The Thing from Another World* and in several other films and TV programs. Disney staffers viewed Arness, 31, in *Them!*, a sci-fi film about giant ants, which debuted in theaters on June 19, 1954. In fact, Arness' agent provided Disney with a print of the film. Arness was impressive as the leading man, Robert Graham, an FBI agent. But a bit player portraying Alan Crotty, a Texas rancher-pilot, caught the attention of the Disney people. The character was played by Fess Parker.

Fess' only scene was set up by a close-up of a telegraph message sent to the special FBI office handling reports of unidentified flying objects and other giant ant-related accounts. The message read:

BROWNSVILLE, TEXAS
ALAN CROTTY, LAZY K RANCH FOREMAN INSISTS REASON FOR CRASHING HIS PLANE WAS DUE TO SEEING FLYING SAUCERS SHAPED LIKE ANTS. CROTTY BEING HELD PSYCHIATHIC WARD MERCY HOSPITAL.

In the film, Graham and his assistant, Dr. Patricia Medford, played by Joan Weldon, visit the detained pilot. Wearing a simple bathrobe and being politely cognizant of Medford's presence, Fess' Crotty is a friendly soul who displays down-to-earth sincerity in his seemingly outlandish testimony about giant flying ants. Graham and Medford believe Crotty's story but do not allow him to leave in fear that his public remarks might start a panic.

Dallas Morning News film critic John Rosenfield cited Fess for his "good comedy."

Whatever it was—his restrained but thoughtful performance, his subtle Texas accent, his height, his good looks, his tussled hair—Fess made a unique impression on the Disney staffers who viewed the film.

"We were looking for somebody to play *Davy Crockett*," said Tom Blackburn, who wrote the *Davy Crockett* script. "I remember seeing Fess in his scene and noting that this was our guy! I immediately called the projectionist to get information about him, his identity, his studio, things like that. He certainly seemed to be just what we were looking for in the role. And when we finally contacted him and I met him, well, I fell in love with the guy! He was perfect! Really, Fess was the only one that was genuinely considered for the role."

Fess echoed Blackburn's recollections.

"Walt Disney actually picked me out during a screening room viewing of *Them!*" explained Fess. "Among the others in the screening room were Tom Blackburn, who wrote the *Davy Crockett* screenplay and 'The Ballad of Davy Crockett,' producer Bill Walsh, and matte artist Peter Ellenshaw. They were initially interested in James Arness, who starred in *Them!* But Walt Disney wanted me. Tom Blackburn called Warner Brothers, the studio that made *Them!* to ask about me. Shortly thereafter, around late June or early July 1954, I was called in by the Walt Disney casting office."

Nolie Fishman, who was married to Walsh at the time, remembered her husband's enthusiasm when he arrived home after the screening.

"Bill told me, 'There's the most perfect guy we saw in a scene with Jim Arness today,'" said Fishman, who later married Hal Fishman in 1976, a year after Walsh's death. "He said, 'This guy is just incredible; he looked so impressive.' I finally met Fess and thought he was absolutely gorgeous and easy to talk to."

Had *Island in the Sky*, a 1953 film starring John Wayne which featured Arness, been screened instead, the casting for *Davy Crockett* could have been different. In the film, Arness played Mac McMullen, a man with a backwoods bucolic drawl and confident style that could have easily impressed Walt Disney. Ironically, Fess appears in an uncredited co-pilot in the film. Arness, of course, didn't get the role of *Davy Crockett*, but a year later he started a twenty-year run as Marshal Matt Dillon on TV's *Gunsmoke*. And John Wayne was on hand in the first episode to introduce him.

Ebsen was disappointed when Director Norman Foster told him that he was not selected to play Crockett.

"I was crushed, of course, but then he called me to tell me about the role of Georgie Russel," noted Ebsen in his 1993 autobiography, *The Other Side of Oz*. The Russel character was crafted to be Davy's sidekick, a life-long friend who accompanied him on all of his adventures.

"His role as George Russel was created for him by Walt Disney as a favor," stated Blackburn. "Disney liked Ebsen, but his career, to many, was over by the 1950s. In a way, his role—a television role—as Russel was seen by some as a definite step backwards in his career. You must remember that TV was still a relatively new medium, especially color programming. But of course, Buddy, one of the dearest people I have ever known, went on to great successes on television."

Ebsen later became Jed Clampett, the family patriarch of the enormously popular *Beverly Hillbillies* (1962–71) and later starred in the title role of private investigator *Barnaby Jones* (1973–80). But for young Baby Boomers, he was George Russel, Davy Crockett's loyal companion. "Buddy was just perfect," said Fess.

Disney's offer to play Crockett couldn't have come at a better time for Fess

"I had already completed a number of films, including *Them!* the previous year," he said. "I had just finished *Battle Cry* in the spring of 1954, and I believe I had just worked on a project with Jim Davis called *Outlaws of the Century*. Still, I wasn't doing a lot. I wasn't at a point in my acting career that I'd consider a watershed. There was some movement by Gary Cooper's production company to get me to be a part of it and there was a possible contract offer coming from Warner Brothers, but both of those arrangements never materialized. At the time, I had given myself three years to do something in the business or do something else. And I was about to review that policy when I was approached by Mr. Disney's people. Things changed drastically when I signed with Mr. Disney. Within a few months we were on location for the first episode."

Despite Blackburn's enthusiasm, Fess wasn't guaranteed the part. He would have to convince Walt Disney—in person—at his Burbank office.

"I was brought out to see Walt by Bill Walsh when he thought it was the right time," noted Fess. "I went down the hall and we sat at a little writer's cubicle which only had two chairs, a desk, phone book, and telephone. For some reason, I brought my guitar. I couldn't play the guitar very well and I couldn't sing any songs that anybody else had done so I wrote my own. And I wrote a little song called 'Lonely.' And when Walt said, 'What have you done,' I said, well, I did this and that and I'm from Texas. 'I see you brought your guitar. Would you like to play me something?' I said sure. So I hauled it out and I sang this little song called 'Lonely.' Now then, 'Lonely' was the sound of a train whistle that you used to hear across the prairie: 'I lost my gal/I lost my pal/Never going back/Cause I'm lonely.' And then some little verses. So I sang it to him. It never occurred to me that Walt Disney was an absolute train buff. He had a train in his back yard! I think it was one-quarter scale. And I learned that later on. But I never realized that connection until only recently. Two weeks later he gave me 'Davy Crockett' to sing. Funny, though: when the sheet music was first presented to me to take a look at, I noticed that my name was spelled F-E-Z at the top of the front page. Obviously, I wasn't exactly a household word at that time."

Tom Blackburn had written lyrics to what originally was titled the "Davy Crockett Ballad." George Bruns provided the music. Blackburn revised the song and sent a copy of the song with its five verses and choruses to Bill Walsh on August 21, 1954. The lyrics were designated to be performed on *Disneyland's* "Show #1." "Fez" was written alongside the first two verses; "Geno" was written next to the third, and "Fez" was written next to the fourth. The final verse was attributed to "all." Walsh or Blackburn changed the final chorus line from "Immortal volunteer" to "King of the Wild Frontier," the same musical phrase that accompanied the first verse. Fess kept the document and, years later, had the lyric sheet framed and placed on his business office wall.

His friends eagerly waited to hear about Fess' meeting with Disney.

"We were very anxious to know how it went," said Kendrick. "When Fess returned, he seemed very pleased. He was pretty sure he was going to get the part. He was very happy but no there was no 'let's go celebrate' or anything like that. He wasn't a party guy. He'd rather stay home and read or just relax. He loved just sitting around with friends and shooting the bull. That was probably the thing he enjoyed the most."

Fess returned to Burbank on August 4 and signed a sixteen-page "Agreement" with Walt Disney Productions for "three motion pictures tentatively titled 'Davy Crockett No. 1,' 'Davy Crockett No. 2' and 'Davy Crockett No. 3'" that were scheduled to commence filming on September 7, 1954. The three productions would become TV's first mini-series, an important milestone in the history of the small screen. The contract, which was also signed by Gunther R. Lessing, Vice President of Walt Disney Productions, stated that Fess would be paid $550 per week while working and would be guaranteed at least five weeks of work. Furthermore, Fess would be paid additional sums if the films were broadcast more than twice. Beyond the initial contract period, the studio had multiple renewal options that totaled six additional years. According to page fourteen of the Agreement, Fess would be paid $2,500 a week while working during the final option period.

In addition, the contract noted: "In the event the Corporation exhibits or causes any such film to be exhibited theatrically in the

United States or Canada it agrees to pay the Artist the sum of $250.00 for each film so exhibited…" Clearly, Disney prepared for the possibility of releasing the TV episodes as an edited feature film in theaters. Over the years it has been reported that the subsequent release of the edited television episodes as the feature film *Davy Crockett, King of the Wild Frontier* in 1955 was an ad hoc decision based on the popularity of the TV shows, but that was not the case. Walt Disney had the foresight to plan for such an eventuality—and it paid off handsomely for the studio.

The contract also stated that Fess would be paid "ten percent of the gross amounts received by the Corporation pursuant to or attributable to any such merchandising or publishing endeavors in or connection with the Artist's name, photograph, likeness, silhouette, caricature or voice is or are used, utilized or simulated, provided, however, that the Corporation's obligation to pay such sums to the Artist shall not accrue unless or until the moneys out of which shall have been received by the Corporation within the United States of America and are placed at the Corporation's unrestricted disposal."

Disney was always concerned with the image that its actors—both human and cartoon—projected to audiences worldwide, and Fess' contract reflected those concerns. The contract stated: "The Artist agrees that during the term of this agreement, and at all times during the production, exhibition and distribution of any and all motion pictures produced hereunder the Artist will conduct himself with due regard to public morals and conventions and will not do anything which will tend to degrade him in society or bring him into public dispute, contempt, scandal or ridicule or that will tend to shock, insult or offend the community or any substantial group thereof, or public morals or decency, or prejudice the Corporation or the American Broadcasting Company or the then current sponsor or sponsors (or its or their agencies) of any television show or motion picture in which the Artist's performance is used." The contract's provisions were comprehensive and demanding but the studio did not have to worry about Fess' deportment. Ever.

"After I was given the job in August, I recorded 'The Ballad of Davy Crockett.'" stated Fess. "I was dating Marcella at the time and I sang her the song. She didn't care too much for it."

"He's quite correct," replied Marcy. "Well, after he started the Disney series he sang the song to me. I was not too terribly impressed. I told him, 'I thought it stinks.'"

Phil Kendrick wasn't a fan of the song either.

"I first heard the song at Fess' apartment," said Kendrick. "Marcy was there and a few others. We both gave each other the eye like that's the most stupidest song I ever heard."

Jimmy Tittle agreed with Kendrick.

"I went out there visiting him and he was practicing the song on his guitar," said Tittle. "I told him, 'That will never fly.' I was probably just teasing him, though."

In time, Marcy changed her mind about the song.

"I was very wrong about the song," she said. "Very wrong."

"And that became a promotional record while we were still out in the field making the movie—the three one-hour episodes," said Fess.

Fess, dressed in buckskins, was later filmed on a sound stage set singing the song with three frontier-looking backup vocalists in front of Norman Foster and a small crew. That segment was featured on the very first show of *Disneyland*, which aired on October 27, 1954.

"And they made a film that was shown in October and it was Walt Disney talking about what the television show would be about and also about what Disneyland was gonna be," explained Fess. "And I was introduced on that show and I sang 'The Ballad of Davy Crockett.' And that was purported to be my screen test. And that's as close as I ever got to a screen test, by the way."

Disneyland began each week with an animated introduction to one of its "many worlds." The narration accompanying the Frontierland sequence—with Tinker Bell wearing a coonskin cap and carrying a flintlock rifle—stated: "Tall tales and true from the legendary past." *Davy Crockett* was on the way.

Much to his amusement, Fess discovered that his August 16th birthday nearly coincided with the real Davy Crockett's August 17th birthday.

"I probably didn't become aware of it until I was working on the Disney series in the 1950s," said Fess. "I never was aware of it as a child. I had read about Crockett as a youngster, but I can't recall

Fess Parker as Davy Crockett in a promotional still.
© DISNEY.

exactly if I knew about his birthday. I'm not sure about the significance of our birthdays occurring on consecutive days. I'm sure those who believe in astrology make something of it, but I don't really believe in it. However, over the years, I have noticed that a number of individuals who have been born under the sign of Leo usually have had some high prospects about their lives."

Before reporting to the production's location site in North Carolina, Fess traveled to Texas.

"He and I drove there in my new Buick," Kendrick pointed out. "He just had enough time to go home and see his parents and mine. We were going to drive straight through."

And they did just that. The two friends decided to share the driving in order to make the most of Fess' limited time off.

"We talked about girls and politics and eventually religion," said Kendrick. "And we talked about heaven, and going to church, baptism, things like that. When we got to the outskirts of Tucson, Arizona, Fess was driving. A motorcycle cop stopped us and told us we were going seventy miles per hour in a forty zone. But Fess talked him out of it. Well, we got on the other side of Tucson and another motorcycle cop pulled us over for speeding. And Fess talked him out of it, too. 'Well, okay, I guess I'll just let you go,' said the second cop. And then Fess tells him, 'That's funny, the motorcycle cop on the other side of Tucson said the same thing.'"

Kendrick silently moaned, shook his head from side to side and slipped down in his seat. "I thought I was gonna die," laughed Kendrick. "I couldn't believe he said that to the cop. I wondered what was going to happen next."

He and Fess soon found out.

The police officer didn't appreciate Fess' blunt honesty or his attempt at humor and immediately asked him for identification.

"But Fess didn't have any identification on him; he didn't even have a billfold," laughed Kendrick. "Fess kept going through his suitcase. The only thing he had was a publicity shot with him and actress Nancy Hale. So the cop took us in to this little justice of the peace, a big fat woman dressed with a six-shooter hanging from her side. It looked like we were going to jail."

Fess realized that incarceration—even an overnight stay in a rural Texas jail cell—could jeopardize his Disney contract, which forbade him to engage in behavior that would cause "public disrepute, contempt, scandal or ridicule."

The police officer explained what happened at the scene and the judge listened intently. The two speeding Texans awaited the ruling. "I was worried," said Kendrick.

The judge found Fess guilty of speeding and fined him $250, a large sum for a traffic violation in 1954. But Fess had no money. Kendrick immediately offered to pay his good friend's fine with a credit card. "She didn't accept my American Express card," laughed Kendrick. "Finally, Fess had to call his agent back in California to wire the $250 and verify Fess' identification."

Fess and Kendrick waited at the jail. They were tired but their collective worries kept them awake. Finally, the wired payment and identification were received by the judge.

"Our delay was probably about four or five hours," stated Kendrick. "By the time we got to Pecos, we were dead tired. We stayed in a flea-bitten motel and it had one narrow single bed. But we got enough shut eye."

Back on the road, Fess and Kendrick stayed under the speed limit and finally made it home.

"Fess spent several days at my home in Abilene visiting friends and relatives before going to Brownwood to visit his parents," said Kendrick. "He had about two weeks off from Disney to take care of personal business before reporting back to Disney in California. I assume he flew back to California, although flying was our choice of last resort in those days."

CHAPTER 3
THE HISTORIC DAVY CROCKETT

Tom Blackburn was entrusted by Walt Disney to get the story of Davy Crockett to the screen but he was pressed for time. Fess had been signed on August 4, 1954, and filming was about to start four weeks later. Blackburn didn't have the luxury to conduct extensive research on Crockett but fortunately there were a few books that were available to him like John E. Potter's 1865 volume, *The Life of Colonel David Crockett*, which combined elements from Crockett's 1834 autobiography with quasi-fictional elements written by Richard Penn Smith in the 1836 book *Col. Crockett's Exploits and Adventures in Texas*. John M. Myers' *The Alamo* was also in print. Published in 1948, the book graphically described Crockett's final moments. Blackburn found much that was interesting in Crockett's story.

David Crockett was born on August 17, 1786, near the confluence of the Nolichucky River and Limestone Creek in what is now eastern Tennessee. However, it wasn't on the "mountaintop in Tennessee" that the first line of "The Ballad of Davy Crockett" later proclaimed—but he certainly was "raised in the woods." His parents, John and Rebecca Crockett, had nine children; David was the fifth born. "My father and mother had six sons and three daughters," wrote Crockett in his 1834 autobiography.

Life on the frontier was hazardous. "By the Creeks, my grandfather and grandmother Crockett were both murdered, in their homes, and on the very spot of ground where Rogersville, in Hawkins County, now stands," stated Crockett.

Poverty was so widespread on the Tennessee frontier that it became part of Crockett's consciousness; as a matter of fact, it was something that he would be cognizant of for the rest of his life. "I began to make up my acquaintance with hard times, and plenty of them," lamented Crockett.

Crockett met Polly Finley, 18, at a community frolic. "She looked sweeter than sugar," he wrote. The pair married on August 16, 1806, one day before Crockett's twentieth birthday. Polly and Davy had three children: John Wesley (born in 1807), William (1809), and Margaret (1812). Although he was primarily a frontier farmer, Crockett was particularly adept as a marksman. "I began to distinguish myself as a hunter, and lay the foundation for all my future greatness," said Crockett.

The same year that his daughter was born, the United States went to war with Great Britain. The War of 1812 expanded when the Red Stick faction of Creeks attacked Fort Mims on August 30, 1813, in what is now Alabama—and this where Tom Blackburn began his teleplay.

The call went out for volunteers and Crockett volunteered for a 90-day enlistment a month later. Another volunteer was George Russell. The two were considered the "best woodsmen" in the company and were soon sent on special scouting missions. Blackburn turned Russell into Crockett's life-long friend, but dropped the last letter from his name.

At the Battle of Taladega, Crockett noted that the Creeks "made their escape through a part of our line." Blackburn wrote a scene in which some of Red Stick's warriors break through General Andrew Jackson's ranks.

Although his 90-day enlistment had yet to expire, Crockett said that his "sixty days had long been out." He prepared to leave camp for home. "The general went and placed his cannon on a bridge we had to cross, and ordered his regulars and drafted men to keep us from crossing," remearked Crockett. "But, after all, we marched boldly on, and not a gun was fired, nor a life lost." Blackburn also brought this scene wonderfully to life in his script.

On January 8, 1815, Jackson emerged victorious over the British at the Battle of New Orleans. Crockett was not with Jackson at the time; instead, the Tennessean continued skirmishing with the Creeks until he ended his service as a fourth sergeant on March 27, 1815. That same year, Polly took ill and died.

Following the passing of his wife, Crockett found consolation in a relationship with Elizabeth Patton, 27, whose husband had been killed in the War of 1812. The two married but Blackburn did not mention Crockett's second wife and the new family in the scripts.

Crockett became active in community affairs. He was made a justice of the peace in 1817, and the next year was elected a colonel in the 57th Militia. In 1821, he decided to run for the Tennessee State Legislature. His stump-speech strategy was a simple one: "Tell a laughable story, and quit." It worked. But when Crockett arrived at the state capitol in Murfreesboro on September 21, 1821 for his first legislative session, he put his jokes aside and concentrated on representing the poor farmers from his district. Many of his neighbors were "squatters," people who settled on government land and built homes, farms and mills without real estate deeds.

In 1823, Crockett successfully ran for re-election. On the campaign trail, Crockett would offer voters "a great big twist of tobacco, and…my bottle of liquor." Blackburn avoided the crudeness of Crockett's backwoods stump campaign but still managed to create an authentic frontier political atmosphere, and Fess played it perfectly. In the next legislative session, Crockett cast a vote for Colonel John Williams instead of Andrew Jackson for U.S. Senator. It marked the beginning of a rift between Crockett and Jackson.

Crockett entered national politics in 1825 when he unsuccessfully ran for Congress; however, he was elected to the U.S. House of Representatives two years later and promptly renewed his efforts to protect the squatters and poor farmers who he represented. Jackson won the Presidential election in 1828 and Crockett was re-elected in 1829. Crockett's detractors called him the Congressman from the cane—short for canebrake, the stalk-like reed areas that punctuated the lands where his constituents called home.

In the Twenty-first Congress, Crockett antagonized Jackson by opposing the Indian Resettlement Act, a law which was designed to force the Southwestern tribes to move west of the Mississippi River. Crockett's grandparents had been murdered by Native American warriors and he had fought them in the Creek Indian War, but he held no animosity towards the tribes. Crockett thought the law was morally wrong and vigorously spoke out against it. Blackburn's script integrated Crockett's sentiments into the most important political scene in "Davy Crockett Goes to Congress."

Despite Crockett's protests, the bill passed and the canebrake Congressman was defeated in the next election by a candidate who had the support of the Jackson political machine in Tennessee. Jackson won re-election in 1832, but anti-Jackson forces were building and soon come together as the Whig Party. Crockett seemed a perfect choice to join its ranks.

Crockett received a boost in the public consciousness thanks to James K. Paulding's play *The Lion of the West*, which featured Nimrod Wildfire, an exaggerated Crockett-like frontiersman. James French's 1833 book, *Life and Adventures of Colonel David Crockett of West Tennessee*, part *Lion of the West* and part biography, became a best seller. Subsequent editions of the book were titled *Sketches and Eccentricities of Col. David Crockett of West Tennessee.* Crockett clearly benefited from the publicity and won his Congressional seat back in 1833. During his time in the Twenty-third Congress, Crockett began writing his autobiography: *A Narrative of the Life of David Crockett of the State of Tennessee.* Published in 1834, the book quickly became a best seller. On the book's title page was Crockett's motto: "Be always sure you're right—then go ahead." Blackburn eliminated the word "always" from the motto and integrated into his teleplay. Interestingly enough, the motto would help guide Fess Parker for over sixty years of his adult life.

Coupled with Paulding's play and the French book, Crockett became a national celebrity. The newly-formed Whig Party took advantage of Crockett's fame and promoted him on a political tour of the Northeast in an effort to spread the anti-Jackson message. Crockett spoke in all the major cities and was well received along the way especially in Philadelphia where the Young Whigs gave him a fine rifle. Blackburn included the rifle presentation in the script but added a fictitious subplot in which Crockett discovers that the tour was created to keep him away from Congress during the Indian Bill debate.

Crockett's national profile received another boost with the publication of a song, "The Crockett Victory March," and the printing of the first *Crockett Almanac* in 1835. Blackburn wrote a scene in which President Jackson shows Crockett one of the almanacs written

The historic David Crockett. Illustration by Joseph Musso.
AUTHOR'S COLLECTION.

by his friend George Russel.

Defeated in the 1835 election, Crockett declared: "You may all go to hell and I will go to Texas." In the autumn of 1835, Crockett, 49, and several companions headed west. Passing through Memphis, one observer noted that Crockett "wore that same veritable coon-skin cap and hunting shirt, bearing upon his shoulder his ever faithful rifle." Texas, then part of Mexico, was in the midst of a revolution. President Antonio López de Santa Anna centralized the government and created a dictatorship. Protests and revolts sprang up in places like Zacatecas, Gonzales, and Goliad. A large force of Anglos and Tejanos opposed to the Santa Anna regime fought and captured San Antonio de Bexar in December 1835.

Crockett arrived in Texas in January, 1836. He wrote to his daughter, Margaret, and her husband that "Texas is the garden spot of the world. The best land and the best prospects for health I ever saw, and I do believe it is a fortune to any man to come here." Blackburn made sure that the script included a reference to Crockett's appreciation of Texas as Fess gazed at the area for the first time. But the scene was conveniently filmed in California.

Crockett took an oath of allegiance to the Provisional Government of Texas and later joined the Volunteer Auxiliary Corps of Texas. In early February, Crockett arrived in San Antonio de Bexar where William B. Travis and James Bowie led the regulars and volunteers, respectfully. Crockett, a Colonel in the Tennessee Militia, offered his services as a "high private."

On February 23, advance units of Santa Anna's army approached the outskirts of San Antonio de Bexar. The Texans regrouped inside the Alamo, the old Spanish mission that had been converted into a fortress by the Mexicans a year earlier. The siege of the Alamo had begun. However, Blackburn has Crockett arriving during the siege in a daring ride through the Mexican lines. Just before dawn on March 6, 1836, Santa Anna's soldiers stormed the Alamo's walls. At the end of the fighting, one of the non-combatants, Susanna Dickinson, noted that she "recognized Colonel Crockett lying dead and mutilated between the church and the two story long barrack, [his] peculiar cap by his side." Santa Anna ordered that the bodies of the defenders be burned.

News of the Alamo's fall spread. On March 28, the *Louisiana Advertiser* reported: "Col. Crockett is among the slain… [He] fell like a tiger." Blackburn embraced the idea of Crockett's heroic death but was challenged on how to depict it in the script.

"Crockett had great courage and character," said Fess.

CHAPTER 4
"DAVY CROCKETT, INDIAN FIGHTER"

The first episode of the *Davy Crockett* trilogy aired on December 15, 1954. Its story line followed Crockett and Russel as volunteers in General Andrew Jackson's (Basil Ruysdael) army during the Creek Indian War, 1813–14.

Crockett and Russel join Major Tobias Norton (William Bakewell) and a small troop of mounted soldiers on a scouting party which gets ambushed by a Creek war party. The two frontiersmen rescue Norton and his men with the "Crockett Charge," a ruse in which the Creek war party—and the major—believe an entire regiment of reinforcements had arrived. Crockett reports back to Jackson and informs him that Chief Red Stick (Pat Hogan) is leading the warriors. Jackson organizes an attack on Red Stick's camp. Crockett and the other volunteers initiate the battle but Red Stick and many of his braves escape when they avoid Norton's predictable musket volley.

Following the battle, Crockett, Russel, and a few other volunteers depart for home despite orders from Norton to remain in camp. After supplying winter provisions for his wife (Helene Stanley) and boys (Eugene Brindel and Ray Whitetree), Crockett returns to Jackson's headquarters only to discover that the general has left for New Orleans, leaving Norton in command. Crockett and Russel track down Red Stick and his few remaining warriors, but Russel is captured. Crockett challenges Red Stick to a fight in order to free his friend. Crockett wins the tomahawk fight and Red Stick orders Russel's release. Crockett promises Red Stick a fair peace treaty. The episode ends with the antagonists shaking hands.

Walt Disney wanted his action-adventure productions to look as authentic as possible and he found the ideal location for the first episode in the Great Smoky Mountains. Director Norman Foster, Fess, and the rest of the Disney production team traveled east and established their headquarters in Cherokee, North Carolina.

"The production was headquartered at the old Boundary Tree Motel and the wardrobe was stored in the auditorium of the Cherokee School," said Ken Blankenship, Director of the Cherokee Museum.

Located in the Great Smoky Mountains was the Pioneer Farmstead, a group of original structures which provided useful interior and exterior shots for both "Davy Crockett, Indian Fighter" and "Davy Crockett Goes to Congress." Now known as the Mountain Farm Museum, the location is operated by the National Park Service. "It's a collection of nine historic log farm buildings that were moved from their original locations throughout the national park and reconstructed at their current location in late 1952 and early 1953," explained Tom Robbins, a Park Ranger at the Great Smoky Mountain National Park. "When you compare scenes in the episodes with the Mountain Farm Museum now the buildings seem to be in the wrong place, but that's because a number of the buildings were moved a second time in late 1959 and early 1960. This seems to have been done for a number of reasons, probably to move them away from the park visitor center and to create more room due to increasing visitation."

The most important Mountain Farm Museum structure featured in "Davy Crockett, Indian Fighter" is the Davis House. Constructed by John E. Davis around 1900, the home was built of matched chestnut logs in the hand-crafted traditional way, although sawmill-produced logs were readily available at the time. The house makes its first appearance as the interior of the Crockett home. It later serves as the trading post exterior and the land claim office interior in "Davy Crockett Goes to Congress." The Davis House is also featured on the cover of the "Farewell" sheet music, a tune featured in the "Davy Crockett at the Alamo" episode.

"The village of farm houses, which was put together by the state of North Carolina, was already an attraction," remarked Fess.

"There are two log structures that appear in the episodes that I cannot identify," said Robbins several years ago. "One is Davy's cabin exterior, although the interior scenes with his wife were shot in the front room of the Davis House. The other structure I can't identify is the house where Davy confronts Bigfoot Mason. There were some structures still in existence in the park in the 1950s that were later torn down but I don't think that was one of them. Some filming was evidently done in other parts of western North Carolina and possibly eastern Tennessee."

A few weeks before on-location filming, Tom Blackburn was still rewriting the script. The revised script for "Davy Crockett...The Creek War" (production #5575) dated August 17—coincidentally Davy Crockett's 168th birthday—noted a proposed air date of December 8, 1954. On page three, the screenplay identified Crockett's first two sons as Tim and Davy, even though they were actually named John and Billy. By the time the script was finalized, Blackburn utilized the correct names of Crockett's sons. Ray Whitetree portrayed John and Eugene Brindel played Billy.

The August 17 script made reference to an interesting event that Crockett recalled during the Creek War in his 1834 autobiography. Crockett recommended George Russell as a reliable scout. But his choice was questioned by a Major Gibson who noted that Russell seem too young and inexperienced since "he hadn't beard enough." Crockett countered: "I didn't think that courage ought to be measured by the beard, for fear a goat would have the preference over a man." Blackburn included dialogue from the autobiography and gave the lines to Basil Ruysdael's Andrew Jackson character. "Why, thunderation, Crockett, he's hardly more than a boy!" exclaimed Jackson. "Ain't even got a beard." But Buddy Ebsen at age forty-six was "more than a boy." The lines were dropped.

Disney costumer Norman Martien dressed Fess in his iconic buckskin clothes and coonskin cap. And it wasn't the first time that a Disney character wore a coonskin cap. Mickey Mouse wore the unique headgear in *R'coon Dawg*, a 1951 cartoon. Instead of the historically correct center-seam Eastern Woodlands Indian moccasins, Martien gave Fess semi-modernized Plains Indians-styled footwear and tan socks. However, it was a minor historical-fashion faux pas, and kids watching TV would be more focused on Fess' headgear than his footwear. Above all, Fess looked comfortable in his costuming and he cradled his flintlock rifle in his arm just like a real frontier hunter. "I had a limited wardrobe," said Fess. "Those buckskins got to a point where they could stand up without me in them."

Fess was a natural for the role. He created and maintained the appearance of a genuine frontier hero. Fess was tall and strong. And he projected confidence; nothing he did seemed awkward or artificial. Had he appeared or acted in any way artificial, kids everywhere would have dismissed him. Instead, they would embrace him with admiration and affection that would reach unprecedented levels.

And there was something else, something very individualistic about him: his facial mannerisms. With his lips thoughtfully closed and subtly turned to one side, Fess would occasionally deliver a squinty-eyed, restrained smile that became his signature visage—an expression many a young Baby Boomer unsuccessfully tried to imitate.

Since the first two episodes were going to utilize a number of common locations, Blackburn also revised his "I Get Into Politics" script (production #5550) two days later on August 19. While Blackburn revised the scripts, the production was busy casting locals and preparing for the first day of filming.

"Filming began after Labor Day," recalled Fess. "September 8, I think, at the Cherokee Indian Nation in North Carolina. We mostly crawled around the rocks in a stealthy way looking for the Indians." And the Native-American warriors were the real thing. The Eastern band of the Cherokee Nation lived within its own territory, the Qualla Boundary, and many were hired as extras.

"I was about ten years old at the time and everybody was invited to an old gymnasium at the Cherokee Boarding School," said Tom Beck, a local resident. "My cousin and I went up there and they had costumes and people to select who would be in the movie. I was selected to be one of the kids. Ironically, we were selected to be white kids rather than Indians. I'm one-half Chitamacha and one-eighth Cherokee. We were paid five dollars a day, maybe it was ten. I bought a couple of cap pistols and holsters with the money I received. I felt that I had done real well for myself."

Another local hire was Blankenship. "I was in seventh grade at the time and somebody from Disney walked into my classroom, looked around and selected me," stated Blankenship. "And the school let us go. After all, it was quite a big deal for a movie company to be in Cherokee. I think I got thirteen dollars a day. It doesn't seem like a lot of money today but back then it was, especially to a seventh-grader."

Norman Foster and his location crew didn't avoid the public; as a matter of fact, they publicized the production with a large sign mounted on one side of the grip truck. The sign stated:

A GREAT TV SHOW IS COMING!
WALT DISNEY'S "DAVY CROCKETT"
STARRING FESS PARKER AS DAVY
TO BE PRESENTED ON "DISNEYLAND"
DISNEY'S SERIES ON ABC-TV PREMIERING OCT. 27

And the tourists showed up in droves. Today, the expansive Great Smoky Mountains is America's most visited national park with over ten million people entering it each year, but it seemed as if that many were around during filming in 1954. Security on the set was minimal and tourists, many armed with their cameras, clicked their shutters at every opportunity.

During a break in the filming of the scene where Davy Crockett and George Russel leave General Andrew Jackson's camp for home, a honeymoon couple arrived on the set.

"We had just been married in Canton, Illinois on September 5, 1954, and were about to end our honeymoon after about four nights in Gatlinburg, Tennessee, in the Great Smoky Mountains," explained New Jersey's Anne English, then a twenty-year old junior pursuing a nursing degree at the University of Iowa. "We were in the process of driving home when we saw an Indian with war paint riding a horse alongside the road. We noticed some trucks and other activity going on nearby so I told my husband, John, that I wanted know what that was all about. We drove up to what we soon discovered was a film site. Someone told us that the film was being shot in Technicolor but the cast and crew were waiting for the clouds to clear. We struck up a conversation with Fess Parker and Buddy Ebsen, but their names meant nothing to us at the time. After a conversation with them about Big Ten college football, John asked them if they would agree to have their picture taken with me.

While on her honeymoon, Anne English poses with Fess Parker and Buddy Ebsen.
PHOTO COURTESY OF ANNE ENGLISH.

It was the first time he called me his wife. Well, John took the photo and we left. We finally realized who they were when *Davy Crockett* was broadcast on television."

"There were lots of folks around during filming," said Fess. "But we didn't have any problems; it was handled nicely. We may have had a rope placed up or something. That was about it."

Another visiting family's camping trip was interrupted by a battle between the Creeks and Crockett's volunteers.

"Our family at the time of the camping trip to the Great Smokies consisted of my wife, Betty; daughter Wendy, age twelve; and son Peter, age seven," stated Connecticut's Clavin Fisher. "One morning, Peter, who had been exploring a bit before breakfast, came racing back to our campfire, crying, 'There are Indians out there on the warpath! Their faces are painted! And they have knives and

Cast and crew take a break during the filming of "Davy Crockett, Indian Fighter." Fess Parker can be seen in the upper left walking away from the set. Photo courtesy of Clavin Fisher.

tomahawks!' We followed him back along a trail marked with red arrows. To our astonishment, in a natural bowl in the forest, Indians in full war regalia were charging a group of frontiersmen, resplendent in their fringed shirts and coonskin caps. The field was shrouded in smoke."

Fisher's daughter, Wendy, recalled that she and her fellow family members had a perfect view of the action. "We saw everything from a nearby hillside," she said. "I remember seeing Davy and somebody hiding behind a bush so the Indians couldn't see them, but they were easily seen by us. I also remember the re-shooting of the battle scenes because the Indians were laughing and fooling around."

The elder Fisher moved closer to the choreographed battle. "I advanced rather surreptitiously with camera in hand until I was about ten feet behind the cameraman," remarked Fisher. "Then I began photographing the action."

And there was lots of action.

The studio proclaimed that the production featured "some of the most dangerous fight scenes ever filmed." The pressbook that was used for the subsequent theatrical release, *Davy Crockett, King of the Wild Frontier*, noted: "To give the picture utmost realism, the Indians refused prop weapons and fought with genuine tomahawks and clubs. The peak personal hazard was reached when one Indian voluntarily toppled thirty feet into a fast flowing river."

Fess acknowledged the physical challenges associated with the individual fights and large battles scenes in "Davy Crockett, Indian Fighter."

"But that episode was my least favorite, primarily because it was somewhat dangerous," he said. "Buddy and I did our own stunts; there weren't any stuntmen that were as tall as Buddy, who stood over six-feet tall, and me. So we were on our own. Two scenes in particular stand out in my memory. In one, the ambush [of Major Norton and his patrol] had so many arrows flying that you were bound to get hit by one sooner or later—and one got me! Each arrow had a hard rubber tip, and one hit me right above my left eyebrow. It happened when I was firing my rifle. The camera was positioned right behind me. I fired at an Indian. I believe Richard Crow was his name who shoots at me as I shoot him. He falls off a rock into the water, but I was the one who really got hit! If it hit me a half-inch lower, I would have sustained a serious injury to my eye!"

The other scene that Fess frowned upon was the big battle with the Creeks. Foster enjoyed the action and pushed his actors and background performers to be as authentically aggressive as possible. In one sequence, Buddy Ebsen flipped a Creek warrior with considerable force over his shoulder onto the ground as the extras battled around him in hand-to-hand combat with flintlock weapons and tomahawks. "During the big battle with the Creeks, Pat Hogan and I fight," said Fess. "Pat was physically powerful and quick; he certainly looked the part. But when he knocks me out with his tomahawk, well, let me tell you: That smarted!"

Besides almost getting his eye shot out by an arrow, Fess said that another memorable scene from the episode was his grinning attempt during the final tomahawk fight with Hogan.

"The final fight I had with Pat Hogan, who played the Creek

Fess Parker's Davy Crockett shakes hands with Pat Hogan's Red Stick in "Davy Crockett, Indian Fighter."
© DISNEY.

chief, Red Stick, stands out in my mind," remarked Fess. "I thought that the scene in which he has me pinned up against a tree and I give him a grin was one of the silliest things I ever did on camera, but it seemed to work out all right."

But those Crockett grins became an essential part of the story. "Throughout the series, he grins his grin to register amusement, irony, and the awareness of being in a tight spot," explained Richard Boyd Hauck in *Crockett: A Bio-Bibliography.*

Walt Disney and his wife, Lillian, visited the set during the Crockett-Red Stick fight. "He came out to the set where Pat Hogan and I had been fighting in the water," said Fess. "It was a surprise to us. And he came there with Mrs. Disney. But he just wanted to see what was going on. Pat and I got a break from fighting in the water. And our food on the set got better when Mr. Disney arrived. We went from peanut butter sandwiches to pork chop sandwiches. But we still operated on a tight budget."

Years later following the release of Disney's *The Alamo* in 2004, the *Davy Crockett* budget question was raised again. "I remember being asked by one of the producers on *The Alamo*," said Fess. "He asked what all three of those films cost and I said they cost about $700,000. He laughed and he said, 'That's what we spent on lunch!'"

Horses were hired from local ranches like the Johnston Family farm in Cleveland, Tennessee. Some of the mounted extras, like Frank Gleason from Rossville and John R. McGauley from Chattanooga, brought their own horses. When it came time for the actors to select horses, Fess gave Ebsen the first choice. "I told Buddy to pick any horse out of the bunch that were offered to us and he goes and picks the white one!" laughed Fess, who assumed that Ebsen would not upstage him by selecting the light-colored horse that was traditionally associated with the star of a Western production. "Buddy was a good rider."

A horseback ride across an old bridge presented an additional danger.

"Another memorable scene is one that features me and Buddy Ebsen, leaving camp to go home," said Fess with a laugh. "As a matter of fact, Buddy has recalled that scene as his scariest scene in the entire series. We had to cross a high wooden bridge without guard rails and ride towards a cannon crew, and we were rather high up. Buddy was trying to control his horse while he held on to a guitar! We also had some difficulties crossing the streams with the horses that we worked with. The best horses belonged to some of the locals who portrayed the mounted soldiers. But there are a lot of moments in filming where not much thought is given to it. Some directors are very cavalier about what they want and the possible consequences. Foster was not the worst one I ever worked with. We had a lot of dangers in the films because of the high spirits of the Indians."

Flintlock rifles also presented problems.

Although Fess looked a like a natural firing the actual nineteenth century muzzleloaders that Disney provided, the actor had never fired them before. After the barrel received its charge of black powder, the flintlock's pan had to be filled with a priming charge. When the rifle is lifted to be fired, the pan rests near the shooter's face. The subsequent trigger pull allows the flint in the lock to strike the steel frizzen, creating the sparks that ignite the priming charge. The resulting gunpowder flash enters the touch hole of the barrel and ignites the main charge which propels the round lead ball out of the muzzle.

"I hadn't really fired flintlock guns before the Crockett series, but I did shoot them again, of course, in the following two episodes," said Fess. "However, those gunpowder flashes took some toll on my eyebrows. The fellows who loaded the guns occasionally got a little too much powder in the pan. And while we were in Cherokee, one of those things happened and burned Buddy's eyebrows. He was madder than a cat!"

Ebsen explained the incident in his autobiography.

"The most dangerous incident involved a muzzle-loading musket, which blew up in my face," stated Ebsen. "In the explosion and flash, I lost my eyelashes, my eyebrows, and a good patch of my front hairline. It was a scary threat to my eyesight as well, so the crew rushed me to a hospital to have my eyes irrigated."

Ebsen also remembered another incident in which he got hit in the head with his rifle after Fess hit it while dismounting from another horse. Later, Ebsen was thrown from his horse when the animal panicked in mud-based lake water. And he cut his forehead open with his powder horn during a dance sequence that was included in "Davy Crockett Goes to Congress." In the episode, Ebsen joins in the fun of a pioneer settlement frolic and delivers his version of the Bandy Twist, a classic tap routine created by vaudevillian Jim Bandy. Ebsen successfully executed the steps despite wearing moccasins and dancing on the ground. But as he bounced in one direction, his powder horn swung in the other.

"When it struck my head just over my left eye, I almost went down for the count, but through my grogginess I knew I had to carry on for Norman," said Ebsen in *The Other Side of Oz*. "So I staggered back into the circle, dancing toward the camera. Halfway there I felt something warm and sticky trickling down my face." Ebsen noticed that the powder horn left a two-inch gash in his forehead. "We had no doctor on the set, and our medical needs were served by a young ex-Navy pharmacist's mate."

Rather than go to a hospital, Ebsen recuperated on the set.

"As I sat in a director's chair having my brow doctored, a tourist approached," remarked Ebsen. "He was fat, had a Brooklyn accent, and a half-chewed cigar in his mouth. He aimed his 8mm camera at me and commanded, 'Hey, Bud! Move a little closer to the makeup man, will ya! I'm shootin' color an' from here that looks like real blood.'"

Beck recalled an incident in which Fess knocked out Pat Hogan with a tomahawk. "Fess Parker threw a tomahawk at Red Stick," stated Beck. "It hit him in the head and knocked him out. They carried him to my porch, rested him, treated the bump on his head, and filmed the end of the scene." And that bump over Pat Hogan's right eye is briefly visible in the DVD version of the episode. "You know, I don't remember that," replied Fess. "If anything, I should have been the one who was knocked out in that fight. But he made an immeasurable impression on the film. Pat was a very talented guy who became my neighbor in Santa Barbara."

Foster's direction emphasized realistic action, especially in the large battle scene between the Creeks and Jackson's forces. The director even borrowed some exciting battle scenes that had been used nearly fifteen years earlier in another historical film. Robert Foster, Norman Foster's son, said that his father had been an uncredited second unit director on *Northwest Passage*, a 1940 film about the French and Indian War. So it is more than coincidental that a number of actions in the earlier film were recreated by Foster in the 1954 Disney production. For example, the shot of Fess from his point of view as he fires his flintlock rifle at a running Creek warrior is straight out of *Northwest Passage*. Other scenes borrowed from the 1940 film include one in which Crockett stealthily leads the volunteers down the hillside, another features waking warriors and various hand-to-hand combat scenes.

Besides the cuts and bruises, Parker had another difficult experience: working with Helene Stanley, who played his wife, Polly. Stanley was an attractive woman who had been Disney's live-action model for *Cinderella* and *Sleeping Beauty*. She was about 5'4" tall; Fess stood 6'5." When Fess' Crockett returns from the Creek Indian War, he lifts her off her feet and kisses her. And what a kiss the first take was! "One take of me kissing her didn't make it to the final print," chuckled Fess. "I more or less played the scene *hungry*, like any frontiersman would have, being away so long from his wife and family. But Mr. Disney didn't think it was appropriate for the audience."

After the cut passionate-kiss scene, Fess said the chemistry between him and Stanley deteriorated. "I wasn't particularly happy with her, and she wasn't too happy with me either," he said with a shrug.

"Director Norm Foster put her in the script; I didn't," stated Blackburn. "I really didn't want her character in the episode. I thought that it really didn't add anything to the story. I wrote her death into the story and I think that it worked rather well. In any event, it was the best I could do with the story."

Norman Foster wasn't too happy with Fess, either.

"The director was out of the country scouting locations for *Zorro* and when he came back he found out that Mr. Disney had chosen me to play Davy Crockett," said Fess. "And I'm sure he had other people that he'd rather have worked with. The Disney people really didn't have big time experienced directors. He didn't particularly think that I was exuding enough energy and so we had this little tension develop between us. As a matter of fact, he tried to get rid of me. I found that out later. But we kept shooting. He had been in contact with the studio back in California, expressing concerns he had with me but I didn't know those conversations were going on. We finally went to a theater in Tennessee where we had the opportunity to see the dailies; we'd never seen any film. On the way out of the theater, Norman Foster came over and said, 'You're coming off.'"

"Coming off" meant that Fess was going to be dismissed from the production and replaced. The previously filmed days of footage would have to be re-shot with the new actor, perhaps one who had originally been considered.

Foster's disapproval of Fess' performance during the first few weeks of filming was later confirmed by producer Bill Walsh. But Walsh didn't share Foster's opinion. "We had hit it off," said Fess of Walsh. The two became very close friends. Several years later, the producer and his wife played an important role in Fess' personal life. "He was the Best Man at my wedding, and his wife was Marcella's Maid of Honor," explained Fess.

Walsh thought that Foster was wrong in his assessment of Fess.

"Bill told me that Norman had said something upsetting to Fess and he didn't appreciate it," said Fishman. "Bill was one of Fess' biggest fans and he was the producer. He would have handcuffed Fess to the set if he had to. Fess was going nowhere. Norman could have been the one who was going to be replaced."

Fess also had an ally in Tom Blackburn, who wasn't fond of Foster.

"I didn't get along with him either, but things eventually got straightened out," said Blackburn. The cost of re-shooting would push the production over budget and by the time the new actor appeared on the set the summertime look of the Great Smoky Mountains would be changing into autumn. In fact, the high elevation hastened the color changes faster than nearby valley communities like Cherokee. Time was a concern.

A decision was quickly reached.

"Fortunately, Norman Foster acknowledged that what I was doing was going to work," said Fess. "After that, everything was fine."

Although Fess sang some verses from "The Ballad of Davy Crockett" on *Disneyland's* debut show, the song was further developed and incorporated into the screenplay.

"When the first rushes started coming back from the Creek Indian War episode, we noticed that the transition between scenes wasn't as smooth as we would have liked," said Blackburn. "So something had to be done, something like a narration bridge—but set to music. I started writing lyrics to what was to become [the complete] 'Ballad of Davy Crockett' by looking at the daily footage. I made up the first few verses right away and took them over to George Bruns, who came up with the melody. When I first played a tape of the song to my family, they laughed! But when they each got a brand new car from that song a few months later, they didn't laugh anymore."

Besides the memorable song lyrics, Blackburn inserted several important lines of dialogue in the script which reinforced moral ideals. For example, Fess' character reassures Red Stick that forthcoming treaties will be honored. "Davy Crockett don't lie," stated Fess in the episode. It was a great lesson for youngsters.

According to the August 17 script, "Davy Crockett, Indian Fighter" was supposed to conclude with a long shot of Crockett and Russel riding off as Ebsen's character plays guitar and sings "The Ballad of Davy Crockett." Instead, a short animated sequence depicting harmonious frontier communities of Anglo settlers and Native Americans ended the program. Upon completion of the first episode, the final rushes were sent back to California.

Fess acknowledged the efforts of his fellow cast and crew members.

"Billy Bakewell was a delight," said Fess. "He was a very confident actor. One of his early films was *All Quiet on the Western Front*. He'd worked with every big actor and actress you could think of. He was the right guy for the part. Basil Ruysdael was a wonderful person, too. I enjoyed getting to know him. He had so many experiences in the world of broadcasting, theater, and light opera. As for Basil, Billy, Buddy, Bill Walsh, and Tom Blackburn, once we made that movie we were friends always."

With his buckskin clothing, flintlock rifle and coonskin cap, Fess' Crockett emerged from the first episode as a sure-shot man of honor and integrity who seemed very comfortable in the woods. He successfully battled a Creek war party with only one other man, skillfully interpreted moccasin tracks, killed a bear in an off-screen knife fight, accurately imitated the sounds of an owl and a Tennessee Thrush, fired a flintlock rifle with deadly accuracy, walked bravely alone into Red Stick's camp to save his sidekick, and fended off an attack from an alligator—accompanied by background music that sounded almost *Jaws*-like!

By the episode's end, a nationwide audience was not only fascinated by Fess' on-screen persona but it genuinely cared about him as well. And it wasn't because of chance. "Disney was an artist who cared for his audience," wrote Donald F. Glut and Jim Harmon in *The Great Television Heroes*. The master visionary's concern for those who viewed his magical creations had reached an unprecedented level—and Fess was the key to it all. Christopher Finch noted in *Art of Walt Disney: From Mickey Mouse to the Magic Kingdoms* that Fess "plays the hero with a rugged dignity which seems completely appropriate."

Fess' portrayal was so significant that some school kids temporarily forgot about duck-and-cover air raid drills and the threat of atomic warfare. "Davy Crockett, Indian Fighter" was enthusiastically embraced by youngsters across the United States. "It was the topic of the day the next day in school," recalled Len Hekel, a New Jersey schoolboy who later served in Vietnam. "I could hardly wait for the next episode."

"It was the very positive reaction we got from that segment that made us know that the series was going to be a success," said Fess.

CHAPTER 5
"DAVY CROCKETT GOES TO CONGRESS"

The production company remained in North Carolina following the filming of the "Davy Crockett, Indian Fighter" episode. The second episode, "Davy Crockett Goes to Congress," covered the largest portion of Crockett's life: 1815 to 1835. Fess would age gracefully on camera from a twenty-nine-year-old Creek War veteran to a forty-nine-year-old former Congressman.

In the January 26, 1955 episode Crockett and Russel stake a land claim with a local official (Henry Joyner) and defend a Cherokee, Charlie Two Shirts (Jeff Thompson), against Bigfoot Mason (Mike Mazurki) and his gang. The rest of the episode is devoted to Crockett's political career, especially his years in the U.S. House of Representatives. And there are a few scenes that involve Crockett's family.

One of the most amusing—and unintelligible lines—in the entire series is delivered by young Ray Whitetree, who plays Johnny Crockett. As Fess' character bids goodbye to his family, Whitetree says something that is hardly recognizable. According to the script, he supposedly says, "Don't let him shoot all the b'ars afore we get there." It remains a harmlessly funny moment in the episode.

"When Fess Parker and Buddy Ebsen first arrive, I'm one of the kids running by," explained Beck about the scene in the frontier village. "We were also involved in a scene where he did his first speech. We can be seen in front of the people who carry him on their shoulders. I remember looking up at Fess Parker and thinking how tall he was."

Several of the Pioneer Farmstead buildings were used in important scenes in the episodes. To make the structures look like they were part of a large frontier community, a gate and partial stockade was constructed under the supervision of Art Director Marvin Davis.

The John E. Davis building served as the interior of Crockett's home and the place where Crockett and Russel sign land deeds. The historic structure's front porch was also the place where Russel reads the letter which contained information about Polly Crockett's death. Under Foster's direction, the scene is restrained and particularly poignant, and Fess played it with thoughtful introspection. Stunned by the news of his wife's passing, Fess' Crockett reacts by telling his friend that he needs "some time by myself." He stands and walks away towards the woods line. But it just wasn't any walk; as a matter of fact, it was planned and deliberate. And it was based upon another actor's famous walk.

"I took it from Gary Cooper, who played Lou Gehrig, in *Pride of the Yankees*," explained Fess. In the film, Cooper, whom Fess worked with in *Springfield Rifle*, delivers the dying baseball player's "luckiest man on the face of the earth" speech and exits the playing field of Yankee Stadium. "The way he walked off the field and into the stadium's tunnel was memorable. Cooper's character was dealing with approaching death and Crockett was dealing with the news that his wife had died. I wanted to incorporate what Gary Cooper was doing in the way I walked away after Buddy reads me the letter. I essentially did the same thing, and the director, Norman Foster, fortunately bought my interpretation of how to do it. It was a difficult scene but I think it worked well."

Fess' chief non-political antagonist in the second episode was the burly Mike Mazurki character, Bigfoot Mason. Mazurki was a veteran screen heavy, a tough guy who played everything from bouncers and henchmen to fighters and pirates. The *Davy Crockett, King of the Wild Frontier* pressbook noted that Mazurki "weighs 250 pounds, stands six-feet-four-and-a-half, and can open a tin of tomatoes with his bare hands."

"Mike was an amazing man, he was great," noted Fess. "He had some wrestling experience, so he was able to handle me well in my fight sequence. Frankly, I had little or no experience, so when we started the fight and had hold of each other he threw me around like a rag doll. I weighed around 210."

"I've demolished many a movie hero," boasted Mazurki in the film's pressbook. "Strictly business, of course."

Foster directed the "rough and tumble, no holds barred" punch-fest in which Mazurki kicks Fess in the back, Fess bites the ex-wrestler's hand, and Mazurki throws Fess into a split rail fence. "I hurt my back going through that fence," stated Fess. "We had nobody to double us. Mike had a wrestling background and he threw me around quite easily. I was lucky to survive when I went through the split rail fence. The first time I went through, I didn't have any pads. So I took the camera blanket off and stuffed it in the back of my pants. And I went through it again. Without the pads I could have incapacitated myself. But that's how basic it was. Whatever we did—riding, fighting—*we* did. Later on, they started bringing stunt people on board, not that they did much."

"That was a good go," said Mazurki in the Disney pressbook. "We just slammed at each other until the film ran out. After the cameras were reloaded, we'd start again. Nobody got hurt, at least not much. Fess clipped my jaw a couple of times and I raised a lump on his head with a fence rail. But it was all in sport and carefully staged, and we're still the best of friends—off screen."

The action in the rest of the episode slows down once Crockett goes on the campaign trail. The episode traces his political career from his election to the Tennessee State Legislature to the U.S. House of Representatives. And for the first time—after fighting the Creeks and Bigfoot Mason in his buckskins—Fess is costumed as a gentleman, complete with a tailored frock cat and top hat.

One of the most entertaining speeches that Crockett delivers is one in which he is interrupted on the campaign trail by a cricket. Crockett exploits the chirping insect by stating that the six-legged critter was actually saying "Crockett for Congress!" However, Blackburn's script of August 19 originally was going to use Disney stock footage of a flock of geese. Fess' original dialogue acknowledged "them geese that flew over" and the birds' alleged collective campaign call of "Crockett…Crockett." But the bugs bested the birds when the scene was shot.

"I was feeling more comfortable in Nashville," said Fess. "And the gentleman who played General Jackson, Basil Ruysdael, and I were having dinner one night and he said, 'How are you doing with your

Fess Parker's Davy Crockett cradles a presentation rifle in Philadelphia from "Davy Crockett Goes to Congress."
© Disney.

big speech in Congress?' I said, 'I know it.' He said, 'Well, if you'd like, I'd be glad to sit with you. Maybe I can help you with a transition or something.' I said, 'Sure, I'd love to do that.' He helped me review my speech lines over dinner; I got close to the Davy Crockett character on that speech."

Blackburn acknowledged Fess' development in front of the camera.

"The speeches Fess gave, especially his opening one in Congress, and his other dialogue worked well," said Blackburn. "And more importantly, Fess grew a lot as an actor since the first episode. I became terribly proud of him by then."

Nashville's most important historic structure was the Hermitage, Andrew Jackson's home, and the mansion was featured in the episode.

"We filmed the Congress scenes in Nashville at the Tennessee State House and we actually used Andrew Jackson's home, the

Hermitage, in the exterior shots," explained Fess. Disney wanted to use the interior of the seventh American President's home but the Hermitage's staff did not allow interior photography. Fortunately, the home of Rogers Clark Caldwell did. The Tennessee banker's residence was decorated and furnished just like the Hermitage and the Disney production team made full use of it. Caldwell's house was also used as the interior of the White House in later scenes. Matte artist Peter Ellenshaw exquisitely created the exterior of the President's residence along with all the other nineteenth century-looking exteriors in the production. Amazingly, Ellenshaw was able to create the matte paintings within the limited time allotted to produce them.

"Speed was the name of the game," stated the artist in his autobiography *Ellenshaw Under Glass—Going to the Matte for Disney.* "With so many shots required I would often paint a matte a day."

Ellenshaw teamed up with animator-special effects wizard Ub Iwerks to save additional time by having the filmed footage projected on a three-foot-by-four-foot sheet of glass that was backed by mottled plastic. "We could now determine the areas we needed to paint the scene, this we would paint directly on the front side of the glass, leaving an opening through which projected live action would show," explained Ellenshaw. Fess appreciated Ellenshaw's realistic creations and soon became friends with the talented artist.

Crockett's principles, underscored by Blackburn, are clearly depicted when the frontiersman responds to Jackson's request for support. Fess states that his first responsibility is to "them who elected me." It was an implanted lesson of sorts from Blackburn to the Baby Boomer audience which was too young to understand the role played by special interest groups and lobbyists in the workings of government at the time.

In another scene, Jackson acknowledges the Crockett almanacs, even though the first one wasn't actually printed until late in 1834 for 1835, years after he left the White House. Interestingly enough, in the script of August 19, Jackson notes additional almanac titles including *Davy Crockett and the Monster of Reelfoot Lake*, which made it into the final print of "Davy Crockett Goes to Congress." The title reflected Blackburn's creativity for establishing the foundation of a future Crockett episode.

Tennessee's Reelfoot Lake was actually created or expanded by the monumental earthquakes of 1811–1812 in the Mississippi River Valley, and the body of water is home to large snakes and other wilderness creatures. In his 1834 autobiography, Crockett mentions a Red-foot lake, perhaps a misinterpretation of Reelfoot Lake. Still, one can only imagine Davy Crockett defending his title as the "King of the Wild Frontier" against who knows what kind of "monster." But it's not much of a stretch. After all, Disney's creative team has designed and built a full-size giant squid for the 1954 feature film *20,000 Leagues Under the Sea*. With Disney, any dream was possible. However, *Davy Crockett and the Monster of Reelfoot Lake* never made it past a line of dialogue.

During filming in Tennessee, Fess received an interesting message from the front desk of the hotel he was staying in. The message read: "Colonel Tom Parker would like to visit with you."

"I didn't know any Colonel Parker but it sounded all right so I said he could come up," recalled Fess, who first thought that the man might be related to him. He didn't realize that Colonel Tom Parker was Elvis Presley's manager. "So he came up and said, 'I'd like to manage you.' Well, I had an agent—and frankly, I didn't know anything about managers—so I said 'Thank you,' and declined the offer." Had a deal been made, Colonel Tom Parker would have been the manager of the "King of the Wild Frontier" and the "King of Rock and Roll."

Crockett's most important Congressional stand was his opposition to President Jackson's Indian bill. And Fess' passionate speech in defense of the Native Americans is principled and memorable. In a way, some of the words underscored the sentiment found in *Brown v. Board of Education*, the landmark 1954 Supreme Court case which outlawed separate but equal educational facilities for African-Americans. He entered the legislative chamber by slamming open its two large wooden doors. "That was intentional," said Fess about his forceful entrance. "And I wouldn't be surprised if the [sound] effect of the doors wasn't enhanced."

In the powerful scene, Fess stands by his desk and strongly delivers his speech in which he criticizes the legislation, the President, and Congress. Although his opponents applaud his convictions, the bill is passed and eventually Crockett is defeated for re-election.

"The confrontation scene with William Bakewell, who played Major Norton as a lobbyist, was an exciting scene to be a part of," said Fess. "I recall that filming ended on the second episode by Thanksgiving of 1954."

A week after the episode aired on January 26, 1955, the motion picture *Battle Cry* opened in theaters. The Raoul Walsh-directed film, based on Leon Uris' best-selling novel about the U.S. Marines in World War II, starred Van Heflin and Aldo Ray. Fess had a small part in the film as Private Speedy, but kids across the country didn't notice. Even if they did, they probably didn't recognize him without his buckskins and coonskin cap. Also appearing in the film was John Lupton, one of Fess' Hollywood roommates, and Texas buddy Dodo McQueen, whose real name was Justus E. McQueen.

"Fess heard about a part that would be just right for Dodo and had him come and try out for it," explained Kendrick. McQueen played Private L. Q. Jones and made a favorable impression on Walsh. "They expanded Dodo's part at Fess' character's expense. I'm sure that kind of irritated Fess a little bit but he never showed it." Surprisingly, McQueen changed his stage name to L. Q. Jones and had an extensive career as an actor, director, and producer.

The most memorable of all the Crockett episodes was scheduled for broadcast in four weeks: "Davy Crockett at the Alamo."

CHAPTER 6
"DAVY CROCKETT AT THE ALAMO"

After filming ended in Tennessee, Fess and the rest of the cast and crew returned to California.

"When he came back he said that he had a good time," remarked Marcy. "He enjoyed the picture very, very much. He was very enthusiastic about the future—I think really for the first time he was really excited about the future. He was very pleased to the way that Walt responded to everything. The next thing I knew, my golly, everybody was going crazy over him."

But there was still another episode to shoot.

The most dramatic episode in the original trilogy was "Davy Crockett at the Alamo." This was the program that traced Crockett's journey to Texas where he eventually fought and died at the Battle of the Alamo during the Texas Revolution. The modern-day Alamo located in the heart of urban San Antonio was not a possible shooting location and Disney did not have the budget to recreate the entire original mission-fortress. The decision was made to build part of the Alamo and allow matte artist Peter Ellenshaw to create panoramic matte paintings for certain exteriors.

Although some live-action exterior shots were filmed on the Janss Conejo Ranch in Thousand Oaks, California, most of the episode was filmed on Soundstage #3 at the Walt Disney Studios in Burbank. "Roughly the size of a football field…the set was so designed that it could be photographed both from inside and outside its six-foot thick walls," noted the *Davy Crockett, King of the Wild Frontier* pressbook. "A seamless painted backdrop gave the illusion of outdoor space, with misty hills in the distance."

"I thought they did a really fine job with the Alamo set," said Fess. "It was not easy to do, to create the sense that the whole thing was there, which it wasn't. Footage from another production was carefully edited into the episode: a brief, nighttime artillery barrage sequence from *Man From the Alamo*, a 1952 film starring Glenn Ford. Perhaps not to confuse the young viewers, Disney's Alamo Church featured its well-known hump-like façade which had been added a decade after the Battle of the Alamo.

In the early part of the episode Fess' character is confronted by an unscrupulous riverboat gambler—whom Crockett nicknames "Thimblerig"—played by Hans Conried. The eloquent-speaking actor previously had entertained audiences in such diverse films as *My Friend Irma* (1949), *Big Jim McLain* (1952), *Sirens of Bagdad* (1953), and *The 5,000 Fingers of Dr. T.* Conried also appeared as the Slave in the Magic Mirror on Disney's 1951 TV *Christmas Show.*

"Hans Conried is someone who I admired," stated Fess. "I knew about him from his days on the radio and I had watched him in the movies. I never got to know him as I did Buddy and the others, but he was very friendly and fun to work with."

Blackburn enthusiastically agreed.

"Hans Conried was a consummate professional who had been a top radio announcer for years," said Blackburn. "Hans was simply wonderful! I almost had him narrating a special project about the wonders of the world that matte artist Peter Ellenshaw and I were working on."

Later in the episode, Crockett tangles with a mute Comanche warrior—subsequently named Bustedluck—played by the athletic Nick Cravat who had appeared in such action-adventure films as *The Crimson Pirate* (1952), *The Veils of Bagdad* (1953), and *King Richard and the Crusaders* (1954).

"Nick Cravat was a talented stuntman who was fun to work with," said Fess. "He was Burt Lancaster's old aerial partner," added Blackburn. "But as many incorrectly think, Nick could speak, though somewhat inarticulately."

Although Fess, Ebsen, Hans Conried, and Cravat arrive at the Alamo by horse in a soundstage shot, the quartet did not participate in the horseback riding long shots in Thousand Oaks. "That was a second unit shoot," said Fess. "I just wasn't there."

Foster and Art Director Marvin Davis created a realistic, dirt-and-grime laden atmosphere for the Alamo scenes. The characters appear worn out and tired; their patience wears thin with every passing day of the siege. Even Ebsen's character argues with Crockett for not being informed about the helpless Alamo garrison's status. Yet, Alamo co-commander William B. Travis, played by Don Megowan, remains steadfast as hope fades with every day of the siege.

The biggest Alamo legend involves William B. Travis drawing a line in the dirt and asking for volunteers to cross the line and remain with him in the Alamo. And Blackburn included it in his teleplay.

"The drawing of the line in the dirt by Colonel Travis was an important moment," said Fess. "It was a fateful decision by those who crossed it and it played well in the episode. Don was a good choice; he was a nice fellow. You know, he was the nephew of Foster Brooks who worked with me on the *Daniel Boone* series in the 1960s. But I didn't know it while we were working on the Alamo segment. Don, obviously, was a big strong man. But I never worked with him again. He was a heavy smoker who eventually died of cancer."

Arguably, the best supporting acting performance in the episode was delivered by Kenneth Tobey, who played Jim Bowie, the ill Alamo co-commander. Under Foster's careful direction, Tobey's restrained gritty realism reflected the plight of the surrounded garrison. His final struggle against the Mexican soldiers who break into his quarters is particularly memorable: Tobey fires a brace of flintlock pistols against two *soldados* and then dispatches another with his knife before being overwhelmed with bayonets.

"He's a wonderful actor," noted Blackburn, who attended the filming of the "Davy Crockett at the Alamo" episode. "As a matter of fact, I think he's one of the best of all time."

"Ken Tobey was an outstanding actor who did an excellent job," remarked Fess. "The death of Jim Bowie was a very powerful scene that demonstrated the courage of his character. Of course, Ken later played Jocko, one of Mike Fink's men, in the keelboat films."

On February 25, 1836, Alamo commander William B. Travis wrote to General Sam Houston, commander of the rebellious Texans, and stated that "David Crockett was seen at all points, animating the men to do their duty." Writer Tom Blackburn accurately incorporated that sentiment in the episode when Fess shoots one of Santa Anna's artillerists at long range and generates cheers from his fellow Alamo defenders. He later forces the garrison out of its understandable melancholy state when he orders a make-shift hoedown, complete with a Buddy Ebsen dance.

The most poignant scene in the episode occurs when Fess sings "Farewell," a poem traditionally associated as one written by Davy Crockett. The poem first appeared as a twenty-four-line creation in the 1836 book, *Col. Crockett's Exploits and Adventures in Texas*. In the Disney series, "Farewell" was edited to six verses and set to music by George Bruns. Foster directed the scene as a moment of reflection for the men who are essentially living out the last night of their lives. It is a heartfelt moment in the episode and its earthy introspective atmosphere still holds up after repeated viewings.

With guitar in hand, Fess delivers the song as the men around him, including George Russel, provide the subtle harmonies:

> Farewell to the mountains whose mazes to me
> Were more beautiful far than Eden could be,
> The home I redeem'd from the savage and wild
> The home that I loved as a father his child
> The wife of my bosom—Farewell to ye all!
> In the land of the stranger I rise—or I fall

"I went back and visited him at that particular time," said Kendrick. "They had not broadcast it yet. They were still filming out at the studio when I went out back and visited with him. On a Saturday he said, 'Phil, are you going to church like you always do, tomorrow?' I always went to the Hollywood Church of Christ, a little bitty old church. He said, 'You mind if I go with you?' I said 'No, I'd like to have you go with me.' Marcy joined us. At the end of the sermon they would invite people to come down and make a prayer request or meet with the elders or make a request to be baptized. When they sang the invitation song Fess went down front, much to my surprise and to Marcy's surprise. Fess requested that he be baptized. The Church of Christ people liked to know that people are sincere and that they understand what they're doing and why they're doing it before they will baptize you."

Kendrick appreciated his friend's request to be baptized but realized there could be a problem with the ceremony.

"Of course, Fess at six-foot-six and Dr. England, who performed the baptism, couldn't be over five-foot-ten or more than 170 pounds dripping wet," laughed Kendrick. "'I therefore baptize you in the name of the Father, the Son, and the Holy Ghost,' says Dr. England. When he dropped him in the water, Fess' feet went straight up in the air. All you could see was his two legs sticking up and he was thrashing; he was drowning! And so was Dr. England! He had disappeared, too. Marcy gets to giggling, I get to giggling. The rest of the congregation doesn't know what to think or what to do. Finally the two of them get up; they're just drippin' wet. Fess does this little bow to the audience and walks out of the baptistry."

Despite the unintentional humor of the incident, Kendrick saw the baptism as something quite serious.

"Immersion is a very humbling experience," explained Kendrick. "It's our confession of what Jesus wanted us to do. Later, Fess' parents thanked me. But the baptism wasn't mentioned much." Although Fess had not regularly attended church since his childhood, he remained a God-fearing and God-loving man. Fess felt that the baptism reinforced his relationship with God at a very important time of his life. Still, he remained silent about the baptism.

Fess returned to the set where the final battle scenes were being blocked by Foster. As the cameras rolled, scores of extras costumed as Alamo defenders and Mexican soldiers battled with bayonets, swords, and tomahawks; stunt men fell from walls and ladders as flintlocks and cannons roared.

"The final scene was definitely under-rehearsed," said Fess. "We had stunt men and stunt extras working in the scene, and there was a considerable amount of uncertain footing, especially where I was swinging my rifle back and forth. The stunt men were excellent. I do recall Troy Melton and Dick Crockett among a number of excellent stunt men. It was individuals like that who made the hand-to-hand sequences on the walls relatively safe. We were really lucky that no one got hurt during the Alamo episode."

Of course, the most difficult decision for writer Tom Blackburn and director Norman Foster was how to film the death of Crockett. "I never did have a death scene," stated Fess. "What was written was

Fess Parker's Davy Crockett fires at the advancing Mexican soldiers in "Davy Crockett at the Alamo."

written and what was shot was shot. There may have been discussions about a death scene but it was not filmed. There was a concern by Disney to take into account both history and the feelings of all the kids. In general, movie making takes a certain artistic license—and that went for the *Davy Crockett* series as well. The main irony in the film's production was how Crockett was going to die. Certain historical items were changed in the film, but this death was different. Disney kept scratching his head, but he finally came up with the ending that was filmed. He was quite thoughtful, though, in his consideration of how children might view the death. Of course, history raises some doubts about Crockett's death. However, the filmed ending could fit either camp, since Crockett doesn't die on camera."

The Siege and the Battle of the Alamo had lasted thirteen days in 1836, and later a *Walt Disney's Wonderful World of Color* press release proudly stated: "Coincidentally it took thirteen days to film the Alamo sequences for Disney's TV dramatization."

The final episode of the trilogy aired on February 23, 1955, a date which coincided with the 119th anniversary of the beginning of the Alamo's siege. But the episode had an ironic connection to something still a decade away. Only weeks before its broadcast, President Dwight D. Eisenhower had sent direct military aid and advisors to Vietnam for the first time to help counter Communist influence and expansion. In the 1960s, Vietnam became the place where young men who had once toyed with plastic flintlocks and coonskin caps as children would carry M-16s and steel helmets in the "New Frontier" world.

"Davy Crockett at the Alamo" was the most dramatic part of Disney's *Davy Crockett* series and it left an indelible image on a generation of youngsters. The image of Fess swinging his trusty rifle, Old Betsy, at the oncoming wave of Mexican soldiers is not only one of the most famous scenes in television history but it became an iconic moment for every Baby Boomer who ever wore a coonskin cap. Fess' multiple, powerful rifle swings gave the scene a sense of intensity that reflected his internalization with the role of the Alamo's most famous hero. But as Santa Anna's soldiers close in on him the shot shifts to the Alamo flag. The audience never gets to see Crockett's last breath.

"But it was one of those things when you think, 'Gee, I'll be glad when they yell 'cut,'" chuckled Fess. "It was a hard rubber rifle; it was pretty much a shillelagh. Crockett's death scene was a difficult scene to do, but it was handled well by Mr. Disney. For me, well, it was the end."

Davy Crockett may have died at the Alamo, but Walt Disney had other plans for the King of the Wild Frontier, especially since the buckskin hero had elevated *Disneyland* to the Nielsen's sixth highest-rated television program of the 1954–1955 season.

Fess received a 1955 Emmy nomination in the "Most Outstanding New Personality" category, but comedian George Gobel won the award at the ceremonies which were held at the Moulin Rouge Nightclub in Hollywood on March 7, 1955. Chester W. Schaeffer was nominated for "Best Television Film Editing" for "Davy Crockett, Indian Fighter," but fellow Disney editors Lynn Harrison and Grant K. Smith took the award for their work on *Operation Undersea*, which aired one week before the first Crockett episode. *Disneyland* also took top honors in the "Best Variety Series Including Musical Variety" category.

In the April 30–May 6, 1955 issue of *TV Guide*, which featured Fess and Buddy Ebsen on the cover, more than 45,000 readers named *Disneyland* as their favorite program. The issue also noted that *Disneyland* was among the top programs in three different television ratings services.

Fess' friends in Texas were thrilled.

William E. King earned his Doctor of Dentistry degree from Baylor University in 1954, and had joined the Navy when he learned about Fess' success. "I was in Japan when I found out," stated King. "I thought it was great."

Fess took a short break after filming and returned to Texas where he visited his parents and friends.

"After he came back to Texas he took me and my wife, Enid, out to lunch," said Woodward. "We went to Macintosh's Café in Arlington. The waitress kept eyeballing him and finally got up the nerve to talk to him. She said, "Don't I know you?' Fess replied, "Yes, M'am.' She got excited and said, 'I knew it. I knew it the minute you walked in because I watch wrastlin' every Saturday night.' We all had a great laugh."

Although he wasn't identified by the waitress, he was soon to become one of the most recognizable people in the world.

"I was under contract with Walt Disney," said Fess. "I had a seven-year contract. There was more to come."

CHAPTER 7
"THE BALLAD OF DAVY CROCKETT"

"BORN ON A MOUNTAIN TOP IN TENNESSEE
GREENEST STATE IN THE LAND OF THE FREE
RAISED IN THE WOODS SO' HE KNEW EV'RY TREE
KILT HIM A B'AR WHEN HE WAS ONLY THREE
DAVY, DAVY CROCKETT, KING OF THE WILD FRONTIER"

The most memorable aspect of Disney's *Davy Crockett* series was the catchy song, "The Ballad of Davy Crockett," which was written by Tom Blackburn and George Bruns. The composition was initially used to introduce Fess to the *Disneyland* TV audience and later used as a musical bridge that began each episode, connected scenes, and subsequently moved the story line. But the tune eventually became an anthem for the Baby Boom generation once it was recorded and sold on vinyl.

"Bill Hayes was, ironically, the first one to record the song," said Fess of the commercial releases. "He did have the most popular version and I won't question popular, but I sang it in fourteen foreign countries and sold records world wide. I have a copy of the lyrics and the date that I recorded the song. There were several musical activities I was involved with during the production. We had a recording session for George Bruns and Tom Blackburn's 'Ballad of Davy Crockett' in August of 1954, before we started filming the first episode on the Creek Indian War."

The timing of the single's release by Disney was hastened by the competition.

"The single wasn't released by Mr. Disney until other versions of the record started selling following the airing of the first episode in

December," explained Fess. "Bill Hayes, of course, had the biggest-selling version of the single on the Cadence label, although there were many others. The other side of the record, 'Farewell,' was recorded at another time. Of course, I sang the song during the Alamo segment. Weeks before the first episode was broadcast, I also sang some verses of 'The Ballad of Davy Crockett' on Mr. Disney's television program."

Fess admitted that he wasn't the world's greatest vocalist or musician.

"Now, as far as musical training goes, well, it certainly wasn't formal training," stated Fess. "So I really didn't prepare for the music that I sang in the Crockett series. Years earlier, I had purchased a guitar. I learned three chords in two different keys and started playing songs from an old Burl Ives songbook, which I still have. But, my father used to invite me into the backyard to practice when I was home."

Fess' original recording of "The Ballad of Davy Crockett" was released only as a promotional recording on the Gusto label. The Norman Singers provided backing vocals to Fess, who provided one of his compositions, "Lonely," on the flip side of the 45 rpm single.

A music contract was signed by Fess, Gunther R. Lessing, and James A. Johnson, Vice President of the Walt Disney Music Company, on February 25, 1955, two days after "Davy Crockett at the Alamo" aired. The contract covered three story-telling recordings—"Davy Crockett, Indian Fighter;" "Davy Crockett Goes to Congress," and "Davy Crockett at the Alamo"—and four songs: "The Ballad of Davy Crockett," "I'm Lonely My Darlin' (Green Grow the Lilacs)," "I Gave My Love (The Riddle Song)," and "Farewell."

The contract stated that Fess would receive "two and one half percent (2½%) of the suggested retail list price of…double faced records manufactured and sold" regarding the story telling recordings and "five percent (5%) of the suggested retail list price of…all double faced records" featuring music. An additional payment schedule was provided for "78 rpm flexible children's records." However, the contract noted the Walt Disney Music was entitled to recoup half of the approximate $1,500 in recording costs.

The complete title of the Blackburn-Bruns song was "The Ballad of Davy Crockett: His Early Life, Hunting Adventures, Services Under General Jackson In The Creek War, Electioneering Speeches, Career In Congress, Triumphal Tour In The North States, And Services In The Texan War."

Blackburn penned 20 verses in all. Some of the lyrics—"his country's call" and "freedom...fightin' another foe"—seemed to reflect the Cold War posture of the United States at the time, but Blackburn disagreed. "It was just the opposite," stated Blackburn. "For me, the country was basically unchanged, despite efforts by the likes of the House [of Representatives] Committee on Un-American Activities. I merely attempted to take one part of American history and make it into a story."

The Bill Hayes version of the song made a strong debut on the record charts.

"Archie Bleyer of Cadence Records asked Disney if he could lease the song for his label's release," said Fess. "He did, of course, and he had a very big hit with it." Bleyer signed Hayes to record the song and his five-verse rendition debuted at the #16 spot on *Billboard* magazine's "Best Sellers in Stores" chart on February 26, 1955, three days after "Davy Crockett at the Alamo" aired on TV. *Billboard* declared: "Not since Joan Weber's 'Let Me Go, Lover,' has a record taken off with the excitement sparked by this disc since being introduced on a recent TV show."

The following week, Hayes' recording edged out the Penguins' classic, "Earth Angel," at the #9 chart position. Seven days later Hayes' version of "The Ballad of Davy Crockett" leapfrogged over the McGuire Sisters' "Sincerely" at the top of the charts. It would remain a chart topper for five weeks.

Disney—and the rest of the recording world—soon joined "The Ballad of Davy Crockett" bandwagon. Fess recorded another version of the song on the Columbia label and it debuted on the *Billboard* charts at #16 on March 12. *Billboard* proclaimed: "Despite the fact that Bill Hayes' version of this tune got off to an early lead, the demand for the 'original' [by Fess Parker] has continued so strong that it seems likely to follow the Cadence disk on the charts." One week later, Fess' recording reached #11, and Tennessee Ernie Ford's vinyl interpretation on Capitol Records debuted at #19.

"I knew the 'Davy Crockett' series was going to be very popular after I heard 'The Ballad of Davy Crockett' on my car radio as I was driving around Beverly Hills one day," said Fishman. "Bill Hayes had the big hit but I preferred Fess' version because it sounded more authentic."

Besides Hayes topping the charts with "The Ballad of Davy Crockett," Fess' recording reached #5 and Ford rose to the #7 position on the "Best Sellers in Stores" roster. Furthermore, Walter Schumann's RCA Victor recording reached the #14 position on *Billboard's* "Most Played By Jockeys" chart. Popular demand for the song increased after ABC-TV rebroadcast the original three episodes on April 13 ("Davy Crockett, Indian Fighter"), April 27 ("Davy Crockett Goes to Congress"), and May 11 ("Davy Crockett at the Alamo"). And the big-screen color version, *Davy Crockett, King of the Wild Frontier*, which debuted in American theaters on May 25, 1955, only added to the nationwide excitement.

Additional vinyl performances were recorded by such artists as the Sandpipers, Gabe Drake and the Woodsmen, Jack Andrews, the Rhythmaires, Bill Hart with the Mountaineer Boys and Orchestra, the Sons of the Pioneers, Tommy Scott, Steve Allen, James Brown and the Trailwinders, Mac Wiseman, Jack Richards with the Corwin Group, Vincent Lopez and the Forty-Niners, and Rusty Draper. To date, over one hundred artists have recorded "The Ballad of Davy Crockett."

Novelty versions of the Blackburn-Bruns song were also recorded. Bob Campbell ("Dizzy Crockett"), Lalo Guerrero ("Pancho Lopez"), and Homer and Jethro ("The Ballad of Davy Crew-Cut") managed to generate sales. Mickey Katz's Yiddish offering, "Duvid Crockett," was the most quirky of all the parodies with its "Duvid, Duvid Crockett, King of Delancey Street" chorus. Katz, who died in 1985, is father of actor Joel Grey and the grandfather of actress Jennifer Grey.

"The Ballad of Davy Crockett" was such a popular recording that at least one version of it remained on the *Billboard* charts on July 23, 1955, two weeks after Bill Haley and his Comets' culture-changing "Rock Around the Clock" reached #1.

More Davy Crockett music was recorded and released. "Be Sure You're Right (Then Go Ahead)," which was written by Fess and

Ebsen, was issued by Disney with "Old Betsy" on the flip side. Fess also appeared as Davy Crockett on a 1955 U.S. Treasury Department *Guest Star* radio transcription disc that promoted U.S. Savings Bonds.

The staying power of the song presented a problem to the cast of *Your Hit Parade*, an NBC-TV show that featured Snooky Lanson, Dorothy Collins, Russell Arms, Gisèle MacKenzie and others who performed the top song hits of the nation. Each week the producers were challenged to find new ways for their stable of singers to present "The Ballad of Davy Crockett." Frontier settings could only be altered so many times as backdrops for the vocalists. New sets were quickly designed. For example, on the May 7, 1955 program MacKenzie sang the tune while art-school kids drew a fellow student dressed as the famous frontier hero. But the cast members of *Your Hit Parade* kept singing the popular song, week after week.

The *Dallas Morning News* reported in a June 12, 1955 story that the song in its various renditions "became the record industry's fastest seller with more than seven million sales in just about six months."

Despite millions of record sales, "The Ballad of Davy Crockett" did not earn a Gold Record from the Recording Industry Association of America (RIAA) for Hayes, Ford or Fess. The organization only began issuing the award in 1958, three years after the tune dropped off the record charts.

During the song's chart success, Marcy was recruited by TV personality and charitable fundraiser Johnny Grant, who was later named the "Honorary Mayor of Hollywood," to go on tour with the USO. "We went overseas to Europe, South Korea, Taiwan," said Marcy. "Debbie Reynolds was on the tour. It was a lot of fun. I corresponded with Fess while I was gone."

"The Ballad of Davy Crockett" would have another vinyl life after *Davy Crockett* aired on British television a year later. And like the United States, it was recorded by a number of diverse artists who competed in the charts against the most popular American versions.

Bill Hayes generated the biggest UK hit. His "Ballad of Davy Crockett" entered the British charts on July 1, 1956 at #13 and two weeks later he was at the #2 position. However, Hayes never reached number one. He stayed at the number two slot for three weeks, held back by Tennessee Ernie Ford's "Sixteen Tons." Hayes remained on the UK vinyl roster for a total of nine weeks. It fell off the charts in March during the week of the Alamo battle's 120th anniversary.

Ford's "Ballad of Davy Crockett" stayed on the charts for seven weeks, reaching #3. Actually, Ford's version was the first to break the UK charts: Ford entered the charts on January 14, 1956 at the #11 position.

Dick James' rendition of the song (with Stephen James and his Chums) spent nine weeks on the charts, reaching #14 on February 11, 1956. As a matter of fact, James had a two sided hit: "Robin Hood" was the flip side of the single. James, of course, later gained additional fame as the publisher of Northern Songs, the firm which published the original works of John Lennon and Paul McCartney during the duo's Beatles' days.

The fourth British artist to score a UK hit with "The Ballad of Davy Crockett" was Max Bygraves. The popular vocalist, who had received acclaim as a teenage soloist in the 1930s, scored a Top 20 hit with the Blackburn-Bruns tune on February 18, 1956. However, Bygraves' song fell off the Top 20 roster the next week. Surprisingly, the Fess Parker version of the song did not chart in Great Britain.

"The Ballad of Davy Crockett" was a major song on both sides of the Atlantic in 1955 and 1956, and was the musical signal of a merchandising craze that was about to sweep the nation and other parts of the world.

CHAPTER 8
THE DAVY CROCKETT CRAZE

"The Ballad of Davy Crockett" recording was, of course, extremely popular but the subsequent manufacture of thousands of commercially-made items generated a pop culture phenomenon that would soon be called the Davy Crockett Craze.

To be sure, the most desired collectible was the iconic coonskin cap and manufacturers produced hundreds of thousands of them. Most of them were actually rabbit hats (and assorted recycled fur coats) which featured a raccoon tail. The tails were available for just a few cents each in 1954, but in a matter of months the price topped one dollar. The demand continued to increase and the price for fur tails climbed even higher. J. B. Simpson's Alaska-Arctic Furs in Seattle had its two million fur-pelt inventory depleted in a manner of months.

The Associated Press reported that the "Davy Crockett craze has created a $2,000,000 boom in the fur industry." In the article, Louis Cohen, President of the American Fur Merchants Association explained that rabbit, raccoon, and opossum fur were "doing a land office business." The AP report noted that the "headpiece fad had also cleaned out the wolf tail market." In addition, a run was made on Australian rabbit, skunk and imitation fur.

And when the price of furs got even higher, non-traditional suppliers entered the market. "This was when the fat-buck boys took over," wrote Armand Hartley in the September 1955 issue of *Confidential*, the popular scandal bi-monthly. "They exhumed from junk-dealers' cellars every scrap of fur refuse buried there over the years. If the animal had a tail, fine; if not, they rolled and stitched on. Mangy, moth-eaten, mildewed or mouldering—anything from a moose to a mouse was welcome game for the hungry hide hunters."

Confidential escalated the story by suggesting that some of the motley fur caps were causing an epidemic of sorts. "Alarmed and indignant are discovering an appalling crop: aggravated and oozing eczema sores; deep-rooted skin and scalp infections; angry-looking and hard-to-check allergic rashes from cheap but powerful chemical dyes and from unsterile animal hairs," warned the magazine. "And parasites that are notorious disease carriers!" But a national health scare never materialized, except in the form of Crockett mania.

Ironically, it appeared as though not all of the fur-tailed caps Fess wore were coonskins; as a matter of fact, one of his on-screen caps looked more like coyote. "Those were coonskin caps, although there may have been different caps used by me during the filming of the Creek Indian War episode," stated Fess. "It's difficult to remember the amount of costumes that I used during the series. I know some publicity photographs of me that were taken during filming that clearly show a coonskin cap on my head. But I also remember having the cap fall in the water during the first episode. When it was taken out of the water and dried, it looked different. That circumstance may be the reason for the different look of the same cap during that first episode."

But coonskin caps and recordings of "The Ballad of Davy Crockett" did not satisfy the appetite of the under-12 crowd. Manufacturers promptly contracted with Disney the right to sell hundreds of different items under the "Walt Disney's Davy Crockett, King of the Wild Frontier," "Walt Disney's Davy Crockett" or "Walt Disney's Official Davy Crockett" title, among other incarnations. Fess' photo or image was usually on each item. Although Disney was not initially prepared for the merchandise demand, over two hundred different items were eventually produced. Among the retail offerings were plastic rifles, toy pistols, powder horns, knives, paint sets, glasses, bowls, cups, plates, furniture, tee-pee tents, guitars, lunch boxes, belts, jackets, T-shirts, wash cloths, towels, candy, peace pipes, wallets, moccasins, boots, paper plates and napkins, cowboy hats, tool boxes, sweaters, gloves, mittens, stamp books, bread package labels, toy boxes, canteens, coloring books, Christmas cards, boxed

Fess Parker's parents admire an assortment of Davy Crockett merchandise at their Texas home.
PHOTO COURTESY OF THE PARKER FAMILY.

puzzles, night lights, games, pencil boxes, comic books, dolls, shirts, balloons, film strips, school book bags, suit cases, neck ties, bandanas, bracelets, curtains, rings, pin-back buttons, serving trays, crayons, toothbrushes, wrist watches, play sets, soap, and many more items.

Dell Publishing released several *Davy Crockett* comic books. *Walt Disney's Davy Crockett, Indian Fighter* was followed by *Walt Disney's Davy Crockett at the Alamo*. And a color photo of Fess as Crockett graced every cover. Although a comic based on "Davy Crockett Goes to Congress" was never produced Dell's ninety-six page *Walt Disney's Davy Crockett: King of the Wild Frontier* included a section titled "Davy Crockett Goes to Washington." The comic featured a number of interesting educational sections about frontier living and several short biographies about famous pioneers, including Daniel Boone. Dell also published *The Real-Life Story of Fess Parker*, a fifteen-cent magazine that included select lyrics from "The Ballad of Davy Crockett" and a page filled with Crockett collectibles.

"I was supposed to get ten percent of the merchandising deal of Disney *Davy Crockett* merchandise," said Fess. "But there was a problem with a Davy Crockett copyright owner from New Jersey. The studio made money, nevertheless, from all of the merchandise." Fess managed to earn about $200,000 from the various Crockett goods.

Disney had the ownership of *Davy Crockett* with Fess Parker's likeness, but Crockett was a nineteenth-century historical figure whose image resided in the public domain. As a result, thousands of manufacturers joined the merchandising bandwagon and offered their own line of products. The diverse non-Disney items included rings, wooden scrap books, pith helmets, lamps, hat racks, banks, waste paper baskets, plastic trains, hot-iron transfers, clocks, wall hangings, pencil cases, clothing patches, party poppers, bicycle mud flaps, lassos, chalk, board games, horse shoes, belt buckles, pull wagons, record players, cookies, canned oysters, coffee, soda, toy boxes, grills, flashlights, fabric, binoculars, note pads, lariats, card games, slippers, badges, sunglasses, band-aids, and many more. Approximately 5,000 different Davy Crockett items—Disney and non-Disney—were produced during the craze.

Some manufacturers even sold non-Crockett items—as long as they featured the famous pioneer's name or image. For example, the Ajax Plastic Corporation had thousands of unsold plastic rodeo sets that included nondescript cowboys, horses, and fence sections. The company stapled a strip of paper across the front of the box that proclaimed "Davy Crockett Western" and sold them all. The Ideal Toy Company reaped a dividend when it packaged its Fix-It Stage Coach one way for Roy Rogers and another for Davy Crockett. An Associated Press report noted that a "pile of dusty moccasins" at a Boston store were advertised as "Davy Crockett" footwear "and sold 3,000 within a week."

Disney fueled the retail frenzy by re-releasing the original three episodes in the spring of 1955. The national print media also helped promote the Crockett Craze. *Life* magazine featured a major article, "U.S. Again Is Subdued By Davy," in its April 25, 1955 issue. The seven-page spread featured everything from historical notes on the real David Crockett and pictures of Crockett descendants to nineteenth-century lithograph images and photos of coonskin cap-wearing kids in backyards across America battling imaginary Creek warriors and Santa Anna's soldiers at the Alamo.

The *TV Guide* of April 30–May 6, 1955, which featured a photo of Fess and Buddy Ebsen from "Davy Crockett, Indian Fighter" on its cover, also contained a story, "King of the Wild Frontier," which was essentially a short bio of Fess. Besides the basic information on the young actor, the article mentioned that Fess would star in a forthcoming new series titled "Davy Crockett and the River Boatmen." That series, of course, would evolve into two one-hour episodes: "Davy Crockett's Keelboat Race" and "Davy Crockett and the River Pirates." The issue also featured a full-page ad for Davy Crockett recordings from the three initial episodes and a promo for *The Story of Davy Crockett*, a book for young readers by Enid L. Meadowcraft. Davy Crockett was everywhere.

Look magazine joined in with a cover story tag—"Walt Disney, Davy Crockett and Disneyland"—on July 16, 1955, a day before the Anaheim, California-located theme park was to open. One article traced Disney's career and a companion article, "Meet...Davy Crockett," reported on Fess' cross-country tour. "Fess Parker, Disney's celluloid Crockett, has swept across the U.S. in a way that would have warmed the heart of his real-life counterpart," proclaimed the magazine.

Indeed.

The United States—at least those in the population who were under twelve years of age—was caught up in a frontier-flavored malady that generated $300 million in retail sales and dominated the airwaves. That $300 million would be approximately $2.5 billion in 2011 dollars.

The Chicago Daily Tribune sponsored a photo contest of kids dressed up as Davy Crockett. Hundreds of Crockett merchandise items were offered along with a "1st Grand Prize" of one hundred dollars. Even women became part of the craze when a Texas hair stylist offered a "Davy Crockett" hairdo based on Fess Parker's wavy hair with "a lock of hair falling forward."

Two periodic newspaper entries were spawned during the coonskin cap frenzy. One was a traditional comic strip, but the other offering went beyond the realm of goofy laughs and commercialism. It was a Disney-produced series called *Davy Crockett Says*, and it always included a moral lesson for its young readers. In one entry, Fess warned kids about "the dangers of associating with bad company." In another, he urged youngsters never to "forget your family and friends." Others stressed the importance of good health, the lessons of life's "hard knocks," duty to one's country, and overcoming adversity.

The joyous chaos of the Crockett Craze was viewed as a healthy expression of youth. Dr. Ernest Dichter of the Institute for Research in Mass Motivation stated in a *Saturday Review* article: "Children are reaching for an opportunity to explain themselves in terms of the traditions of the country. Crockett gives them that opportunity." In the article, Eugene Gilbert of Gilbert Youth Research added that Fess' Crockett promoted moral values.

Clearly, Disney and Fess were aware of the power of celebrity and its impact on a young audience. And Fess would soon be meeting that audience face to face.

CHAPTER 9
"DAVY CROCKETT, KING OF THE WILD FRONTIER"

Although some may have questioned why Walt Disney filmed the three initial episodes in costly color during a time when the overwhelming majority of American households had black and white televisions, they quickly found out when the motion picture *Davy Crockett, King of the Wild Frontier* was released to theaters nationwide on May 25, 1955. The film also opened in Brazil on June 6, and in Australia on August 4. The release of the film, a 93-minute edited version of the three original TV episodes, coincided with the end of the elementary school year in the United States in order to capitalize on box office receipts. School was out and *Davy Crockett* was in Technicolor!

Disney didn't prepare any merchandising campaign prior to the release of the first episode, "Davy Crockett, Indian Fighter," in December 1954, but a full-scale commercial assault was launched for *Davy Crockett, King of the Wild Frontier.*

The film's oversized pressbook—*Walt Disney's Davy Crockett King of the Wild Frontier Exhibitor's Campaign Book*—was filled with promotional materials designed to maximize the theatrical release's box office impact. The publication featured numerous items that theaters could order to promote the film. Among the commercial offerings were various-sized posters, assorted newspaper ad and scene mats, publicity stills, insert cards, window cards, and a seven-foot tall "cutout standee" of Fess as the famous frontiersman.

The lyrics to "The Ballad of Davy Crockett" were included in the pressbook along with a roster of thirteen artists who recorded the song besides Fess' rendition. "Every Big Name Record Company Cuts a 'Davy Crockett' side!" proclaimed the pressbook, and record labels such as Capitol, Decca, Mercury, MGM, and RCA prominently were listed.

The pressbook heralded fifteen wearing-apparel manufacturers of Davy Crockett clothing and twenty-nine makers of additional merchandise from across the nation including North Carolina's Blue Bell, Inc. (shirts, jackets, and pants), New York's Regal Knitwear Co. (sweaters and bathing suits), Missouri's Trimfoot Co. (boots, shoes, and moccasins), New Jersey's Childhood Interests, Inc. (jointed figures and string puppets), Rhode Island's Hassenfeld Bros, Inc. (pencil boxes and color-by-numbers paint sets), Maine's Withington, Inc. (bow and arrow sets), Ohio's Sun Rubber Co. (vinyl dolls), and Connecticut's United States Time Corp. (watches), among others. Books, sheet music, and comic books were also highlighted in the pressbook. And Fess eagerly looked forward to his 10 percent slice of the retail pie. "There was an unexpected bonanza of merchandise produced," said Fess. "And I had ten percent of the gross amount."

The Daisy Company, which manufactured toy rifles, powder horns, and canteens, urged its retailers to stock up on its products with an enthusiastic ad that elevated Fess' status: "All Daisy Davy Crockett merchandise is colorfully packaged in boxes bearing Walt Disney copyrighted illustrations, logotypes, and—most important—the picture of Fess Parker, who *is* Davy Crockett to all kids and adults who watch TV and go to the movies."

Disney encouraged theaters to utilize TV spot ads at no charge. "The full set consists of a 1-minute and two 20-second spot commercials which can be telecast over your local TV stations," noted the pressbook. "Each of these is packed with Davy Crockett action and is musically backed with the 'Ballad of Davy Crockett.'" Theaters, though, would have to pay for the TV time. However, free radio transcriptions were available to theaters to use as film promotions. The pressbook noted: "The 'Ballad of Davy Crockett,' one of the most popular song hits in years, provides the background music for all of the *Davy Crockett, King of the Wild Frontier* radio transcriptions."

The pressbook also contained numerous publicity articles which carried such approved headlines as "Walt Disney's *Davy Crockett, King of the Wild Frontier*," "Perfect Blend of Historical Fact With Wonderful Entertainment," "Music Enlivens Disney's *Davy Crockett*,"

"Fess Parker—From Texas to Stardom," and "Historical Heroes Figure in Walt Disney's *Davy Crockett*."

Although *Davy Crockett, King of the Wild Frontier* was merely the large-screen, edited version of the three original TV episodes, the theatrical release was still a "new" motion picture and movie critics penned their obligatory reviews.

Bosley Crowther of *The New York Times* wrote that the film "is a straight juvenile entertainment with a story line as simple as a T and enough poker-faced exaggeration to satisfy the most implausible fibber in school. The incidents are tall and transparent. No psychological subtleties to confuse. You know what's happening every single second. And all of it is okay."

The reviewer mentioned that Fess displayed "two" expressions" and looked a "little bit [like] Jimmy Stewart." Crowther was somewhat critical of the TV-screen to theater-screen image transitions. "A certain condescension in construction to the small screen of the television screen is noticeable in the frequency and frankness of the close-ups that run through this film," noted Crowther. "Practically all of the dialogue exchanges are played by the characters' heads. This tends to be slightly annoying on a full-size theatre screen." Ironically, *The New York Times* never mentioned anything about the overuse of "full-size theatre screen" heads in its favorable review of the Beatles' *A Hard Day's Night* a decade later when coonskin cap-wearing Baby Boomers had graduated to mop-top hair styles.

Clyde Gilmour of *The Lethbridge Herald* in Alberta, Canada was more generous. He called the film "a surprisingly enjoyable western comedy-drama." Gilmour was particularly fond of the film's stars. "Fess Parker as Crockett and Buddy Ebsen as his trusty pal are not only tough and valiant but humorous and unpretentious," he wrote. "Davy Crockett [is] a film which many adults probably will enjoy as heartily as their juniors."

Rual Askews's review in *The Dallas Morning News* noted that "Fess Parker is a natural as Davy, and if his stamina holds out, his working future is secure. Fess fills out his buckskins and coonskin cap convincingly and rolls out the backwoods lingo without batting a self-conscious eye." The reviewer added that the film "can hold its poker-face high with pride for keeping a national phenomenon modestly in line."

The *New York Daily Mirror* called Fess "a new star." The *New York Daily News* gave the film three and one-half stars and stated that "Fess Parker is irresistible." And the *New York Herald Tribune* stated: "Fess Parker is a combination of Gregory Peck, Jimmy Stewart, and Gary Cooper—down, girls!" The Disney publicity department promptly placed those comments in its print ads.

But the success of *Davy Crockett, King of the Wild Frontier* didn't depend on advertisements; it spread by word of mouth—the best form of advertising and the cheapest. Kids loved the film's action and its select moments of audience participation. One scene in the film always generated a reaction from youngsters in movie audiences. When Crockett instructs Major Norton to whistle "like a Tennessee thrush," movie theaters turned instantaneously into audio aviaries as hundreds of kids mimicked the bird call.

An interesting aspect of the feature film was the addition of nine new or altered verses to "The Ballad of Davy Crockett" that were not part of the original 20-verse collection in the sheet music. Of course, kids joyously sang along.

The most important ingredient in the promotion of *Davy Crockett, King of the Wild Frontier* was Fess who participated in a cross-country tour. "It was forty-two U.S. cities starting in the spring of 1955," he said. "I started out on the tour by myself and then Buddy joined me in June."

Fess' itinerary was basically the same for each city: a promotional stop for the film, a visit to an area hospital or civic organization, a meet-and-greet with local or state government officials, rushed meals, and a quick night's sleep at a hotel. And the next day he would be off to the next city to do it again.

Besides the promotional visits, which were sponsored by the Hudson Motor Car Company, Fess willingly participated in hundreds of interviews. "If some poor guy wanted me to meet him for breakfast at six o'clock for an interview, I'd do it," he said. "I tried to do the best I could to service who was interested."

Fess was amazed by the receptions he received.

"It was so strange because many of the places I went were adult," said Fess. "I did go to schools. Schools were named Davy Crockett; they changed the names. But I met a lot of business people, civic leaders, and so on."

One of Fess' most important stops was Tennessee, the birthplace of Davy Crockett.

On May 28, Fess arrived in Chattanooga where he was greeted by T. Vance Price, the head of the Price Auto Company, the city's biggest Hudson dealership. Price had a sign made up that read:

Official Car
Hudson Welcomes
Davy Crockett
Fess Parker, star of the picture
"King of the Wild Frontier"
Price Auto Co.
Your Hudson Dealer

Fess appeared at Engel Stadium in the morning where he was entertained by such diverse activities as a model airplane club demonstration, an archery exhibition, and a performance by the Chattanooga High School band. He participated in a media luncheon at the Read House, an historic hotel, and later visited the T. C. Thompson Children's Hospital. The next day he was on the road again.

"Fess was here in Morristown, Tennessee on May 29, 1955, in the afternoon," said Sally Baker, who now serves as the director of the Crockett Tavern and Museum in Morristown. The Morristown *Daily Gazette* reported that 2,000 people were on hand to greet Fess. "He was at the Crockett birth site earlier that morning in Limestone. In Morristown, he was at the historic Crockett Well site for about six minutes; as a matter of fact, he stood there surrounded by majorettes! Then he went downtown for fourteen minutes on a hay wagon that stopped in front of the Princess Theater. But the theater didn't show the Disney movie until weeks later."

Despite the quick visit, Fess acknowledged the city. "Always the gentleman, Fess Parker wrote a thank-you letter to Morristown Mayor C. Frank Davis," noted Baker. In the letter, Fess told the mayor that he appreciated "the courtesies and hospitality" but respectfully declined an invitation to the city's August centennial celebration due to his upcoming filming of the next *Davy Crockett* episodes.

Fess Parker is greeted by the citizens of Morristown, Tennessee on May 29, 1955.
PHOTO COURTESY OF SALLY BAKER.

"From Morristown, he went to Knoxville where he spoke to a Boy Scout group and then flew out the next day from McGhee Tyson Airport," said Baker. While in Knoxville, Fess was welcomed by Mayor George Roby Dempster, an unpopular Democrat who was voted out of office later in the year because he raised taxes.

On the eve of *Davy Crockett, King of the Wild Frontier's* debut in many Tennessee theaters, Volunteer State Governor Frank G. Clement proclaimed June "Davy Crockett Month."

Phil Kendrick remembers when Fess returned to his home state.

"He invited me to join him on part of the tour," said Kendrick. "I was with him in Oklahoma City, Fort Worth, and San Antonio. But San Antonio was something else. The crowds were huge. One newspaper said that it was the largest crowd that had ever turned out for a celebrity in the city's history. It was unbelievable!"

The Associated Press reported that when Fess showed at Halliburton's Department Store in Oklahoma City, over $28,000 worth of Crockett merchandise was sold. "It could have easily been more," said a store spokesman, "but our stock ran out."

Over 2,000 people greeted Fess when he arrived at Beaumont, Texas' small airport, and in Austin 5,000 fans of all ages were on hand to meet him. While in the Texas capital, Fess presented a painting of the Alamo to Governor Allan Shivers. The governor also made Buddy Ebsen an honorary Texan. And during a stop in Houston, Fess dined with two of Crockett's great-great grandsons.

On June 10, Fess and Ebsen arrived at Dallas' Love Field and was greeted by 1,500 children, a "coonskin cap color guard," and a lineup of airline hostesses, who all wore white coonskin caps. The pair was ushered away to a Hotel Adolphus brunch where they met various dignitaries, the press, and a group of *Dallas Morning News* newspaper carriers. Dallas was a special part of the tour because his parents were there. Later, Fess and his parents were driven in a motorcade of Hudson automobiles.

The Dallas Morning News welcomed him as "Texas' own: Fess Parker." Jeweler Frank Everts, who knew Fess years earlier, presented his childhood friend with a solid gold powder horn that was inlaid with diamonds. Fess was also reunited with Captain Paul Rafferty, who commanded the minesweeper *YMS334* during World War II. The skipper remembered Fess as "a long, tall youngster with a chronic slouch from dodging the low overhead" on the ship. Sheriff Bill Decker made Fess and Ebsen honorary deputy sheriffs. Nine years later, Decker would be in the spotlight again as he sat in the backseat of the lead car in President John F. Kennedy's fateful motorcade.

At the Majestic theater in Dallas, Fess and Ebsen were scheduled to appear on stage five times before each showing of *Davy Crockett, King of the Wild Frontier.* At every appearance a packed house of youngsters and their parents greeted Fess and his sidekick with high-volume enthusiasm. Ebsen told *The Dallas Morning News*, "In all my years as a performer, this was the greatest thing I've ever experienced." Charley Freeman, the road show booker for Texas' Interstate movie chain, stated: "I've seen 'em come and go for forty-seven years, but I've never seen any celebrities receive the kind of reception these kids gave Parker and Ebsen today."

Fess managed to find time in Dallas to promote a summer reading program sponsored by County Librarian Bess Ann Motley. He showed up to meet fifteen youngsters who signed up for the program which was designed to stimulate an interest in reading.

Another reading-related program welcomed Fess.

"Anticipating a scheduled visit to Little Rock by Fess Parker, the Arkansas Gazette commenced a sixteen-part series on Crockett geared especially for children," wrote Manley Cobia in *Journey into the Land of Trials: The Story of Davy Crockett's Expedition to the Alamo.*

In Birmingham, Alabama, Fess was greeted by 10,000 people at the airport. He had a little breathing room later in the day when he made an appearance at The Club, an exclusive private dining facility where he cut watermelons with some Hudson Car dealers. On hand to coordinate the event was Charlie Levy, Disney's Eastern Public Relations Director.

It was a hectic schedule for Fess but the 30-year-old actor didn't complain.

"That tour was part of my job," he said. "I just did it."

"He was a calm, cool cat," said Kendrick. "He never really got that much excited."

Shillito's department store in Cincinnati, Ohio created one of the biggest promotional buildups. The store took out a large ad in the *Cincinnati Post* on June 3, 1955, which proclaimed,

**"Get out them shootin' irons, podner
Davy Crockett's
comin' to town!"**

The store was well prepared for the afternoon arrival of Fess and Buddy Ebsen on June 15, the same day that *Davy Crockett, King of the Wild Frontier* was opening at the city's Palace theater. The newspaper ad stated that the store had "official Davy Crockett regalia at Shillito's Frontierland Shops on the Balcony and Second Floor and in the Basement."

But the department store offered an additional incentive: "Davy's Honor Guard."

The store devised a promotion in which "25 children between the ages of 3 and 12 will be chosen to meet Davy Crockett and Buddy Ebsen at the airport and escort them back to town in a Shillito-Hudson motorcade." Of course, kids would have to come to the store in advance and register. "Come in early and sign up," urged the store, who expected the kiddies' parents to buy an armload of

Crockett merchandise while they were there. The motorcade, with police sirens blasting away, arrived in the city where Mayor Carl Rich proclaimed "Davy Crockett Day" to the masses and presented Fess and Ebsen with keys to the city. The two buckskin-wearing TV stars were also appointed officers in the Cincinnati Chapter of the Hudson Triangle Club, which recognized car sales. "Sure hope I prove to be a good Hudson salesman and I appreciate the honor of being head of the club," stated Fess in the July 8, 1955 issue of the *Hudson All-American Go-Getter*, a corporate newsletter.

Fess made a stop in Washington D.C. where he presented a rifle to Robert B. Anderson, the Deputy Secretary of Defense. While in the nation's capitol, he associated with high-ranking military officers and powerful politicians like Texas Senator Lyndon Johnson, Speaker of the House Sam Rayburn, and Tennessee Senator Estes Kefauver, who had worn a coonskin cap in his 1948 Senate run and in 1952 when he sought the Democratic Presidential nomination. And many more of the Washington elite stood in line to get Fess' autograph.

One June 17, 1955, he landed at Philadelphia airport where he joined a 22-car motorcade of Hudson automobiles. The motorized caravan arrived across the street from Independence Hall at the Commodore John Barry statue where representatives from the National Rifle Association presented Fess with a fine early nineteenth-century .50 caliber rifle that had been built by J. Bender, a Lancaster, Pennsylvania gunsmith. Participating in the ceremony was Congressman William A. Barrett (D-PA) and Medal of Honor recipient Merritt Austin Edson, a World War II U.S. Marine veteran who earned the nation's highest military award during the successful defense of the Guadalcanal Airport on the Solomon Islands in 1942. Fess, as usual, was dressed as Davy Crockett for the occasion.

The inscription on the rifle reads: "Presented to Fess Parker by the National Rifle Association of America, June 17, 1955 in commemoration of the rifle given to Davy Crockett by the Young Men of Philadelphia, July 1, 1834." The inscription concludes with Crockett's motto: "Be sure you're right then go ahead."

"I used to visit a lot of fellows who fired Kentucky long rifles and made guns during promotional tours in the 1950s following the success of the Crockett series," said Fess.

One lucky Florida girl still recalls her memorable day with TV's frontier hero."I had a photo taken with him in June, 1955," exclaimed Bev Friberg Cameron. "I was six years old at the time and was a big fan. I had the complete outfit. Fess was visiting a local children's hospital, the Variety Children's Hospital, which is now Miami Children's Hospital. I am not sure how we knew about the visit, perhaps because my dad worked for the *Miami Herald*. I don't remember a big crowd. Unfortunately, my dad is gone so I can't give you the details of the visit. I even have a picture of me next to his official car with a sign saying, 'Hudson welcomes Davy Crockett.' My memories of the day I met 'Davy' was one of excitement. I bragged about it for weeks. I remember feeling sad when he started to drive away and I tried to reach out to his car. Fess showed concern over my safety and had the car stop until my dad had firmly grabbed my hand. I just didn't want him to go."

Fess' gregarious nature in which he treated everyone with friendly respect originated with his father. "He told me to be nice to the people on the way up because you'll see them again," explained Fess.

New York greeted Fess and he even made a visit to Coney Island.

"I've kind of lost the sequence of what happened then," confessed Fess. "But all of a sudden, I went to New York. And while I was there I was treated for a sinus infection with penicillin. And I became allergic. I was sitting in the hotel room with a Disney fellow, Bob Dorfman, and I just kind of fell over in a chair. My heart was going like a hummingbird's wings. So they called the doctor who was on call. He came in and gave me a shot of something and stopped it. When I went over to England—from then on for many months—when I was in the cold, suddenly my face would swell, my hands would swell."

Perhaps Fess' most memorable visit was a particular stop in Michigan.

"The biggest thing I can think of was when Buddy and I were in Hudson's Department Store in Detroit, and there were three main roads that enter that section of downtown Detroit. Hudson's—which is no longer there—was a very big store and they had a very big marquee. They let all of the school kids out in Detroit. It was kids as far as you could see. And Buddy and I were up there on the

Bev Friberg Cameron meets Fess Parker in Miami.
Photo courtesy of Bev Friberg Cameron.

[marquee] singing 'Bang Goes Old Betsy.' And we couldn't leave Hudson's for a while. There were just too many people."

Detroit was also the home of the American Motors Corporation, which had been created the year before as a result of the merger of Nash-Kelvinator Corporation and the Hudson Motor Car Company. Detroit's Hudson dealers and the American Motors' top brass, led by its President George Romney, welcomed Fess to the company's headquarters.

The film grossed a solid $2,401,000, according to Hollywood reporter Bob Thomas. Considering that the tenth biggest film of 1955, *East of Eden*, took in $5,850,000, Disney and Fess did well with their edited TV-series release.

And while *Davy Crockett, King of the Wild Frontier* was playing in the theaters, Davy was getting ready to revive the life and legend of Davy Crockett despite the frontier hero's death at the Alamo.

CHAPTER 10
"DAVY CROCKETT'S KEELBOAT RACE" & "DAVY CROCKETT AND THE RIVER PIRATES"

Walt Disney had a problem with Davy Crockett: the buckskin hero perished at the Alamo. "Historically, of course, Davy Crockett died at the Alamo," stated Fess. "But the show had become so popular by then that Disney was considering extending the series."

But how?

Clearly, there could be no sequel about the illustrious frontiersman's life after March 6, 1836. But Disney came up with a brilliant solution: a story about Crockett *before* his days at the Alamo. The result was the first prequel in TV history: "Davy Crockett's Keelboat Race." And it was followed by another episode, "Davy Crockett and the River Pirates."

Davy Crockett was back!

Celebrity newspaper columnist Hedda Hopper proclaimed: "Take off those black armbands, kids, and put on your coonskin caps, for Davy Crockett will hit the trail again."

The two episodes were escapist fun with lots of action, river locations, and a supporting cast worth its weight in action, adventure, and laughs. The two programs made no reference to an exact time or to Polly Crockett and the children. Still, there was an element of historical truth to them because after his Congressional election defeat in 1825, Crockett and some hired hands set sail down the Mississippi River on two boats stacked with 30,000 barrel staves. However, before he could reach New Orleans, the boats crashed and started to sink. Crockett almost drowned; the boats were destroyed and the staves were lost.

"Davy Crockett's Keelboat Race" traces Crockett and Russel's attempt to beat legendary boatman Mike Fink in a race to New Orleans. Crockett and Russel join Capt. Cobb (Clem Bevins) and his crew on the *Bertha Mae*. Mike Fink, enthusiastically portrayed by Jeff York, and his crew navigate the *Gullywhumper.*

"Off the top of my head, it's somewhat difficult to remember all of the details, but shortly after the completion of the Alamo episode the Disney people and ABC television agreed that something else was going to be filmed because of the popular reaction," recalled Fess. "But I do know that Mr. Disney was backed by ABC, and it was something he wanted to do. So in time, the cast and crew was out at Morganfield, Kentucky working on the Ohio River on keelboats. Like everyone else, though, it was my formal baptism on a keelboat. I did have a break from filming when Buddy Ebsen and I went back to California for the opening of Disneyland."

Disney sent a cast and crew of about fifty led by Director Norman Foster to the Ohio River where they shot along thirty miles of the waterway including Illinois' Cave-In-Rock, a place where river thieves operated over a century earlier. Co-writers Tom Blackburn and Foster did their homework: they even included a character named Sam Mason, who was an eighteenth-century river pirate. The cast was augmented by approximately seventy-five local men who worked as extras in the production.

The shoot was physically demanding because Fess and his fellow keelboat men powered their vessel against the stream by shouldering long poles and pushing the boat along from the deck sides. Furthermore, some choreographed skill was necessary for the crew members to place their respective poles uniformly in the muddy river bottom without losing them.

Fess enjoyed the on-location shoot but he did not appreciate the oppressive summer heat. "Oh, man, was it hot back there!" laughed Fess. "Buddy and I were really glad to get away from there." But Fess was in for another surprise when he returned to California in mid-July.

"Buddy and I found out that we were going to the Hollywood Bowl on Walt Disney Night, which was actually a two-night event," said Fess. "We sang 'Bang Goes Old Betsy' and 'Be Sure You're Right, Then Go Ahead' and 'The Ballad of Davy Crockett' in front of about 25,000 people. Besides those songs, I also sang 'Farewell' with a full orchestra and chorus. It was some experience. When the second night was over, Buddy and I began rehearsing for opening day in Disneyland."

The grand opening of Disneyland on July 17, 1955 was televised live. It was actually an "International Press Preview" event since the park didn't officially open to the general public until the next day. TV personalities Art Linkletter, Bob Cummings, and Ronald Reagan shared the hosting duties. Walt Disney beamed as he greeted those in attendance and those watching on TV screens: "To all who come to this happy place—Welcome! Disneyland is your land. Here age relives fond memories of the past. And here youth may savor the challenges and promise of the future. Disneyland is dedicated to the ideals, the dreams, and the hard facts that have created America—with the hope that it will be a source of joy and inspiration to all the world."

It may have been Disney's land but the star of the day was Fess. Joined by Ebsen, Fess and his loyal side kick rode their horses to the main TV camera area where they were introduced by Linkletter. The frontier buddies actually had rehearsed part of their ride earlier in the morning sans buckskins. They promptly sang "Bang Goes Old Betsy" amidst a chorus line of athletic, pioneer-garbed dancers.

When the performance was over, Fess took a break. "The crowd was so huge that I didn't even walk around," explained Fess. "Instead, I went to Walt's private place above the fire house and we had a drink."

Disneyland's Frontierland became the capital of official Davy Crockett merchandise. The Emporium on Main Street U. S. A. sold everything from dinner plates and toy flintlock pistols to clothing and wallets. At the Frontier Arcade, kids of all ages could test their marksmanship at a shooting gallery which was identified with a large, rustic-looking wooden sign that read: "B'ar Country: Try Your Skill With Ol' Betsy.'" The rifles were equipped with a light beam that stopped a moving bear and forced the bruin to stand and change his direction. It was pure fun.

The most unique feature in the Frontier Arcade was a photo display area that featured full-sized figures of Fess as Crockett and Ebsen as Russel. Kids would be posed with a toy rifle and a coonskin

Fess Parker's Davy Crockett, boatmen, and livestock aboard the *Bertha Mae* in "Davy Crockett's Keelboat Race."

cap and have their photograph taken. The finished print was a handsome product and a wonderful keepsake. Another collectible was a personalized record titled "Davy Crockett and His Friend."

Following the Disneyland opening, Fess and Ebsen traveled back to the Ohio River where they boarded the *Bertha Mae* for more filming. In one scene, Fess and his boat mates provide a ride for a farmer and his livestock. "Pigs were on the deck and, well, it was pretty stinky!" chuckled Fess. "And we didn't have much room to move around on the deck either."

Most of the action on the river involved fights between rival crews and the river pirates. "I remember all the guys on the keelboats," laughed Fess. "I believe a lot of them were locals. And it seemed that every time one of them would get knocked in the river, we would have to stop and rescue them. Yeah, they couldn't swim. They ran from water!" Other factors occasionally stopped the cameras from rolling: modern-day objects in the river, like trash, people, and boats.

Conceptual art for "Davy Crockett and the River Pirates."
© DISNEY.

Fess had another brief break from filming when he returned to Disneyland in August to guide Vice President Richard Nixon and his family around the park. Fess had lunch with the Nixons at the Red Wagon Inn, the park's only complete-meal eating establishment. Fess also joined Cornelius Vanderbilt Wood, the park manager who had developed Disneyland, in a ceremony where the Vice President was presented a special silver key to the park. Fess later made other occasional appearances at Disneyland, including a special Thanksgiving showing with Walt Disney as they both rode horses down Main Street.

The October 15–21, 1955 issue of *TV Guide* featured a front-page headline that stated: "Davy Crockett Rides Again." A two-page article, which featured five color photos from the production, alerted readers that a new episode was on its way. "Davy Crockett's Keelboat Race" aired on November 16, 1955, and was followed the next month by "Davy Crockett and the River Pirates" on December 14. Thanks to the two prequels, *Disneyland* ended up as the fourth most popular television program of the 1955–56 year.

"Davy Crockett and the River Pirates" would become the last of the five *Davy Crockett* episodes but Disney considered reviving his frontier hero in a new series about Jean Lafitte. According to a United Press International story filed by Henry Gris, the legendary pirate was scheduled to join General Andrew Jackson at the Battle of New Orleans in a new Legends series, and Fess was going to make an appearance as Crockett. But the Lafitte proposal never got beyond the idea stage.

Stores were stocked with new *Davy Crockett* merchandise for Christmas of 1955. Montgomery Ward offered a steel covered wagon for $4.69, a towel set for $1.59, and an Alamo Model Set for $4.59, among many other items. Sears, Roebuck and Company promoted a three-piece dinner set for $1.59, a camera outfit for $4.79, and a lamp for $3.95, plus additional toys and games. One independent retailer sold a Davy Crockett Pogo Stick for $6.95.

But the Crockett Craze was peaking in the United States.

"Although interest in Davy Crockett has by no means died, it no longer is at the white heat it reached earlier this year," reported the *Newark Advocate* in December. The newspaper article noted that Fess was somewhat pleased by the situation. "I'm just as happy about that," stated Fess, who quickly clarified his words. "I could never hate Davy Crockett. Not when Mr. Disney gave me ten percent of the sales of Davy Crockett merchandise. Not when my record of 'The Ballad of Davy Crockett' sold 1,000,000 copies. No sir. I couldn't be mad at Davy. Why, I've got a new house up in Benedict Canyon. You might say it was the house that Davy built. It has been said that I contributed to the demise of Hopalong Cassidy. In turn, I could be happy to step aside for something new like the Mickey Mouse Club."

Fess and Buddy Ebsen appeared on *The Mickey Mouse Club* on December 23, 1955, as a kind of final reminder for parents who had yet to purchase the requisite *Davy Crockett* merchandise for Christmas. Their appearance coincided with the program's Talent Roundup Day, and end-of-the-week performance fest. And on Christmas Day, the Mike Fink Keelboat Ride debuted at Disneyland. In fact, the boats were the actual ones used in the episodes, although they were rechristened with each other's names, restructured, and modified for guests of all ages. As for powering the vessels, the keelboat poles were replaced by 70 horse-power motors.

Buddy Ebsen and Fess became good friends. They even became neighbors when Ebsen gave Fess a real estate tip about an available house—the aforementioned "house that Davy built"—across the street from him in Beverly Hills. "The house cost $30,000," stated Fess. "It had two bedrooms. It was a cute little house. We became neighbors. Buddy had six daughters. His wife at that time had gone to Vassar and she couldn't forget that."

In late 1955, the nation's two major political parties began planning for the 1956 Presidential election. While speculation centered on the Democratic challenger to Republican incumbent Dwight D. Eisenhower, *Cockeyed* magazine, a Fawcett publication, "nominated" Italian actress Gina Lollobrigida and Davy Crockett as political running mates! The magazine's December 1955 issue proclaimed the unique pairing as a cover story with Lollobrigida wearing a strategically-placed "I Like Davy" campaign button. A photo of Fess from "Davy Crockett, Indian Fighter" was placed behind the actress. Of course, the twenty-nine-year-old Italian-born actress was constitutionally ineligible to run for President and Crockett had been dead since 1836. No matter.

The Crockett Craze was finally crazy.

In 1956, "Davy Crockett and the River Pirates" earned an Emmy nomination in the "Best Single Program of the Year" category; however, *Producer's Showcase* production of *Peter Pan* with Mary Martin won the award. Still, *Disneyland* won the 1956 award for "Best Action or Adventure Series" and Walt Disney won the Emmy as "Best Producer—Film Series." Thanks to the popularity of the various *Davy Crockett* episodes, *Disneyland* became the fourth most popular television program in the country, according to the Nielsen ratings.

Like the original three episodes which were edited and released as a major motion picture, Disney edited the two prequels and released them as a theatrical release on July 18, 1956, as *Davy Crockett and the River Pirates*. Disney promoted the film as a "thrilling new adventure." The motion picture's pressbook listed a "vast array of *Davy Crockett* merchandise set for local exploitation efforts" and included a twelve-part "Davy Crockett and the River Pirates Story-In-Pix" series that daily newspapers could use to stir interest in the film. And the film generated favorable reviews. *The Dallas Morning News* called it "a frolic for youngsters."

In 1956, the Crockett Craze crossed the Atlantic Ocean when Fess went on a promotional tour for *Davy Crockett, King of the Wild Frontier*. Fess arrived in London via Pan American Airways on March 31. He left the plane wearing a modern-day top coat but quickly changed into his buckskin jacket and coonskin cap before he walked off the tarmac. He was greeted by a huge crowd that included Deidre Butchins, 14, the founder of the British Davy Crockett Fan Club. He appeared on BBC's *In Town Tonight* show and then made appearances in Glasgow, Edinburgh, Newcastle, Liverpool, Manchester, Leeds, York, Sheffield, Dublin, Belfast, Birmingham, and Cardiff.

"My schedule there was more intense than it was [in the United States], a city a day," recalled Fess. "I had a regular routine: an interview for breakfast, orphanages, hospitals, department stores, lunch with the Lord High Mayor and a whole bunch of people. In the afternoon, maybe a department store again or some other location. I was busy all day. At dinner, I usually had an interview in that city, and then I would get on a plane or train."

Fess' visit to Cardiff on April 19 was typical. He arrived at General Station and was greeted by a number of designated youngsters including Graham Lewis, 13, and Gareth Thomas, 6. While in Wales' capital, Fess, dressed in his buckskins and coonskin cap, visited Frank Chapman, Lord Mayor of Cardiff. At city hall Fess shared a greeting from Los Angeles and stated that the city owed "an immense debt to its citizens of Welsh origin." Fess also made an 11:30 a.m. appearance at Littlewoods' department store where a "Trading Post" section had been set up with *Davy Crockett* merchandise. Fess paid a visit to Cardiff's Whitchurch Hospital where he sang "Whirlwind," a Stan Jones song performed by Gene Autry in 1951, to Ian Smith, a five-year-old boy who, according to his father, was not expected to live more than a few years. "It was wonderful," exclaimed Smith in a *South Wales Echo and Express* newspaper interview. "I've always wanted to see him and now I have." Later that evening, Fess made a 7 p.m. appearance at the Odeon theater where a huge crowd greeted him. The Cardiff crowd was so enthusiastic that he had to be "rescued by the police"

And then Fess was off to another city.

Unfortunately, Fess suffered another allergic reaction in Scotland.

"I remember a day in Glasgow when I got up one morning in a very primitive room—something probably a hundred years old—and I turned on the faucet and the water was cold," explained Fess. "I splashed my face with it. Oh, my eyes! It took three or four hours until I could go out. It was really weird."

At one stop, Fess' celebrity status interfered with British transportation.

"One of the great moments was in Edinburgh," said Fess. "I was unavoidably late. But there was a railroad train that was legendary for its departures on time. The station master was in a frock coat and top hat. We arrived at the station to catch that train, but we were late. And they held the train. The station master met us at the station. We walked out. It was a big train. We walked almost the length of that train to get on board. I was thinking, 'Gosh, this is something!'"

As usual, Fess was dressed in his buckskins and coonskin cap as the train's passengers looked out of their windows to see what had delayed their departure. "I was dressed in costume," said Fess. "I worked in that thing a lot and very seldom could I get out of it."

While Fess was in Europe, fellow actor Gregory Peck was returned to the United States and became a victim of the Crockett Craze. *Davy Crockett* producer Bill Walsh shared the story with his wife, Nolie.

"Bill told me that Gregory Peck had been in Europe for a while and was flying back home," explained Nolie Fishman. "When he returned to the states and deplaned some kids in the airport caught a glimpse of him and excitedly started yelling, 'Fess! Fess!' as they pointed at him. He turned to the studio rep who was meeting him and asked 'What's a Fess?' It was quite funny."

Fess recalled that he didn't do much electronic media in Europe.

"In a number of those countries, they didn't have television," he said. "So I had to go into a theater or a dance hall. It was kind of interesting to do that." Sometimes Fess made appearances at large dance halls where young fans were joined by adults who were drinking. "I always dreaded that because they had to stop and be introduced to some funny looking guy in a costume."

He returned to London on April 20 where he met the Lord Mayor at an official reception. Later in the day he departed for Paris and over the next several days made stops in Stockholm, Oslo, Copenhagen, Amsterdam, Brussels, and Rome before returning to London on May 3 where he met an old friend.

"I was in the Air Force stationed at the Royal Air Force base in Molesworth when Fess contacted me and invited me to see him for a few days," said Milstead. "I wasn't that far away from London so I went to see him. He was staying in a suite at the Dorchester Hotel. Fess had a bottle of Bushmills Irish Whiskey that the Lord Mayor of Belfast had given him. Well, we had a good time with that. We later went to a club where Eartha Kitt was performing and went back stage to meet her. I had a great time."

Several nations had witnessed *Davy Crockett, King of the Wild Frontier* before Parker arrived on the European continent. It opened in Italy as *Le avventure di Davy Crockett* on February 7, and in Hong Kong on March 19. *Davy Crockett, præriens bedste mand* debuted in Denmark on March 23.

"None of the five television episodes were ever aired here in Denmark," said Crockett researcher Gert Petersen. "After the first film's release in March, 'Davy Crockett and the River Pirates' debuted here on October 6, 1956. And two Davy Crockett comic books were published."

While Fess was touring Europe, *Davy Crockett roi des trappeurs* opened in France on April 11. The movie posters identified him as Fier Parker since fesse in French meant buttock! Fier meant proud—a much safer choice. French children sang their version of "The Ballad of Davy Crockett" with such chorus endings as "*Davy, Davy Crockett, L'homme qui n'a jamais peur, qui n'a jamais peur.*"

On April 13, *Davy Crockett, koning van de wilde grenzen* graced the theater screens in Belgium. West Germany greeted *Davy Crockett, König der Trapper* on August 3, and *Davy Crockett, erämaan kuningas* made its debut in Finland on August 31. In December, the film opened in Japan and Sweden.

Fess made an impression on European kids, too.

"I happened to grow up at a time when Walt Disney's Davy Crockett movies, starring Fess Parker, were out and I became that character," said British music superstar Phil Collins in *Music of the*

Alamo: From 19th Century Ballads to Big-Screen Soundtracks. "I became Davy Crockett. I thought I was the only one. Wrong! I even won a few talent contests singing 'The Ballad of Davy Crockett.'"

"Fess Parker came to the big stores in Copenhagen," said Gert Petersen. "I remember that the school children bought raccoon tails which they placed on their bikes."

Fess' busy European schedule reminded him of his U. S. tour the previous year. "I wore out six sets of guitar strings playing 'The Ballad of Davy Crockett' and nearly wore out my pipes while singing it," said Fess in a May 25, 1956 article in the *Oakland Tribune.*

European merchandising rivaled American products in their diversity. For example, the Danish-produced Davy Crockett book series written by Tom Hill featured exciting frontier adventures, and the British published an impressive three-dimensional pop-up book. The sheet music to "The Ballad of Davy Crockett" was also a big seller in Great Britain. One of the most impressive French products was a colorful plastic percussion pistol that came with a sturdy cardboard holster.

Stateside, the Topps Chewing Gum Company, best known for its baseball cards, issued two eighty-card *Walt Disney's Davy Crockett* picture bubblegum sets in 1956. The cards came in wrapped twenty-four to a box with a five-cent per pack price, and 120-count boxes with a penny price tag per pack. The cards featured scenes and promotional color photos from *Davy Crockett, King of the Wild Frontier* on the obverse of the card with such lively phrases as "Davy Senses Trouble," Face To Face With Death," "Deadly Arrows," "Vicious Battle," "Storming The Walls," "A Bullet Finds Its Mark," and "Fighting Finish." The reverse of the cards featured text descriptions of the front-side image. The initial run of cards featured orange-colored backgrounds on the reverse side; the second run was characterized by the green-colored background on the flip side. Both sets of cards today command high prices from collectors, especially the ones with the green-colored backgrounds.

That same year, a sixteen-card set of non-Disney—misspelled "Davey Crockett"—exhibit cards was issued. The cards featured illustrations of a generic-looking Crockett in such situations as "Davey Crockett fighting a bear with a knife," "Davey Crockett—Buffalo Hunter," and "Davey Crockett at the Alamo awaiting the attack."

The Crockett Craze also manifested itself in a number of off-beat ways. For example, an enterprising Pikesville, Maryland entrepreneur rechristened his truck-mounted whip-ride the "Davy Crockett Kiddy Whip Ride." The mobile attraction was advertised for use at such events as birthday parties, church carnivals, day camps, school fairs and shopping center promotions.

Over the years, the phenomenology of the international coonskin cap-flavored zaniness was dissected by academics, assorted social scientists, and political pundits like William H. Buckley. Margaret J. King even earned a Ph.D. from the University of Hawaii in 1976 for her *The Davy Crockett Craze: A Case Study in Popular Culture* dissertation. King credited a "special matrix" of kids and the new medium converging together at the right time. The Cold War, the U.S. economy, the communal aspect of TV viewing in the 1950s, the aspirations of the Baby Boom generation, and other assorted factors were cited by the so-called experts as reasons for the pervasive popularity of *Davy Crockett*. Perhaps, though, it was nothing more than a great story vividly told by a great storyteller, Walt Disney—and embellished by a hook-laden song and a larger-than-life performance by Fess Parker on national TV.

Davy Crockett was everywhere in the mid-1950s. But soon, like all fads, it soon came to an end. *Disneyland* slipped to the fourteenth position in the TV ratings. However, Fess and Walt Disney were only getting started.

CHAPTER 11
AFTER DAVY CROCKETT AT THE WALT DISNEY STUDIOS

Still under contract to Walt Disney Productions, Fess was assigned the starring role in *The Great Locomotive Chase*, a Civil War film about a daring 1862 Union railroad raid in Georgia. Fess played the role of James Andrews, a spy who commanded a small group of Union soldiers in an attempt to destroy Confederate telegraph lines and railroad bridges by hijacking a train on the Western and Atlantic Railroad. Fess was joined by his fellow cast members and Walt Disney in a special *Disneyland* program about the film that aired on May 30, 1956.

The Great Locomotive Chase was released on June 8, 1956, and like the release of *Davy Crockett, King of Wild Frontier* a year earlier, it coincided with the beginning of summer vacation for school kids nationwide. The film also starred Jeffrey Hunter as the indefatigable Western and Atlantic Railroad conductor William Fuller who helped thwart the mission. The Francis D. Lyon-directed motion picture also included a lineup of actors who appeared in the *Davy Crockett* series including Jeff York, Kenneth Tobey, and Don Megowan. One of the featured performers was John Lupton, Fess' old Hollywood roommate. Veteran stuntmen Chuck Roberson and Dale Van Sickle had minor roles. Fess also invited his friend Morgan Woodward to be a part of the film.

"He told me, 'Disney is going to a live action motion picture and there's a great part in it for you,'" said Woodward. Fess explained to producer Bill Walsh that he had a friend with acting experience. Walsh agreed to let Woodward try out for the part. "So I came out, did the test and got the part. The part wasn't great but it was a part as this mean-ass Confederate master sergeant who almost discovers

James J. Andrews on the train. I had a concept of who the character was: a farm boy, a dedicated rebel. He raises a lot of hell singing rebel songs and screaming and yelling and that kind of thing."

Although Woodward's part was small it marked the beginning of an acting career that would span five decades and include numerous roles in such TV Westerns as *Cheyenne, Sugar Foot, Broken Arrow, The Life and Legend of Wyatt Earp, Wagon Train, Death Valley Days, Bonanza,* and *Daniel Boone*. Woodward was later featured in such productions as *Hill Street Blues, Fantasy Island,* and *The Incredible Hulk*, among many others. He also appeared in a number of motion pictures.

In *The Great Locomotive Chase*, Parker was costumed as a mid-nineteenth century civilian so there was not a coonskin cap, flintlock rifle or tomahawk to be seen in the film. But there was plenty of suspenseful action as the cast and crew brought the true story to life by using the old Talulah Falls Railroad and classic railroad engines borrowed from the Baltimore & Ohio Railroad (the *William Mason* locomotive doubled for the *General*) and Paramount Studios (the *Inyo* locomotive became the *Texas*). As Andrews, Fess' character primarily uses deception and falsehoods to achieve his goals. Only after he is captured does Andrews engage in action: a prison-break fight. It was somewhat of a disappointment for fans of *Davy Crockett* to see Fess in anything that didn't resemble the wild frontier.

Walt Disney was on hand in Clayton, Georgia, the production's headquarters, when location filming began on September 26, 1955, not long after "Davy Crockett and the River Pirates" wrapped. One day, while riding in a car that included Disney and Jeffrey Hunter, Fess received some startling news.

"We were engaging in some simple conversation and Jeffrey Hunter explained to me about an exciting project he just finished with John Wayne and director John Ford," said Fess. "It was *The Searchers*. Walt leaned over to me and said, 'They wanted you for that.'" Fess was stunned.

The Searchers was one of Wayne's greatest films and, perhaps, his finest Western. Hunter played Martin Pawley, the nephew of Wayne's Ethan Edwards, who joins his uncle in a quest to find a long-lost family member who had been kidnapped by Comanches. Hunter was only two years younger than Fess, but he successfully portrayed the Martin Pawley character with calculated, youthful immaturity. Fess later learned that John Ford was angry with him. "He thought I rejected the part," he said. "But it wasn't my decision. I had met him at a party not too long before that where he playfully ate some food off my plate and gave me a rough-house shove with his arm. I thought we had gotten along."

Fess was extremely disappointed but he did not share his feelings with Disney. However, teamed with a new agent, Ray Stark, Fess and Disney agreed on a new contract on July 1, 1956. "Ray Stark became my agent in 1956," stated Fess. "I was at a meeting with Bill Walsh at the studio when I met Ray Stark." The new one-year contract, co-signed by W. H. Anderson, Vice-President in Charge of Studio Operations, gave Fess $1,000 per week "for each week the Artist is actually engaged in rendering services hereunder" and higher amounts for six 52-week option periods that would conclude with a weekly salary of $4,000. The contract also included higher royalty payments for any recordings Fess would make.

Fess received a double-dose of disappointment when Disney informed him that the production company of *Bus Stop* wanted to cast him in the motion picture. "Mr. Disney said that he thought the film wasn't right for me," said Fess. "He thought that the story line was inappropriate for a family audience."

Disney was somewhat correct about the Joshua Logan-directed adult dramatic comedy which starred Marilyn Monroe as a small-time café singer and Don Murray as a lovesick Montana cowboy. The movie, which was released on August 31, 1956, was promoted by theater posters which depicted the two stars in a suggestive stance, hardly the kind of artwork that Disney would have approved. Nevertheless, the film was a commercial and critical success.

"And Don Murray received an Oscar nomination for Best Supporting Actor," lamented Fess.

The *Corpus Christi Caller-Times* reported that another studio wanted Fess "to portray a famed hillbilly song writer. But Disney refused, because the character was depicted as tussling with the bottle."

Fess' next Disney film, *Westward Ho, the Wagons!*, followed on December 20, 1956, just in time for school kids' Christmas vacation. The William Beaudine-directed western was an innocuous production that had Fess playing the role of John "Doc" Grayson, a steady but uncomplicated man who sings songs and saves the day in the process. One song, "Wringle Wrangle," written by Stan Jones, was recorded by Fess and was a chart hit. Bill Hayes, who had the most success with "The Ballad of Davy Crockett," also recorded the tune and managed to reach #33 on the *Billboard* charts. But this time Fess had the more popular version when his recording reached the #12 position. The flip side of "Wringle Wrangle" was "The Ballad of John Colter," another Tom Blackburn-George Bruns collaboration.

Westward Ho, the Wagons! was shot on location on the Janss Canejo Ranch in Thousand Oaks, California, the site where some "Davy Crockett at the Alamo" exteriors had been filmed. The motion picture took advantage of the popular *Mickey Mouse Club* television program by including such Mouseketeers as Cubby O'Brien, Karen Pendleton, Tommy Cole, and Doreen Tracy. The eclectic cast also featured David Stollery, who played Marty in *The Mickey Mouse Club* series *Spin and Marty*, and Jeff York, Mike Fink from the *Davy Crockett* keelboat episodes. TV's *Superman*, George Reeves, was also a prominent member of the cast. Even Morgan Woodward, Fess' friend, appeared as Obie Foster in the production. However, the film did not resonate with critics or the public. Peter Ellenshaw, the film's matte artist, called it "a very dull movie."

"It was kind of an awkward production because I'm not sure whether it was originally designed to be a film for TV or a theatrical release," remarked Fess, who made a special Disneyland appearance in June, 1956, with co-star Kathleen Crowley, to promote the film. "In fact, I wasn't exactly sure why the studio was making it. And I didn't have much to do in that film. But as a result of 'Wringle Wrangle,' Buddy Ebsen and I created Musicland, our own ASCAP publishing company. I later got a chance to sing the song on the *Ed Sullivan Show* in 1957." Fess made his appearance on the program on January 20, 1957, which also featured three performers with top 20 chart hits: Sonny James ("Young Love"), Ivory Joe Hunter ("Since I Met You Baby"), and the Tarriers ("Banana Boat Song"). With a smile on his face and a guitar in hand, Fess confidently delivered his song.

The motion picture was later edited for television and debuted on *Walt Disney Presents* as the two-part "Westward Ho the Wagons!: Ambush at Wagon Gap" in February 1961.

Fess had even less to do in his next Disney film, *Old Yeller*. Released on Christmas day in 1957, the memorable Robert Stevenson-directed film was based on the popular Fred Gipson novel about a struggling western family and its beloved dog. Gipson, by the way, was an acquaintance of Fess' father during the time the author worked for the *San Angelo Standard-Times*. The film's scene in which the rabies-infected dog is put to death by the oldest boy in the family is poignantly heart breaking and painful. However, Fess is absent from the screen throughout much of the film because his character, Jim Coates, was scripted as being away on a cattle drive.

When he wasn't filming or making special appearances on behalf of Disney, Fess and Marcy continued to date. The couple was occasionally seen at some of the best restaurants and clubs in and around Hollywood, rubbing celebrity elbows with the likes of Cary Grant, Jimmy Stewart, Robert Wagner, and Frank Sinatra.

"Frank had actually come to see me at the Townehouse in the early fifties," said Marcy. "I admired Sinatra as a singer. I loved his talent. But we didn't know that many Hollywood people. We chose not to; we had enough Texas friends."

Fess and one of his Texas friends, Phil Kendrick, who had joined his family's oil and natural gas business after graduating college, became partners in some oil-drilling operations. "He invested some money in an oil deal that I set up," explained Kendrick. "I would put together prospects and tried to get partners to help spread the risk, and Fess was limited to a sixteenth share. We all made some money from it, and the tax deductions were good back then. On his second investment, he had a one-eighth share, and he later invested in a third prospect. We made a little money on each of those wells but they weren't that successful. We eventually plugged them and that was that as far as Fess' involvement was. He didn't stay in oil too long but it gave him the right to say that he was an oil investor."

In 1957, Fess revisited his Davy Crockett character when he recorded another version of "The Ballad of Davy Crockett." It was released on a Buena Vista Records promotional single and was also included on a Disneyland LP titled *Yarns and Songs*. The album, which also included "Farewell," was reissued four years later as the Disneyland LP *Yarns and Songs of the West*. Fess' new recording of "The Ballad of Davy Crockett" was also included on the 1958

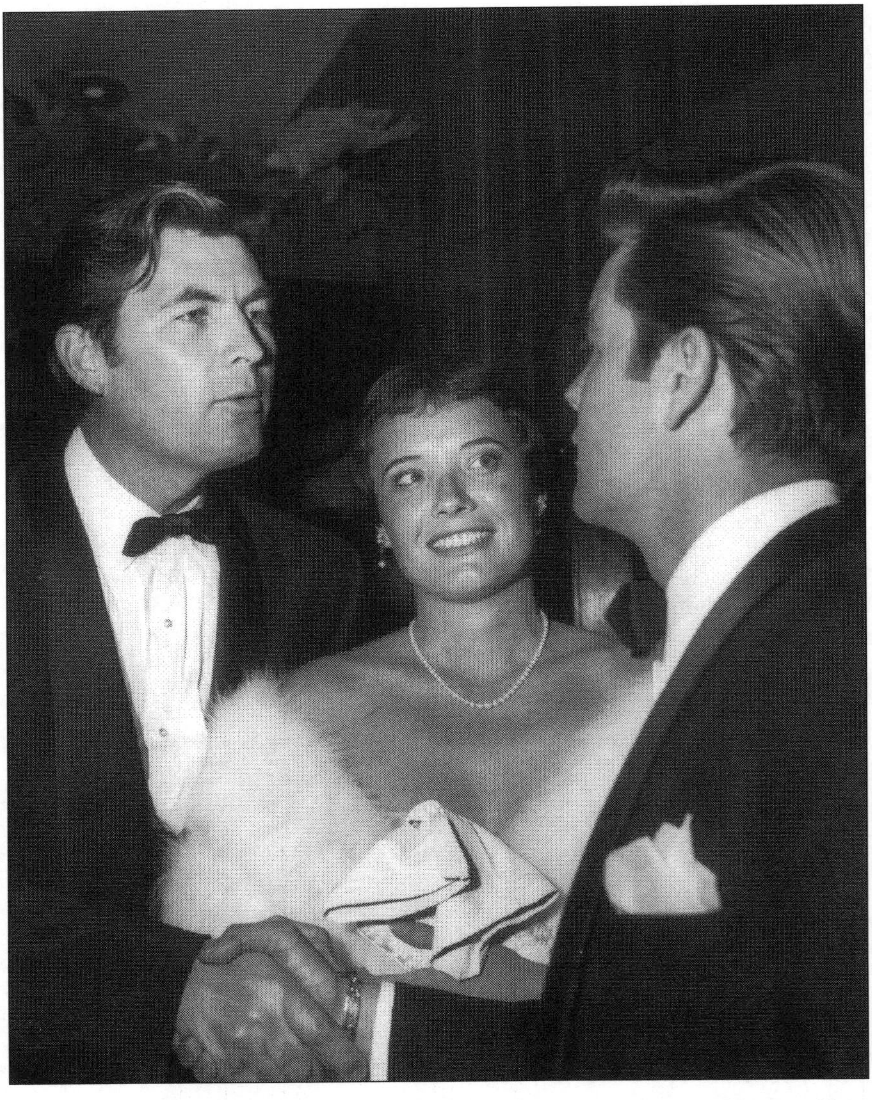

Fess Parker and Marcy Rinehart meet actor Robert Wagner at Romanoff's in Beverly Hills in March 1957.
AUTHOR'S COLLECTION.

Disneyland LP *Songs About Zorro and Other TV Heroes.*

Although Fess kept his dissatisfaction over the missed *Searchers* and *Bus Stop* opportunities to himself, an interesting item appeared in the December 13, 1957 issue of *Variety*. "Good Morning: Two Davy Crocketts?" reported entertainment columnist Army Archerd. "When

Fess Parker read that John Wayne would play *Crockett* in his forthcoming *Alamo*, Parker volunteered to play one of the other top roles." Wayne went on to play the famous frontiersman in his epic 1960 film and Fess, of course, was not in the cast. Fess was still under contract with Disney in 1957, and Archerd said nothing more in the column about *The Alamo* project (except for a quirky Fess quote that "Most Texans would rather be Governor of Texas than President of the United States"). However, when Wayne was on the eve of production for his film, Fess sent him a coonskin cap inscribed with the following note: "I hope this does as much good as it did me."

While Fess appeared in the various films, the original *Davy Crockett* episodes were regularly rebroadcast on television. And *Davy Crockett, King of the Wild Frontier* continued to pop up on theater screens. The motion picture played at the Tex Theatre in Corsicana, Texas during Easter week in 1958, three years after its big-screen debut. A newspaper ad in *The Corsicana* on April 4, 1958, promoted the film and its companion featurette, the third chapter of the *Adventures of Frank and Jesse James*, a thirteen-chapter, 1948 Republic Pictures serial.

Fess had more screen time in his next Disney film, *The Light in the Forest*. The motion picture, which was released on July 8, 1958, was based upon Conrad Richter's novel about a white youngster who returns home after living among Native Americans. Despite Fess' top billing, the real stars of the film were James MacArthur, who played Johnny Butler (aka True Son), and antagonist Wendell Corey. The film deviated somewhat from the book's central theme of racial and cultural animosity by adding a love interest for MacArthur's character in the person of Carol Lynley. Fess essentially had a supporting role as the trustworthy scout Del Hardy. One of the uncredited Native American actors, Eddie Little Sky, would later appear in three episodes of *Daniel Boone*.

While *The Light in the Forest* was finishing its run in the theaters, another Fess Parker-John Wayne item popped up in the newspapers. Hedda Hopper reported about a "Wayne, Fess Parker in Business Deal" in the *Los Angeles Times* on August 4, 1958. "There's a deal brewing between Fess Parker and John Wayne for the latter's Batjac company. It's also a funny titled *The Old Maiden*, which Harold Shumate wrote, about a race horse that never won a race." The

Texas-born Shumate had written many Westerns for film and television, including the small-screen's horse saga, *My Friend Flicka*. It seemed like an interesting project, although Hopper failed to tell her readers that Fess was still under contract at Disney. But since Shumate's tale was much tamer than *Bus Stop*, it was possible that Disney might have approved Fess for the production. However, the Parker-Wayne collaboration never got beyond Hopper's column.

Fess was slated to appear in the next Disney film, *Tonka*, a story about a horse that starred Sal Mineo as a young Native American. However, Fess was not scheduled to receive important screen time; in fact, he was going to have less to do than he did in *Old Yeller*. "It just wasn't right," stated Fess, who was hoping for better roles. "I wasn't being used in the right way, so I ended my contract with Disney."

Producer Bill Walsh sympathized with Fess.

"Bill was in complete agreement with Fess," said Fishman. "My husband thought that Fess had so much presence on camera; he simply wasn't being used correctly."

But Fess' *Davy Crockett* sidekick had an idea that could have revived the Parker-Disney relationship. During a Chicago radio station interview years later, Buddy Ebsen mentioned that the idea for another prequel was considered: "Davy Crockett at the Battle of New Orleans."

"I don't recall any specifics for such an episode extension of the Crockett series or a special pilot episode," countered Fess. "However, I wouldn't be surprised that it was considered at the time. I know that the ABC television network, which carried the *Davy Crockett* series, would have liked to have a continuing series, but Walt Disney wasn't interested."

In any event, Fess walked away from Disney with three years left on his contract. "After I left the studio, I was not that financially well off as some people thought."

CHAPTER 12
Post-Disney TV and Film Work

Fess made his last big-screen appearance as Davy Crockett in Bob Hope's 1959 comedy *Alias Jesse James*. In the film's outrageous shoot-out conclusion, Hope is outnumbered by a gang of gunslingers. But the veteran comedian manages to survive because some of the biggest TV and movie Western heroes come to his rescue—including Gary Cooper, Roy Rogers, Jay Silverheels (*The Lone Ranger's* Tonto), Hugh O'Brian (*Wyatt Earp*), Gail Davis (*Annie Oakley*), Ward Bond (*Wagon Train's* Major Seth Adams), and James Arness (*Gunsmoke's* Matt Dillon). Fess defends Hope with a successful flintlock rifle shot and quips, "Shoot at my friend, will ya."

However, all the Western stars received no final credits in the film. But they were reimbursed for their services.

"I got a boat engine for my appearance in that film!" laughed Fess. "But I had a sailboat at the time and the engine was too big for it; it was more appropriate for a power boat. Well, my agent at the time had such a boat and I gave it to him. I always wondered if he got me the job so he could get the engine!"

Fess missed out on an opportunity to appear in *The Horse Soldiers* with John Wayne. He approached John Ford, who apparently had forgotten the misunderstanding over *The Searchers*, and sought the co-starring part of Major Henry Kendall. "It was a good role and Mr. Ford seemed as if I would be right for it but he already cast Bill Holden in it," explained Fess. Despite missing out on *The Horse Soldiers*, Fess worked in two additional 1959 Westerns.

Fess' first non-Disney production in which he had a major role was *The Hangman*, a cerebral Paramount Western that was released on June 17, 1959. The film starred Robert Taylor in the title role and Tina Louise. Fess, as Sheriff Buck Weston, was third-billed in the Michael Curtiz-directed film. However, the film lacked the splendid action of such earlier Curtiz classics such as *The Charge of the Light Brigade* and *The Adventures of Robin Hood*. Clearly, no one confused *The Hangman* with Curtiz's *Casablanca* but Taylor delivered a first-rate performance and Fess was workmanlike in his role. *Dallas Morning News* film critic Tony Zoppi noted that "Parker, cast as the sheriff in the town, still drawls his way through the dialogue and walks with a loping stride reminiscent of his Davy Crockett portrayal." One of the uncredited lawmen in the film, Lorne Greene, would become a household name in less than three months when *Bonanza* debuted on NBC-TV.

Before the year was out, Fess appeared in yet another Paramount Western, *The Jayhawkers*. Released on October 15, *The Jayhawkers* screenplay was set in pre-Civil War Kansas, a bloody territory characterized by the violence generated between abolitionists and pro-slavers. Jeff Chandler was top billed in the Paramount film as Fess' antagonist, an egocentric leader with empire-like visions. Fess successfully tackled the role of Cam Bleeker, a character who was more complex than his mainstream persona in *The Hangman*. Surprisingly, the script avoided the issue of slavery.

Film critic Rual Askew wasn't too pleased with Fess' low-key performance. "Fess Parker isn't as functional as cord-wood but acts and moves that way as the jailbreaker who kills on principle." A studio press release even noted that in order to prepare Fess for the film's romantic scenes co-star Nicole Maurey had to sing "Gallic love songs to Fess before the cameras roll for their *clinch* scenes." As a side note, Don Megowan, who played William Travis in "Davy Crockett at the Alamo," appears in *The Jayhawkers* as a character called China.

Fess used some of his earnings from the two Paramount films to launch the Cascade Records Company with partner Al Kavelin, who led a popular dance band in the 1930s, and had a chart-topping single, "I Give You my Word," in 1941.

Fess released a single on Cascade, "Strong Man" b/w "Eyes of an Angel." "Strong Man" was somewhat similar to Jimmy Dean's chart-topping 1961 hit "Big Bad John" but it failed to make the record charts. "Eyes of an Angel," an innocuous mid-tempo love song, also failed to generate airplay.

Cascade expanded its roster of artists when Dennis Weaver was signed to the label. The *Gunsmoke* actor recorded "Girls Was Made to be Loved," but the single failed to chart.

Fess got a tip from someone who knew Ed Carrell, a Texas food salesman who wrote songs in his spare time. One of Carrell's tunes was "The Gila Monster," a rhythmic novelty song that anticipated the release of the low-budget sci-fi flick *The Giant Gila Monster* in June, 1959. Carrell had local bandleader-tenor sax player- singer Joe Johnson record the song—along with another composition, "Cool Love"—and sent it to Fess who was impressed. Unlike Weaver, Johnson was an experienced performer who had been an instrumentalist on recordings by Nat "King" Cole, Joe Turner, and Ray Charles, among others.

Fess flew to Dallas on May 21, and checked in at the Hotel Adolphus, the same place where he had made an appearance four years earlier during his promotional tour for *Davy Crockett, King of the Wild Frontier*. Fess met Johnson, who had been performing at Club Vegas, an Oak Lawn-neighborhood nightclub run by Jack Ruby, the man who would later murder President Kennedy's assassin, Lee Harvey Oswald. Fess signed Johnson to a Cascade recording contract and within weeks "The Gila Monster" was released. *The Dallas Morning News* reported on July 21, that the song "climbed into the Top Ten circle here last week." Despite its local success, the song didn't have the legs to break onto *Billboard's* Hot 100 national chart.

The most unusual Cascade release was *Fess Parker Presents Behind the Veil: Modern Melodies of the Near East*. Produced by Kavelin and written and conducted by Gene Von Hallberg, the album's dozen orchestral tunes featured such tracks as "Bashraf Aman," "Song of Zulieka," "Dervish Dance," "Drum Dance of Damascus," and "Chant of the Snake Charmer." Obviously, none of the selections recalled the arresting chorus of "The Ballad of Davy Crockett."

"They were mistakes," laughed Fess. "And those songs, of course, were released on Cascade, which was my record label. It just shows what unfettered optimism will do! Of course, I spent some time trying to relate to the music industry back in the 1950s, but it didn't quite work out."

Another Cascade album, *Fancy Feathers*, was a musical fantasy for kids that featured Fess as the farmer-story teller and tunes performed by former Disney Mousketeer leader Jimmy Dodd, Disney voice-over artist Paul Frees, and vocalist Gloria Wood of "Woody Woodpecker" song fame.

The LP's liner notes revealed some interesting financial information about Fess and his two Paramount Westerns: "The studio reaction to Fess' work before the camera is best summed up in the fact that his one picture a year contract (which had several years to go) was torn up and replaced by a new pact calling for twelve films over the next six years. Fess will realize a little over $2,000,000 under terms of his new deal." However, Fess made only one more film for Paramount.

Fess was considered for another TV series, *The Code of Jonathon West*. His title character debuted in *G. E. True Theater* episode titled "Aftermath," which aired on April 17, 1960. The program, which was actually the pilot for the proposed series, was directed by veteran director Jacques Tourner. The veteran French filmmaker, best known for such motion pictures as *Cat People* and *I Walked With a Zombie*, had directed Buddy Ebsen in eight episodes of the 1958–59 TV show *Northwest Passage*. However, no studio expressed interest in the proposed series.

But 1960 was a significant year: Fess finally married Marcy.

"We went together for six years," said Marcy. "It was the end of November or the beginning of December in 1959, and we were sitting in a car outside the Talk of the Town in Santa Barbara. It was after dinner and he said, 'Do you think we should get married?' I said, 'What do you think?' Fess said, 'I think we should.' I replied, 'I'm ready!'"

Marcy was elated but Fess didn't give her an engagement ring.

"He gave me a wedding ring, no engagement ring," said Marcy. "It was a simple gold wedding ring. Then I got a diamond later on. And pearls!"

Fess and Marcy wanted Bill and Nolie Walsh to stand up for them at the ceremony in early January 1960.

"Bill and I were thrilled to be asked, but we were committed to a winter week at Sun Valley," said Fishman. "So they graciously postponed the wedding. But we got sick with bad colds on the train ride home. Our doctor told us not to do anything—including the wedding—until we felt better. Despite being sick, Bill and I agreed

Mr. and Mrs. Fess Parker walk down the aisle on January 18, 1960.
PHOTO COURTESY OF THE PARKER FAMILY.

that we were not going to make Fess and Marcy postpone the wedding yet again. We went anyway. Since I was sick, I didn't wash my hair. I wore a beige silk dress with pearls and a cashmere beige hat partially pleated with a *large* pearl pin. To this day Marcy claims that I was her 'matron of honor' in a ski cap straight off of the slopes!"

The couple finally exchanged vows at the Presbyterian Church in Montecito, California on January 18, 1960.

"We had about two hundred people," stated Marcy. "Bill Walsh served as Best Man and his wife, Nolie, as Maid of Honor." Tom Blackburn gave the bride away. "Tom and his wife were good friends of ours and since my father died, Tom was kind enough to walk me down the aisle."

Marcy and Fess avoided the trappings of a fancy wedding. Marcy didn't wear a traditional wedding gown; she wore a high-neck, knee-length dress that was belted at the waist and a matching hat with a short veil. Fess wore a two-button business suit. "Actually, Fess didn't want me to wear a wedding gown," remarked Marcy. "That's what he wanted so I complied."

"After the reception, we had a two-week honeymoon in northern California—Carmel, San Francisco, and so forth and then on to Seattle," explained Marcy. After the honeymoon, Marcy continued to sing professionally. "But only for a while. I wanted to be a housewife." The couple settled into their new home in Santa Barbara.

Another project interested Fess: Max Evans' novel, *The Rounders*, the story of two modern-day cowboys. A copy of the author's manuscript was among several novels and short stories that cluttered a resource table at MGM Studios in 1960. "They called it a 'slush table,' explained Evans. "Writers, directors, and whoever else wanted to explore he possibility of turning something onto a motion picture could pick up something off the table and develop it. Burt Kennedy found *The Rounders* and just happened to pick it up."

Kennedy had written a number of minor Western films but, according to Evans, "wanted to launch himself as a director in motion pictures." Kennedy thought that *The Rounders* would be an ideal project for Fess.

"Burt showed it to Fess who, in turn, showed it to Tom Blackburn," said Evans. "Burt Kennedy and Tom Blackburn would write the script, Fess would produce and star in it, and Burt would have his first director's credit."

But Fess wanted to develop the entire production himself and have an experienced director behind the camera. He persuaded the celebrated William Wellman to come out of retirement. Wellman had directed such classics as *The Public Enemy, Beau Geste, Battleground, The High and the Mighty,* and *Lafayette Escadrille*, his last film, in 1958. He had also directed Fess in *Island in the Sky*.

As a result of Fess' move, Wellman was in and Kennedy was out.

"I was in a real turmoil because the person who originally wanted to direct my movie, Burt Kennedy, was replaced by someone else," confessed Evans. "Burt had to be hurt deeply but my copper mining business was in debt and I needed the money so I went with Fess." Evans and Fess agreed on a short option of four months in which they both felt that a production deal could be made. Evans drove to California to meet Fess and Wellman.

Evans and Wellman quickly became friends. Evans explained his life as a cowboy, a World War II soldier, a painter, a miner, and a self-confessed wheeler-dealer. "I told Wellman that I wasn't a professional actor but I did some serious acting on various deals through my life," laughed Evans. "We really hit it off, but I still felt terrible for Burt." Later, at a party with Fess and Wellman at Tom Blackburn's house in California, the veteran director said to Evans that he would like him to work in the movie. Fess and Evans didn't interpret the comment to be serious. "In fact, I told Fess that I didn't even want a part in the film," explained Evans.

While he was in California, Evans met Fess' friend Morgan Woodward, who had established a number of screen credits since his debut in *The Great Locomotive Chase.* "Morgan and I shopped around another novel of mine, *The Hi-Lo Country*," stated Evans. "We got David Dorttort, who was a successful TV producer and writer, interested but he decided to take another series. Our project was dead."

Near the end of the option period, all the principals and their respective representatives met at United Artists to seal the deal.

"The script that Wellman and Blackburn wrote was really good," stated Evans. "They stayed true to my story and eighty-percent of their dialogue came right from my book. We were getting along famously."

And then Wellman dropped a bombshell.

"He said, 'I want to cast Max as one of the leads, the part of Wrangler,'" recalled Evans. "Wrangler had a busted face and so did I. But Fess threw a fit. He stood up and told Wellman that he had some other people in mind for the part. It was all true but I couldn't believe anyone would stand up to Wellman. He never took anything from anyone—studios, producers or actors. Wellman just sat there for a moment, got up and said, 'I'm through.'"

Wellman walked out of the meeting and was followed by Evans.

"He told me, 'I want to tell you how sorry I am, but I can't work with an actor who is casting my movie,'" stated Evans. Minutes later, Evans walked back in the room where Fess told him, "I'm not going to pick up the option."

The Rounders was dead—at least the version with Fess Parker.

But the film was eventually made in 1965, with Henry Fonda and Glenn Ford, who was given the role originally slated for Evans by Wellman. And Burt Kennedy wrote the screenplay and directed the film.

Fess and Evans didn't speak for a long time.

The Parker's first child, Fess Elisha Parker III, was born on June 17, 1961. He was called Eli. "It was short for Elisha," explained Marcy. "Fess and I just started calling him that from when he was very young."

At the same time Disney launched *Daniel Boone*, a four-part series which starred Dewey Martin in the title role. The episodes aired on December 4, 1960; December 11, 1960; March 12, 1961; and March 19, 1961. In reality, Boone's life was more adventurous than Crockett's, but the success of the earlier *Davy Crockett* episodes undermined the new series' potential. According to Tim and Terry Todish in *Alamo Sourcebook 1836*, "the combined genius of Walt Disney and Fess Parker made this historical reality so insignificant that when Disney got around to telling the story of Daniel Boone, it barely registered on the national psyche." Martin was pleasant enough but lacked the charisma that Fess effused as *Davy Crockett.* Twenty-seven years would pass before the Disney would depict another famous frontier character on the small screen.

In 1961, Fess reportedly was involved in a TV pilot about the prolific Western painter Charles Marion Russell, but it failed to generate interest. Perhaps producers thought that in Fess' hands a paint brush was a poor substitute for a flintlock rifle.

Still, the movie roles finally had generated some money for Fess and he decided on making what he considered his first luxury purchase. "I bought a sloop, a Cal 42," said Fess. "It was forty or fifty feet long." But the boat was more than a recreational toy: it

The King of the Wild Frontier signals Poseidon, the god of the sea, off the California coast.
PHOTO COURTESY OF THE PARKER FAMILY.

served a purpose. There were a lot of people who were influential in my career. It was a way of entertaining folks and meeting folks." He sailed along the coast, occasionally heading to Catalina Island, which was about twenty-two miles from the mainland.

Fess was involved in other enterprises besides acting. He invested in a number of Motel 6 Joint Ventures and developed three mobile home parks: Rancho Santa Barbara, Rancho Goleta, and Rancho San Vicente in Santa Barbara. "Dad was the money guy and Fred Rice—Uncle Fred as we called him—was the builder," said Ashley Parker Snider, Fess' daughter. "Uncle Fred went way back with dad."

Rancho Santa Barbara also became the new home for Fess' parents. They were getting older and Fess wanted them close by in order to provide better care for them. The Texans' move was celebrated in a local publication. "They were featured on the cover of some magazine which amusingly stated, 'Parkers Park in Parker's Park,'" remarked Ashley.

His two year absence from dramatic roles on TV was noted by a press release in January 1962. "Fess Parker marks his return to television as a star of the true and exciting *Death Valley Days*' drama 'Miracle at Whiskey Gulch.'" Dressed as preacher for his role as Reverend Joel Todd in the January 26, 1962 broadcast, Fess looked more out of place than he did when he abandoned his buckskins and coonskin cap for a gentleman's frock coat in "Davy Crockett Goes to Congress." It was work but the part wasn't significant.

Fess' last big-action motion picture was *Hell Is for Heroes*, a World War II action drama which was released by Paramount on June 26, 1962. Fess, who played Sergeant Pike, was billed third after Steve McQueen and pop singer Bobby Darin. L. Q. Jones—the former Justice E. McQueen—also appeared in the motion picture as Sergeant Frazer. The Don Siegel-directed film depicts the exploits of a squad of U.S. Army infantrymen who are ordered to hold a precarious position near the German Siegfried Line.

A favorable review in *The Dallas Morning News* noted: "Personalities like McQueen, [Nick] Adams and Parker have a knack for projecting dimensional characters through sparse dialogue. They succeed vividly here."

Fess actually had more than "sparse dialogue" in the original script.

"That was an interesting film," explained Fess. "But the film people ran out of money and they abruptly ended it. And they ended it before my big dramatic scene!"

After Fess completed work on *Hell Is for Heroes* he returned to television. "I left the film business but I had the opportunity to work on *Mr. Smith Goes to Washington*," said Fess, who starred as Senator Eugene Smith in the 1962–63 series. The ABC-TV show was loosely based on the Frank Capra film of 1939 that starred Jimmy Stewart but the programs were more comedic than the dramatic big-screen original. Fess co-produced the series with Hal Stanley.

ABC-TV sent Fess and Marcy on a press tour to several major media markets prior to the show's debut. And Fess assisted the ABC-TV publicity department by promoting the show himself. He wrote letters and postcards to various reporters about the program. On June 9, 1962, Fess sent a postcard of the U. S. Capitol to Mike Connally of the *Hollywood Reporter*. "Hi Mike," wrote Fess. "Thought you might like to see my new home for 1962–63 on ABC-TV with Mr. Smith Goes to Washington. Checked with Otto P. [Preminger] and he said, 'Go Man! It's a crazy town!'"

Fess played down the inevitable comparison to Jimmy Stewart in the original motion picture.

"We did about thirty half-hour films but I never tried to copy Jimmy Stewart's character," said Fess. "Our programs featured great comedians from Hollywood's past like Harpo Marx and Buster Keaton, and an up and coming talent by the name of Jim Nabors." Among the other performers who appeared on *Mr. Smith Goes to Washington* were pop singer Kay ("Rock and Roll Waltz") Starr, *Bowery Boys* alum Leo Gorcey, comedian Doodles Weaver, and country music star Red Foley, who portrayed Uncle Cooter in eight episodes. Like other sit-coms, the comedic moments in the episodes were augmented by a noticeable laugh-track.

Fess and co-star Sandra Warner appeared on the October 28-November 3, 1962 cover of *American T-Vue Time*, a regional TV magazine distributed in the greater Baltimore-Washington D. C. area. The issue is interesting because one of its articles focused on "a new redhead" on TV's *The Rifleman*—Patricia Blair. After appearing in twenty-two episodes of the Western in 1962 and 1963, Blair would later co-star with Fess in *Daniel Boone*.

The *Mr. Smith Goes to Washington* episode with Harpo Marx is arguably the most interesting of the all the programs. In "The Musicale," Marx, who was nearly 73 years old at the time, performed a beautiful rendition of "Red River Valley" on the harp before an audience which included Fess' character and an actor depicting President John F. Kennedy. However, the Chief Executive's face is never seen; the audience only hears his voice when he speaks to Senator Smith. The episode aired on October 20, 1962, during the Cuban Missile Crisis. Four weeks later, President Kennedy was assassinated. "The Musicale" was also Harpo Marx's last television appearance.

Interestingly enough, the next-to-the-last show, "The Lobbyist," which aired on March 23, 1963, featured Trevor Bardette. The veteran actor played Davy Crockett ten years earlier in *Man From the Alamo*, a Glenn Ford Western. Lacking strong ratings, *Mr. Smith Goes to Washington* wasn't renewed for the 1963-64 season.

Fess explained that during the run of *Mr. Smith Goes to Washington*, movie producer Cubby Broccoli considered the native Texan as the big-screen's James Bond. But Broccoli already had his James Bond: Sean Connery. Surprisingly, Ian Fleming, the author who created the James Bond character, had his doubts about casting Connery because he thought the 6'2" actor was too big for the part. Fess, of course, was three inches taller than Connery, who had worked in the 1959 Disney production, *Darby O'Gill and the Little People*. Furthermore, *Dr. No*, the first Bond film, was released on October 2, 1962, just a few days after *Mr. Smith Goes to Washington* made its debut. So it appears that Fess may have misinterpreted Broccoli's interest. Still, it would have been quite an amusing transition if Fess had uttered, "Bond, James Bond," after stating years earlier, "I'm Davy Crockett. I'm half-horse, half-alligator!"

Morgan Woodward believed that Fess maintained a certain acting style: consistent, even-keeled, unflustered, and straight-forward. "Fess had a self image," said Woodward. "And as an actor Fess had an impossible time of acting outside that self image. Fess was not a character actor." But Fess believed that his restrained on-screen performances were not because of any restrictions on his ability. Like Gary Cooper, he simply approached his craft with understated emotions. And he wanted to display his skills in the character part he wanted most: Atticus Finch, the lead in *To Kill a Mockingbird*. He sought the part but Gregory Peck secured the role and delivered a magnificent performance in the 1962 motion picture, which earned the veteran performer a Best Actor Oscar.™ "I wouldn't have been surprised if Fess got the part and did a good job," said Marcy.

In 1963, Fess returned to the stage.

The classic Rodgers and Hammerstein musical, *Oklahoma*, was celebrating its 20th anniversary in 1963, and producers Lee Guber, Frank Ford, and Shelly Gross hired Fess to portray Curly McClain, the male lead in the touring company. Joan Weldon, who was cast as Laurey Williams in the Richard Barstow-directed production, had appeared with Fess in *Them!* Before every performance, the production's hair and makeup department turned Fess' wavy locks into curls.

Although Fess did not have the powerful vocal delivery of such performers as Alfred Drake (the original Broadway Curly), Howard Keel (the 1947 London production's Curly), or Gordon MacRae (the 1955 motion picture Curly), he handled such songs as "Oh, What a Beautiful Mornin'" and "People Will Say" with unassuming charm and confidence.

"I could never replace Howard Keel, but I was his substitute for that season," said Fess. "But that pretty much ended my musical career on stage."

Over the next two TV seasons, Fess worked occasionally in small roles on a number of programs—from *Destry* and *Amos Burke, Secret Agent* to *The Alfred Hitchcock Hour.* His performance as Sheriff Ben Wister in *The Alfred Hitchcock Hour* episode, "Nothing Ever Happens in Linvale," which aired on November 8, 1963, is interesting because in various scenes viewers can see the scar near his left ear that was caused by the 1946 knife attack.

But Fess would soon be returning to the frontier. And he would be wearing another coonskin cap.

CHAPTER 13
CREATING "DANIEL BOONE" FOR TELEVISION

Daniel Boone came first. The intrepid trailblazer was born nearly 52 years before Davy Crockett. But two centuries later it was Davy Crockett who helped make the *Daniel Boone* TV series happen.

"NBC television had an interest to do a series about Davy Crockett," said Fess. "But Mr. Disney didn't approve since it obviously conflicted with the original episodes that he created. NBC avoided the issue by simply going with another frontier character, Daniel Boone," said Fess. "I didn't know if it would work."

It worked.

Daniel Boone ran successfully on NBC-TV for six seasons.

"Now I don't know if I was the first to suggest it, but I suggested to Fess, 'What about Daniel Boone?'" said Woodward. "I remember Fess going, 'Hmm?'"

Fess, Twentieth Century Fox, NBC-TV, and producer Aaron Rosenberg discussed the project in late 1963. On January 7, 1964, a license agreement between the network and Twentieth Century Fox Television approved a $175,000 pilot and an option to produce the first year at $115,000, with options for successive years. The document stated that after the pilot's costs were recouped, "Divisible Monies" would be shared among Fess Parker (30%), NBC (25%), 20th Century Fox (25%), and Aaron Rosenberg (20%).

Before it went into production, the series received media attention when Fess, Marcy, and Eli were invited to participate in the commissioning ceremony of the nuclear submarine *USS Daniel Boone* on April 23, 1964, at Mare Island Naval Shipyard in Vallejo, California.

On May 13, 1964, NBC-TV took out a large ad in *Variety* which proclaimed: "Look who's joining Dr. Kildare: Daniel Boone—and he's just what the doctor ordered." The network heralded *Daniel Boone* as the 7:30–8:30 p.m. lead-in to *Dr. Kildare* for the upcoming fall season. NBC-TV called *Daniel Boone* "a rousing adventure set in pioneer America," and its star as "every inch the frontiersman—from buckskin britches to Boone-skin cap."

Later, a joint venture agreement was signed by Twentieth Century Fox Television; Fespar Enterprises, Fess' company; and Arcola Pictures, Aaron Rosenberg's company on April 15, 1966. The agreement created The American Tradition Company "for the purpose of producing, distributing and otherwise exploiting a filmed television series (the pilot film thereof, having been produced and financed solely by Fox) tentatively entitled 'Daniel Boone.'"

Fess came up with the name American Tradition.

"It represents how much this country has offered to previous generations and to me, and to my children," recalled Fess in the October/November 1985 issue of *Santa Barbara Magazine.* "The tradition is that you can start with nothing, pursue your dreams, and achieve anything." He later clarified the meaning of the expression in a December 1999 interview in the *Robb Report.* "American Tradition simply means that if you're willing to work hard and have a reasonable appreciation of your possibilities and a little luck, you can live the American dream."

In return for receiving a share of the net profits from the new series, Fess accepted a lower salary. But it was still better than the $550 a week he earned with his first Disney contract.

"Fess Parker will be drawing about $5,000 in his first week as Daniel Boone in the new NBC series produced by 20th Century Fox," wrote Bob Thomas, a reporter for the Associated Press in June of 1964.

In the article, Fess confirmed that the *Daniel Boone* series was actually prompted by the *Davy Crockett* episodes.

NBC-TV sent out a publicity release in early September, 1963, which proclaimed: "The fabulous exploits of Davy Crockett—one of America's most exciting frontiersmen and one of TV's most popular heroes of a decade ago—will be retold, for the first time in color, in three full-hour parts on NBC-TV's *Walt Disney's Wonderful*

World of Color Sunday, September 8, 15 and 22."

"This show probably wouldn't be going on the air if NBC hadn't broadcast the three Crockett films at the end of last summer," explained Fess. "They created such a sensation all over again that a new series was suggested."

Fess immediately thought that teaming up with Disney again would be worthwhile.

"We went to Disney with the idea but they weren't interested," remarked Fess. "Because of contractual matters, they wouldn't sell the rights to the character. We thought about going ahead with a series about Davy on our own, but no insurance company would take a risk on protecting us against an injunction."

The reporter asked Fess if there would be much of a difference between the famous Kentucky pioneer and the Tennessee hero. "Not very," quipped Fess.

Daniel Boone was the most famous eighteenth century pioneer in American history. Born in Pennsylvania during the autumn of 1734, Boone was one of eleven children born to Squire and Sarah Boone. The family moved to North Carolina in 1750. Boone never received much formal education but developed a self-taught literacy.

At the outbreak of the French and Indian War, Boone served as a civilian teamster in General Edward Braddock's disastrous march to Fort Duquesne in 1755. A year later, he married Rebecca Bryan. He served with the North Carolina militia in campaigns against the Cherokee in 1759 during the war.

Boone's reputation as a skilled hunter was established during the 1760s. He made an initial trek into the Kentucky region in 1767, and returned two years later. On June 7, 1769, he began his historic exploration of the bluegrass land. Months later, however, Boone was captured by the Shawnee but later released. He returned home but quickly renewed his Kentucky hunting expeditions with "Tick Licker," the name given to his trusty flintlock rifle. In 1773, he led his family and several dozen settlers into Kentucky but when his son and several others were captured and killed by the Native American warriors, the settlement effort was stopped. Boone subsequently participated in Dunmore's War, a military action called by Lord Dunmore, the Royal Governor of Virginia, in 1774. The martial operation was successful and the Shawnee yielded their claims on the region.

A year later, hostilities began between Great Britain and her thirteen American colonies when shots were fired at Lexington and Concord in Massachusetts. The War for American Independence was underway. At that time, Boone led a small group of settlers through the Cumberland Gap into Kentucky. Boonesborough was established in September of 1775.

In the summer of 1776, Boone's daughter, Jemima, and two other girls were kidnapped by the Shawnee, but Boone led a scouting party and successfully rescued the girls.

The following spring, the Shawnee attacked Boonesbourgh and wounded Boone. The intrepid pioneer recovered but a year later was captured while on a hunting excursion by Chief Blackfish of the Chilocothe Shawnee. Discovering that the tribe was planning an attack on Boonesborough, Boone devised a plan to delay the assault. Boone informed the warriors that he would surrender the fortified settlement without a fight if Blackfish and his braves held off their attack until the following spring. The Shawnee chief agreed. Boone's deception was so convincingly portrayed that some of his fellow captives believed him to be a traitor.

Boone and some of the other prisoners subsequently were adopted by the Shawnee. However, when Boone discovered that Blackfish was planning to attack Boonesborough in the late spring of 1778, he fled the camp and managed to make the difficult 150+ mile journey—on horseback and on foot—back to the settlement. Although he helped defend Boonesborough against Blackfish's attack, some settlers believed that he had betrayed the others who were still in captivity. Official charges were brought against Boone but he was declared not guilty.

While the Revolutionary War continued, Boone led various settlers into Kentucky. He collected a large sum of money from a number of settlers and traveled to Williamsburg, Virginia to file claims. However, while there, the money was stolen. Boone promised to repay the funds and he did, although it took several years.

Boone later served in various official positions. He was elected a lieutenant colonel in the militia, a representative in the Virginia Assembly, and a county sheriff.

In the autumn of 1780, Boone and his brother, Ned, were attacked by a band of Shawnee. Ned was killed. In August of 1782, Boone's son, Israel, was killed during the Battle of Blue Licks. Boone later joined George Rogers Clark in a series of raids against Shawnee settlements, which were among the last military engagements of the Revolutionary War. The Treaty of Paris in September 1783 formally ended the war and recognized the independence of the United States of America.

After the war, Boone worked as a businessman in various enterprises, participated in land speculation and served as an elected representative. In 1799, Boone and his family moved to Spanish-controlled Missouri. He remained there for the rest of his life. His wife, Rebecca, died in 1813. Boone died at age 85 on September 26, 1820; Davy Crockett had just turned thirty-four.

Boone's life was filled with exciting adventures and it seemed a natural fit for the man who had brought Davy Crockett to life on television a decade earlier. Fess planned to use as many media resources as possible to publicize his new series.

Fess promoted *Daniel Boone* in song on his 1964 RCA album, *Great American Heroes*, which was recorded on August 6, 25, and 26, 1964, at RCA Victor Studio A in Hollywood. He sang the program's theme song on the first track and added tunes about such historical figures as Jim Bowie, Abraham Lincoln, George Washington, Patrick Henry, and Andrew Jackson. The LP also included Fess' third version of "The Ballad of Davy Crockett."

The first episode, "Ken-Tuck-E," aired on September 24, 1964; the last episode, "Israel and Love," was broadcast on May 7, 1970. And like the *Davy Crockett* series, each *Daniel Boone* episode began with a title song. The new show's theme was written by Vera Matson (lyrics) and Lionel Newman (music). The first line of the song introduced the character and the man who played him: "Daniel Boone was a man, yes a big man."

But it would take more than a "big man" to make *Daniel Boone* successful.

It appeared to be a difficult sell since the eighteenth century-based teleplays were juxtaposed against a contemporary American society that witnessed major civil rights marches; urban rioting; the Beatles invasion and rise of the counter culture; war in Vietnam; the assassinations of Robert Kennedy and Dr. Martin Luther King; Apollo 11; and Woodstock.

Furthermore, genre-wise, *Daniel Boone* was almost going it alone.

A decade earlier, Walt Disney's *Davy Crockett* was subsequently joined by scores of TV Westerns. But by the mid-1960s, most of the TV Westerns had either gone to Hollywood's happy hunting ground or were sliding in the Nielsen ratings. *Daniel Boone* had only a few small-screen Western allies of significance, like NBC-TV's *Bonanza* and *The Virginian*, CBS-TV's *Gunsmoke*, and ABC-TV's *The Big Valley*.

The stories did not follow the actual events in Boone's life the way the Disney episodes followed Davy Crockett's life. Instead, the *Daniel Boone* episodes loosely traced the famous pioneer's adventures during the 1770s. The 165 episodes of *Daniel Boone* were somewhat similar to the basic characterizations established in the *Davy Crockett* series but instead of another frontiersman as a sidekick, Daniel Boone's favorite companion was an Oxford-educated Cherokee named Mingo, played by Ed Ames, the youngest of the popular singing Ames Brothers.

After the Ames Brothers act broke up in 1960, Ed Ames studied acting at the Herbert Berghof Studio in Manhattan for a couple of years. He delivered a strong performance as John Proctor in an Off-Broadway production of *The Crucible* in 1961, which led to featured Broadway roles in such plays as *The Fantasticks* and *Carnival.* However, his 1964 role as Chief Bromden in *One Flew Over the Cuckoo's Nest*, which starred Kirk Douglas as McMurphy, helped him secure his part *Daniel Boone*.

"Probably because I had done *One Flew Over the Cuckoo's Nest* on Broadway, people from Twentieth Century Fox must have seen me in it and invited me out," said Ames. "I came out to California—I was living in New Jersey—and met Fess. I had never met Fess before but I knew him from *Davy Crockett.* I had no idea what the role was going to be. We didn't have much interaction then because there were five or six guys talking to me. And, lo and behold, they called my agent and said that they would like me to do the role. I got the part of Mingo."

Fess and company didn't know exactly how Mingo should speak in the series.

Ed Ames as Mingo. "Silent Concern."
ILLUSTRATION BY INAHLEE BAUER.

"At first we were going to do it with a real strong British accent because, after all, Mingo was educated at Oxford," explained Ames, who had—and still has—a rich bass-baritone voice. "But he was a Native American guy. We finally decided on a cultured accent, but not real British." This was not the first time that a Daniel Boone production featured a Native American sidekick for example,

George Regas played Black Eagle to George O'Brien's title role in the 1936 RKO film *Daniel Boone*.

Ames was optimistic about *Daniel Boone* and Fess.

"I really thought that it would be a success because of his enormous success as Davy Crockett," remarked Ames. "And we had more fun working together. We had many, many laughs at ourselves and everything that happened around the set. I was surprised at how intellectually aware he was, how really smart he was. I nearly didn't give him credit for being as well educated a guy as he was."

Ames' visibility on the program helped boost his solo singing career. He scored over a dozen solo Adult Contemporary hits during the run of *Daniel Boone* including the popular "Try to Remember," "My Cup Runneth Over," and "Who Will Answer?"

Fess' new TV family—wife Rebecca (Patricia Blair), son Israel (Darby Hinton) and daughter Jemima (Veronica Cartwright)—played a more prominent role in the series than his Crockett family did in the Disney series. Albert Salmi co-starred in the first season as Yadkin, another frontier side-kick of sorts. And a tavern keeper named Cincinnatus (Dallas McKennon) was a regular throughout the series.

Salmi, a trained actor who studied under Lee Strasberg, was a wonderfully quirky performer who added a rich texture of restrained complexity to his character. Interestingly, he played Bo Decker in the opening night Broadway cast of *Bus Stop* on March 2, 1955. Though he possessed more formal training than his fellow cast members, Salmi considered himself just one of the cast, and he would go out of his way to help others on the set. In his biography, *Spotlights & Shadows: The Albert Salmi Story*, author Sandra Grabman detailed an incident in which Dallas McKennon accidentally picked up a camera operator's carefully-placed tape measure. The camera operator screamed: "Who the hell moved my floor mark for this shot?" Salmi immediately spoke up and said, "Somebody must have kicked it during the noon break." Peace on the set was restored. Salmi easily fit in with his castmates; however, the actor wanted more creative challenges and left *Daniel Boone* after the first season.

"Albert was only there for the first couple of years, so I was five when I met him and six when we started working with him," said Hinton. "I can't really remember that much about him. All I

The Daniel Boone Family: Veronica Cartwright, Fess Parker, Darby Hinton, and Patricia Blair. Courtesy of Dan Markovich. "'DANIEL BOONE' © 1964 Twentieth Century Fox Television. All rights reserved."

remember is that he had a great voice and a deep laugh."

Hinton's character wasn't even originally in the script. His mother had taken him for an open call audition for *The Sound of Music* at the Twentieth Century Fox Studios. And she dressed him for the part, complete with lederhosen, knee-high socks, and a frilly white shirt.

Fess Parker and Albert Salmi. Courtesy of Dan Markovich. "'DANIEL BOONE' © 1964 Twentieth Century Fox Television. All rights reserved."

"I was late for the casting so my mother dropped me off at the studio and went to park her car," explained Hinton who immediately saw a line of boys and stood behind them. A casting assistant brought him inside. "I met a lot of nice people, but they were not from *The Sound of Music*. I was in the wrong line; I was in the 'Final Casting for Daniel Boone' line. By the time my mother found me she was upset that I was in the wrong line but I told her that I thought I got the part."

Hinton impressed the casting department so much that the original part of an older son for *Daniel Boone* was altered to favor a young boy like Hinton, who was only six years old.

The Sound of Music also played a part in Veronica Cartwright getting the role of *Daniel Boone's* daughter.

"I had auditioned for a part in *The Sound of Music* as did my sister, Angela," said Cartwright. "And she got the part of Brigitta. I went over to Austria with my family while Angela did the film. I was in Salszburg in 1964 when I was called directly to play the role of Jemima Boone and was asked to fly home immediately. I flew back with my father and I was soon on location in Kanab, Utah to shoot the pilot."

Blair, like Parker, was born in Fort Worth, Texas. Her attractive looks led to a modeling career and, later, motion pictures. Her screen debut (billed as Pat Blake) was in the 1955 film, *Jump Into Hell*, which told of the Vietnamese siege of Dien Bien Phu. Regular work in television followed. By the early 1960s she had appeared in such TV Westerns as *Yancy Derringer, The Rifleman, The Virginian, Bonanza,* and *Temple Houston*.

On October 17, 1964, Marcy gave birth to a girl, Ashley. Growing up, Fess' kids only knew their father as a TV performer called Daniel Boone.

"They loved it," said Marcy. "But they'd ask, 'Who's Daniel Boone?' and 'What's Daniel Boone all about?'"

Eli in particular enjoyed his visits to the set.

"I remember getting up at 4:30 or five o'clock in the morning and riding out to the Fox Ranch in a vehicle that looked like a taxi on steroids," said Eli. "I had a lot of fun hanging around with Darby Hinton. It was fun to hang out with him. We used to get ourselves in a little hot water once in a while, but most of the time it was just for being in a place where we weren't supposed to be. I do remember that Darby didn't have the usual kind of pets: he had raccoons and snakes. Once one of his boa constrictors got out, either accidentally or intentionally, and it terrorized the set!"

Eli's playful association with Hinton was monitored by Fess, who stressed proper behavior to his children at all times.

"Fess was consistent with Eli and Ashley growing up," noted Marcy. "As a matter of fact, we both were pretty much the same

Darby Hinton, Fess, Eli, and Ashley Parker on the *Daniel Boone* set.
COURTESY OF DARBY HINTON.

when it came to parenting. But I was easier on my kids than my parents were on me. I wasn't as old fashioned. Fess established certain rules for Eli and Ashley when they were growing up—like restrictions about their hours at home and hours away from home, things like that. And there were no-smoking and no-drinking rules that had to be followed. Fess set a good example because he did very little drinking and he smoked only a few cigarettes."

"Dad was a great parent," stated Ashley. "When he was home—filming and business kept him away a fair amount of time—he was very hands on. Dad had a 'tell it to you straight' sort of style. He was very honest and didn't sugar coat things. He was such a keen observer of people and situations and he often used those experiences to make his point about manners or dress or decisions that people made. Dad was always interested in our thoughts on subjects and was eager for us to share our opinions, but he was not interested in us being disrespectful and was never a fan of *colorful* language. He wouldn't tolerate profanity as he thought it was unimaginative."

Years later, Ashley recalled an incident in which Fess taught her a lesson in responsibility.

"There was nothing worse than disappointing dad," explained Ashley. "He taught me to drive and was very 'cool' about it, allowing me to drive around in Hope Ranch—the unincorporated area where we lived—in order to get lots of practice. He was very patient and seemingly unflappable when it came to teaching me to drive. So after getting my license I promptly got into a head on collision with four girls from my high school tennis team in the car. Both cars were totaled and it was completely my fault but, most fortunately, nobody was seriously injured. I had a bad bruise on my chin and my legs were banged up but otherwise I was okay. The day after the accident, dad drove me to school for the first time in a long time. As he pulled over to the curve to let me out he said, 'Do they still have that driver's ed class here at school?' I responded in the affirmative and that's when he got me. He said, 'You might want to go in there today and show them your face and tell them how you almost killed all those girls. It might prevent someone else from driving recklessly.' He picked his moments well."

During breaks in filming, Fess and Ames would engage in lengthy conversations.

"We would talk about world affairs, tell jokes, swap stories and we'd talk about the business," said Ames. "When we first started working together—when the day's work was over—we would swap stories about our youth growing up. We had a lot of intimate conversations."

Surprisingly on a network known for its color programs, *Daniel Boone* was originally filmed for NBC television in black and white. "When I took the job, I said I'd like for us to do this in color and they said, 'Fine.'" said Fess. "When I found that we were going to do it in black and white I got mad."

"We had shot the pilot film in color and we certainly thought that it was going to be done in color," said Ames. "It was like a double cross."

"It was an unfortunate situation that they created," said Fess.

However, strong first-season ratings and demands by Fess forced Twentieth Century Fox to make the visual change. Starting in the second season, all the *Daniel Boone* episodes were filmed and broadcast in color.

Fess was saddened by the loss of his father who died on January 31, 1965, during the first season of *Daniel Boone*.

"It was a very difficult time for Fess," said Marcy. "He took his father's death hard."

"I always got the feeling that dad was frustrated that F. E. died so young," stated Ashley. "He was only sixty-four. I knew that dad blamed cigarettes. I think that once dad got past sixty-four, he thought he could live forever."

With the death of his father, Fess and his family spent more time visiting his mother. Ashley fondly remembers her visits to her grandmother's mobile home. "She used to peel apples for apple pie and I would sit at her feet and eat the peelings," she said. "I enjoyed that."

After his father's funeral, Fess returned to the set. Establishing camera angles and lighting positions for each scene was a time-consuming task, so stand-in performers frequently were hired to take the place of the principal actors before the actual filming took place. Fess found his stand-in on a polo field.

"I was going to school at Santa Barbara City College, 1962–63, and I was dating someone who was playing polo," explained Carol Toso. "Fess was learning to play polo at the time and they met, and as a result, I met Fess, too. And then I met Marcy. Later, she and I ran into one another through a mutual friend. Marcy told me that she was going to drive cross country to see Fess perform in *Oklahoma* and she invited me to go along. She and I got into the car and traveled all over. We first went to the Bay area and then on to Iowa where she visited her family. We went to Minnesota to visit some of her friends and then to Baltimore. But I never got a chance to see Fess perform in the musical. Another year went by. I was modeling and then I went to Europe for about six months. When I returned, I saw Marcy again; she had just given birth to Ashley. We had dinner and Fess asked me, "Carol, why don't you be my stand-in?'"

And she did.

Toso, an attractive model, stood 5'8" but she was still much smaller than Fess. The crew came up with a solution to make her fit Fess' frame for proper camera and lighting angles.

"They built a stool for me that brought me up to Fess' height," laughed Toso. "I still have the stool; as a matter of fact, I use it often."

Toso's stand-in job for the 1965–66 season of *Daniel Boone* was unique.

"I was the first female stand-in for a male TV star," said Toso. "I later learned that Marlon Brando used a female stand-in for some of his pictures but that was film not television."

Despite her sex and height, the cast and crew never joked about her because Fess had established an atmosphere on the set that accentuated the positive.

"He was as gracious as could be to everyone on the set," said Toso. "It was a family environment. He had a dynamic personality that made you want to get to know him better. He was so down to earth. He was always interested in other people and what they had to say. It wasn't just about *him*."

Toso managed to make a few appearances as an extra on *Daniel Boone*.

"Just some silent bits, walking down the street or riding a horse," said Toso. "It was fun."

Fess was more than Toso's employer.

"The Parkers not only introduced me to my future husband but Fess gave me away at the ceremony, which took place on May 21, 1966," said Toso. "Marcy was one of the bride's maids and Eli was the ring-bearer."

The costuming and sets vividly were recreated on *Daniel Boone* but they were sometimes a bit too pristine to be regarded as authentic recreations of early America. Fess was costumed in standard Hollywood frontier wear, a mix of eighteenth and ninteenth century-flavored clothing instead of the common linen hunting clothes and broad-brimmed felt hats worn by Boone and his contemporaries. The prop substitutes used for Boone's "Tick Licker" rifle were anachronistically bulky and awkward, and the frontiersman's hunting bag was

Fess Parker in a casual pose during a break from *Daniel Boone*.
PHOTO COURTESY OF THE PARKER FAMILY.

awkwardly wrapped around his powder horn. Still, Fess looked good no matter what he wore and he always seemed comfortable in the clothing. However, the Eastern tribes on *Daniel Boone* frequently were costumed as Plains Indians with teepees instead of wood and bark lodges. And Bowie knives, which were not popular until the ninteenth century, occasionally were seen in the hands of performers. These were minor flaws and they never interfered with the stories or the characters. For television in 1964, *Daniel Boone* was frontier America in all its small-screen glory.

Ames vividly remembered his costuming and makeup.

"It was the first episode," said Ames. "I came down for makeup in the morning, and costumes, wigs. They had a lot of extras playing Indians."

Ames expected to have his makeup carefully sponged on.

"But they hit me with a bucket—it was icy cold—of body makeup!" laughed Ames. "They sloshed me! I said never again. That was the first and last time they ever did that."

Despite Ames' unfortunate makeup orientation, *Daniel Boone* was essentially an even-keeled production, thanks to the friendly and professional tone that Fess established.

"We had a pretty smooth operation, I thought," said Fess.

"We had lots and lots of fun together," said Ames. "Fess was always fun on the set."

"Fess never changed from the man I first remember to the last day I had the privilege of talking to him," said Hinton. "Fess was genuine, real. You got what you saw and you liked what you saw. Fess was the show. He set the tone for the show. There were no egos, there were no tantrums. There was never a scene or anything thrown. He never had to showboat or show his authority. It was a very smooth-running set. I really didn't appreciate it that much until I did other work. He certainly knew everybody's name. He certainly was friendly with everybody. It was a big family. And if there were any squeaky wheels, they just quickly disappeared."

Ames concurred with Hinton's assessment of the *Daniel Boone* set.

"Fess would come on the set in the early morning and have a cup of coffee, and as he wandered through the set he would greet everybody with warmth," said Ames. "He knew their names, he knew their children, he knew their families. He just wouldn't say 'Hi' and go on; he would stop, like a friend. He would have a conversation. These people would die for Fess. They'd do anything for him and to make the show a hit."

Hinton, who lost his father in a 1958 plane crash, saw Fess as more than an actor-dad.

"We just had a great relationship," explained Hinton. "I happily accepted him as the role of my dad because I didn't have a dad. The set takes on the atmosphere of whoever the star is. Fess was always

Away from the *Daniel Boone* set, Fess Parker prepares to order from a restaurant menu with Eli and Ashley.
Photo courtesy of the Parker Family.

caring and loving. He had this wonderful family relationship that he was drawing on from home and bringing to the screen."

Cartwright's assessment of Fess matched the comments of her co-stars. "Fess was wonderful and kind," she said.

Fess arrived at the set most of the time by plane.

"Flying down from Santa Barbara was more fun than driving," said Fess, who would land in Santa Monica before being driven to the set nearby. "They didn't want me to fly solo so there was usually a pilot alongside me.

Daniel Boone was primarily filmed at the Twentieth Century Fox Studios in Los Angeles. "All the interiors, like inside the fort, and a lot of the 'exteriors,' like outside of Boone's cabin, were shot at the Western and Sunset Avenue Fox lot," said Hinton. "It's now a mini mall."

Real exteriors were filmed at different locations.

"Most of the exteriors were shot on the Fox Ranch, which is now Malibu Creek State Park," said Hinton. "They shot one episode in Florida but 'Israel' didn't get to make that trip. I did get to go to Kanab, Utah where we shot two, maybe three, episodes. And we would sometimes go to Frazier Park, California. One of the things I keep remembering is how much fun and easy going Fess made the set wherever it was, and especially when we were at the ranch. I also remember Ronald and Nancy Reagan used to ride over from their nearby ranch to have lunch with Fess and how nice they were."

CHAPTER 14
"DANIEL BOONE": 1964–1970

The series debuted on September 24, 1964 with "Ken-Tuck- E." Filmed in color, it was an action-packed episode that had a number of *Davy Crockett* touches in it. For example, Fess wears a fringed buckskin shirt and coonskin cap, and has a dependable sidekick. And the pilot also contained stock footage of wildlife that was characteristic of the *Davy Crockett* episodes.

Fess' *Daniel Boone* is quickly established as a man of action in "Ken-Tuck-E." Fess easily hoists himself on a tree by way of a limb, runs like a deer through snow and rock covered terrain, survives a Shawnee gauntlet with power and skill, and catches a tomahawk that is thrown at him by stuntman Chuck Roberson's Dark Panther character. "I happened to actually catch that tomahawk on the first take," quipped Fess, who also commented on the incident in the *Daniel Boone* DVD set.

The big battle in which the Indians attack the settlement's fort is augmented by a number of uncredited scenes from *Drums Along the Mohawk*, a 1939 film that starred Henry Fonda. The color match between the original John Ford-directed motion picture and the 1964 pilot is quite good, as is the editing effort of Louis Loeffler. In one scene a flaming arrow fired from a warrior in *Drums Along the Mohawk* is extinguished in the next shot by Darby Hinton, who bravely tosses dirt on the burning gunpowder barrel after kicking the projectile aside. In another scene, boiling water that women in *Daniel Boone* pour upon the attacking braves is actually an edited clip from the 1939 film.

In the original pilot, Hinton portrayed a character called Nathan; Bobby Horan played Israel. Thanks to some careful editing and final credit alterations, Horan's character became Nathan, a friend of the Boone's. "However, they didn't re-shoot or edit the final scene, though, where the Boone family walks away from the fort, arm in arm, including the character played by Bobby Horan," explained Karen Dusik, who serves as the webmaster of danielboonetv.com, the site of the unofficial Daniel Boone TV Fan Club. "Fans who had never seen the original pilot were very, very confused."

Besides Horan, another casualty of the pilot's editing was George Lindsay, who played a character named Wigeon. Lindsay appears in the debut program but his role was nothing more than one of the fort's defenders, although Fess quickly removes Wigeon's shirt as a makeshift flag of truce. Lindsay, of course, went on to a successful television career in such programs as *The Andy Griffith Show* and *Mayberry R.F.D.*, among other productions.

"Ken-Tuck-E" was punctuated by enough enjoyable family moments to elevate the production from its pilot status to the kick-off episode of the series. "The premier pilot has more scenes with the Boone family and has more Daniel-Rebecca interaction than did the original pilot, which had some fight scenes and footage of Daniel and Mingo being chased by the Shawnee," explained Dusik. "Those scenes were replaced with Daniel singing to Rebecca and interacting more with the family. I saw it as a move to be a bit less like Disney's Crockett and establish Daniel as a solid family man."

Daniel Boone featured lots of action including flintlock shoot 'em ups, hand-to-hand fights, and Mingo's nasty bullwhip skills.

"But there never was graphic violence," said Ames. "Fess was very, very adamant about that. He said, 'This is a show where a huge part of the audience are kids, and I don't want to be associated with that kind of violence.' We would have fist fights with the Red Coats instead of knife fights or bayonet fights."

Boone historian Robert E. McDowell saw it differently and criticized the TV show. "The real Daniel Boone was five-feet, eight-inches and heavy set," said McDowell in a newspaper interview. Surprisingly, the historian saw more violence than was actually depicted on the program. "He avoided fights and got along splendidly with the Indians most of the time. Fess Parker kills scores or more of Indians every week. He even caught some Aztecs lurking around Kentucky and bagged them."

Ames later co-hosted *The Mike Douglas Show* and reluctantly displayed his skills with a bullwhip when prodded by the crew. "I was actually instructed on how to use the whip by an Israeli self-defense guy," explained Ames. "And he trained me well. But I was not about to use it on this woman on the show, who they positioned with a cigarette in her mouth, because I could easily disfigure her if I missed. Well, I didn't miss. I took the cigarette right out of her mouth. And the payoff came when a few moments later another bullwhip wrapped around my neck. It was my teacher, the guy who originally instructed me!"

Cartwright remembers "The Choosing" that aired on October 29, 1964, as her favorite episode. "It was basically my show," said Cartwright. "I get kidnapped, I wear buckskins; it was fun."

Cartwright also remembers "The First Beau," which was broadcast on December 9, 1965. The young actress was sixteen years old and her "beau," Fabian Forte, the singer who had three top ten hits in 1959 ("Turn Me Loose," "Tiger," and "Hound Dog Man"), was twenty-three years old. "My first kiss on screen was with Fabian, who was playing my love interest on the show, and he kissed like his age," laughed Cartwright. "When he kissed me it was my first French kiss, and the director told him, 'You can't do that; it's a family show.'"

During the first season's filming of *Daniel Boone*, a casual meeting between Fess and another actor blossomed into a long-term friendship. The actor was Ron Ely, who would later star as *Tarzan* on the NBC-TV series that ran from 1966 to 1968.

"I stopped by the set to pick up a friend who was working with Fess on *Daniel Boone,*" said Ely. "Fess recognized me and came across the set to introduce himself. He greeted me without artifice and without that common pretense that he did not know who I was. 'Hi, Ron, I'm Fess Parker,' was exactly what he said upon our first meeting. I had previously done two series on CBS, *The Aquanauts* and *Malibu Run*; Fess, of course, had done the series on *Davy Crockett.* That was enough for us to be aware of each other. We chatted briefly before he was called to the set, and I did not see him again for a few years. I was impressed with his demeanor and with the feeling of his set. There was a noticeable lack of tension, which to my experience up to that date, was somewhat rare on a TV series.

A very short time after my first meeting with Fess, I was on my way to Brazil to begin the shooting of *Tarzan*, Although both his series and mine were NBC shows, we never had the occasion to see each other in those years. My show was shot on location in Brazil and Mexico, and he was, for the most part, doing his show on a sound stage or a nearby Hollywood location."

Fess treated his guest performers as if they were visitors to his parents' home in Texas. He remembered his parent's hospitality, especially the way his mother catered to his friends.

"It was unlike any other show," said Ames. "When you're a guest on somebody else's television show, the star of the show minimally welcomes you and you go on to do your work and get it over with. Fess wasn't like that. Fess would welcome them with great warmth and make them feel that they were important. He was very hospitable. He gave them the best dressing rooms. It was a very happy set. He was very cordial between shots. He would sit with the guest star and make them feel very, very welcome."

And guest performers kept coming back. Over 200 actors made repeat appearances on *Daniel Boone.* Fess' friend Morgan Woodward, who had accumulated dozens of film and television credits since *Westward Ho, the Wagons!*, appeared in two *Daniel Boone* episodes during the first season. "Fess was always a pleasure to work with," said Woodward. "It was thoroughly enjoyable to work with an old friend."

At the end of the first season, Fess hit the road and made public appearances to spark interest in the series. He even showed up dressed as *Daniel Boone* at the All American Soap Box Derby in Akron, Ohio in August of 1965. Fess appeared on a celebrity podium that was constructed in front of the Sheraton-Mayflower Hotel. Glenn Ford and Frankie Avalon, who also attended the event, battled Fess in the celebrity Oil Can Race which Fess won.

Each episode followed a standard procedure after a director and cinematographer were assigned and a writer was hired. Take "A Christmas Story," for example, an episode that aired on December 23, 1965. George Geraghty directed and Jack Swain was behind the camera. Writer Stephen Lord submitted a revised final draft of "A Christmas Story" on September 30, 1965. The teleplay was scheduled for a seven-day shoot commencing on Monday, October 11 and

Fess Parker shows off his Oil Can Trophy at the 1965 All American Soap Box Derby.
COURTESY OF DAN MARKOVICH.

ending on Tuesday, October 19. The cast had Saturday and Sunday off. Augmenting the regular cast members were Fess' good friend Morgan Woodward, Jay Silverheels, Ted White and other supporting players.

Fess was scheduled to report each day at 7:30 a.m. for makeup and wardrobe; Patricia Blair usually had to report at least a half hour earlier. Veronica Cartwright and Darby Hinton usually had later calls, but on Wednesday October 13, and Monday October 18, the youngsters had to report at 9 a.m. for school. The work day usually ended no later than 7 p.m. for everyone.

A sum of $19,131 was paid to the show's contract players—regular cast members, episode performers with speaking parts, and stunt players—for "The Christmas Story." Fess earned $5,100; Ed Ames earned $1,350. Patricia Blair was paid $1,150, Veronica Cartwright $850, and Darby Hinton $650. An additional $2,752 was paid for the extras.

Besides the regular crew, mechanical effects personnel were hired to provide the artificial snow, which would be featured in over fifty different camera shots. The artificial snow dressing was budgeted at $2,500. The entire episode's estimated cost was $138,221.

The first three seasons, George Sherman served as the program's primary producer; Vincent M. Fennelly produced a half-dozen others. Sherman had directed dozens of B-Westerns in the 1930s and 1940s, and a number of action-adventure feature films including the Errol Flynn swashbuckler *Against All Flags* (1952) and Victor Mature's *Chief Crazy Horse* (1955). But at the end of the third season, Sherman sought a better deal from Aaron Rosenberg. Sherman, in fact, had been courted by Ivan Tors Productions, best known for its popular TV show *Flipper*, to produce *Gentle Ben*, a prime-time family show about a Florida Everglades game warden, his family, and a friendly bear named Ben.

Rosenberg, who was in Florida producing *Tony Rome* with Frank Sinatra, didn't appreciate Sherman's posturing. He refused to negotiate with Sherman and promptly severed ties with him. The executive producer, however, needed a new producer. And fast.

Barney Rosenzweig offered his services to Rosenberg, who was his father-in-law.

"In 1964, I went to work for Aaron," said Rosenzweig. "He wanted me to use my publicity acumen to help him promote his material and to liaise between the production and the publicity department of Twentieth Century Fox, and in return for that he would teach me his craft. I could learn how to be a producer from Aaron, which is what I wanted to do. To this day, ninety percent of what I've learned in the business, I learned from Aaron, one way or another."

Despite the family connection, Rosenberg was reluctant to give him an opportunity to produce until the Sherman-*Gentle Ben* issue manifested itself.

"Aaron told me, 'You take the job,'" said Rosenzweig, "'You're ready. I'll pay you a thousand dollars a week.' By the time he came back from Florida, I was wearing a coonskin cap, my way of saying I'm ready to take the job. But it wasn't his job to offer."

According to Rosenzweig, since Rosenberg only owned 20 percent he didn't have the authority to hire Sherman's replacement. Subsequently, a meeting of all the principal owners or their representatives—including, of course, Fess—met to determine who the new producer would be. And there was already some tension in the room before the discussion began.

"Fess and Aaron weren't getting along," said Rosenzweig. "Fess perceived himself as being in the hands of an absentee landlord. Aaron was off with Frank Sinatra making movies; he was doing other stuff. He would only come down to Western Avenue once a week."

Fess was also concerned about the Rosenzweig-Rosenberg family connection.

"He was nervous about the idea of having Aaron's son-in-law running the show," said Rosenzweig. "But I told him what my vision of the series was. I told him that I didn't think it was as good as it could be and that I thought it could be a lot better. I thought he deserved better. I told him what I would do with the show and how I thought I could make it better."

Rosenzweig's focus was on the scripts and the forty-six minutes of actual screen time that was needed in each program. He told Fess that he wanted improved writers and more of them. "He listened," said Rosenzweig.

Fess and the others had a few additional candidates to interview but he later phoned Rosenzweig with a friendly "Hello, boss!" greeting.

"I decided to introvert the show," stated Rosenzweig, who emphasized the interrelationship among the show's characters. He hoped that this change would not only retain *Daniel Boone's* audience but add to it. "When I took over *Daniel Boone* in 1967, it was about to enter its fourth and, some thought, last season," he said. "It had never rated higher than in the 39th position in the Nielsen ratings, which was, at best, tenuous in those days. It was over one million dollars in deficit, and had never received a favorable critical notice. We lost to *Batman* and *The Flying Nun*."

Still, *Daniel Boone* remained an important part of NBC-TV's Thursday night lineup which included *Ironside, The Dean Martin Show,* and *The Tonight Show*. But a new CBS-TV program challenged its time slot: *Cimarron Strip*, a big-budget, ninety-minute Western that starred Stuart Whitman and, ironically enough, Randy Boone, who supposedly was related to *Daniel Boone*.

"*Daniel Boone* had a budget of about $154,000 an episode when I started," Rosenzweig pointed out. "*Cimarron Strip* had a budget of $350,000."

Everyone started to worry. Veteran producer George Sherman was gone and a twenty-nine year old was in his place; the ratings hadn't been particularly good for years; and a big-budget program from the network which had previously won every ratings battle of the week—except Thursday—was on its way. To make matters worse, CBS-TV was debuting *Cimarron Strip* on September 7, 1967, one week before *Daniel Boone* returned for its fourth season.

Rosenzweig said that he had a lunch-time conversation with Paul King, a former *Daniel Boone* co-producer/producer and writer who was aware of the situation. "He told me, 'Enjoy your year as a producer,'" said Rosenzweig. "'You guys are going to be murdered by the show.' No wonder Fess was depressed."

But *Cimarron Strip* turned out to be a bust. Low ratings and high production costs added up to just twenty-three episodes. Its last original episode aired on March 7, 1968, the same night that "The Far Side of Fury" episode aired on *Daniel Boone*. Surprisingly, two of Fess' old friends from Texas, Dodo McQueen and Morgan Woodward, appeared in a few episodes of *Cimarron Strip*. "I was unaware of the competition between the shows," said Woodward. "For me, it was just work." And Bobby Horan, who played Israel Boone in the original *Daniel Boone* pilot, appeared in an episode of the CBS Western.

"During my tenure, which lasted three seasons totaling seventy-eight episodes, the show averaged in the top twenty-five, getting as high in the rankings as ninth," stated Rosenzweig. "It was not only no longer in deficit but was being made at or below the license fee. With summer reruns, that made *Daniel Boone* the only hour show in the history of Twentieth Century Fox to be in profit in its initial run. Finally, in 1967, '68, and '69, we received outstanding notices each year, my favorite being my first, naturally, when 'Variety' termed it 'a well-crafted oater." The publication used "oater" as a nickname for a Western.

Daniel Boone not only survived into its fourth season, it was a genuine TV hit. Hollywood reporter Dick DuBrow identified Fess' characterization as a key to the show's popularity: "[Parker] has a deceptive, rugged, masculine style that wears well."

"A strange thing was happening," added Rosenzweig. "The scripts, which were now about something, started stimulating better writing. And the writing brought in better casting."

Rosey Grier, Fess Parker, and Jimmy Dean. Courtesy of Dan Markovich. "'DANIEL BOONE' © 1964 Twentieth Century Fox Television. All rights reserved."

Fess was particularly proud that his guest stars on the series came from a cultural cross section of America. *Daniel Boone* featured African-Americans (Woody Strode, Roosevelt Grier, Raymond St. Jacques, et al.), Hispanics (Carlos Rivas, Armando Silvestre, Félix Gonzáles, et al.), and Native Americans (Eddie Little Sky, Jay Silverheels, et al.).

"Rosey Grier was a big guy, a fun guy," said Ames.

"There were always practical jokes going on," said Hinton, who remembered a prank played on Grier, a former defensive lineman for the New York Giants and Los Angeles Rams. "Rosey was supposed to lift a bucket of water. Well, they took a bucket and filled it with lead and just put a mirror on top of it with a little bit of water on it so it looked like it was water all the way down. When he tried to lift it, he had a little challenge." Grier and the rest of the cast and crew all laughed at the joke. Grier so impressed Fess and Rosenzweig that he appeared as Gabe Cooper in eight episodes during the 1969–1970 season.

Throughout the run of the series, a number of episodes focused on the issue of slavery and race relations, and Grier starred in one of them, "Mama Cooper," which was one of Fess' favorite episodes. The program, which aired on February 5, 1970, featured guest star Ethel Waters, the gifted African-American performer, as Rachel, Gabe's long-lost mother. In Lionel E. Siegel's teleplay Grier's character finds his mother, who had been given her manumission papers, and promises to take her to free territory. However, Waters' character is dying and she perishes on the journey. Gabe threatens to burn the plantation where he found his mother but honors her death-bed promise not to destroy the place.

Earlier, Yaphet Kotto was featured in "Jonah," another slave-oriented program, which was broadcast on February 13, 1969. And former heavyweight boxing champion Floyd Patterson appeared in "The Road to Freedom," which was first broadcast on October 2, 1969.

"Fess understood that we were making the show relevant," said Rosenzweig. However, there had been other relevant shows earlier in the series. For example, Brock Peters portrayed the title character in "Pompey," an episode about a runaway slave who is befriended by Boone. The show aired on December 10, 1964, five months after President Lyndon Johnson signed the Civil Rights Act of 1964 into law. And Rafer Johnson, the former Olympic Gold Medal winner, portrayed the title character in "My Name is Rawls," an episode about another runaway slave which first aired on October 7, 1965. The issue of the legality of slavery in colonial times was the centerpiece of "The Wolfman," which aired on January 26, 1967.

Fess was sensitive to the plight of African-Americans in the 1960s and thought it appropriate to address civil rights issues through specific *Daniel Boone* episodes. And his concerns were genuine.

"In all the time I knew Fess Parker, I never heard a whisper or a statement or a gesture of any kind that was bigoted," said Ames. "He went out of his way when he spoke of other races or religions. He was a pure soul. He wanted his show to have people of color, and he always portrayed them with dignity."

"I was glad that we had the opportunity to do shows like that," said Fess.

"I'm more proud of *Daniel Boone* than anything I've ever done," added Rosenzweig, who later served as Executive Producer for the Emmy award-winning *Cagney and Lacey*.

Chuck Bargiel, Fess' friend and attorney, stressed the importance of the *Daniel Boone* series. "He was very appreciative of *Davy Crockett* and enjoyed doing it and was grateful for the fame that it gave him," said Bargiel. "But the show that reflected him most of all was *Daniel Boone*, by the number of stories and body of work in which racial issues were dealt with."

A number of *Davy Crockett* cast members also appeared on the show: Pat Hogan (Red Stick in "Davy Crockett, Indian Fighter"), Mike Mazurki (Bigfoot Mason in "Davy Crockett Goes to Congress"), Kenneth Tobey (Jim Bowie in "Davy Crockett at the Alamo" and Jocko in both keelboat episodes), Don Megowan (William Travis in "Davy Crockett at the Alamo"), Jeff York (Mike Fink in both keelboat episodes), and Hank Worden (Fiddler in "Davy Crockett and the River Pirates"). The most appearances on *Daniel Boone* made by *Davy Crockett* alumni were Chuck Roberson and Ted White, two uncredited stunt men in "Davy Crockett at the Alamo." White actually had fourteen credited appearances as various characters on *Daniel Boone*, but occasionally did double-duty as Fess' stunt double.

Tom Blackburn, who wrote the *Davy Crockett* scripts and the lyrics to "The Ballad of Davy Crockett," was hired to write three *Daniel Boone* episodes: "The Tamarack Massacre Affair" (1965), "Gun-Barrel Highway" (1966), and "The Spanish Horse" (1967). In fact, Blackburn seemingly inserted some "Davy Crockett, Indian Fighter" moments in "The Tamarack Massacre Affair," which he co-wrote with David Duncan. For example, Boone's instructions to his children before he leaves home, his interpretation of tracks in the ground and the descending hillside approach of the militia before the Indian camp are Disneyesque to say the least. And the some of the climactic battle scenes between the British regulars and the militia conveniently were borrowed from Walt Disney's *Johnny Tremain*.

Fess and Walt Disney crossed paths at a TV studio dinner during the first season of *Daniel Boone*. It was somewhat of an awkward moment until they exchanged greetings. "He wished me well with my new show," said Fess, who did not know that his former boss was going to be in attendance. "I appreciated that." Fess interpreted the brief conversation as a thaw in their relationship.

Comedy is an element not usually associated with *Daniel Boone* but it punctuated a number of the episodes.

"Fess had a great sense of comedy," said Ames. "Sometimes it was very sly. He was very good at it and kept in all within the character. We were constantly tossing off comments and barbs that were very good natured."

Fess occasionally recruited comedians or actors with comedic backgrounds like Jimmy Dean, Doodles Weaver, and George Gobel who made a guest appearance as Francis Clover in "Four-Leaf Clover," an episode which aired on March 25, 1965. An unintended part of Gobel's portrayal was his appearance. "And he was wearing a crew cut in colonial times," laughed Ames. "I don't think that was the normal hairstyle in that period." Ten years earlier in March 1955, of course, Gobel had won the Emmy for "Most Outstanding New Personality," a category in which Fess had been nominated for *Davy Crockett.*

Jimmy Dean enjoyed working with Fess. "Fess Parker is one of the finest human beings around," said Dean to *The Dallas Morning News.* "He's been trying to get me to move away from New York and settle in the open air. Fess isn't show biz and he found someone who wasn't either…me."

Veronica Cartwright remembered Fess' height. "He was six-foot six and always had a good sense of humor about villains having to stand on apple boxes or him having to stand in a hole when he played a scene," said Cartwright. "It always amazed me this big imposing person could get out of the tiny Porche that he used to drive."

Fess always towered over his fellow cast members except when Hugh "Slim" Langtry got the role of Bartollo in the "Beaumarchais" episode which aired on October 12, 1967. Langtry was 6' 8" tall, and Fess didn't mind being the second tallest performer on the set. "I liked it," said Fess. "Looking up to a fellow is very good for the chin."

One of the interesting aspects of *Daniel Boone* is that the episodes featured both fictional and non-fictional characters. Among the more prominent names in early American history that graced the credits of the show were Benjamin Franklin, John Adams, Patrick

Henry, Aaron Burr, the Marquis de Lafayette, and George Washington.

A future President of the United States visited the set one day.

"One time at lunch time two guys came riding over the horizon at Fox Ranch and one of the guys was the Governor, Ronald Reagan, who was, by the way, a friend of Fess, a good friend of Fess," explained Ames. "They rode down over the hill and the Governor said, 'Can I have lunch with you people?' We said, 'Sit down.' That was the only time I ever met Ronald Reagan."

A number of prominent actors appeared on *Daniel Boone* including such distinguished thespians as Sam Jaffe, Michael Rennie, Maurice Evans, Walter Pidgeon, Vincent Price, and George Sanders, who made a memorable appearance as Colonel Roger Barr in "Crisis By Fire," a 1966 episode.

"George Sanders couldn't remember line one," laughed Ames. "Scene after scene. He go would go up, he would laugh, and forget his lines. It was misery for the director—even made more so because between each take he used to make up limericks—not such clean limericks. And would go on three pages of limericks and remember every single one. Then we'd go and shoot the scene and he'd blow the line. And that's the way it went. And, by the way, it turned out to be one of the best shows we ever did. He came off terrific!"

"And he could play guitar and sing," added Fess. "He did that between takes, too." Fess remembered another memorable George Sanders moment during the episode.

"An actress had to get on a horse as part of the scene and he was part of the scene," chuckled Fess. "So the director would say 'action' and the scene would start. She would climb on the horse and he would blow the deal. She got very exercised after more takes. She told Sanders, 'If you do that again I'm gonna get down or this horse and kick you right in the ass!' He got it right."

A spin-off film from the series, *Daniel Boone: Frontier Trail Rider*, was released in 1966. Like *Davy Crockett, King of the Wild Frontier*, which was the edited theatrical production taken from the three original *Davy Crockett* episodes, *Daniel Boone: Frontier Trail Rider* was an edited combination of "The High Cumberland: Part 1" (April 14, 1966) and "The High Cumberland: Part 2" (April 21, 1966). Primarily aimed at European audiences, the film's one-sheet

Vincent Price, Fess Parker, J. Pat O'Malley, and Darby Hinton during a break from the "Copperhead Izzy" episode.
Courtesy of Darby Hinton.

poster proclaimed: "Storming Across The Western Plains—With A Dream Big Enough To Settle A New Land And Courage Great Enough To Take On Indian, Outlaw, Or Any Man Who Tried to

Stop Him!" In France, the film was released as *Daniel Boone: Le Trappeur*. Once again, Fess Parker was bringing the American frontier to audiences on both sides of the Atlantic.

That same year, Fess appeared as Clint Barkley in the motion picture *Smoky*, a family-oriented film about a cowboy and a horse. Directed by George Sherman, the film was an awkward mix of 20th-century ranching, muted romance, and brief World War II moments. *Dallas Morning News* film critic Kathy Flanery called the film "a fascinating human story to be enjoyed by the whole family" and remarked that "Fess Parker plays a convincing role." Nevertheless, the 1966 Arcola Pictures productions was Fess' last big-screen acting performance.

On December 15, 1966, Walt Disney died, twelve years to the day after "Davy Crockett, Indian Fighter" debuted on television. Disney's passing brought up mixed emotions in Fess. He certainly was eternally grateful for the opportunity that Disney gave him yet he perceived his professional relationship with him as one which hindered his growth as an artist.

"He told me about Disney and how disappointed he was and the treatment they gave him," said Ames. "He was always disappointed. Although he maintained friendships with certain people in the Disney company, he never felt that Walt Disney treated him right. Disney felt that he had a property and the property was Fess Parker playing *Davy Crockett*. But Fess was an actor; he wanted to do things. But I do remember him telling me that he did have opportunities to do other things and Disney kept him on the end of a tether; he just never let him go and Fess always felt bad about that. He also felt bad that they didn't give him the rights to do the *Further Adventures of Davy Crockett*. It turned out fine in the end, but he was always a little hurt by Walt Disney for limiting his career."

Fess returned to his alma mater, the University of Texas, in 1968 where he received the Distinguished Alumnus Award. According to the July/August 2003 issue of *The Alcalde*, the university's alumni publication, "When the Alumni Center was built in 1965, Fess donated money, and the courtyard was named in honor of his father, Fess Parker, Sr., and when the courtyard was enclosed in 1989, the creekside deck at the south end of the Alumni Center was named The Fess Parker Deck."

In 1968, Fess received an honorary Doctor of Letters degree from the University of Eastern Kentucky. He was now Dr. Fess E. Parker. But, in typical Fess fashion, he never used the title.

The popularity of *Daniel Boone* generated several front page cover stories for *TV Guide* magazine. Fess, wearing a coonskin cap, and co-star Patricia Blair appeared on the August 21–27, 1965 issue's cover, and a hatless Fess, Patricia Blair, and Darby Hinton graced the May 11–17, 1968 issue's cover.

Daniel Boone was also promoted by a Gold Key comic book series that ran from 1965 to 1969. Fess' American Tradition Company held the copyright to the books. The first of the fifteen issues was particularly interesting because among the generic illustrations of the title character were actual drawings of Fess. Issue #1 also included the "Official Handbook Fess Parker as Daniel Boone Trail Blazers Club." The comic book's special section included information about such frontier skills as tracking, hunting, establishing a camp site, starting a fire, and loading and firing a flintlock. In fact, primitive weapons—from flintlock rifles to hunting knives—graced the cover of every issue—except one: issue #11 featured Fess' character with a fishing pole. The most interesting *Daniel Boone* comic book cover was issue #13 which featured a photo of Fess taken from the *Davy Crockett* series!

Besides the comic books, *Daniel Boone* was popularized by an assortment of merchandising. The number of products offered for sale were dwarfed by the thousands of items that were produced during the Crockett Craze, but there were enough items—from toy action figures, board games, View-Master reels and Super Slates to lunchbox and thermos sets, a Spanish-produced TV card set, balloons, playsets and, yes, coonskin caps—to keep young *Daniel Boone* fans happy.

As each season passed, the main cast members on *Daniel Boone* developed their characters with subtle touches of complexity.

"You knew your character; you knew how he would behave," said Ames. "You began to think like your character. You would try and see everything from your character's eyes. There was a lot of time spent learning the lines."

Ames explained that as time passed by he and Fess understood their respective characters better than some of the writers.

"New writers would come along from week to week," said Ames. "These new guys would come along and they'd have the outline of the story but they didn't have our characters. They weren't familiar with them; the audience was. We each had developed a character that was identifiable. By the time we got rolling, I knew Mingo much better than anybody else. If they wrote things that I would never say, I would get it changed if possible. Fess did it all the time, too."

"I got the opportunity to revise some scripts," added Fess, who pointed out that he never had that opportunity before.

The growing friendship between Fess and Ames helped develop their respective on-camera characters.

"We had wonderful conversations, sometimes long after the shooting was over," said Ames. "I remember one time we went out to have a beer together and there was Dean Martin sitting there saying, 'Hey fellas, I've been watching you guys. All right! You're doing well.' Our relationship was so strong off camera that it showed on camera. They talk about chemistry, well, we were pals and it showed in the scenes as well."

Besides his work in front of the camera, Fess also directed a number of episodes. "I'd like to continue as an actor the rest of my life," he told Gene Handsaker of the Associated Press. "But I think these other things give me a better bite into my craft." He debuted in the director's chair on February 8, 1968 in the fourth season with "Then Who Will They Hang from the Yardarm If Willy Gets Away?" He followed with "The Plague That Came From Ford's Run" (October 31, 1968), "The Patriot" (December 5, 1968), "Hannah Comes Home" (Christmas 1969), and "An Angel Cried" (January 8, 1970).

Fellow cast member Dallas McKennon had high praise for Fess.

"He's as natural as Boone," said McKennon in an interview. "He is a marvelous man to be associated with. You know he's developing into a good director. He's come up with some very inventive camera angles among other things."

"Hannah Comes Home" and "Mama Cooper" were among Fess' favorite episodes, along with "Ken-Tuck-E," "Empire of the Lost," "A Christmas Story," and "The Williamsburg Cannon, Parts 1 and 2."

"Hannah Comes Home," broadcast on Christmas 1969, is a touching story about a woman who returns to her husband after spending fifteen years among the Chickasaws. The woman, Hannah, played beautifully by Mary Fickett, believed her husband had been killed in the raid in which she had been captured; her husband, Jonas, played wonderfully by Ford Rainey, believed that she had been killed. Jonas never remarried but his Hannah had bonded with the son of the tribal chief and later gave birth to a son, Jason, played by Ted Eccles. The emotional struggles that all three confront are further complicated by the reaction of the Boonesborough community, particularly the heartless school teacher played convincingly by William O'Connell. Under Fess' direction, Fickett and Rainey deliver memorable performances. Rainey's prayer in the final scene acknowledged the "happiness and love of a family bound together" clearly reflected Fess' appreciation of his own family.

Fess' on-camera family continued to get along famously.

"Ed was always, and still is, great to me," said Hinton. "I have a lot of fond memories about him. He would show me how to use the whip and throw the tomahawk. Patricia Blair was very nice to me. Later in the show—I was probably eleven or twelve—she hugged me tight in a scene and we had to hold that position while they lit it. I looked over to one of the camera guys and said, 'She is my bosom buddy,' as that is where my face was pressed. The crew cracked up and I think she got a little embarrassed."

Fess kept busy with other projects while working on *Daniel Boone*. "Fess had an office practically set up on the set," said Ames. "He was very busy doing all sorts of business things. He was always very busy in between shots." Despite his hectic activities, one newspaper report called Fess "by far the most relaxed actor in the business." Fess pointed out that "Texans are not noted for being nervous."

An Associated Press articled titled "Horse Trading, Hollywood Style" on April 20, 1967, noted that Fess made an interesting exchange while working on *Daniel Boone.* Fess traded a twenty-four-year-old plane for a 300-horsepower truck, a two-bed wheeled camper, and a 45-foot trailer with "two stalls for his polo ponies."

Also during the run of *Daniel Boone*, Fess made guest appearances on a number of TV programs including *The Danny Kaye Show, The London Palladium Show, The Jonathan Winters Show, Today, The*

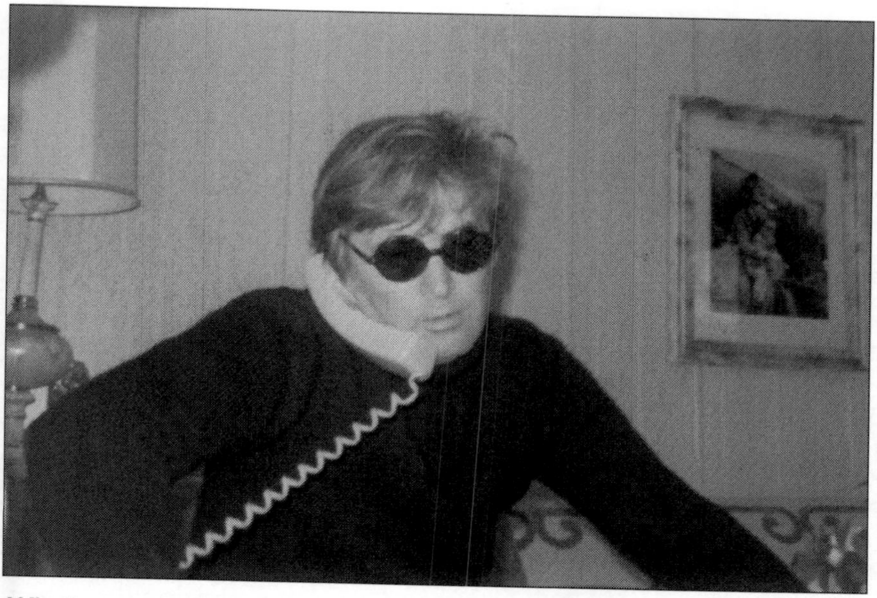

Whether on the Daniel Boone set or at home, Fess Parker was constantly on the phone promoting the show, making deals and "horse-trading."
PHOTO COURTESY OF THE PARKER FAMILY.

Beautiful Phyllis Diller Show, and *The Soupy Sales Show*, among others. On the zany *Soupy Sales* show, Fess did a soft-shoe dance; told a corny joke about a Daniel Boone stagecoach ride; greeted White Fang, Sales' oversized "dog;" and observed the host getting hit in the face with a pie.

He also spoke before various groups and organizations, and made appearances at fairs and rodeos. "I did rodeos all over the country from Florida to Washington State," said Fess. At the end of *Daniel Boone's* second season Fess appeared at the15th annual J-Bar-H Championship Rodeo in Camdenton, Missouri during July 1-5, 1966. At the 1966 Indiana State Fair, one of the seventy-two beauty contestants asked Fess for a kiss; however, all the girls lined up to pucker up with him. "I got to the tenth girl and I got so breathless I had to stop," quipped Fess. At the 1967 Kitsap County Fair and Rodeo teamed Fess up with the Polack Brothers Circus. In 1968, he appeared in his *Daniel Boone* costume at Cheyenne, Wyoming's Frontier Days where he fired his rifle and sang with a local vocal group. Fess returned to his birthplace in 1969 where he performed twenty times at the Fort Worth Stock Show Rodeo.

"Fess Parker was the guest at the Emerald Empire Round-up on July 8, 1970 in Eugene, Oregon," recalled Judy Southwell. "I was eleven. He sang a little for the rodeo audience and afterwards he signed autographs. My folks had purchased an 8 x 10 photo of *Daniel Boone* for each of us kids—I was the oldest of five kids—and we got in line. He shook hands with each of us, signed my photo and my little autograph book, and shook my hand again when I told him that *Daniel Boone* was my favorite show. He had huge hands."

Ed Ames was also called on to bring his Mingo character to various events around the country.

"I did some rodeos and some shows for the circus," stated Ames. "I would come flying out on a white horse, dismount and then tell a story and sing a few numbers. I had Mingo's bullwhip and I actually became quite adept with it."

He also became adept with tomahawks. In fact, the most memorable—and unplanned—moment in Ames' entertainment career resulted from throwing a tomahawk. He appeared on the April 29, 1965 episode of *The Tonight Show.* Host Johnny Carson stood by as Ames, dressed in a handsome suit and tie, threw a tomahawk at a wooden target that featured the outlined sketch of a frontier lawman. Ames' tomahawk hit the target in the figure's crotch with the blade's handle pointed up at an obvious phallic angle. The audience went wild with laughter. Ames laughed uncontrollably and walked towards the target to retrieve the weapon, but Carson grabbed his arm and spun him around for more laughs. Every so often the camera would focus on the target. The laughter went on for over a minute in what has been regarded as the longest sustained live audience laugh in TV history. Ames was joyously embarrassed and laughed at himself with self-deprecating honesty. Carson hilariously exploited the moment for maximum laughs when he quipped to Ames, "I didn't even know you were Jewish." The laughs continued.

Ames explained that he wanted to hide his embarrassment as soon as he saw the tomahawk land. "I immediately started walking towards the target in order to remove the tomahawk," laughed Ames. "I was also thinking about standing in front of the tomahawk in order to conceal it but Johnny grabbed my arm. He knew he had something at that moment but was still trying to figure out what to say or do. Well, the next day I'm in New York and people are staring at me, cab drivers are looking at me. It was something. I was a hero in New York for one day."

"Yes, we did give him a hard time for the Johnny Carson appearance," said Hinton.

Fess thought Ames' appearance on the *Tonight Show* was free advertising for the show. "I felt as if more people tuned into our show as a result of what Ed did on Johnny's show," suggested Fess. "It helped."

Fess' on-screen image as a loving and responsible parent did not go unnoticed.

"While I was filming the *Daniel Boone* series for Twentieth Century Fox Television, I was named Father of the Year," said Fess. "I was invited to attend an awards-presentation ceremony in New York and, of course, I attended. It was one of a number of very special awards that I received during my career." As "Father of the Year," he was recruited by the *Encyclopedia Britannica* to pitch the company's 24-volume set. "Except for a twist of fate, I might have been a history teacher instead of an actor," stated Fess in a print ad that he wrote for *Encyclopedia Britannica*. "And I'm still something of a bookworm." In the ad, Fess reminded parents to "show a genuine interest in what their youngsters are learning in school."

After the Kentucky's Cumberland National Forest was renamed the Daniel Boone National Forest in 1966, Fess participated in a renaming ceremony at the national park with Secretary of the Interior, Stewart Lee Udall. Fess was also involved in promotion of the U.S. Post Office Department's issuance of a six-cent commemorative Daniel Boone stamp on September 26, 1968 in Frankfort, Kentucky. And the American Humane Association named Fess as its National Chairman for its "Be Kind to Animals" campaign. That same year, Ohio sculptor Mike Makras created a life-size bronze bust of Fess, who placed it in his office at Twentieth Century Fox. "I appreciate all of the time and talent you contributed to it, and I look forward to seeing you the next time I am in Cincinnati," wrote Fess to Makras on April 10, 1969. Years later, Fess donated the sculpture to the Alamo.

In 1969, Fess entered the RCA studios and recorded two folk-flavored songs: "Comin' After Jinny" and "Sittin' Here Drinkin."

The label promoted the 45 rpm single with the somewhat inaccurate advertising slogan, "America's favorite frontiersman embarks on the recording frontier." After all, Fess had made a number of recordings a decade earlier, including his big "Ballad of Davy Crockett" hit. But the RCA release failed to break the charts.

Daniel Boone's final episode, "Israel and Love," aired on May 7, 1970. The story included a one-sided puppy-love romance between Darby Hinton's Israel and Robin Mattson's Brae. Israel is heartbroken after the girl leaves Boonesborough with her father but Boone comforts his son with some thoughtful words. Israel raises a question about who to share the important things in life with. "With your wife if you're lucky," says Boone. "With your son if you're even luckier." Even though the words came from the pen of script writer Melvin Levy, it was pure Fess Parker. Hinton's pay stub, which is currently in *Daniel Boone* fan Dan Markovich's memorabilia collection, stated that the young actor earned $875 for the episode. After taxes and a U.S. Savings Bond purchase of $218.75, Hinton's net pay was $430.50. Little did he know that it was going to be his last regular paycheck from the series.

Daniel Boone came to an end in a rather uneventful way.

"As of yet we have not heard as to the seventh season on 'Daniel Boone,'" wrote Fess in a February 18, 1970 letter to MCA executive Jennings Lang.

But Fess soon found out about season seven.

"Networks are always looking for the next hit," said Rosenzweig. "And unless everybody's on the same page and pushing for it to be renewed, unless everybody wants to keep going—the producer, the executive producer, the star, the studio—well."

As *Daniel Boone's* final season wound down, Fess made plans for the immediate future. Days before "The Homecoming" episode aired on April 9, 1970, it was announced that Fess signed a multiple motion picture and exclusive film contract with Warner Brothers. Part of the deal included the development for a new TV series to debut in the 1971–1972 season, but nothing ever materialized.

During production of the *Daniel Boone*, Fess traveled to Vietnam to visit the troops, many of whom grew up on *Davy Crockett* a decade earlier. "I felt for them," said Fess. "They had grown up watchin' me, but they were still young."

Fess Parker visits wounded U.S. soldier Alan Jerome "Jerry" Greenwood in Long Binh hospital in Vietnam.
PHOTO COURTESY OF ALAN JEROME "JERRY" GREENWOOD.

The "grunts" appreciated his visits.

Alan Jerome "Jerry" Greenwood was a nineteen-year-old soldier in the 9th Infantry Division's 5/60 Mechanized Infantry when two pieces of enemy shrapnel ripped into his abdomen on April 22, 1968. He was removed from his .50 caliber machine gun position atop an armored personnel carrier and taken to Long Binh hospital where he recovered.

And then Fess arrived at the facility.

"My first reaction was, 'Wow, it's Davy Crockett!'" said Greenwood, who received three Purple Hearts in Vietnam. "I had only been in Vietnam for a few months and seeing Fess Parker brought back memories of home. I think his visit was really an up day for everyone. To this day, I have always had lots of respect for those who put their lives as risk to visit and entertain the troops."

Brian Smith, an Army officer in Vietnam, relayed a story about Allen Reid, a fellow graduate from Fort Benning's Infantry Officer Candidate School, and Fess. Fess visited Reid's firebase in the Central Highlands west of a village called Dakto in 1968.

"Allen was very impressed that a celebrity such as you would visit a small firebase, which was much farther into *Indian territory* (as we used to say) than a large base camp," explained Smith to Fess in the *Fess Parker Winery & Vineyard* summer newsletter in 2007. "Allen, a 2nd Lieutenant and Recon Platoon Leader with Co. B, 1/8th Inf, 4th Infantry Division, spoke with you that visit and mentioned that there was a Specialist 4th Class named Daniel Boone under his command, but he was out in the jungle on a mission and would miss seeing you. Allen told me that he asked you if you would talk with Specialist Boone if the soldier could be reached by radio (very primitive radios used in the field forty years ago). They did raise him on the radio, and you got on the 'horn' and said, 'Hi, Daniel Boone? This is Davy Crockett calling.'" Allen has never forgotten that gesture—it added tremendously to the morale of a young enlisted man named Daniel Boone who was in harm's way every day for a year."

Entertainment writer Army Archerd reported on Fess' visit to the troops in his May 8, 1968 column: "Fess Parker, back from 21 days in Vietnam, is already planning a return. However his next trip will not be handshake tour, he sez—he's taking girls—three beautiful girls and a club act." Archerd noted that while Fess was in Kon-Tum playing cards with some soldiers one night, one of them announced to a fellow soldier outside their quarters that Fess Parker was with them. Fess told Archerd that the soldier on guard duty wasn't impressed. "The other one answered, 'Hell, I'd rather meet Faye Dunaway,'" laughed Fess who joked about bringing female entertainment with him if he ever returned to Vietnam. But on a serious note, Fess told Archerd, "This was the greatest trip of my life," he explained. "I sure got a lot of new and different thoughts."

Marcy was concerned about her husband's safety while he was in Southeast Asia.

"I was worried but I thought it was phenomenal what he did by going over there," said Marcy. "I had made some USO tours to South Korea and I was aware of the dangers. It wasn't easy. You just don't know what could happen if a security mistake was made. And he would go to remote places. But that was his style. He would do things that other people wouldn't do. While in Vietnam the military assisted him in making several phone calls home to me and I

Fess Parker distributes supplies to Vietnamese civilians.
PHOTO COURTESY OF THE PARKER FAMILY.

appreciated that. Fess had a great experience being over there. He had quite a time but I was glad when he returned home."

At home, Fess continued to assist various U. S. military efforts. He traveled to Detroit where he took part in the U. S. Marines "Toys for Tots Jamboree" at the city's Edgewater Park. He also narrated *The Silver Rifle*, a half-hour documentary about the meaning and tradition behind the Combat Infantryman's Badge for the U. S. Army Information Department in 1969. Dressed in a sport jacket and tie and holding a flintlock musket, Fess traced the history of the American rifleman from Daniel Morgan's rifle company in the Revolutionary War to the conflict in Vietnam. "And in Vietnam," states Fess in *The Silver Rifle*, "the infantryman meets his greatest challenge: a jungle war with an ever-shifting front that demands military competence and individual courage of the highest degree." Fess concluded the documentary by reading portions of *I Am The Infantry*, a poem written by Lieutenant Colonel Stephen H. White in 1955.

Fess also made time to record a public service announcement for Project Hope, the humanitarian project of the *S. S. Hope,* America's peacetime hospital ship. He also appeared on thirteen National Rifle Association-sponsored radio programs in 1970 in which he touted conservation education.

After the *Daniel Boone* series ended, Fess returned to Vietnam, where *Daniel Boone* was reportedly the most popular American television program. According to the military publication *Stars and Stripes*, on December 12, 1970, he was in Da Nang where he helped unload a plane that contained "Christmas trees, turkeys and other gifts for troops in five areas of the war zone in Vietnam." And once again, he made time for his friends.

"Fess had a made a tour to Vietnam while I was stationed in Taipei," said Milstead, who had risen to the rank of Lieutenant Colonel. "He had moved on to Okinawa and he invited me to stop by if I could. Since Taipei was only about a two and one-half hour flight away, I went. It was good to see him again and what he was doing."

And Fess made time for his family. He frequently brought his children to his mother's mobile home where they enjoyed casual visits, birthday parties, and anniversary celebrations.

In 1968, Fess had a plan to construct a 180-acre theme park called Frontier Worlds on a 1,500-acre site in Kentucky's Boone County near the intersection of two interstate highways, I-71 and I-75. The park's theme would include "the various frontiers during the history of the country." He designated approximately 140 acres for the park; the rest of the land would be developed for commercial and residential construction with some acreage designated for public parks and open land. The location, which was near Cincinnati, Ohio, was selected because it was within several hours driving distance of such metro areas as Louisville and Lexington, Kentucky; Dayton and Columbus, Ohio; and Indianapolis, Indiana. Fess liked the demographics and the overall transportation facilities. Construction cost estimates ranged from $13.5 million to $20 million.

Clearly, Fess was going to model his park after Disneyland, specifically the Frontierland section. But Frontier Worlds was going to be more. A replica of the Pilgrims' *Mayflower* would grace the entrance. And among the nearly two dozen planned attractions

Fess Parker with his mother, Mackie, and Ashley and Eli at his mother's mobile home at Rancho Santa Barbara.
PHOTO COURTESY OF THE PARKER FAMILY.

would be a showboat with live entertainment, a Huck Finn raft ride, a Klondike gold town, and an outer space rocket ride. And the park was going to have its own Hall of Presidents; as a matter of fact, Fess approached sculptor Mike Makras to create the heads of the nation's chief executives. "I was ready to make them if the park was going to be built," said Makras. Once a land deal could be reached, ground was expected to be broken before the year was out and the project would be completed by 1970. However, Fess couldn't line up enough investors and the idea was scrapped.

But Fess was determined to build a theme park—somewhere. And he found that location not far from home.

He located 452 acres of land in Santa Clara, California with the idea of developing one hundred acres of it into the theme park there. At first, Fess tried to team up with the local Santa Clara government but such a commercial venture was beyond its authority. He would have to fund the project with help from private investors.

Fess needed legal guidance. He hired attorney Arthur Henzell and the two quickly hit it off.

"With Fess, you almost become his friend immediately," said Henzell. "He's a warm person, a gentleman in the old-fashioned way. We clicked and over a period of time we became better friends."

Henzell recalled that Fess had initial success securing the property.

"He was able to acquire options on all this property, but he had a horrible time trying to get it financed," said Henzell. Fess saw an investment partner under the golden arches of McDonald's. And he went straight to the top: McDonald's founder, Ray Kroc.

Fess, accompanied by a lawyer from Kindel & Anderson, met Kroc at the fast-food giant's Illinois headquarters and discussed the theme park plan. Kroc listened politely to Fess, and then they went to a private dining room to eat. "Just as they were sitting down at the table—Fess told me he would never forget this—Kroc spontaneously said, 'I'll give you $50 million for a half interest in the project,'" explained Chuck Bargiel, who later became one of Fess' most trusted lawyers. "But before Fess could respond, his attorney began to 'chum' Kroc for more money and advantages. The whole thing came off as a 'what else are you going to do for us?' arrangement. Kroc was offended. He politely rebuffed the effort by Fess' attorney. They finished lunch, and that was the end of that. Fess never forgave the lawyer for blowing what he thought could have been a done deal if only he had kept his mouth shut."

But the Frontier Worlds project wasn't dead.

The Marriott Hotel group was interested but it wanted major ownership in the finished park. Fess refused the offer.

"It didn't work out so I sold the land to Marriott," said Fess. "But I was still interested in doing something in the real estate business."

Henzell negotiated the sale of the land with Marriott and remembered Fess' reaction. "The check was handed to me and I gave it to Fess," explained Henzell. "I said to him, 'I think you made a very good deal.' He didn't smile at all and said, 'But I lost my project.'"

Although the land was worth several million dollars at the time of the sale it later appreciated to unprecedented levels. "All the vacant land around the proposed theme park site is now part of Silicon Valley," said Henzell. "He had to give that up."

But he didn't give up his service to various charities and educational institutions. Fess served as Chairman of the National Cancer Society's Crusade and 1970, and served as a Director of the Santa Barbara Medical Foundation Clinic. He was presented a Doctor of Fine Arts degree in 1970 by the University of Santa Clara, where he had served as Regent Emeritus of the Board of Fellows and chaired the school's capital development campaign in the Santa Barbara area. The Fess Parker Studio Theatre at the university remains a testament to Fess' association with the institution of higher learning. Fess also served as a Trustee of the Foundation for the University of California at Santa Barbara and the Motion Picture Relief Fund.

CHAPTER 15
Show Business after "Daniel Boone"

The *Daniel Boone* series was over but Fess remained relatively active on the small screen during the early 1970s. He even made one more cameo appearance as Davy Crockett. He appeared on *The Red Skelton Show* on March 17, 1970 in a comedy sketch titled, "He Died with His Boots on Cause He Had Cold Feet to Start or He Died with His Boots Off, That's Why He Stubbed His Toe." Coincidentally, one of the show's other guests was singer Mac Davis who fifteen years later would portray Davy Crockett on Shelly Duval's TV series *Tall Tales & Legends.*

Still another TV offer came his way: *McCloud*, the drama about a modern Western lawman who travels to New York City where he takes on the bad guys. The lead, Sam McCloud, would follow in the footsteps of Walt Coogan, the character portrayed by Clint Eastwood in Don Siegel's 1968 film, *Coogan's Bluff.* Herman Miller, who co-wrote the motion picture's script, directed the new TV series. And Fess Parker seemed to be a perfect choice for the starring role.

"He was pondering the opportunity of whether it was a good idea or not," said Eli.

But Fess was going to do something that the historic Davy Crockett didn't do: he was going to spend more time at home with his family. Fess passed on the role, and it was given to Dennis Weaver, a veteran of TV's *Gunsmoke* and *Gentle Ben.* Weaver did an admirable job on the series which ran from 1970 to 1977.

"I did have kind of an idea that he was near the end of his career," said Eli. "We were sitting around the dining room table and he was wrestling with the idea of walking away from the roles that he had been associated with."

However, Fess continued to make guest appearances on a number of television programs during the early 70s. He was seen on *The Andy Williams Show, The Dean Martin Comedy Hour,* and the game show *Hollywood's Talking*.

Fess and Ron Ely crossed paths again.

"It was the spring of 1970 that we actually became well acquainted and ultimately close friends," said Ely. "I was on my way to play a tennis event in Orlando, Florida for a professional tennis player friend, John Newcombe. On the flight with me were Fess and his wife, Marcy, who as it happened were on their way to the same event. That is when we began to talk and learn about each other. It was a fairly quick-setting friendship as we learned we had so many common interests and connections in our backgrounds—not the least of which was the fact that we both came from Texas. We spent that weekend playing tennis and talking; we even flew back together to California. From that time on, I spent countless hours with Fess and Marcy. And over the years, Fess became my closest friend."

Ely introduced a fellow actor, Robert Loggia and his wife, Audrey, to Fess.

"We became close friends with Fess and Marcy about thirty years ago as a result of knowing Ron Ely, a mutual friend," explained Audrey. "We were invited to their home at Hope Ranch and had a great time. We spent several weekends there."

Loggia, who starred in the title role of Walt Disney's *The Nine Lives of Elfago Baca* in 1958, enjoyed hanging out with Fess.

"I loved the guy," said Loggia. "I loved everything about him. I especially enjoyed hanging out with him and Ron Ely. We were like the Three Musketeers."

Fess was still acting but he was also exploring a few real estate projects. In the early 1970s, he envisioned the undeveloped Goleta Slough near Goleta, California as the next Marina del Rey, a place that would feature moorings for boats, hotels, and restaurants. Since coastal development involved the Army Corps of Engineers and the federal government, he once again went straight to the top for help: he telephoned the President of the United States.

"Fess was in Art Henzell's office and asked the receptionist at the White House to get President Nixon on the phone," explained Bargiel. "She called back to apologize that the President wasn't available but she said she had Rosemary Woods on the phone." Woods, President Richard Nixon's personal secretary, who would later gain notoriety when she confessed to erasing a portion of a crucial White House tape recording during the Watergate investigation, informed Fess that General Alexander Haig, White House Chief of Staff, would take his call.

Henzell was astonished at Fess' influence. "I almost fell out of my chair," laughed Henzell. Fess conversed with Haig but found out he would be unable to assist him in his effort to develop the project. Years later, Fess made a direct call to Secretary of Defense Donald Rumsfeld during the George W. Bush administration on another matter. That was part of Fess' approach to business matters: talk to the highest-ranking person first.

Fess continued to explore various real estate projects and his business savvy was viewed with interest by UCLA which invited him to lecture about his mobile home parks during the fall semester of 1970.

The last film Fess worked in was *Climb an Angry Mountain*, a TV movie which aired on December 23, 1972. Fess' character is an old-school California law man on the trail of a fugitive, Joey Chilko (Joe Kapp). The story is compounded by a New York cop (Barry Nelson), who has different ways of doing things, and the fugitive's hostage: Sheriff Cooper's son, Michael (Clay O'Brien). The cast also included Arthur Hunnicutt, who portrayed Davy Crockett in *The Last Command* (1955).

"I can tell you that it was not very comfortable working in January on the 11,500-foot level slopes of Mount Shasta in northern California for *Climb an Angry Mountain*," said Fess. "I know we experienced a white out on the set because of the snow and wind; it was quite dangerous. As for Arthur Hunnicutt, I don't know if it was the first time I worked with him in a film. But he was quite a good actor; in fact, he was a very strong character actor." Actually, Hunnicutt had appeared on *Daniel Boone* as a character named Gabe in a 1966 episode titled "Run A Crooked Mile."

Climb and Angry Mountain was repeated on NBC-TV's *Saturday Night at the Movies* program on June 1, 1974. The movie's publicity promo stated: "Fess Parker stars as Elisha Cooper, a widowed California rancher who supplements his meager income by working as a sheriff."

Fess also became a real life rancher.

"He purchased the property somewhere around 1972 or 1973," said Eli.

"It was a time when I started to acquire land around Santa Barbara," added Fess.

"The ranch was called Rancho de las Dos Hermanas," explained Eli. "It was 2,514 acres and was located on Highway 166, just outside of Santa Maria, California. We spent many great weekends out there riding motor cycles and working cattle. Great memories!"

Ashley also enjoyed spending time at the ranch.

"We used to go camping up there, work cattle, and drive around in an old Army jeep," said Ashley. "It was awesome."

Fess and Marcy lived in a number of houses during their marriage, from Beverly Hills to Palm Springs, but they settled into a wonderful home in Hope Ranch in Santa Barbara, a place that exceeded their expectations.

"The house was 14,000 square feet with an Olympic-sized swimming pool and tennis court on eighteen acres," stated Marcy. "And we had an eleven-car garage. We had a few cars, a tractor, and a jeep. But the garage came in handy when we had guests or entertained, and we entertained everyone there, including the Reagans. We were there from around 1972 to 1984. The house itself had seven bedrooms upstairs and two downstairs bedrooms. On the property were two guest houses. It was absolutely phenomenal; it was my favorite house."

And Santa Barbara was Fess' favorite community.

"What they say about Santa Barbara is that when you die and go to heaven you won't like it: you'd rather be in Santa Barbara," said Fess in an interview years later. He spread the word about Santa Barbara's beauty to Peter Ellenshaw and his wife who eventually moved there. "It was Fess who introduced me to life in Santa Barbara," stated Ellenshaw. "It was truly beautiful."

Fess' last acting job was for *The Fess Parker Show*, a 1974 Don Fedderson production that featured him as Fess Hamilton, a recently-widowed construction foreman who is having a difficult time raising his three daughters: Susie, 16 (Cindy Eilbacher), Beth (Dawn Lynn), and Holly, 6, (Michelle Stacy). His best friend, Boomer (Norman Alden), who is also widowed, has three sons.

John McGreevey, who had written other on-screen situations for another widower-lead family in *My Three Sons*, wrote the first draft of the pilot, "The Essential Susie," on December 10, 1973. He penned rewrites of the teleplay on January 7, 22, 25, and 29. Shooting started several days later.

The half-hour show aired on March 28, 1974 as the first of four CBS-TV "Four Funny Families" pilots. *The Fess Parker Show* aired at 9 p.m. and was followed by *Dominic's Dream* (9:30), *Pete 'n' Tillie* (10 p.m.), and *Change at 125th Street* (10:30).

The Fess Parker Show story line revolves around Fess' oldest daughter, Susie, who suffers through the pains of teenage romance and anti-establishment lectures from one of her friends. The pilot also included a story line about daughter Beth and an unscrupulous businessman named Johnson (Woodrow Parfrey) who sells tomato seed packages. McGreevey added Julie Weston (Linda Dano) as Parker's love interest, a loveable mutt named Amby, and a quirky old housekeeper named Mrs. Esther Crowe (Florence Lake) to the teleplay.

The major problem with *The Fess Parker Show* was that its multi-family story line had been produced before in a number of series which audiences had lost interest in; as a matter of fact, *The Brady Bunch*, which debuted in 1969, and *The Partridge Family*, which first aired in 1970, both ended production in 1974.

Fess' last lines in the pilot became the final professional acting lines of his career: "And one thing I never do is argue with a liberated lady!"

Although the pilot wasn't picked up by any network, Fess took the decision in stride. "I learned that if they name a show with your real name, it was the end," he joked.

But not quite the end.

"Somewhere around 1974, one of the networks approached Fess about returning to TV for another series," stated Ely. "I remember discussing it with him, and he did not seem too keen on getting back in to the game. The series, as I remember it, was about a logging family and Fess was to be the patriarch. Obviously, he did not accept it and the series did not go forward."

On January 27, 1975, Bill Walsh, the producer of the *Davy Crockett* series, died.

"Fess gave the eulogy when Bill died, too," said Fishman. "And years later when Fess was honored at Disneyland, he invited my son, David, and me to go with his family because he thought that Bill's contributions had long been ignored by the company. He had us stand up and introduced us and described Bill's credits. I appreciated that."

CHAPTER 16
"AFTER SUNDOWN"

While he was working on *Daniel Boone*, Fess was fascinated by a short story he read in *True* magazine titled "The Apaches vs. the Sodbuster."

According to the article's author, Bill Hafford, the story was based upon an oral history account told in 1940 by an old Apache named Billy Goat John who had described in graphic detail how two settlers held off an Apache attack in 1864.

Fess thought the three-page story would make a terrific movie and he turned it into a screenplay.

"I adapted it from a story written by Bill Hafford," said Fess. "It was based on a true story, a story about an older man on a ranch that he built in Arizona. It's a story about how he and his wife survived an Apache attack during the Civil War when there were few soldiers in the West. But these are not blood-thirsty savages; they have their own internal problems."

The main characters in the screenplay were Martin and Rosa Baylock. Fess described Martin as "a tall, lanky man with a stubble of red beard" and Rosa as a woman with "dark Mexican features ...high cheekbones and incongruous blue eyes that sparkle, even with fatigue." Their primary antagonists were Delsha, Maasi, and Haskay, determined Apache warriors who, according to a screenplay note, would speak Apache in the film. Supporting characters named Bob Hayes and Amos Jennings, augmented Fess' script.

Fess finished the screenplay during mid-1967 after *Daniel Boone* finished filming the last episode of the series' third season. Through 111 pages and 464 camera positions, Fess' characters displayed behavior in *After Sundown* that had clearly been missing on *Daniel*

Boone. Like "The Apaches vs. the Sodbuster," Fess' screenplay was filled with graphic language and violence. For example, in scene number 68, Delsha promises, "They will not die easy deaths. They will die very slowly…and I will be the one who peels the skin from their bodies. My knife…and my knife only…will touch their flesh." In scene number 186, Maasi stands next to a fallen prospector and instructs his fellow warriors to "strip the clothes from him, then stake him to the ground and cut his eyelids away." And the screenplay's final action-packed battle is filled with descriptive blood and gore.

Fess gave his screenplay to his literary agent, Evarts Ziegler, who promptly shopped it around to a number of production companies and actors.

Surprisingly, one of the first actors considered for the film was the Japanese performer Toshiro Mifune, who appeared in such classic motion pictures as *Seven Samurai* and *Rashomon*. On August 17, 1967, Ziegler sent a copy of the script to the Beverly Hills law office that represented Mifune. One week later, the firm acknowledged receipt of the screenplay and promised to submit it to the busy actor who was slated to work in two films that would carry through July 1, 1968. The surviving correspondence did not identify what role Fess wanted Mifune for but it was probably the Apache lead, Delsha. In any event, there was no reply from the actor. Fess put *After Sundown* on the back burner until *Daniel Boone* was in its last season.

A pitch to MCA Studios producer Jennings Lang in early 1970 resulted in the following letter to Fess on February 10, 1970: "While we feel that you do have writing talent and that your story is quite absorbing, we unfortunately have a number of projects similar to this one already in the works."

Of course, MCA did not "have a number of similar projects" about a besieged frontier couple "in the works." It was obvious that MCA wasn't interested. However, Fess replied with a diplomatic letter eight days later in which he said to Lang, "I am glad that you like the story and I appreciate your comment as to my writing talent. Hopefully, we will have it under way relatively soon."

Fess had noted in his letter that he expected a production "understanding with Steven Broidy," the head of Motion Picture International. "Before long we hope to have it off the ground," added

Fess optimistically. But that didn't happen either.

More copies of the script were sent to other studios.

Richard E. Lyons, who produced the 1962 Western *Ride the High Country*, wrote back from his MGM office on August 10, 1970. "*After Sundown* is quite a script," noted Lyons, who sent a copy of his message to *Rounders* Director Burt Kennedy. "I've read my share of Westerns over the years but can't remember many that top this for mood, inventive off-beat action, and the Goddamndest hundred and eleven pages of two people trying to stay alive for a principle that I've ever read. With all the paperweight material hitting the screen these days this script has to be made."

Despite his enthusiasm, Lyons didn't say that he would make the film.

In April 1971, Fess sent a copy of *After Sundown* to Charles D. Champlain, the Entertainment Editor of the *Los Angeles Times*, and followed it up with a lunch date with the writer. He waited months for a reply and finally got one on September 7. Champlain stated that the script was "a professional job" and was filled with "suspense, surprise and action." But he added, "It's not my cup of tea."

Champlain pointed out that the violence in the script "does not sit as well as it used to, and the reason, I believe, is that we are no longer so naïve (as audiences) as we used to be."

Finally, Champlain got to the point rather bluntly: "To me, it just seems a bit late for *After Sundown*. It tells us nothing new and indeed relies on a fairly stereotyped basic situation—nice white settlers imperiled by senselessly cruel redskins."

Fess was disappointed with Champlain's comments but not discouraged. He knocked at MGM's door again. But this time, he went straight to the top. He sent a copy of the screenplay to George L. Killion, MGM's Chairman of the Board. On October 6, 1971, Killion wrote Fess and told him that he would read the script and pass it on to Doug Netter, MGM's Executive Vice President and Chief Operating Officer. "I am hopeful that MGM will express great interest in the property and I shall certainly keep you advised," concluded Killion.

Netter read the script and penned a quick note to Killion on November 15, 1971. "I appreciate very much your submitting *After Sundown*," wrote Netter. "We have reviewed the screenplay carefully again as it was submitted to us twice before and do not believe it is a picture that we would like to do at this time."

Another rejection.

Fess also approached Stan Kamen of the William Morris Agency.

"I believe the first question to be answered is—do you agree this to be material which would be of interest to you?" asked Fess in a letter dated October 8, 1971. "If you like the material my proposal is that my production company would produce and supply the director. I would play the role of Martin."

The William Morris Agency also passed on the project.

With no interest from the major studios, Fess sought assistance from International Cinema, a Louisiana-based production, advertising, and distribution company. He met representatives from the small firm as a result of a previous appearance he had made at Frontier Days, an event held during Colfax, Louisiana's Pecan Festival.

International Cinema's Gordon C. Ogden replied to Fess on April 12, 1973, with a pathetic low-budget reply: "I agree with you that your film could be very successful but as I told you at the Pecan Festival, our group is not interested in producing another film until more positive results are forthcoming on *The Player*."

The Pecan Festival? *The Player?*

Fess was getting desperate but he was not giving up, so the wild frontier king contacted a duke: John Wayne. But Fess didn't want to be the first to contact Wayne about *After Sundown*. He thought that if someone else enthusiastically recommended the project Wayne might agree to do it via his Batjac Production company. Fess dictated a note to his secretary, Karla Grady, who sent it to Olive Carey, the widow of Wayne's on-screen mentor, Harry Carey. He also sent Carey a copy of the screenplay and later discussed the project with her over the phone. Fess followed with a note on August 24, 1973: "If you care to follow through on our conversation, please forward this on to Duke," he wrote. "Would value his opinion." However, Wayne was involved with his next film, *McQ*, and passed on *After Sundown*.

Fess was also involved in *The Fess Parker Show* pilot during the winter of 1973–74, and when the program wasn't picked up he refocused his attention on *After Sundown*. He considered shooting locations in the Southwest and contacted Ruth W. Armstrong, the

Director of the New Mexico Motion Picture Industries Commission, about potential filming sites. Armstrong, who worked out of Governor Bruce King's office in Santa Fe, sent Fess the commission's Local Manual and additional literature about the state. "Mrs. Agnes Dill, a member of our N. M. Motion Picture Industry Commission, is a member of the Isleta (pueblo) Tribe, President of the American Indian Women's Association, and one whose judgement I trust," wrote Armstrong in an April 19, 1974 letter to Fess. "With your permission I will ask her to read the script with me, and let you know if we think it will be offensive to today's Indian people."

Fess sent a copy of *After Sundown* and a note to Armstrong on April 22.

"I appreciate your approach, cooperation, interest and your candor," he wrote. "Obviously, I am excited at the thought of going through with this film and will be grateful for your thoughts and assistance."

And then Fess heard from Agnes Dill.

"The Apaches were cruel and very revengeful, but I can't imagine they did all the story says, such as what they did to the eyes," stated Dill to Armstrong, who forwarded the comments to Fess in May 7, 1974 letter. "I just can't say if it is really a true representation of the period it is trying to depict. It may be a good movie to some people and could be very popular."

Armstrong added some comments of her own.

"The settlers wanted to *own* the land to work it, to graze cattle on it, to fence it in," she wrote. "The Apaches did not think of 'owning' the land—they passed over it, hunting, riding, moving from place to place, occasionally forming into clusters of shelters for a season or two. Any intrusion into the vast area through which they roamed, whether by white man or another Indian tribe, was an encroachment on their domain. Four generations later, descendants of these people still live in New Mexico and each believes his ancestors were right."

Despite the criticism, Armstrong concluded her letter on an upbeat note.

"I liked your script," she confessed. "I have to admit, there is more violence in it than I care for personally, but that is only my opinion and I am no critic." Armstrong provided Fess with information about Apache Reservations and location sites. She stated that her office would "be delighted" to transport him around to possible shooting locations.

Fess finally found a potential financial backer for his project. He was pleasantly surprised to discover from Armstrong that one of tribes had financed a motion picture a few years earlier. The 1971 Paramount Pictures film, *A Gunfight*, which starred Kirk Douglas and Johnny Cash, was produced by the Jicarilla Apache Tribe, known to historians as the only tribe that failed to provide assistance to the Federal government when the U.S. Cavalry tried to capture the celebrated warrior Geronimo.

On May 10, 1974, Fess sent a letter to Wallace P. Wolf at the Pacht, Ross, Warne, Bernhard & Sears legal firm in Los Angeles and informed him that Armstrong was "going to contact the Jicarillas with regard to their feelings about cooperating and doing the film."

A week later, Armstrong followed up with a letter to Fess.

"I have talked with Richard Tecube, director of Industrial development for the Jicarilla Apache Tribe about your project," wrote Armstrong. "He discussed it at a meeting of his development committee and he said they are interested. He did not ask a single question about the script, so I did not pursue it. At the very beginning of the conversation, I told him the period, gave him a very brief idea of the story and let it go at that."

Armstrong provided more encouragement.

"I know you can make the film and we would be happy to work with you anyplace in the state," she added. "There are plenty of Indian people who would like to work with you also. It is wonderful of you to be so concerned about their opinion of the story."

On May 20, Wolf informed Fess that he was excited that Armstrong liked the script and was willing to approach the Jicarilla Tribe. He told Fess that he "did the production work" on *A Gunfight*.

"The film did not do sensational business, but it is anticipated that when the television sale is totally paid for the Jicarillas will have totally recouped their negative cost contribution of $2,000,000," noted Wolf, who also informed Fess that he would be willing to "discuss" all matters regarding *A Gunfight*.

While preliminary negotiations began between Fess and the Jicarillas, Armstrong scouted various locations in New Mexico.

"I was in Santa Fe for three days over the 4th of July holiday," wrote Armstrong to Fess on July 10. "While there, I was taken to the Jemez Pueblo also was impressed in the possibility en route to Jemez of a pueblo about 22 miles out of Santa Fe along the river. We are moving slowly, but with optimism."

Fess had also flown to New Mexico during the July 4, 1974 weekend.

"Sorry I didn't see you when you were in New Mexico," wrote Armstrong on July 16. "You may want to look at other areas, such as the Las Vegas area or the Mescalero-Apache country in the south-eastern part of the state." She organized ten color photos of the terrain outside of Las Vegas, which was situated about sixty-five miles east of Santa Fe, and sent them to Fess as side-by-side images which helped depict the panorama of the pristine region.

Fess was informed through Armstrong that Tecube had suggested that his tribe provide "a mature, knowledgeable person as a technical advisor and perhaps a half dozen grown men, various ages, as actors." Fess responded on July 10, and told Tecube that the "film would give an opportunity for ten or twelve men and a small group of women or children." Fess added that he was "excited about seeing the people and their countryside."

Several months later discussions continued between Fess and the Jicarilla Tribe. Although no documentation can be found, some sort of an agreement was arrived at—either with the tribe or an entity known as Cine Group—because Fess approved a Production Budget on May 24, 1975. It appeared that *After Sundown* was going to be made after all.

A twenty-eight-page Direct Picture Cost-Budget included everything except the named individuals who would compose the cast and crew. One exception: Fess Parker was identified as the Writer and the Producer. He would receive $25,000 for each job description.

Principal photography was scheduled for twenty-eight days and the production headquarters would be in Albuquerque. The unnamed Director would receive $35,000. The actor who played Martin Baylock would earn $25,000, the actress who portrayed Rosa Baylock would receive $15,000, and the actor who played Delsha would be paid $10,000.

The supporting cast salaries ranged from $2,250 for the Bob Hayes and Amos Jennings characters to $4,000 for the roles of Haskay and Maasi. Day players would earn $173. An additional $10,400 was allotted for stand-ins and a core band of Apaches. With stunt costs, the on-camera talent totaled $82,765.

A budget of $8,000 was allotted for the interior and exterior construction of the Baylock's adobe home complex. The cost for horses and their feed totaled $8,400, and a snake and snake handler added up to another $450. Most of the wardrobe was coming from Hollywood rental sources, but the principals would have custom items made for them. The total for all costumes, labor, cleaning, and crew was $15,850.

Fess wanted *After Sundown* to be a big screen film so he provided for Todd-AO cameras, the same equipment that was used on such epic films as John Wayne's *The Alamo.*

The entire motion picture was scheduled to be filmed within a month for a total cost of $956,451. Translated into today's adjusted-for-inflation dollars, *After Sundown* would carry a budget of nearly $4 million, a very modest amount for a modern film.

Fess was ready to go ahead with casting and other pre-production activities despite a letter that was sent from Charles A. Pratt of Bing Crosby Productions to Rowland Perkins at the William Morris Agency. "Enclosed I am returning subject screenplay," wrote Pratt. "The theatrical market for westerns today is dead as a doornail and BCP will have to pass on this one."

The letter was prophetic. The financing never materialized and *After Sundown* became dead as a doornail.

Or was it?

CHAPTER 17
"DANIEL BOONE" AND HOTEL HEADACHES

It had been a remarkable twenty-year run of TV for Fess since the debut of "Davy Crockett, Indian Fighter." And although his frontier hero days were behind him, his frontier hero headaches had just begun.

Besides his salary and residuals from *Daniel Boone,* Fess' deal made him partners with the studio, Twentieth Century Fox, and the Executive Producer, Aaron Rosenberg, and included ownership of the 165 episodes that were produced plus a share of the series' net profits. But he never received any net profits. He turned to his friend and lawyer Art Henzell, who represented him in business and real estate ventures once Fess had moved to Santa Barbara, and to Chuck Bargiel, a new young lawyer at the firm. Bargiel, had first met Fess in 1977, when he saw him sitting in a conference room at the law firm of Cavaletto, Webster, Mullen & McCaughey, which became Mullen, McCaughey and Henzell in 1982, and later, in 1991, Mullen & Henzell. Bargiel joined the firm as its newest associate when he moved to Santa Barbara from Chicago in 1976. "Fess spoke to Art Henzell, Art called me in, handed me copies of the contracts and the accountings, and asked if I would look into it," said Bargiel. "I was excited as I could be to be able to do legal work for my boyhood hero."

With Bargiel as his legal sidekick, Fess sued Twentieth Century Fox.

The litigation was very public.

The battle even made it to nationwide television when it was examined in a *60 Minutes* segment titled "We're in the Money?" a few weeks before Christmas in 1980. Harry Reasoner introduced the program with an explanation of what "creative bookkeeping" in

Filming "We're in the Money?" segment for *60 Minutes* (L to R): Arthur Henzel; Mike Wallace; Marion Golden, segment producer; Fess Parker; and Chuck Bargiel.
PHOTO COURTESY OF CHUCK BARGIEL.

Hollywood was all about: "bookkeeping that guarantees that no matter how successful a television series or a feature film, it may never earn a dime in profit for the actor, the writer or the director who was supposed to share in that profit." Fess and fellow actor James Garner were interviewed separately by *60 Minutes* correspondent Mike Wallace who visited the actors at their respective homes earlier that summer.

"I believe that when my attorneys have an opportunity to present this before a jury and a judge I think we will be able to show it wouldn't have made any difference if I had had ninety nine and nine-tenths percent of the net profits," declared Fess. Wallace later stated that *Daniel Boone* "grossed almost forty million dollars" but was "still more than a million dollars in the red."

"The salary that I did take was less than I could have taken had I not gone the participation route," said Fess, who noted that he made $5,000 an episode. "My contemporaries were making from twelve to eighteen thousand an episode. When a venture, a joint venture, between a major corporation, such as Twentieth Century Fox, NBC, and a top producer, such as Aaron Rosenberg—when we came together and that venture produced forty million, and Aaron and I between us did not get two cents—that's a penny apiece—on the face of that, something is wrong."

At Fess' insistence, and to the consternation of his law firm, Chuck Bargiel sat next to him on the show and explained to Wallace what his client's next step would be. He cloaked his reply to a Wallace remark about "barefoot boys" going up against experienced Hollywood legal departments with an obvious touch of pure Davy Crockett. "Well, Mike, when Fess and I go to Los Angeles on this case, we both put our shoes on," said Bargiel. "And I'll tell you something very candidly about that, sir. When I was seven years old, I first met Mr. Parker on a television screen along with another generation, a whole generation of American youth. And he told me something. He said, 'Be sure you're right and then go ahead.' He still feels the same way about it. So do I. We're sure we're right, we will go ahead."

Finally, with Bargiel's help, Fess and Twentieth Century Fox negotiated an out-of-court settlement that was amicable and a confidentiality agreement.

Having made peace with his Twentieth Century Fox, it was time for Fess to move on.

Fess Parker's entertainment career may have ended, but he already was well into another professional phase of his career: real estate development. A 32 ½ acre parcel of undeveloped beachfront property in his adopted hometown of Santa Barbara interested him.

"I had been living in Santa Barbara for sixteen years and I wondered why that property hadn't been developed," recalled Fess in the October/November 1985 issue of *Santa Barbara Magazine*. "In 1976, I asked about it."

On December 15, 1976, the 22nd anniversary of the "Davy Crockett, Indian Fighter" broadcast, Fess signed an agreement with the Santa Barbara Cabrillo Corporation, a subsidiary of the Southern Pacific Railroad, which gave him an option to purchase 32½ acres of waterfront property in Santa Barbara where earlier in the century two locomotive roundhouses once stood. The first one had been destroyed by an earthquake in 1925, but the damaged structure was rebuilt in the style of the *Plaza de Toros de la Real Maetranza*, the famous bullring in Seville, Spain. The Southern Pacific Railroad used the roundhouse facility until 1961. The locomotive turntable was then removed by the railroad and the building was converted into a warehouse, which eventually went into a state of non use and disrepair.

The so-called East Beach waterfront area where the 32 ½ acre parcel was located had been the focal point of various park development efforts since the 1920s. In 1924, area residents formed the East Boulevard Improvement Association and with the help of the local chamber of commerce obtained assistance from the Olmsted Brothers, the architectural landscape designers who had shaped the appearance of college campuses, state and local parks, and government grounds across the United States. Interestingly enough, the Olmsted Brothers designed the roadways in the Great Smoky Mountains, the same place where Fess had filmed parts of *Davy Crockett*.

The Great Depression and World War II placed park development plans on hold. In 1964, the Santa Barbara City Council essentially reaffirmed the vision of the Olmsted Brothers, but that view of the future from the distant past had been replaced by deteriorated area that became a haven for drifters. However, cognizant of the sad condition of the acreage, seven years later the government body altered its vision of the area by adopting a study recommendation that included the development of "specialized motel facilities" and an "urban conference center."

Fess' early plans for the site included a 500-room luxury hotel, a 1,500-seat conference center, tennis courts, 200 condominium units, and large underground parking area. The completed development originally was planned to be managed by the Hyatt Corporation. Extending his hand is a reciprocal way, Fess promised to donate several acres of the property to nearby Palm Park if the Santa Barbara City Council would add seven acres to the recreational area. But his plan met immediate resistance from those who opposed virtually any commercial development along the waterfront, particularly environmentalists who recalled the impact of the 1969 Santa Barbara off-shore oil spill. Fess faced another lengthy and formidable challenge: besides the human opposition forces were layers of government bureaucracy which easily could discourage most developers. But not Fess.

Fess called upon his lawyer, Arthur Henzell, to help him navigate through the choppy legal waters that lay ahead.

Confronted with questions and concerns raised by the environmentalists, the politics of the Santa Barbara City Council, the statewide pressures of the South Coast Regional Coastal Commission, and the local Environmental Hearing Board, Henzell flat out told Parker that he could not succeed.

"He appreciated my advice," said Henzell. "I'm a very conservative guy; he was a visionary. When I thought he was off the mark, I told him. I told him, by the way, that he would never be able to develop the hotel on the beach which is now there. I thought Fess was, obviously, not as mature with regard to business matters probably at the beginning, like none of us are. But Fess has always been able to accomplish these things. He's so personable."

Not long after Fess took up the challenge after being advised by Henzell, Dave Davis became Santa Barbara's City Planner in 1978. Davis was a *Davy Crockett* fan. As a youngster, Davis had a *Davy Crockett*-themed birthday party in 1956, and even made his parents stop at the Alamo during the family move from Louisiana to California. "On day one I walked into my office in Santa Barbara and sitting at my desk is *Davy Crockett*," said Davis. "He is so charming and disengaging—one hell of a charming guy. He just wanted to welcome me to Santa Barbara. We talked for about an hour." Although pleasantly surprised by Fess' visit, Davis thought it un-businesslike to explain his childhood affection for *Davy Crockett.* Since he represented the city he always maintained a distance from Fess. "I was always an arms-length away—and this is the way it should be between the regulator and client," said Davis.

The California Coastal Commission further complicated Fess' plan by instituting a halt on projects that negatively could affect what were called local coastal plans. However, Fess believed that his development plan—which he called The Santa Barbara Park Plaza Project—would not have an adverse impact. Moreover, he believed that the project description was congruent with the guidelines established by the State Coastal Commission. Fess, who had modified his plan by reducing the size of the conference center from 1,500 to

1,000 seats, wanted cut through the red tape and explain his project directly to the State Coastal Commission instead of going through the city council. But the Santa Barbara City Council voted four to three against Fess' modified conceptual plan and blocked his effort to speak directly with the Coastal Commission. Fess was angry and publicly threatened to abandon the project entirely. But he later calmed down and told the *Santa Barbara News-Press* in its January 23, 1980 issue that, "I certainly won't abandon my interest in the property."

Undeterred and embracing Davy Crockett's motto—"Be always sure you're right, then go ahead"—Fess revised his original plan and his modified plan and submitted yet a new one. "I have had so much encouragement that I just cannot quit," said Fess in the January 31, 1980 edition of the *Santa Barbara News-Press*. "I continue to look forward to a good faith and objective comparison of my plan to what the opponents of my project would have, and what the possibilities can mean in the years to come." Aware of the overall economic environment, Fess added: "I have no reason at this time to believe there has been a thorough and objective study of the pros and cons, no balancing of advantages to the City in dollars, in housing, and in renewed economic vitality affecting the entire South Coast."

Despite his conflict with the City Council and other government agencies over his project Fess was still named the Grand Marshall of the 1980 Santa Barbara Old Spanish Days Fiesta Parade, an annual event which began in 1924. He made a political statement when he rode in the procession on a mule which he called "City Council."

With the national economy suffering from high unemployment and inflation, local business groups began to organize around him because they believed that Fess' project would be beneficial to the community. The Downtown Organization, for example, saw a hotel and a conference center as a way for Santa Barbara to generate jobs and tax revenue.

Seemingly energized by the inauguration of his good friend, Ronald Reagan, as President in 1981, Fess viewed the New Year with renewed optimism. Upbeat and strategically conciliatory, he made his plan more appealing to the local government and others by eliminating the underground parking garage and 100 hotel rooms. The city's Environmental Review Committee accepted the plan. When it did, Fess exercised his option and purchased the 32 ½ acre Southern Pacific Railroad property. He subsequently submitted an official—not conceptual—plan to the city council for approval.

Davis' office raised concerns over several issues including traffic, building size, "view corridors" from the beach below and "view issues" from the hillsides above. Once again, avoiding the bureaucratic red tape that a written debate would generate, Fess responded in person. And on numerous occasions the two would engage in spirited debates and difficult discussions over the potential development of the waterfront property.

"In his dealings with me, he was always straight forward," said Davis. "He was always a gentleman, a real gentleman. He would charm everybody in the office when he walked in—not just by his personality as a celebrity but by his personality as a human being."

Additional details complicated the rough-and-tumble wrangling among Fess, the City Council, Davis' office, the environmentalists, and others: sub-divisions creations, rezoning; hotel, conference center and parking facility designs; open space; and landscaping. A public meeting was held on May 14, 1981. Those who opposed Fess' plan cited its size and the resulting motor vehicle traffic; those who supported him mentioned the economic benefits of the hotel and convention center. Public debate raged for months in the *Santa Barbara News-Press*. In the meantime, Fess served as Honorary Chairman for his community's United Way Campaign.

Fess sensed that for the most part public opinion was in his corner. While he was steadfast on certain aspects of his plan he was still willing to compromise somewhat in order to get his plan approved. The City Planning Commission's major issue involved the maximum number of hotel rooms. Fess originally wanted 500 rooms, but he later scaled that down to 400; he finally agreed to 360. In June, the Planning Commission voted five to one to approve Fess' Santa Barbara Park Plaza Project. A month later, after public hearings, the City Council concurred with the Commission in a six to one vote.

Fess' focus on the project temporarily halted when Bargiel suddenly took ill.

"It was on a Friday night in early December of 1982 when I had an appendicitis attack," said Bargiel. "They did the surgery on Saturday and on Sunday I was pretty much out of it. On Monday morning I awoke in my hospital bed and there sat Fess Parker in my room with a copy of the newspaper. 'I just wanted to make sure you got your morning paper,' he said to me. And every morning that week when I awoke, Fess Parker was there with my newspaper. It's the first time in my life that I enjoyed any celebrity because I became known throughout the hospital as the man to whom Fess Parker brought his morning paper."

Bargiel recovered but another legal matter presented itself.

Although the Santa Barbara City Council had approved Fess' plan, others in town challenged the decision. Fred Eissler, who created a one-member entity called Scenic Shoreline Preservation, circulated a petition which sought to place the issue directly in the hands of the voters. Eissler contended that a referendum by a vote of the public should decide whether the hotel should be built. The petition was circulated to obtain enough signatures to get the question on a ballot. The effort was supported by Helen Yost, President of Santa Barbara's League of Women Voters. The signatures were collected and presented to town clerk Richard D. Thomas, who was expected to count and verify the signatures. But it was the city attorney who had the authority to decide if the question was to be on the ballot. Thomas refused to count the signatures at the instruction of the city attorney since he considered the issue not subject to a referendum. A lawsuit was filed to have the clerk count the signatures and Fess won in Superior Court. However, on further appeal in *Yost v. Thomas* (1984), the Supreme Court of California reversed the lower court decisions. In its decision, the Supreme Court declared that the "City Council of Santa Barbara was acting legislatively" in approving Fess' project and, as a result, the decision by the city council was "subject to the normal referendum procedure."

Fess was stymied yet again. But he was sure he was right. He went ahead.

The referendum was set for a vote and both sides drummed up their respective support but a non-related legislative decision interfered with the timing of the vote.

Martin Luther King, Jr. Day had been signed into federal law on November 2, 1983, by President Reagan. The holiday would be celebrated every year on the third Monday in January, which coincided with King's January 15th birthday. But not every state followed the federal holiday; as a matter of fact, it wasn't until 2000 that all the states officially acknowledged the celebrated Civil Rights leader's birthday.

"Between the time the City Council acted and the January 22, 1985 date, the California Legislature—in the fall of 1984—designated Martin Luther King as a State holiday to be celebrated on the third Monday in January," explained Davis.

And that created a problem for the date on which the referendum could be held.

"But the city council had set the third Tuesday in January for the referendum question," said Bargiel, who understood that local elections could not be held on the same day as the holiday or the day before or after.

"The law said that you could not have a vote or election on the day before or after a holiday," confirmed Davis. "The referendum was delayed again."

The referendum was postponed for two months. Fess had to wait one more time.

"Fess tore his hair out once again," said Henzell.

Finally, the referendum took place on March 12, 1985.

"He won overwhelmingly," said Henzell. According to a newspaper report, 72% of the voters, 16,594, favored Fess' plan, and only 6,359 opposed it.

Fess brought another attorney into the project: Chuck Bargiel.

"Fess said, 'I want you to draft a joint venture agreement and a management agreement for this new hotel if we go with the Red Lion people,'" said Bargiel. "And I said, 'I'm honored that you would want me to do that, but I don't know my butt from my elbow about such things.' Fess said, 'I know you don't. Here's the textbook by the Cornell School of Hotel Administration. Read the book, look at the appendices and you can do this! You're a smart guy.' So I did it."

Bargiel developed both agreements—each forty-five pages thick—for Fess and the Red Lion Hotels Corporation. A key aspect of the deal was that Fess negotiated a $32 million construction price-tag cap for the hotel because he believed that construction costs would eventually top that mark. If costs went above that, Red Lion interests would be responsible. Bargiel called it typical Fess "good horse-trading."

But another roadblock popped up.

As Fess realized, actual construction costs were going to top the $32 million mark but representatives from the Red Lion didn't want to be responsible for it despite the contract.

"Fess replied, 'In a pig's eye,'" said Bargiel. Red Lion refused to budge. The matter went to arbitration before a three-member panel that included a lawyer, a certified public accountant, and an architect. The arbitration went on for forty-two day-long sessions spread out over months from January through July of 1986.

"Every Tuesday, Wednesday, and Thursday we would meet at the Biltmore Hotel in Montecito," said Bargiel. Then the arbitrators came up with the idea to compare and contrast various hotels in the company's chain that had been shown to Fess by the Red Lion principals, Pietz and McClasky, before they made and signed their deal in early 1982. So a decision was made to visit a dozen of them. "One week we all went hotel hopping," said Bargiel. "We leased a Lear jet for the arbitrators and the rest of us flew in the Red Lion's jet, which I recall was a Cessna Citation, and went to Red Lion hotels in places like Seattle, Portland, Sacramento, and San Jose."

The arbitration board examined their comparative data and rendered a decision.

"They went for Fess!" exclaimed Bargiel. "The board upheld the contract and the guaranteed maximum with the exception an additional $135,000 which was designated to add glass to the arches around the Plaza that had been added by the city after the contract was signed." And the decision awarded attorney fees and expenses for Fess.

"It was finally over," said Bargiel. "Finally."

As fate would have it, one minute skirmish erupted on the local level.

"The Architectural Board Review and the Landmark Commission each had two separate meetings where the principle issue on the agenda for the project was whether the cyclone fence around the construction site was to be black or green," mused Bargiel.

A view of the Pacific Ocean from the Fess Parker Doubletree Resort in Santa Barbara, California.
PHOTO COURTESY OF THE PARKER FAMILY.

Fess Parker's Red Lion Resort opened in 1987, eleven years after Fess purchased options to buy the property from the Southern Pacific Railroad. The facility was later renamed Fess Parker's Doubletree Resort after Red Lion sold its interest. The beautiful Spanish colonial-styled facility, which offers views of the ocean and the Santa Ynez Mountains, features four restaurants and numerous recreational activities. "I started with the Red Lion Hotels Corporation and now with the Doubletree we're partnered with the Hilton Corporation," said Fess.

Years later, Dave Davis retired from public service.

"I remember my last day on the job," said Davis. "My last day at work, Friday, August 30, 2002, concluded with a party to celebrate my leaving the employment of City of Santa Barbara after almost twenty-five years. Where else would I want that party to be but in the new Chase Palm Park expansion created through the City's partnership with Fess. He had donated the western half of the property to the City and the park was developed by City Redevelopment Agency which was part of my Department's responsibilities. The party was held in the large grassy amphitheater area on the east end of the park. As I and my family—wife, our two kids, my siblings, and their kids—were approaching the gathering from the west just past the children's play area, there was Fess, standing alone to the side. He stepped out to greet us, graciously introduced himself to the family, and then pulled me aside to say he wouldn't be staying for the party. But he had one last item of business for me: he wanted to personally congratulate me, let me know that he had highly valued our working relationship, even through all of the hotly-contested battles and arguments over the development of the area; he sincerely hoped we'd continue that relationship now on the basis of our personal friendship. He presented me with a bottle of his wine, one that he said he hoped I'd enjoy with my family on this special day. We drank that bottle at the table that evening, with a special toast to my friend, Fess Parker."

After Fess Parker's Red Lion Resort was built, Fess and his Red Lion partners refinanced the property.

"Fess' first refinance of the hotel allowed him to acquire acreage in the Santa Ynez Valley," said Bargiel. With the proceeds, Fess purchased a 714-acre ranch in Los Olivos, in Santa Barbara's Santa Ynez Valley. But Fess had no intention of raising horses or cattle on the land. He had other plans.

"The best is yet to come," he said confidently.

CHAPTER 18
NOSTALGIA AND RECOGNITION

On September 13, 1978, Fess and Buddy Ebsen were among the special guests on *NBC Salutes the 25th Anniversary of the Wonderful World of Disney*. The pair, dressed in handsome business suits, reminisced about the *Davy Crockett* series. The segment included a portion of the October 27, 1954 *Disneyland* show in which Fess sang "The Ballad of Davy Crockett" and a colorful clip from "Davy Crockett's Keelboat Race" in which the Crockett out shoots Mike Fink within the confines of a riverfront tavern.

On the program, Fess and Ebsen discussed if they should sing *the* song. Fess went slightly off script and declared, "If you don't do it for me, how about doing it for Mr. Kefauver or that guy from Illinois who just turned to his wife and said, 'Isobel, when we cleaned out the attic did you see my coonskin cap?'" Fess had made a reference to his Chicago-educated lawyer, Chuck Bargiel, and his wife at the time. Then Fess and his sidekick sang a few modified verses of "The Ballad of Davy Crockett" and Ebsen reprised the dance he did in "Davy Crockett Goes to Congress."

"It was a great appearance and I was thrilled to be referenced by Fess," said Bargiel.

Fess' mother had a stroke in 1981.

"She was never the same after that," explained Ashley. "Dad and I found her on the floor of her mobile home. She had been vacuuming. He always felt horrible that she had lain there overnight before he and I found her. He had phoned a few times and she didn't answer, but since she was always so active and busy he didn't think too much about it. During her recovery he made sure that someone was with her all the time for her meals at the rehabilitation institute. Eli and I would take turns going when dad couldn't be there and he hired extra help, too. Later, when she was able to come home, he paid for round-the-clock care for her and we visited a lot. Dad was so good to her."

In the mid-80s, Fess considered running for Congress as a Republican. Fess subscribed to such ideas as freedom of enterprise, private property, the profit motive, competition, economic opportunity, and limited government, and felt that the Republican Party best reflected those fundamental concepts. Years later, he called himself "a good old Republican boy with Libertarian principles."

Fess set his sights on the U.S. Senate.

"Dad did consider a run vs. Alan Cranston," said Ashley about Fess' challenge to the liberal Democrat who won the first of four U.S. Senate elections in 1968. Cranston also launched an unsuccessful bid for the Democratic Presidential nomination in 1984. Of course, some thought it was novel that an actor would turn politician, but Fess would not have been the first California-based actor who sought and won an elected political office. George Murphy, who had appeared in numerous films like *Broadway Melody of 1938*, *This is the Army*, and *Battleground*, was elected to the U.S. Senate in 1964. Shirley Temple Black ran unsuccessfully for an open Congressional seat in 1967, but was later appointed U.N. Ambassador by President Nixon. And then, of course, there was Ronald Reagan.

Like Murphy, Temple-Black, and Reagan before him, Fess already had the name recognition factor that all politicians need to establish their campaigns. And Fess' celebrity was primarily based on two all-American heroes: Davy Crockett and Daniel Boone. It certainly didn't hurt to be associated with resourceful historic leaders of honor and bravery. Furthermore, Fess didn't carry the political baggage that Murphy and Reagan held since both had been active in politics for years before they sought office.

Fess started to test the political waters.

One of his political concerns was education. He proposed a unique idea about improving quality teaching in a speech: "Is it possible to get some of the best college graduates to remain in the classroom as teachers?" questioned Fess. "I believe we can. I believe we must. There will be a cost. But nothing of value in our nation's history came cheaply. Freedom, for example, our most valuable asset, has been very costly indeed. In order to get quality teachers in the classrooms, quality salaries should be paid. And those teachers who excel beyond expectations should receive additional compensation. I'm not suggesting that local communities shoulder the entire burden. The national government can help. For example, it can help by exempting teachers from national income taxes, a program that would increase teachers' purchasing power while not increasing the revenue responsibilities for local districts. But teachers should be held accountable for their teaching. A program, perhaps a national system of standards, should be established. Clearly, something should be done."

National educational standards and a federal income tax exemption for teachers were bold policy proposals, but Fess never delivered the speech or ran for Congress.

"He consulted with Ed Rollins and ultimately decided that it would be very costly and tough on the family, too," explained Ashley. "Obviously, dad had name recognition going for him but the idea of traveling back and forth or relocating the family was not taken lightly. I think dad was very tempted but reason prevailed."

Most of the prevailing reasoning came from Marcy Parker.

"And Marcella was not enthused by the idea," said Fess with a smile.

Interestingly enough, the Bush Administration and Congress enacted national educational standards in 2001 with the No Child Left Behind Act.

Buddy Ebsen also made political news in the 1980s. When fellow *Beverly Hillbillies* cast member Nancy Kulp decided in 1984 to run for Congress as a Democrat from her home state of Pennsylvania, Ebsen sent her a note that read, "Hey, Nancy, I love you dearly but you're too liberal for me—I've got to go with Bud Shuster." Shuster, the incumbent Republican, defeated Kulp for the 9th Congressional district, 117,203 to 59,449.

But Fess wasn't completely out of the national political arena.

"He was on the short list to be named Ambassador to Australia after representing President Reagan at celebrations commemorating the Battle of the Coral Sea," explained Ashley. On his 1985 visit, Fess proved that he was no mere celebrity during his press conference at the Regency Sydney hotel, which was packed with newspaper and television reporters. Briefed by the U.S. State Department and in command of the issues, he smoothly commented on the problem with ANZUS, the Australia, New Zealand, United States Security Treaty. The controversy began when New Zealand backed out of the 1952 treaty with the United States in 1984 due to a dispute over port rights for the U.S. Navy's nuclear fleet. When asked about the awkward relationship among the three nations, Fess diplomatically replied: "We're very hopeful that the ANZUS will be put back in the spirit of its original founding."

One reporter asked Fess to comment on President Reagan.

"Well, I think his job is a tough job, and I think he's doing a fine job," stated Fess.

While in Australia, Fess traveled to Sydney drug rehabilitation centers on behalf of Mrs. Reagan, who was leading the "Just Say No" campaign, an anti-drug effort in the United States. Despite Fess' impressive role as envoy, Laurence Lane, a former U.S. Ambassador-at-Large, was named Australian Ambassador in 1985.

"I really don't know if I'll ever get appointed or elected to anything," joked Fess in the *Santa Barbara Magazine*. "I look at it like this: life unfolds in a certain way; there is a rhythm and an ebb and flow to it."

Fess' mother passed away on June 24, 1985, nearly twenty years after her husband's death. "She was such a tough gal," said Ashley. "But so sweet. I think it was really hard on dad because he was so devoted to her. But I think he felt like he had done right by her—and he had. It meant a lot to him for her to be in her own home until the end."

Fess made another pitch to the Disney Studios about reviving the Davy Crockett series. "I had a screenplay called *Return to the Alamo*, which I thought was a natural for the Disney Studios," said Fess. "It was a charming little fictional vignette about Crockett and Russel."

The *New York Daily News* reported the story on January 2, 1987.

"New findings by scholars indicate he may have survived the Alamo," claimed Fess about the historic Davy Crockett in the article. The story about Crockett surviving the Alamo had been around since the year he died at the Alamo. On April 5, 1836, the Rochester, New York-based *Monroe Democrat* erroneously reported: "We are happy to state, on the authority of a letter from Tennessee, that the report of the death of the eccentric Davy Crockett is not true."

But it was true.

Fess clarified his statement.

"I don't know if that's true, but I have a script treatment for what might have happened to Crockett if he did survive—purely fictional, set 25 years after the Alamo," said Fess. "You know, I look around today and see some of the films. I see *Star Trek* doing so well, and it was a unique show, but, and it may be immodest of me to say so, I do believe there is a much larger audience for a well-made and well-conceived Davy Crockett film starring Buddy Ebsen and Fess Parker."

Despite Fess' enthusiasm, the project never materialized.

"Unfortunately, I didn't get the right kind of support from them," he remarked.

Fess was presented a 1986 Golden Boot Award by the Motion Picture and Television Fund. The award is presented to those who have made important contributions to the genre of the Western. Fess' roles as *Davy Crockett* and *Daniel Boone* plus his work in such westerns as *Untamed Frontier, Springfield Rifle, Westward Ho, the Wagons!, Old Yeller, The Jayhawkers*, and *The Hangman* easily warranted the award.

Fess was joined in the fourth annual induction ceremony by *Gunsmoke* star James Arness, stuntman-actor Jock Mahoney, author Louis L'Amour, actor Cesar Romero, *Gene Autry Show* musical director Carl Cotner, actor Guy Madison, singer-actor Burl Ives, actor Fred MacMurray, stuntman Glenn Randall, actor George Montgomery, and singer Texas Ritter.

A few of Fess' fellow inductees shared professional paths with him. Arness worked with him in *Them!* and *Island in the Sky*; Burl Ives and Tex Ritter recorded versions of "The Ballad of Davy Crockett;" Jock Mahoney appeared in a 1967 episode of *Daniel Boone*; and George Montgomery starred as Davy Crockett (actually Crockett's nephew) in the 1950 film *Davy Crockett, Indian Scout.*

Fess remembered that one of the other award recipients had a hidden talent. "You know who was a good singer—James Arness!" exclaimed Fess. "Jim was from Minneapolis and had sung in the Minneapolis Choir."

Associating with other film stars may have generated another idea.

"Now, for the first time in years, I'm without a demanding project," said Fess to the *Disney Channel Magazine* in 1986. "And so I'm thinking about returning to the motion-picture industry. That was my first love, and you never forget your first love. I have a number of ideas which I've presented to the new generation of filmmakers at the Walt Disney Company. Who knows? After all that time, I may be back among friends at the studio again."

A year later, Fess returned to Texas to help promote the Alamo.

"In the summer of 1987, Fess Parker traveled to San Antonio to lend support to a new foundation that was established to save and promote the vast history of Alamo Plaza," said Gary Foreman, who worked with the Alamo Foundation. "His enthusiastic response to help this fledgling cause was precipitated by a visit I had made to Santa Barbara a few months earlier. Upon his arrival to Texas, he immediately became one of the first financial donors to the foundation and undertook a series of public engagements and interviews where he articulated the preservation philosophy with his typical Texan authenticity." Fess was eventually named National Spokesperson for the Alamo Foundation. The organization's goals included the restoration of Alamo Plaza, the establishment of scholarships, grants to public schools, and the creation of a "forum for the constructive dialogue between the countries of Mexico, South America, and the United States."

At the ceremony which officially launched the Alamo Foundation, Fess proclaimed, "History tends to be yesterday. But this hallowed ground will have even greater meaning in our troubled future. I'm here to help if I can." During the day he viewed a living history demonstration enacted by historical interpreters in front of the Alamo. Hundreds of people showed up to see Fess, and a number of adults and children wore coonskin caps. The *San Antonio Light* featured a photo of Fess carrying a four-year-old boy who was wearing the iconic headgear in its July 10 edition.

Fess later arrived at city hall where he was made an honorary mayor of San Antonio. "When he walked into the City Council chambers, the entire room erupted into the chorus of 'Davy Crockett,' followed by a roar of applause," said Foreman. "As he graciously bowed to his admirers one could not help but think it was another 'Lion of the West' moment where Fess met himself coming back."

San Antonio Mayor Henry Cisneros welcomed Fess. "You cannot know the influence you had on Texans and San Antonians," said Cisneros. "It was impossible to grow up in that era and not wear a coonskin cap."

The next March, Fess sent a Western Union telegram to the Alamo Society when the organization held its annual symposium in San Antonio.

"To the Alamo Society: Best wishes for an enjoyable and successful get together," wrote Fess in the March 2, 1988 message. "Your interest in the Alamo heritage forms one of the stronger fibers in our democracy. You sure are right so go ahead."

And Fess wasn't completely out of Disney's plans for a new television series about Davy Crockett.

In 1988, Disney revived Crockett's life with four new episodes starring Tim Dunigan. "Davy Crockett: Rainbow in the Thunder" (November 20, 1988), "Davy Crockett: A Natural Man" (December 18, 1988); "Davy Crockett: Guardian Spirit" (January 13, 1989), and "Davy Crockett: A Letter to Polly" (June 11, 1989).

Dunigan's Crockett was joined by Gary Grubbs who played George Russell—that is, a Russell with two L's, unlike Buddy Ebsen's George Russel. And Disney wanted Fess to be a part of the program.

"I was invited to do a part for the new show but I wasn't approached as one, well, who had busily worked on his [acting] craft," said Fess. "Disney wanted me to play a character in the Dunigan series. But the story didn't have an authentic feel, [it was] somewhat modernized. So I declined to be a part of it. I had my Crockett story which would have been different and easier to do."

Fess also pointed out that the contract for the new series was restrictive.

"Furthermore, the final contract went beyond the original time schedule," he said. "For example, they expected me to be available for additional film bits and voice-overs. Obviously, that conflicted with other personal obligations so I walked away from the role."

The series did not do well; as a matter of fact, the first episode, "Davy Crockett: Rainbow in the Thunder," which focused on the Creek War, ranked 47th among sixty-five weekly programs. There were a number of obvious problems with the new series. The British Columbia locations hardly looked like the green hills of Tennessee. Costuming and props were not particularly authentic, and the script was punctuated by anachronisms. For example, in a conversation with President Andrew Jackson (David Hemmings), Dunigan's Crockett talks about his wife, Polly, who "died about ten years ago." Polly Crockett died in 1815, fourteen years before Jackson was first inaugurated. One would expect that Crockett knew when his beloved wife died. But more than anything, the new series lacked creative magic, the ineffable ingredient that is characteristic of all successful Walt Disney productions.

Years later, the Disney CEO acknowledged the series' failure to Fess.

"I was at a function with Michael Eisner and we talked about the new Crockett series," said Fess. "He turned and looked at me and said, 'Next time we do it, we'll get it right.'"

Fess traveled to the U.S.S.R. in 1988 and logged about 10,000 miles over the country's vast landscape. He didn't particularly enjoy his visit. "The food was basic and bad," he said. "Our 26-year-old, well-educated guide, who spoke four languages, lived in a single twelve-foot by nine-foot room. I was glad to return home."

And when he got home on American soil, he decided to do something with it.

CHAPTER 19
"KING OF THE WINE FRONTIER"

Fess was excited about land he had purchased in Los Olivos, California.

"It was December of 1987, I believe, and I was living in Goleta, California and my dad called," recalled Eli. "He told me that he had some new property and wanted me to drive up and look at it."

Eli drove up and was impressed at what he saw.

"Dad had a nose for dirt," said Eli. "However, at that point he never mentioned anything about wine. But between December of 1988 and January of 1989, we were getting started in the wine business."

"At about that same time, mom decided that she was tired of 'running' the large Hope Ranch house," said Ashley. "She wanted to spend more time in Palm Springs so mom and dad bought a place down there and were in the process of fixing it up. Dad understandably needed a place in Santa Barbara because he was working on a plan for the property next to the hotel. When he wasn't in Palm Springs with mom he stayed at the Mountain View Inn in Santa Barbara. But he wanted to buy a little place in Santa Barbara to 'hang his hat.'"

Fess found the property.

"But the house was in pretty bad shape," noted Ashley. "However, it had the most amazing view. It was situated right on a bluff in Hope Ranch and had a panoramic ocean view. Mom had a bad feeling about it from the start; she was concerned about the quality if its construction. But she agreed to oversee the renovation."

"It just bothered me," said Marcy. "I could just tell by the way it was shaped and positioned on the side of the cliff."

Marcy was proved right.

"And then it happened during one of those big rains that we had," noted Marcy.

"Essentially it was a real estate nightmare," explained Ashley. "They had the house completely gutted and rebuilt. But as soon as the hardwood floors, cabinets, and appliances were installed it slid off the bluff! Torrential El Niño rains that winter plus an undisclosed flaw in the foundation were both factors in the destruction. It was such a shame. As I recall, the insurance company came through but I think dad also filed against the realtor who placed the listing. For a long time dad's stock answer to why he got into the wine business was, 'Well, at the time I was homeless and unemployed so it seemed like a good idea.'"

Fess consulted with Dale Hampton, who established his Santa Maria, California-based vineyard management and winery company in 1972.

"I had met him up at his ranch, the Rancho de las Dos Hermanas, and got to know him and Marcy pretty good," explained Hampton. "Later on I was hosting a wine event, a wine tasting, and I asked Fess if he would emcee the event. He agreed and we all had a good time. I remember he enjoyed the Riesling that we offered; as a matter of fact, Fess and Marcy both liked the Riesling so much that their first planting, about five acres, was Riesling."

Fess planted 5½ acres of Johannisberg Riesling in 1989, and he promptly spread the word that he had just entered a new frontier.

"I just wanted to drop you a note to tell you about my latest and most exciting venture—the winery and vineyard business," wrote Fess in 1989, the year of his first harvest. "I have spent most of my career in the entertainment field. I've done motion pictures and T.V. shows, developed theme parks, and beachfront resorts in Santa Barbara. Now I'm indulging myself and entering the ultimate business—a winery. This story, like every other, is actually more involved. You see, I have spent thirty years in Santa Barbara County and have witnessed the birth and maturation of our local wine and grape industry. It is now at a stage where the wines are so good, and their recognition so broad, that it is an irresistible calling. I have been beckoned by Bacchus and am paying him my ultimate tribute: I am now a vintner."

Fess Parker and his son, Eli, at the Fess Parker Winery.
PHOTO COURTESY OF THE PARKER FAMILY.

Fess also had another reason for starting the winery.

"There has been another very strong motive," explained Fess. "My son, Eli, and I have joined creative forces before, and we have always wanted to work together in a traditional family business, one that future generations will grow up in. The catalyst for all this was finding the perfect vineyard site on the Foxen Canyon wine trail. We purchased this 714-acre ranch in December of 1987 and promptly set about planning our winery and establishing the vineyard."

Besides the winery, Fess operated another ranch in San Luis Obispo County. During a casual walk along the far boundary of his vineyard property one day, Fess was confronted by some private security guards who informed them that he was a bit too close to the property line of his neighbor. The neighbor was none other than Michael Jackson. Fess politely acknowledged the guards' responsibilities and told them to say hello to the singer. The King of Pop and the King of the Wild Frontier eventually met on October 6, 1991, at Neverland Ranch where Jackson hosted the wedding of Liz Taylor and Larry Fortensky. And Fess provided the wine for the wedding party. The media coverage of the event was extensive with helicopters hovering dangerously above such star-studded celebrity guests as Liza Minnelli, Nancy Reagan, Eva Gabor, Merv Griffin and Eddie Murphy. "Frankly," said Fess in *People* magazine story, "some pretty stalwart men of the screen felt nervous." As everyone waited for the ceremony to begin an unannounced skydiver made his appearance. "We were waiting for the wedding to begin and all of a sudden that skydiver came down about six feet away from us," recalled Fess years later. "That was the doggondest afternoon I ever had." Fortunately, everyone survived Mrs. Fortensky's wedding.

The next year, Fess planted twenty-five acres of Syrah and Chardonnay, and later added Viognier and Marsanne. Additional plantings of Syrah, Chardonnay, and Merlot followed.

Fess was enthused about the family winery.

"Building a winery, not quite completed as of this writing, has proven to be a wonderful revelation," he noted. "The challenge is combining the natural beauty of the surroundings, the architecture, and the vineyards with a state of the art facility for the production of fine wines. With the challenge, however, comes the reward of growing our own grapes, making wine, and entertaining our friends on the ranch where we live. I assume my enthusiasm for the wine business should be obvious to you by now."

He recalled that wine wasn't the alcoholic beverage of choice in his early Hollywood days. "I don't remember many folks drinking wine at restaurants back then," stated Fess. "Whether it was the Brown Derby or wherever Marcy was singing, cocktails were the thing."

The biggest event in the Parker Family in 1991 was Ashley's wedding to Rodney Shull, her Bishop Garcia Diego High School high school sweetheart, who had lettered in three sports and served as the student body president. Shull later attended Santa Barbara City College where he established all-star football records as a receiver. He later went to Stanford University. The pair wed on August 31, 1991.

"Rodney and I dated on and off for ten years—through high school and college, post college," explained Ashley. "Rodney graduated from Stanford in 1987, a year after I graduated from Bates, because he had another year of eligibility for football. We had an amazing wedding at Our Lady of Mount Carmel Church in Montecito, and the reception was held at mom and dad's country club, Birnam Wood."

Shull, who had been working as a stock broker at the time of the wedding, was later hired by a pair of mutual fund companies. At that time, Shull was helpful to the family. "He was working with dad on all projects," said Ashley. "He worked with bankers, city officials, and anyone else dad was meeting with." Fess recognized Shull's business sense and recruited him as the winery's Chief Financial Officer in 1997. "Rodney's title was Vice President—Fess Parker Winery," added Ashley.

The Parkers also traveled to France in 1991.

"Marcy and I took a wonderful trip to France this Fall to the Alsatian and Rhone winemaking regions," noted Fess. "What a way to learn the business! Part of the trip included a week-long barge trip down the Rhone canals. I want to deny that I ever said 'after the first three days it was like prison with really good food.' I enjoyed it, every minute of it and we came back home feeling fortunate to be a part of such a romantic industry."

Besides the trip to France, Fess and Marcy took other international travels. They also enjoyed relaxing sojourns with friends and family to places like Italy, Japan, Taiwan, and China. Fess considered himself a dedicated businessman but he took time to enjoy himself. "You've got to have a little fun each day," he said.

Fess' children would soon be playing a more significant part of the wine business. Following a harvesting stint at the Byron Winery and Vineyard in the Santa Maria Valley and University of California at Davis coursework, Eli sought expert tutelage.

"I apprenticed with Jed Steele from 1993 to 1996," explained Eli, who assumed the title of President and Director of Marketing for the Fess Parker Winery in 1996. Steele was a highly regarded vintner who helped elevate the Kendall-Jackson Winery in the 1980s before establishing his own successful wine-making and consulting business.

"Fess had called me and asked if I would consult with him about his winery," said Steele. "I was reluctant at first, especially since I resided in the northern part of the California wine district and he was in the Santa Barbara area. He was persistent. He called about three or four times. Eli called me up and asked me if I would consider coming down to meet them, so I agreed to meet with Fess and Eli, who became a very astute pupil. He learned very quickly. And Eli was the winemaker."

Steele came to respect Fess' perspective on wine making.

"He took a no-nonsense approach to what was in his glass," said Steele years later.

Eli was soon joined in the winery by his sister. But before Ashley joined forces with the King of the Wine Frontier she had to sever her ties with the President of the United States.

Ashley had graduated from Bates College in 1986 with a B.A. in English and had joined President Ronald Reagan's White House staff where she served as one of four Presidential Trip Coordinators in the Office of Presidential Advance. She got the job after her parents opened up their home to White House staffers and the press corps in 1984. "When the Reagans were at the Western White House in the summer, our neighbors across the street used to host members of the President's staff and the White House Press Corps," explained Ashley. "Well, one summer they couldn't do it so mom and dad let them use our facilities—just about everything, including the tennis court." The Parker's gracious hospitality was so well received, that the "open house" became a regular summer event. White House staffers and reporters frequently joined members of the Parker Family in tennis matches.

One summer, Ashley was playing tennis with William F. Sittmann, Special Assistant to the President and to Michael K. Deaver, Deputy Chief of Staff. "He asked me if I wanted to work in Washington D. C. the next summer," said Ashley. "I agreed." Fess and Marcy were proud of their daughter and knew that she would exceed expectations.

"I became a White House intern before it was a bad thing," laughed Ashley.

At the same time, Fess set up a series of charity tennis tournaments which benefited the First Lady's "Just Say No" campaign and raised over two million dollars for the Nancy Reagan Drug Abuse Fund. "He was always carrying a tennis racket during those years," said Ashley.

After President Reagan left office in 1989, Ashley left the White House staff and became a Special Assistant to the Deputy Secretary of Public Affairs in the Office of Housing and Urban Development under Secretary Jack Kemp during the George H. W. Bush Administration. But she soon left Washington D. C. for the vineyards of Los Olivos.

"Eli and Ashley were raised in a very level-headed manner by Fess and Marcy," said Steele. "Very level-headed."

Fess shared his early vintages with friends like Ron Ely.

"I believe I first tasted some of Fess' wines when he was in what I would call the experimental stage in developing them," remarked Ely. "But as I remember, this was before Fess' own vineyards had matured, meaning that he was buying his grapes from other local vineyards. It was not long after that, however, that Fess' vineyards were the source for his very excellent wines."

The labels of Fess Parker Wines featured a small coonskin cap. "Nothing grandiose," explained Fess. "Just a small, tasteful one." And the corks were embellished with a coonskin cap and Fess' signature.

That iconic logo, of course, was a cultural symbol to those who grew up with him during the *Davy Crockett* and *Daniel Boone* years. It was an identifiable connection to those who wore coonskin caps in their youth and were now clearly old enough to consume his wines. Fess also recognized the importance of the historical figures he played on television and never hesitated to speak about them when he was given the opportunity. He usually discussed the nostalgic value of his characterizations but on occasion he placed them within a modern context as a way of educating an audience. For example, Fess, ever the diplomat, issued a statement about cultural appreciation and acceptance to members of the Alamo

A label from a bottle of Fess Parker Syrah, complete with a small coonskin cap.
PHOTO COURTESY OF THE FESS PARKER WINERY.

Society which appeared in the March 1990 issue of *The Alamo Journal*.

"If I may make a statement to the members of the Alamo Society, I would remind them that the symbolism of the Alamo remains so very important on this day," stated Fess. "War is always an unfortunate event, and a war, of course, underscores one meaning of the Alamo. But the warfare associated with the Alamo should not necessarily be associated today with any ongoing tensions between people. It should not be an historical event that maintains, for example, Anglo-Latino conflicts today. I hope we've all grown past the particularization of that famous battle. In fact, we should all come to appreciate a better understanding of all the Alamo battles' participants. In particular, we should appreciate the sacrifices made by both the Alamo defender and the Mexican soldier. Devotion to duty was a characteristic of both participants; it was something they both shared. The Alamo, then, can be seen as a real positive."

Despite his involvement in the winery he had plans to revive his *After Sundown* film project.

Fess re-examined his files which not only contained the rejections from the mid-1970s but additional pieces of correspondence from years later. It appeared that while the project had originally been categorized as "dead as a doornail," Fess thought otherwise. He discovered an old letter written by actor Robert Loggia, who received a copy of the script in March of 1979. "The action is good and by itself can almost carry the film," wrote Loggia. But Loggia raised a few questions. "Are the characters strongly developed?" "How have they reached us emotionally to root for them?" "Is there something in this play that keeps the intellect working other than the ways to survive?" "Is the dialogue strengthening the action?"

Fess pitched his project around and managed to secure the interest of Ron Maxwell, who had made such films as *Little Darlings* and *The Night the Lights Went Out in Georgia*, among others. A joint venture agreement between Ronwell Productions and Fess Parker was subsequently drafted on July 5, 1990, and indicated that "principal photography of the Picture is scheduled to commence within a twenty-four month period." The document also identified Maxwell as "producer and director" and Fess as "producer and actor."

Although nothing concrete followed the joint venture agreement proposal, Fess remained hopeful that *After Sundown* would finally reach the pre-production stage. As the two-year time period neared its end, Fess informed Hollywood reporter Army Archerd about the project in the August 18, 1992 issue of *Variety*. "I'd like to make one more picture," remarked Fess. "The Whites are no better than the Indians in this story." A similar story later appeared in Boyd Magers' "Western Clippings" column in *The Big Reel*, a publication devoted to Hollywood history and memorabilia.

But the joint venture agreement was never activated. By 1992, Maxwell was turning Michael Shaara's Pulitzer Prize-winning novel, *Killer Angels*, into a screenplay which became *Gettysburg* the following year.

The final doornail had been hammered into *After Sundown*.

Despite the demise of the *After Sundown* project, it was a good time in Fess' life. He was a robust 66-year-old man whose children were working alongside him in the family's successful wine business. And he was having "a little fun each day."

Fess' annual medical checkup with Dr. Vernon Freidell in March, 1991, included a routine PSA test, which measures the level of prostate-specific antigen in the blood. The test was standard procedure for most men over the age of fifty. The test result indicated an elevated PSA number which suggested that Fess may have had prostate cancer. Dr. Freidell referred him to a specialist, Dr. Donald Rhodes, who biopsied his prostate, confirming the diagnosis.

"As his physician I explained to him the nature of the disease," explained Rhodes. "Most people who hear those results are upset; some experience panic. But not Fess. For him it was basically, 'All right, what do I do next?' I told him about the two basic options: surgery or radiation therapy. He consulted with several physicians and chose to have radiation, and was given 64 Gy of external beam to his prostate from February through April, 1992. I preferred he have surgical removal of the cancer, but he elected to have radiation. Fortunately, this cured his prostated cancer, but left him with urinary control problems."

Radiation treatments notwithstanding, Fess continued cheerfully to work at his office and the winery. And he accepted all appropriate invitations.

On October 22, 1991, Fess was inducted as one of the Disney Legends at ceremonies held at Walt Disney Studios in Burbank. Disney CEO Michael Eisner hosted the event and Roy Disney introduced the award recipients. Fess, dressed in a jacket and tie, was brought to the award-site on a horse-drawn coach—accompanied by Mickey Mouse. He got off the coach and took his seat with the other recipients and guests. As soon as Disney said "Fess Parker," a band played "The Ballad of Davy Crockett." Fess was escorted to the presentation area by Goofy, who was wearing buckskins and a coonskin cap.

"Fess' name has become synonymous with the King of the Wild Frontier, Davy Crockett," said Disney. "His portrayal of this backwoodsman set off a national craze. Coonskin caps became the fad—and almost on the Champs Elysees at one point, actually, Fess. As Davy Crockett, he paraded down Main Street in the opening day festivities at Disneyland. His other Disney credits include *Westward Ho, the Wagons!*, *The Great Locomotive Chase*, and *Old Yeller*. Fess has written screenplays, composed songs, and is currently a successful businessman. And just with the tiniest hint of blame on you, you got me started in sailboats. It's my honor, Fess, to present you with the Disney Legends Award."

"I'm honored to receive this," stated Fess. "The year 1954 was the year I met Marcella, who became my wife, and joined the Disney family. And it's been a wonderful, positive influence in every way. I'm so proud to be here today. Thank you very much."

Julie Andrews, who later received a Disney Legends Award at the ceremony, was the first to greet Fess when he returned to his front row seat next to Marcy. Others receiving awards were Carl Banks (animation and publishing), Claude Coats (animation and Imagineering), Don DaGradi (animation and film), Ken Anderson (animation and Imagineering), and Sterling Holloway (animation-voice). Bill Walsh (film and television production) and Mary Blair (animation and Imagineering), received their awards posthumously. Later, Fess placed his handprints and signed his name in wet cement. The casting was later made into bronze and placed on display at the Disney Studios along with the other Disney Legend Award recipients. Disney archivist Dave Smith acknowledged Fess' award in *Disney A to Z: The Updated Official Encyclopedia* and noted that he was "perfect as Davy Crockett."

One month later, Fess proved that he still was *Davy Crockett.*

Director David Zucker had been a fan of Fess' since his childhood and made it a point whenever possible to include something related to Davy Crockett in his films. In his *Naked Gun 2 ½: The Smell of Fear*, which was released in June 1991, the opening scene of the film features a White House Announcer standing in front of a Davy Crockett painting. A coonskin cap, a buckskin jacket, and framed images of the Alamo and Crockett are among the items that decorate the apartment of Leslie Nielsen's character, Frank Drebin. Later in the film, Zucker, dressed as Crockett, and fellow Fess-fan Robert Weil, costumed as George Russel, fire flintlocks during a zany SWAT-team shoot sequence.

Zucker subsequently invited Fess to a flintlock rifle frolic at his ranch in Ojai, California on November 23, 1991. Fess showed up appropriately in a coonskin cap and his *Daniel Boone* jacket, much to the delight of the other shooters who were there. But everyone wondered if Fess was still the same guy who outshot Bigfoot Mason in the "Davy Crockett Goes to Congress" episode thirty-six years earlier.

Fess didn't disappoint his fans.

Fess Parker and the author at David Zucker's 1991 Flintlock Rifle Frolic in Ojai, California.
Author's collection.

"We set up oranges and water balloons at about fifty yards," said Weil, who helped organize the frolic. "Fess fired the first time and one of the balloons exploded. Everybody cheered. Then he did it again!"

Zucker seemed to enjoy it more than anyone.

"I was definitely thrilled, as we all were, to have him there, live and in person, as our guest," said Zucker, who was dressed in buckskins and a coonskin cap for the event. "For one day at least, we could all be kids again, transported back to another time, the feeling not lessened by the fact Fess, at six-foot-five, was every bit as tall as my dad looked to me in 1955."

Visitors to the Fess Parker Winery would occasionally meet Fess as he made his daily rounds around the vineyards. Fess enjoyed autographing bottles of his wine and talking about *Davy Crockett* and *Daniel Boone*. Part of his charm was his ability to make everyone feel as if he or she was the only person on earth. It appeared to be a unique gift, but it was more than that: Fess was genuinely interested in everyone. Of course, he answered numerous questions about his television and film career. "I spend five to ten hours a weekend meeting people, and they come up and say, in effect, 'My life values were shaped by that show,'" stated Fess.

The lack of Crockett and Boone memorabilia in the winery's tasting room prompted visitors to ask questions about coonskin caps, buckskins, and Old Betsy.

"I don't have anything from the series now," explained Fess about items from the Disney series. "A couple of coonskin caps that I had either fell apart or were given away. I do remember, however, two wax dummies that were made of Buddy Ebsen and me that were on display in Disneyland years ago. Each of them had some of the costumes that we wore in the series, but I don't know what happened to them. The rest of the clothing that I wore stayed in wardrobe; some of the outfits could be in Western Costume or the Disney Studios on racks for all I know. I didn't even take any props from the shows!" However, one of Disney artist Charles Boyer's *Fond Memories*, a limited edition lithograph which depicts Fess as Crockett surrounded by kids and Disney cartoon characters, hangs proudly at the Fess Parker Winery's wine tasting room.

The news of Helene Stanley's death on December 22, 1991 came as a shock to Fess. Stanley, who portrayed Polly Crockett in the Disney series, and her husband had tried to contact Fess shortly before her death. "I was unable, for some reason, to meet her," he said. "That's a shame. I'm truly sorry I didn't get a chance to see her again."

Fess provided his handprints and signature in cement at a special ceremony held at Walt Disney World's Theater of the Stars in Hollywood Studios on Jan. 29, 1992. The next month he appeared on the cover of the February issue of *The Alamo Journal.*

Later in the year, he attended a ribbon-cutting ceremony for a Walt Disney exhibit at the Museum of Broadcast Communications in Chicago on June 13. "I had a great weekend," said Fess.

The next month, Fess opened up a tasting room at the winery. "Thirty two acres is a modest-sized vineyard but as a small family operation, this crush put everyone to the test," wrote Fess in the autumn of 1992. He also noted that work continued on the main building and its grounds. "We now have a beautiful grassy meadow around the main building, perfect for fall picnics under the oak trees."

Fess Parker in his *Daniel Boone* outfit on the cover of issue #80 of *The Alamo Journal*. Robert Weil assembled the composite image by placing a photo of Fess at the 1991 David Zucker Flintlock Rifle Frolic against a photo of the modern-day Alamo church. Author's collection.

Fess made special appearances at various events including the Walt Disney World International Food and Wine Festival in EPCOT where he graciously spoke about his wines and his experiences as *Davy Crockett* and other Disney film characters.

"The first Disney Food and Wine Festival that we attended was in 1992," stated Ashley. "And the reason that I remember was because dad, Eli, Mark Shannon, our first wine maker, and I went there and had a great time."

Fess was pleased that his wines were going to be showcased at the festival but was concerned about the competition.

"Dad was pretty excited to be included at the festival but Chappellet Winery was there and they were really big deal—very Napa!" said Ashley. "Also the Cline Brothers were there with their Rhone wines. Our wines weren't very good back then but we made up for it with enthusiasm and dad's star power."

At the Disney event, Fess spoke with many attendees and politely autographed wine bottles and posed for photographs. He returned home confident that the next International Food and Wine Festival at Walt Disney World would be represented by better Fess Parker Wines.

Thanks to the efforts of Jed Steele and Eli, the quality of the wines increased. "We made improvements," said Fess.

In October 1992, Fess accepted an invitation to attend Rutherford, Tennessee's annual Davy Crockett celebration. The town of 1,300 residents was embellished with "Welcome Fess" signs. Fess participated in a parade, visited the reconstructed Davy Crockett Cabin-Museum, signed autographs, and posed for photographs. Approximately 7,000 people showed up to see their favorite frontier hero. The local newspaper praised his visit: "The legendary pioneer heroes, Boone and Crockett, were portrayed by a younger version of the man Rutherford met Saturday. Somehow, however, the character and integrity that stamped those historic figures, embodies Fess Parker. What else would compel a man as enterprising as Parker to accept the modest invitation of a small town to join in the celebration of a local icon?" Upon returning to California, he autographed a rifle stock that was later mounted on the wall of Club 33, Disneyland's exclusive dining facility.

In February 1993, he approached the Disney Studios with a project he had pitched six years earlier.

"I'm a history lover," stated Fess. He read about the scholarship regarding the papers of Mexican officer José Enrique de la Peña which suggested that Crockett survived the Battle of the Alamo and was subsequently executed. Inspired by the debate among Alamo historians about the authenticity and content of the documents, Fess dusted off his rough draft about Crockett and Russel surviving the famous 1836 battle.

"Crockett and Russel are taken back to Mexico and are imprisoned," explained Fess. "But they manage to escape—Buddy and I were older so I made the escape twenty-five years after the capture. Well, they end up having more adventures before returning to the Alamo on the anniversary of the battle."

Fess had hopes for the project. "But Disney wasn't interested in the story," he said.

On April 15, 1993, William Bakewell, who played Tobias Norton in the *Davy Crockett* series, died. In the wake of his prostate cancer, Bakewell's passing—even though he was 84-years old—was a reminder to Fess of his own health.

"I talked with William Bakewell just two weeks before he died earlier this spring," said Fess at the time. "He had been hospitalized at the Motion Picture Country Hospital. There were many who attended his funeral, since he appeared in many motion pictures, like *Gone With the Wind*, for example. Among the people who attended his funeral were Ginger Rogers and Cesar Romero."

Fess was always willing to contribute to worthwhile charities and in June 1993, he was one of the celebrities who played a round of golf in the Philips Charity Classic in Bella Vista, Arkansas. Proceeds from the event benefited cancer research and treatment. "It's kinda nice to have one genre to hang your hat on, even if it was a coonskin cap," said Fess to the Associated Press. He and Marcy also supported the Performing Arts Scholarship Foundation in Santa Barbara which "helps develop young musicians vocally and instrumentally for future careers."

In 1993, Fess hosted an Independence Day Celebration at the winery. It proved so successful that it became a yearly tradition in Los Olivos. Other events became mainstays such as the Harvest Festival Winemaker Dinner and the Annual Release Day Weekend, which featured a barbeque, live music, bottle-signings, and other activities. He also made a strong connection between his frontier hero portrayals and his wine when he produced a special edition magnum Pinot Noir in 1993 that was etched with Davy Crockett's motto and an image of him as *Daniel Boone*. The commemorative bottles were subsequently produced with additional images of Crockett in various sizes over the years. He later returned to the Museum of Broadcast Communications in Chicago on November 2,

1993, for "An Evening With Fess Parker." The event was hosted by the museum's curator, J. Fred MacDonald and moderated by Gary Deeb of WLS-television.

But another medical problem manifested itself.

"He had blood in his urine and an X-ray that was taken showed a tumor in the kidney," said Dr. Rhodes. There was no time to discuss additional consultations or options. Two weeks later, on November 17, 1993, Dr. Rhodes removed his right kidney for a tumor of the kidney along with his right ureter.

Fess recovered without complaining.

Since he had been out of the acting business for twenty years, questions popped up in the media about Fess' whereabouts. He was one of a number former film and television stars who were featured in the December 1993 issue of *Luxury Lifestyles*, a special edition tabloid publication that asked the front-page question, "Where Are They Now?" In his article Fess noted that, "I've walked around for thirty years in a warm glow from people enjoying Davy Crockett."

In 1994, Fess attended the Alamo Society Symposium in San Antonio. As he was introduced, the opening music from "Davy Crockett, Indian Fighter" filled the conference room. He emerged from a waiting room wearing his *Daniel Boone* jacket and a coonskin cap. The room, mostly filled with Baby Boomers, erupted in cheers and applause. He approached the podium and said, "I'm Davy Crockett, fresh from the backwoods." Fess hadn't uttered those words since the autumn of 1954 during filming of "Davy Crockett Goes to Congress." The Alamo Society members thought they had entered the time zone of their youth. They were gleefully stunned.

Fess continued with his introduction as if he were Davy Crockett.

"I'm half horse, half alligator and a little tetched with snappin' turtle," he said. "I've got the fastest horse, the prettiest sister, the surest rifle and the ugliest dog in Tennessee."

The men and women in the audience had momentarily become boys and girls once again.

But Fess had a serious message to share with the group. He was very concerned about the commercialization of Alamo Plaza which stood in the shadows of the famous mission-fortress. "My feeling is that this city and this state should be large enough, wise enough and creative enough to pull back away from the Alamo and give it space," said Fess, who explained that it was important that the Alamo be properly showcased to the millions of visitors who came to the Shrine of Texas Liberty each year.

At the meeting, Fess was presented a special award plaque which read:

The Alamo Society
salutes
Fess Parker
star of
"Davy Crockett, King of the Wild Frontier"
for inspiring a generation
with his dignity, humility and compassion
in helping us to
Remember the Alamo

After the plaque presentation, Fess sat at a table and patiently chatted with every person who approached him with an item to autograph. In typical fashion, he made everyone feel special when they asked him to sign a poster or pose for a photo.

Joan Headley of San Antonio stood in line with three of her friends. "I told him about March 6 being my son's birthday and that he was attending Baylor University," said Headley. "I also said we were going to Waco to have dinner with him that evening. After my other friends visited with him, he turned back to me and said, 'You have a wonderful birthday dinner with your son tonight.' I will never forget his kindness and thoughtfulness to me. Most celebs would not have given it another thought but Fess was not that kind of man."

Fess had toured extensively in 1955 and 1956 to promote *Davy Crockett, King of the Wild Frontier* and in the 1990s made promotional visits around the country on behalf of his winery. On May 16, 1994, he was the featured attraction at "Dinner at Disneyland Hotel with Fess Parker" and on July 3, he hosted a "Davy Crockett All American Independence Day Celebration at the Winery," which included a Mountain Man rendezvous, live country music, and a reading of the Declaration of Independence.

One of the most advertised visits was his appearance at New York

The author presents Fess Parker with The Alamo Society plaque in 1994 in San Antonio, Texas.
AUTHOR'S COLLECTION.

City's Sherry-Lehman, an upscale Madison Avenue wine shop on September 17, 1994. The shop took out a full-page ad in *The New York Times* which read: "Meet Fess Parker. Mr. Parker, the proud proprietor of Fess Parker Winery, will appear at Sherry-Lehman as Davy Crockett for a tasting of his fabulous wines."

Fess didn't show up in buckskins as advertised but that didn't prevent hundreds of fans from attending the event. He autographed bottles of his three featured 1992 wines—Chardonnay, Chardonnay reserve, and Syrah—and posed for photographs. A delegation from the Alamo Society even showed up to greet the King of the Wine Frontier. "We came just to show our respect and admiration for the man who embodied the positive qualities that we felt Davy Crockett stood for in his lifetime," said Michael Boldt, a New Jersey-based artist and musician who had been a fan of Fess' since his *Davy Crockett* days on television. "And Fess did not let us down."

"As always, it was a pleasure to meet all the wonderful people who came to see me," said Fess about his Sherry-Lehman appearance. "It was fun, too."

Fess later wrote an endorsement for *The Alamo Journal*, the official quarterly of the Alamo Society: "I always enjoy the continuing scholarship and research in *The Alamo Journal*. Who says history is dead and dry? Interest in the deeds that took place in 1836 will continue to intrigue and fascinate all men and women who love freedom. Long live the Alamo on the pages of history and in our hearts!" The statement was published in the December 1992 issue of *The Alamo Journal* and has been featured on the second page of every issue since.

The Fess Parker Winery increased its output.

"By 1993, we were producing about 18,000 cases a year," reported Eli. "By 1995–1996, we were producing about 35,000 to 40,000 cases."

And his wines were generating attention and praise.

"What I can tell you is that 1994 has been a banner year for awards and writeups," wrote Fess in his winery's fall/winter 1994/95 brochure. "Of particular note is the 1992 Syrah that not only earned a Gold Medal at the Farmers Fair in Riverside County but recently received another Gold at the World Wine Competition along with the National Championship Award for that varietal. Not bad for the first time out, huh?"

During 1995, the Fess Parker Winery began its wine club. Now fans across the country could savor his wines without ever visiting Los Olivos. The wine club shipments were accompanied by a no-frills, quarterly newsletter that described the wines, related merchandise and winery events. The carefully-crafted booklets also included employee profiles, recipes from Marcy and occasional words of wisdom—"The Fess Files"—from the man himself. The newsletter booklets eventually evolved in glossy publications with full color photography.

And that same year, Eli got married at the winery. "I actually met my wife, Laureen, at a wedding that was held at the winery two years earlier. The winery is an excellent spot to get married at, and with my connection to the winery it seemed like a perfect fit." It was Laureen's second marriage; she had been divorced and had two girls,

Artist Howard Bender salutes the "King of the Wine Frontier."
PHOTO COURTESY OF HOWARD BENDER.

Tessa and Tara. "She's been a wonderful daughter-in-law," remarked Marcy.

In 1995, Ray Herbeck, Jr., an Alamo Society member and executive producer of the IMAX film *Alamo...The Price of Freedom*, crossed paths with Fess.

"I have never been star struck and have worked with a few legends including Jimmy Stewart, Robert Mitchum, Liz Taylor, and Olivia De Havilland, but in the case of Fess Parker, it wasn't the case of meeting a 'star,' it was a case of meeting an inspirational role model," explained Herbeck. "I found that Fess Parker was again proving to be a role model for me—in showing how to ease gracefully and graciously into the 'twilight years' with a sense of humor, a feeling of accomplishment and a twinkle in the eye."

In 1995, Fess qualified for inclusion the newly-created West Texas Music Hall of Fame due to his two chart hits, "The Ballad of Davy Crockett" and "Wringle Wrangle." He was joined on the organization's "Honor Roll of Vocalists" by such singers as Buddy Holly, Roy Orbison, and Ernest Tubb, among many others. According to Sid Holmes, the Director of The West Texas Music Hall of Fame, the establishment's memorabilia collection features several Fess Parker items including framed photos, recordings, and one of the performer's shirts from *Smoky*.

Fess and Marcy loved to travel and they continued to do so in the 1990s. They particularly enjoyed traveling with friends, especially those who worked with him on *Davy Crockett*. They went on a trip to Europe with Peter Ellenshaw and his wife, Bobbie. On another trans-Atlantic journey, Fess and Marcy were joined by Bill and Nolie Walsh at Thornbury Castle in England during Christmas week of 1995. The 500-year old castle, which at one time housed King Henry VIII and Anne Boleyn, has extensive gardens and its own vineyard.

"We stayed at the castle, which was near the Welsh border," said Fishman. "Some of Fess and Marcy's other friends were with us and it was quite nice; as a matter of fact, it was one of the most wonderful Christmas times I ever experienced. We attended a reception and everyone was standing around talking. Fess noticed that my twenty-year-old son was sitting alone. Fess quietly detached himself from his group and went over and sat down next to David and started talking to him. A kindness a mother never forgets."

In 1996, his wines helped elevate the profile of his area. "Santa Barbara County is the Napa Valley of Los Angeles," proclaimed Frank J. Prial, the *New York Times*' wine columnist, on April 7, 1996. The article, which featured a photo of Fess at his winery's entrance,

Fess Parker and his vineyards.
PHOTO COURTESY OF THE PARKER FAMILY.

noted, "Fess Parker chardonnay is outstanding." And the *Fess Parker Winery* winter 1996 newsletter proudly proclaimed that Douglas Bailey of the *Boston Globe* named the 1993 American Tradition Reserve as "one of the top five Syrahs in the world." That same year, Fess won six Gold medals and five silver medals from various competitions, including the California State Fair and the Cincinnati International Wine Festival. One wine in particular, his "Santa Barbara County" Chardonnay won several medals.

As the winery grew, Fess considered other projects and he brought new young talent into his business family.

"I first met Fess Parker in 1996," said Richard E. Fogg. "I was twenty-five years old and a brand new lawyer right out of law school. Mr. Parker had been a long standing client of Mullen and Henzell L.L.P., the Santa Barbara law firm at which I got my start. I was brought into a meeting with him about some real estate matter a few months into my time at the firm. Having been born in 1971, I really was not aware of Mr. Parker's celebrity. But I could tell immediately that he was larger than life: the manner with which he conducted himself; his ownership of the room; his confidence and gracious manner; the deference that he was given by everyone at the office."

He appreciated working with Fess but a member of Fogg's family seemed to appreciate it even more.

"But the thing I remember most was my father's reaction later that night when I called to tell him that I had met Fess Parker," said Fogg. "As a kid my father always seemed to me completely unaware of television, movies, and popular culture. Now he was born in 1944. So when he acted like a ten-year-old boy who had just met his hero from me simply telling him I met Fess Parker, I knew this was a serious matter!"

Fogg went on to be one of Fess' most trusted associates.

"I started working on more and more of Mr. Parker's legal business from 1996 to 2000, mostly real estate purchases and financings," he remarked. "Over that time, Fess started calling on me directly with greater frequency. I was always impressed by his vision, his personal attachment to real estate opportunities and the fact that he really seemed to respect my input. Whenever we would meet, even though I was only in my late twenties with little experience, he would solicit my input and really listen. It was a huge boost to my confidence. Mr. Parker took me to breakfast in 2001 and asked if I might consider coming to work for his family full time, a proposal I ultimately accepted. That began about seven or eight years of acting as his 'general counsel,' 'confidant' and 'sounding board.'"

Fess looked to Fogg for his input. He liked having a wide range of advisors from different age groups to provide him with advice. And he appreciated those who disagreed with him, as long as their counter proposals and ideas were better than his.

"I was involved in pretty much all aspects of his interests to one degree or another, along with his family, trusted CFO Bill Osterbauer, and other advisors," noted Fogg.

In 1996, Fess donated some of his waterfront property to the city of Santa Barbara.

"The land was dedicated by Fess on August 13, 1996," said Dave Davis. "A dedication ceremony was held on site by the Parker family. It was at this event that Fess introduced me as almost a 'part of the family,' since it seemed he had spent more time with me in the past fifteen years than his own kids! That got a good laugh. The grand opening of the newly constructed park was May 30, 1998."

In 1997, Fess Parker Wines received some important critical attention.

Wine Advocate guru Robert M. Parker, Jr.—no relation to Fess—gave impressive scores of 89 to the 1994 "American Tradition Reserve" Chardonnay, the 1995 "Central Coast" Muscat Canelli, and the 1994 "Santa Barbara" Syrah.

On August 16, 1997, Fess celebrated his seventy-third birthday.

"No big deal," wrote Fess in his winery's fall 1997 brochure. "They're just like buses, or maybe the Swallows of Capistrano. They'll be another one along any minute."

The Disney Channel aired the original "Davy Crockett, Indian Fighter" episode on Sept. 21, 1997. And the remaining four episodes, the two originals and the two prequels, followed. When informed about the upcoming broadcasts, Fess was elated. "That would be wonderful to see the original episodes airing again," he said. Despite his success with *Daniel Boone*, Fess held his portrayal of *Davy Crockett* in the highest regard. He told the *Dallas Morning News* a year later: "I never really had a good part other than Davy Crockett."

Fess got a call another call from Disney. The studio requested his contribution on the video re-release of *Old Yeller*. He agreed. Fess went into the studio and provided some voice-over narration on the 1957 motion picture, and while in Hollywood he participated in twenty satellite media interviews. Fess noted the family values that were inherent in the film. "If you're a child, you learn responsibility for another being, a pet," he explained. "And then, of course, this family, this Texas-ranch family in the late 1800s exemplified a lot of very positive values."

Ashley and her husband, Rodney, planned a vacation during the winter of 1998. They were going to take their kids, Spencer and Greer, and Rodney's sister and his parents along. They left their house on February 8, 1998.

"Our entire family was in the car driving to LAX to catch a flight to Colorado for a family ski trip," said Ashley. "Rodney was behind the wheel when he started to lose consciousness. His last words were, 'Dad, take the wheel.'" Bob Shull managed to guide the car over to the side of the road and I called 911. An off-duty sheriff had seen us pull over and he stopped to help. He and Rodney's sister, Amy, pulled him out of the car and took turns performing CPR until the ambulance got there. They airlifted him to the hospital and we followed a California Highway Patrol unit to the hospital in our car. After about thirty minutes, they brought us back to a little room and told us that he had died. It was literally unbelievable."

When Ashley returned to Santa Barbara she was consoled by Fess and Eli.

"Dad was amazing during that horrible time," said Ashley. "He told me to pick out a plot in the Catholic Cemetery here in town. He made a point of wanting to pay for Rodney's funeral and the memorial. He was so supportive and wonderful. He did his best to come to school events for the kids in the months following Rodney's death even though he was always so busy. Anytime there was an event, like the time when Bishop High School retired Rodney's jersey and inducted him into the Athletic Hall of Fame, dad would always go with me."

Fess was obviously concerned about Ashley and her children, but he also felt their loss.

"I think Rod's death was a huge blow to him," said Ashley. "They had become very close and at that point I think dad viewed Rodney as a key player as far as the family business was concerned. Rodney had been instrumental in securing some financing for the vineyard expansion and so when he passed away Eli thought it would be fitting to name a vineyard for him."

In 1998, Parker purchased the Grand Hotel in Los Olivos and transformed the thirteen-year-old building into the Fess Parker Wine Country Inn & Spa, an upscale, twenty-one room, neo-Victorian facility.

That same year, on April 11, Fess and Eli were invited to the Jed and Marie Steele Tasting/Dinner at the Oregon Grill in Hunt Valley, Maryland. The event, hosted by Robert M. Parker, Jr. and his wife, was a benefit for Maryland's St. James Academy. Fess and Eli, who were joined by eleven other guests, enjoyed a vertical tasting of nineteen outstanding Penfolds Grange Hermitage wines.

Being in the company of talented wine consultant Jed Steele and influential wine critic Robert M. Parker meant a lot to Fess and Eli. "It was quite an event," remarked Eli. "Dad and I were glad to be a

The front entrance of the Fess Parker Wine Country Inn & Spa in Los Olivos, California.

PHOTO COURTESY OF THE PARKER FAMILY.

part of it."

Prior to the dinner, Robert M. Parker hosted a reception at his home where he presented a 1924 Bordeaux to Fess in honor of his birth year. Before departing to the restaurant, the wine critic asked Fess if he could spend a few minutes with his bedridden father. Fess, of course, obliged.

Fess and Eli were pleased to learn that an increasing number of the nation's finest restaurants were serving their wines—from Brennan's in New Orleans and Renaissance in Aspen to L'Etoile in San Antonio and The Mansion on Turtle Creek in Dallas. But they were not content to have their winery be one-dimensional: they wanted it to be the place where special cultural events took place, a location where all the creative arts could converge. An early example was the July 18, 1998 performance of the Coast Valley Symphony in its First Annual Summer Pops Concert.

On August 2, 1998, Fess was featured in a revealing interview in *The Dallas Morning News*. Besides the usual Hollywood resume information and updates on his winery, he responded to several unique questions

My hero is: "For a lot of reasons, Ronald Reagan."

Guests at my fantasy dinner party: "Daniel Patrick Moynihan, Newt Gingrich, Henry Kissinger, Colin Powell, Jeanne Kirkpatrick, Cindy Crawford."

I wish I could sing like: "Perry Como"

I'm happiest when: "Three times day—breakfast, lunch and dinner."

My last meal: "Red beans and corn bread, onions, green peppers."

I regret: "That my interests have taken me so far away from Texas, although my heart remains there."

The newspaper article also focused on the winery and Eli's concern that his father's wine might be dismissed out of hand simply because of the celebrity factor and the name on the label. "We wanted to be known for what's *in* the bottle," stated Eli.

The hard work paid off.

By the late 1990s, the multiple wine competition awards and positive reviews in various wine publications and newspapers influenced fine restaurants from across the country to carry Fess Parker Wines. New York City's China Grill, Seattle's Canlis, New Orleans' Gautreau's, Dallas' Star Canyon New Texas Cuisine, and Denver's Brasserie Z's wine lists soon featured bottles with small coonskin caps on the labels.

"As the first anniversary of Rodney's death approached I was dreading how hard it was going to be for everybody," said Ashley. "I talked Eli into going to Australia with me on a regional Shiraz growing trip in January run by a viticulturalist named Dr. Richard Smart. Eli was all set to go but had to cancel at the last minute because Laureen was having some problems with her pregnancy. I think everybody thought that I would cancel but it had been a pretty tough year and I really wanted to get away."

Ashley went by herself.

On the first night of the trip, she attended a wine tasting where she met Tim Snider.

"Tim had gone to Williams, a small liberal arts college in Massachusetts, and I had gone to Bates so we had that in common," said Ashley. "He was just very nice and fun and a good diversion for me. We flew back to California—separately—on Valentine's Day and I was surprised when he told me that he would like to call me and get together when we were both settled back in the states. I was surprised that he was up for that given the fact that I was widowed and had three kids."

She saw him a few times after that at San Francisco-based wine functions.

"At the time, Tim was working in the marketing department at Gallo after working his way up the ladder in the sales and management arenas," said Ashley. "He had been with the Gallo Company for eight years and was looking for a change, something less corporate."

But first, Snider would have to meet the King of the Wine Frontier.

"Tim first visited Los Olivos on Vintners Festival Weekend in April of 1999," said Ashley. "He met my folks, Eli and a few of my really close friends. He really hit it off with everyone."

Eli was particularly impressed by Snider's knowledge and a few months later he offered him a job.

"Tim moved to Santa Barbara in August of 1999 to come on board as our new Vice President of Sales and Marketing," said Ashley. "It was great working with him, and he made some very timely changes to the way we did business."

Fess' seventy-fifth birthday in 1999 was celebrated in grand style. And he never knew a thing about the surprise celebration until he stumbled upon the event—from above!

The party was planned by Eli and Ashley and set up on the Rodney's Vineyard section of the Fess Parker Winery. "Surprise was of the utmost concern so to that end Eli lured Fess into taking a helicopter tour of the winery's vineyard resources and then dropped him on the mesa to be greeted by his guests," said Ashley. "Many old friends from his Texas days were in attendance including Jimmy Tittle from Abilene, Phil and Kay Kendrick, Gus and Harrriet Vietas, and Morgan Woodward."

And "Davy Crockett at the Alamo" was the theme.

"Framing the scene was a 33' high by 63' long replica of the Alamo romantically recreated from Disney photographs by artist David 'Mad Dog' Norton," said Ashley. "An enormous white tent shaded the two hundred guests who dined on Texas BBQ provided by Tom Perini of Buffalo Gap, Texas. The tables were adorned with bandana tablecloths and the centerpieces were cowboy boots with local wildflowers cascading out the top. Music was provided by Tom

Celebrating Fess Parker's 75th birthday (L to R): Morgan Woodward, Gus Vietas, Kristopher Parker, Fess Parker, Phil Kendrick, and Jimmy Tittle.
Photo courtesy of the Parker Family.

Leatherwood and his band Brushfire."

Perini first met Fess in 1955 during the actor's promotional tour for *Davy Crockett, King of the Wild Frontier.*

"Fess as *Davy Crockett* arrived in San Antonio, and he was staying at the Menger Hotel," recalled Perini. "My father knew Phil Kendrick and his father so he kind of knew some of Fess' friends from Abilene. My father met Fess and introduced me to him. I was thrilled."

In the 1970s, Perini became one of Fess' friends.

"He would come back to Abilene all the time to see his friends, and that's when I got to meet him again and know him," said Perini. "I was about eighteen years younger than he was but because I knew some of his friends we became friends. Years later, I provided the food for his seventy-second birthday and I did it again for his seventy-fifth."

Perini opened the Perini Ranch Steakhouse in 1983 and quickly established his food emporium as one of Texas' best restaurants. "Fess loved to eat," stated Perini. "He really enjoyed mesquite-smoked pepper beef tenderloin, ribs, brisket and sausage—the down home food."

Fess Parker's 75th birthday party in Los Olivos, California. Standing in front of the imitation Alamo church façade (L to R): Jeff Harris, Kim Harris, Fess Parker, Ashley Parker Snider, Krissy Thomas, Brad Thomas, Tim Snider, and Adrienne Scheule.
PHOTO COURTESY OF THE PARKER FAMILY.

A special twenty-seven minute video chronicling Fess' life and career was produced by Ashley for the birthday bash. The production was filled with humor and heart-felt sentiments from his family, friends and employees. Following the video, Marcy sang "Happy Birthday" to her husband.

In 1999, Dr. Rhodes examined Fess again and detected several cancerous tumors in Fess' bladder and after surgery, initiated BCG—Bacillus Calmette-Guerin—therapy. "He looked in good shape for his age," remarked Rhodes. "He was a young seventy-five, but he had cancer." The BCG treatment, which is used to treat bladder cancer directly through a catheter, was applied during Fess' visits to the doctor's office.

Like his battle with prostate cancer, Fess maintained a let's-deal-with-it-and-move-on attitude. He sought sympathy from no one but his family was obviously concerned. "That was dad's way, but we were worried," explained Ashley.

"He later had a recurrence which had to be removed surgically," said Rhodes. "And I subsequently admitted him to the hospital. But I wanted to maintain his privacy so I asked him if it would be all right if I could make up a phony name for him upon his admittance. He said, 'Okay.' No one knew that he was in the hospital until the day of the surgery. As he was being wheeled down the hallway on the way to surgery and he sat up and said, 'Hi, I'm Fess Parker,' to people we passed. I said to him, 'Hey, I tried to keep you anonymous!'"

Ashley recalled a similar incident.

"When he was hospitalized in the early 90s—I can't recall what for—he registered under the name 'Johnny Walker,'" noted Ashley. "I thought it was very funny."

Released from the hospital, Fess returned home to recuperate—not to complain or seek sympathy.

Dr. Rhodes later crossed paths with his patient.

"I remember having to speak at a pharmaceutical conference of district managers from Pfizer at Fess' Wine Country Inn," said Rhodes. "I didn't know it at the time but Fess was having a board meeting there as well. He found out I was there from a waiter and promptly left his meeting for mine. He walked into the meeting and said to the managers, 'Listen to this guy, he saved my life.' And then he just walked out. That was Fess."

Robert M. Parker tasted more of Fess' wines in November of 1999 and stated that they were "the finest efforts of date. The bottom line is simple—this looks to be one of the more serious, up and coming players in Santa Barbara." *Wine Enthusiast* magazine awarded a 93 to the 1996 Syrah Rodney's Vineyard "American Tradition Reserve" and a 92 to 1996 Syrah "Santa Barbara County."

"Nineteen ninety-nine was a year of growth for our vineyard operations," said Eli. "We currently have approximately 450 acres under vine between Rodney's Vineyard, Marcella's Vineyard, and Ashley's Vineyard. Eli also announced that the Fess Parker Winery purchased an additional 1,400 acres in the Santa Ynez Valley where 250 acres were designated for planting.

Fess and his son were pleased at the praise but continued to strive for even better wines; as a matter of fact, Eli started developing his own wines: Epiphany Cellars was launched in 2000 when a separate tasting room was opened in Los Olivos.

"Over the course of seven or eight years in order to perfect Fess Parker Wine we experimented with a number of different vineyards and wine-producing techniques," explained Eli. "As a result of an experimental program and a fun way to showcase these new wines, Epihany was created."

That same year, Fess expanded the Wine Country Inn & Spa by landscaping a new lawn and garden area. The space was designed to host garden receptions, special luncheons and dinners for up to 120 guests. He had battled two cancers but remained active, upbeat, and optimistic.

"By 2000 we were producing approximately 100,000 cases annually," said Eli. "And our output continued to increase."

Another big family moment manifested itself.

"Tim asked me to marry him on Memorial Day Weekend of 2000," said Ashley. "We were married on November 4th at the Mission Santa Ynez and held our reception in the barrel room at the winery."

Fess volunteered his services to the California Department of Transportation's Adopt-A-Highway program. The state agency came to the winery where Fess filmed four promotional spots for California television audiences.

"Fess was something else when it came to trash on the streets," laughed Ames. "One day, we were walking down Grand Avenue, the street that his Inn is on in Los Olivos, and he spotted some litter on the street. He walked over to it and picked it up. I wonder how many other celebrities would have done that. He really loved his community and wanted it to look the best at all times."

CHAPTER 20
"FAREWELL TO THE MOUNTAINS"

Fess Parker Enterprises entered the twenty-first century with considerable real estate, hotel, and wine-making operations. Fess looked for some professional assistance outside his family and found it in the form of Bill Osterbauer, who was named Chief Financial Officer in 2001.

Osterbauer, a Baby Boomer with considerable experience in corporate finance, found out that his job description expanded when Fess asked him to do more. "Quickly he started pulling me away," said Osterbauer. "He'd say, 'Could you look at this mobile home park deal?'" Osterbauer quickly assumed more responsibilities.

"I found the interaction with Fess to be personally satisfying and interesting," said Osterbauer. "I could almost tell from his demeanor what the day was going to be like. If I got there at eight o'clock in the morning and his Mercedes was already parked there, he's loaded for bear! He's got some ideas and some concepts and some things that he wants to get onto. So he and I would get together and he would often times lay out ideas or concepts or problems that he was concerned with or things of that nature and we would kick these things around."

Osterbauer was impressed by Fess' business style.

"His style was very informal," said Osterbauer. "He loved being with people. But not everybody was to his liking; he didn't like those who were disrespectful. He was much more discerning in terms of his real likes and dislikes than his public persona. He was a very stubborn guy. If somebody said something could not be done, he would see it as a challenge, not as an obstacle or threat. And he certainly knew when to hold 'em and when to fold 'em."

Osterbauer also appreciated Fess' creative visions. But sometimes they seemed a bit too unique.

"He was always looking for things that could be developed in a different way," said Osterbauer who remembered the day when Fess approached him with the idea of acquiring control of the old Los Angeles Union Station. Fess envisioned transforming the railroad facility into a mausoleum.

"It wasn't consistent with the city's vision of what they should have in their downtown area," laughed Osterbauer.

Fess not only managed his business interests, he actively promoted them. And he constantly sought out opinions from others.

"His ability to reach out and touch people who might have some perspective or some valuable information on certain subjects was uncanny," said Osterbauer. "And he would travel all over the country to help establish his winery."

"He was a great ambassador for his label," said Eli. "And he enjoyed doing it."

And those visits, to say nothing of the increasing quality of Fess and Eli's wines, helped generate some critically-acclaimed dividends.

Fess and Eli introduced a new label in 2003: Parker Station. The label featured the caricatured face of a raccoon. The Parker Station Pinot Noir was promoted as "The best wine you can afford to drink daily," a tagline created by Tim Snider.

"We actually topped 140,000 cases by 2004, but we cut back on our quantity and redirected our operation," said Eli. "We pulled away from certain offerings and ended up being lean and more focused."

The San Francisco International Wine Competition is the largest—and arguably the most prestigious—wine competition in the United States. Vintners from around the world submit thousands of bottles of their best wine in an effort to be judged in a number of elite categories. In 2006, the competition received over 3,000 entries, but only forty-two wines qualified for recognition. One of them was a Fess Parker Wine (the 2003 Syrah "Rodney's Vineyard" won Best Syrah) and two were Eli Parker's Epiphany Cellars' wines (the 2005 Grenache Blanc, Camp 4 Vineyard won the Best of Show White Wine; and the 2003 Revelation earned a Double Gold). Eli

Parker was also named the 2006 Andre Tchelistcheff Winemaker of the Year.

"I'm honored to be recognized with an award inspired by a great winemaker, Andre Tchelistcheff," said Eli.

Fess was particularly proud.

"Yes, he was very proud of that," said Eli. "He was pleased that I was recognized but I was more happy that we as a family, as a business, worked together and were successful. We had—and still have—a great team."

Attention was also generated by the 2005 motion picture *Sideways*, which filmed a number of scenes at the Fess Parker Winery. The production company renamed the Parker enterprise as "Frass Canyon." One of the most memorable scenes in the film is where Paul Giamatti, a Pinot Noir afficianado who loathes Merlot, requests a "full pour" of wine in the Fess Parker Winery's tasting room.

The R-rated film impacted wine sales in a big way.

"Not until this crazy little movie was released did Pinot Noir firmly solidify its niche with mainstream wine consumers," said Eli. "As a result of increased interest we are up 16 percent in Pinot Noir sales in the wholesale market and up 22 percent here in the tasting room. We have sold out of every Pinot Noir we sell in the wholesale market well ahead of schedule."

Fess, however, had mixed opinions about *Sideways*.

"I was pleased because the film alerted people about our winery and the wineries in our area," remarked Fess. "But I was not pleased with some of the language in the film."

Nevertheless, the Fess Parker Winery had emerged as a major player among Santa Barbara County's wineries. "I'm not sure my father realized that his winery would get to be what it has become," said Eli. "Its success originated with him. Ranching and farming were in his blood and there's an agricultural connection between them and wine making."

The Parker Family's wine operation expanded to four labels: Fess Parker, Parker Station, Frontier Red, and Epiphany. The Fess Parker label constitutes about half of the production; Parker Station generates about 20 percent of the output; Frontier Red represents about 12 percent of all the wine produced; and Epiphany the rest.

When the work day was over, it was time for entertaining. Guests called it "Parker Hospitality."

"Routinely after dinner we would adjourn to the living room and somebody would have a guitar and somebody would sit at the piano," said Bargiel. "And virtually every dinner party concluded with some kind of sing-a-long."

After the Parkers sold their spacious Hope Ranch house and moved into smaller quarters in Los Olivos, the song fests ended. But just for a while.

Marcy incorporated singing as a regular part of Thursday evenings at the Fess Parker Wine Country Inn & Spa. Accompanied by pianist Bill Powell, Marcy would deliver a wide range of standards and her signature "blues and ballad" tunes.

Powell had been playing piano at the Alisal Guest Ranch in Solvang, California in the mid 1990s when Marcy walked in one night, sat down next to him and started singing. "Then Fess came in for a nice visit," said Powell, who had actually met both of them for the first time in the late 1950s when the musician was working in a Santa Barbara record store. "Fess was this tall handsome man and Marcy was a real dish, just stunning! I thought to myself, "What a striking couple they make."

After meeting them at the Alisal Guest Ranch, Powell met Fess and Marcy several months later.

"They later invited me and my wife to a Billy Taylor concert that was held at their winery," said Powell. "Then they hired me to play a few times at the winery and one thing led to another. We became friends and ended up playing every Thursday night at the Inn. I began playing there in April of 1999. Fess always wanted to have a venue to spotlight Marcy's vocal talents and to create a place where people could enjoy some fine music and vocal talent—thus, Thursday nights were born."

Marcy, of course, handled every song with ease. Fess was a willing vocalist but needed a bit of assistance.

"Fess enjoyed singing on Thursday nights, too, but he wanted to be prepared so he would sometimes come up to my house to rehearse," said Powell. "One day he stopped in and he told me that he had been 'just driving along and singing to the cows.' Fess had very eclectic musical tastes as a singer—everything from Hank

Williams' 'Your Cheatin' Heart' to Kurt Weil's 'September Song.'"

Powell pointed out that guests would regularly request "The Ballad of Davy Crockett."

"I remember a guy from Scandanavia was there on his birthday and Fess sang the Happy Birthday song to him," said Powell. "The guy was thrilled. He said, 'I never thought that Davy Crockett would sing "Happy Birthday" to me.' Fess was so generous with his time. And he was the most gracious person."

The Parkers would also encourage others to join in on the musical fun.

"Everyone sang there at one time or another from Ed Ames and Jane Russell to Cheryl Ladd," said Bargiel. "I even remember a woman who sang 'Amazing Grace' in Cherokee."

Ladd and her husband, Brian Russell, had met the Parkers through mutual friends and charity events in the early 1990s. They also enjoyed the Thursday nights.

"I sang, too, of course," said Ladd, who scored a top 40 hit with "Think it Over" while she starred on TV's *Charlie's Angels*. "But when I went to the Inn I preferred when others sang, especially Marcy. But when they wanted me to sing, I did."

And on one occasion the Thursday night event helped revive someone's career.

"I had stopped singing for years because I was just finished with the *business* of show business," explained Jeanne Arnold Ames, Ed Ames' wife, who attended one of the Thursday evening sing-a-longs at the Inn. She had an extensive career sharing the stage with the likes of Tony Bennett, Bob Hope, George Burns, Chuck Berry, Shecky Greene, Rich Little, Joe Piscopo, and Ike and Tina Turner, and she recorded with such diverse artists as Ringo Starr, Peter Allen, Loudon Wainwright and Albert King. "I really didn't want to sing, but he gently got me back into singing and I had some of the richest moments of just being a person, an entertainer at that little place, the Inn. I was terrified, though. I mean, I had sung in front of thousands and thousands of people but this was a place where you had to sing with people in your face. I told Fess I just couldn't do it. He didn't put me down; he didn't say, 'Oh, come on, that's silly.' He gently suggested from week to week until I ended getting a show out of that little room."

Jeanne Ames' show was *Sondheim Reviewed*, an adaptation of the popular Broadway production *Side By Side By Sondheim*. Joined by Angelina Réax and Michael Sokol, Ames renewed her career in June 2003 at the Center Stage Theater in Santa Barbara.

"The show ran for three months," beamed Jeanne Ames. "Here I was singing again, and with two opera singers no less. And it was all because of Fess and his encouragement."

Fess and Marcy loved to host parties of all kinds. If there was a reason to celebrate something, they would.

"My husband, Brian, was born in Scotland and raised in Canada," said Ladd of her spouse who had recorded two albums for Elton John's Rocket Records and wrote songs for such diverse artists as songs for Chaka Khan and Ann Murray. Russell's music was subsequently sampled by the likes of Jay-Z and Kanye West. "But he wanted to become a U.S. citizen. When he did, Fess and Marcy threw a party for him. That's the way they were."

Generosity was clearly part of the Parker social equation. Bill Powell remembered a particular incident in 1998.

"One evening Fess called and asked me to accompany him to Santa Barbara in the morning because he had some business to take care of down there," said Powell. "I said sure, I always enjoyed the time we had driving around, conversing about everything from politics to diets. He picked me up in Marcy's Mercedes and we drove down to the local Mercedes dealer. When we arrived, Fess turned to me and handed me the keys and said, 'Here you go. Take her home.' I was at a total loss for words, obviously not expecting this. I told Fess that I couldn't accept it. He said, 'We've got too many cars. It's a done deal; we'll get the paperwork straightened out later.' Concerned because there wasn't a current license tag on the car and the only registration was a few years old I asked Fess what I should do if I got stopped on the way back home. He smiled that impish smile and said, 'Just tell them the Governor is a friend of mine.'"

Since childhood, Fess loved to read. As an adult, he read everything from periodicals and newspapers to business reports and books. He particularly enjoyed David McCullough's Pulitzer Prize-winning *John Adams*. "You know, the Adamses wrote everything down," noted Fess in the 2003 *Alcalde* interview. "Our nation is so enriched by that trove of letters and by the character of Abigail. It was one thing for John to sacrifice and do the things he did. It was another that she could live alone, maintain a farm, feed herself, still be able to support her family in all the circumstances of their lives."

Unlike John and Abigail, Fess and Marcy did nearly everything together, including collaborating on a music album. The sing-a-long Thursday nights at the Inn became so popular that guests wanted to know if any prerecorded music was available. Marcy soon entered the recording studio and emerged in 2000 with *Marcy Parker Sings Love Songs*, a carefully-produced collection of fifteen classic tunes that featured Bill Powell on the piano. Her husband wrote the CD's liner notes which included his recollection when he first saw that "beautiful girl with an unforgettable voice."

Whenever possible, Fess and Marcy enjoyed providing their own transportation whether by land, sea or air. Over the years the couple owned several aircraft and boats.

"The first plane that dad owned was a Piper Twin Comanche," said Eli. "Then he had a Beechcraft Twin Bonanza, a Beechcraft Queen Air—which I'm not sure that he actually owned—a Cessna 182, a Cessna Skymaster, a Cessna 340, and a Cessna Citation."

"We flew everywhere together, even across the country," remarked Marcy. "He was a good pilot."

Fess persuaded Peter Ellenshaw to buy a plane. "Fess Parker invited me to share in the purchase of an airplane," said Ellenshaw in his autobiography. "I would be able to fly back and forth whenever I wanted! He had a pilot ready, a mechanic, it was a twin-engine plane; it was all very nice and useful. Very expensive though, I don't know why I ever thought of doing it!" Ellenshaw explained that another person joined in on the purchase but Fess soon said, "I don't like this plane very much, it won't fly on one engine." Ellenshaw recalled that the "nightmare" investment was "costing us plenty." The plane was eventually sold and Ellenshaw was glad to get rid of his "plane thing."

On the high seas, the Parkers sailed in the *Cholita*, a 46-foot sloop, the 52-foot long *Sea Isle*, and the *Coho*. "The *Coho* was a modified fishing boat," said Ashley. "She was smaller than the *Sea Isle*. Fess, of course, had served in the U.S. Navy so boating came somewhat naturally to him. Marcy, however, was from Iowa. But that didn't stop her from sailing on her own. On more than one occasion she sailed the *Cholita* on her own to Catalina Island and back. "I sailed all the time, sometimes with Fess and sometimes by myself," said Marcy. "Of course, when we sailed together he was the captain, but I put in a lot of time at the helm. I actually learned how to sail from that old Norwegian boyfriend of mine." Marcy noted that her husband enjoyed the stress-free atmosphere of being on a boat. "When we were sailing he relaxed the most. Fess was basically a stay-at-home guy, but he enjoyed sailing so very much. And I must say, he was a very good sailor."

Since Fess portrayed both *Davy Crockett* and *Daniel Boone* some people were confused as to who was who. Print media would occasionally identify a photograph of Fess as one of the frontier heroes while the companion article discussed the other famous pioneer. Online auction-site sellers contributed to the confusion when they made similar mistakes. The situation was addressed in a History Channel documentary—*Boone and Crockett: The Hunter Heroes*—that first aired in July of 2001. The production, directed by Gary Foreman, featured historians who traced the lives of the celebrated figures and explained how their personalities became intertwined in the public consciousness due to Fess' portrayal. "Unintentionally, Fess Parker confused generations of Americans about the difference between Daniel Boone and Davy Crockett because he simply played both," stated Michael A. LoFaro of the University of Tennessee at Knoxville. But Fess didn't mind the mix up since those "confused" folks still appreciated his thoughtful portrayals of both men.

Fess was always quick to come to someone's assistance when an emergency happened.

"My father suddenly died on September 4, 2001," said Ladd. "Of course, one week later was the September 11 tragedy. It was a very stressful time for me. Fess and Marcy stepped forward after the funeral and said, 'Don't worry about anything.' They were so generous with everything, from food to caring. It was just their way."

Two months later, *Davy Crockett* made a twenty-first century comeback of sorts.

The original TV episodes were finally released on DVD on December 4, 2001 as part of the Walt Disney Treasures series. Titled *Davy Crockett: The Complete Television Series*, 150,000 copies of the five original episodes were carefully restored to about 99% of their original length. A few short sequences were not included, like part of the animal roundup in "Davy Crockett's Keelboat Race," and a few clips are in sepia tone since some of the original color negative film was missing.

The restoration effort was primarily entrusted to veteran editor Tony "Skip" Malanowski, an appreciative fan of Fess' since his childhood who treated the project with reverence. "I was thrilled to work on the project," remarked Malanowski. "I spent seven months working as chief editor restoring the shows, matching the original color negative against a black and white 35mm Fine Grain Master of the original broadcasts. This gave me the chance to use the color sections, where available, to restore the show as closely as possible to the original broadcast—only in color. Remember, the original negatives were used in the shortened theatrical versions, so sometimes we would be short a couple of frames here and there, which we would have to account for. And other times, the shots would be missing altogether. So to keep the overall feel of the show, we had to use the black and white sections rather than leave them out entirely—which is a decision I still agree with. This is why, on occasion, you have shots that are in black and white—or sepia—on the DVD."

Fess was elated about the Walt Disney Treasures release.

"I think it's wonderful!" stated Fess. "And it certainly interests me since I know I will recall some memories about it. I haven't seen the entire production in quite some time. Oh, I've seen bits and piece of it over the years but not all of it. I was invited to participate in an event to mark the occasion of Walt Disney's one hundredth birthday at Walt Disney World in December, the same month that the DVD is being released."

Davy Crockett: The Complete Television Series is not without its flaws, however. Not everyone who was involved in the project maintained the same level of care that Malanowski demonstrated. For example, the cover features a reverse image of Fess as *Davy Crockett* and DVD host Leonard Maltin, a genuine Fess Parker fan, provides the wrong air date for the "Davy Crockett Goes to Congress" episode. Surprisingly, the DVD box notes suggest that Crockett never fought in the Creek Indian War: "General Andrew Jackson enlisted Crockett to fight Chief Red Stick. But instead of going to war with the Indians, Davy convinced them to sign a peace treaty."

The Supplemental Features feature a limited amount of production stills and interviews. But some errors are included. For example, "The Ballad of Davy Crockett" was not a "#1 song for three months." It was a chart-topper for five weeks. And a described account between Crockett and John Q. Adams never happened.

Still, *Davy Crockett: The Complete Television Series* is an essential piece of TV history and Malanowski's reverential editing elevates its visual quality. And even the edited film version, which was also available in DVD format, still held up in the eyes of twenty-first century reviewers. Jim Craddock's *Videohound's Golden Movie Retriever*, said it was "well done by a splendid cast."

A Davy Crockett exhibit opened at the Bob Bullock Texas History Museum in Austin, Texas in 2002. Fess attended a pre-opening gala and was impressed by the collection of nineteenth-century historical items and pop culture collectibles from the 1950s and 60s.

"It was a very pleasant experience," said Fess. "They really did a nice job. I appreciated the turnout. I enjoyed the Crockett exhibit because of the generosity of those people who contributed to it. It's a very functional museum and it will grow to be an event center where people will discover their heritage."

Fess was particularly interested in the historical artifacts, especially those of Crockett's March 6, 1836 antagonist, General Santa Anna. "Yes, Santa Anna's sword and scabbard," noted Fess. "I'm in awe that the museum had that. And also the figurehead from the clipper ship *David Crockett*. And the rifles."

One of the nineteenth-century flintlock rifles on display was used in "Davy Crockett Goes to Congress."

"That was great," said Fess, who had one suggestion for the museum. "Well, the only thing missing was music. I would have liked to have heard 'Farewell' or even 'The Ballad of Davy Crockett' being played in the background. Still, I'm thankful not only for Fess Parker's legacy but for old Davy. I've traveled with him for quite some time."

And there was a chance he was going to travel with him one more time on the big screen.

Disney's Touchstone Pictures was about to film *The Alamo* in January 2003, and there was speculation that Fess might make a cameo appearance in the film which featured Billy Bob Thornton as Crockett. Immediately, comparisons between Thornton and Fess—and Thornton and John Wayne—popped up in the media. "All I can say is that I would never underestimate a successful actor," said Fess about Thornton's ability.

On March 25, 2003, Fess was presented the Texas Medal of Arts award by the Texas Cultural Trust Council (TCTC) for Media-Film/Television and Acting in ceremonies held in Austin, Texas. According to the TCTC, the award "spotlights and celebrates the creative excellence, exemplary talents and outstanding contributions by Texans in selected categories, ultimately featuring the best in Texas." Fess' award was in the Film/Television and Acting category. He was joined by such other award recipients as singer Charlie Pride and dancer-choreographer Tommy Tune.

"When Fess, Tim and I traveled down to Texas for the Texas Medal Arts ceremony in Austin, we knew that Disney's *The Alamo* was being filmed just outside the city," explained Ashley. "There had been rumblings that they might want dad to do a cameo in the film. It seemed to me that dad was reluctant to 'mess' with his Davy Crockett legacy, but some of us in the family thought it might be fun and encouraged him to do so. It came up during our visit that it might be nice for dad and Billy Bob Thornton to meet while we were in town. So during the dinner party at the Driskill Hotel following the Medal Arts ceremony, we excused ourselves and dad and I were ushered into a ballroom. Dad was having a good time reminiscing as we walked through the public space at the Driskill as he had been to a lot of parties there during his college years. We waited for Billy Bob to arrive in this big empty ballroom where someone had arranged a seating area. Dad was wearing coat and tie, dress slacks, and his best cowboy boots; he looked every bit the former UT Fraternity man. Suddenly the double doors to the ballroom opened and in walked this rather diminutive man in a pea coat and beanie hat. He couldn't have been more than 5'9" and he was very scruffy. I think the idea was that dad and I were supposed to be very impressed about having the chance to meet Mr. Thornton—but the reality was that Billy Bob looked scared to death. Dad stood up and strode halfway across the room to meet him with his hand outstretched. Billy Bob looked up—and I do mean up—at dad and must have felt like he was standing at the foot of the Lincoln Memorial. Dad's hand absolutely engulfed the smaller man's hand and he gave him a 'How ya doin,' Billy Bob!' It was hilarious. Billy Bob looked like a field mouse that senses an eagle shadow circling above him. It wasn't a long meeting, but it was very cordial. I'm guessing Billy Bob was thinking that maybe he had bit off more than he could chew trying to replace Davy Crockett in the hearts and minds of America."

Fess was finally contacted by Touchstone Pictures, which was filming just miles outside of Austin in Dripping Springs.

"When I was in Austin I was invited to go to the set but because of the timing it didn't work out," explained Fess. "I returned to Austin again and got a call from the second assistant director who said that I 'have a call at nine o'clock the next day' to appear in the film. I asked him what the scene was and he said, 'I haven't got a clue.' I told him that I would be willing to be a part of a scene but I didn't want to bring attention to myself."

Fess explained that he didn't want to upstage Thornton and told the second assistant director that he would appreciate hearing more about the role and the scene from John Lee Hancock, the director of *The Alamo*. "I was expecting to hear from the director but he never called. So I said, 'I'm outta here.' It was quite an unprofessional experience."

Later in an interview, Thornton said that he "never intended to play the character as John Wayne or Fess Parker. I wanted to make him more than a one-dimensional guy." When Fess learned of Thornton's critical comment he shook his head. He was disappointed in Thornton's public assessment of his memorable performance as Davy Crockett, but Fess refused to get angry or counter the actor's remarks. He simply said, "That's unfortunate."

Ashley was glad that her father didn't work in the film.

"When the dust settled and the reviews came out, as usual, dad's instincts were better than most and he definitely made the right decision not to participate," said Ashley. *The Alamo* tanked at the box office and became Disney's all-time biggest film bomb.

Fess and Buddy Ebsen had been friends since 1954, and they continued to make appearances together at occasional Disney events, especially select anniversary specials on television. Ebsen was presented a Disney Legends Award in 1993, two year's after Fess received his. The event was the last important public appearance that the multitalented performer ever made.

Ebsen died on July 6, 2003. He was 95.

"I spoke to him earlier in the year and I spoke to him later when he was in the hospital," said Fess. "When he was home, I asked him how he was getting along and he told me some days were good but some days were tough. His house had a lot of steps and he and his wife, Dorothy, were going to sell the house and move. They had a condo in Long Beach, but the next thing I heard from Dorothy was that he was in the hospital. I spoke to him two days before he died. I phoned the hospital and Dorothy answered. She told Buddy, 'It's Fess Parker.' Buddy got on the phone and said, 'Hi, Fess,' but I couldn't understand everything that he said after that. I said to him, "You get yourself well."

Fess later attended Ebsen's funeral service.

"He was such a talented man," stated Fess. "He will be missed."

Some wondered what had happened to Fess, too.

Following Ebsen's death, a letter appeared in the February 1, 2004 edition of the Sunday *Parade* magazine which asked, "Is Fess Parker, who played TV's Davy Crockett in the '50s, still alive and kickin'?" Page editor Walter Scott responded with, "Not only alive but a busy entrepreneur." Fess found such periodic inquiries about him amusing. "Yeah," chuckled Fess, "I'm still kickin.'" However, as he approached his eightieth birthday he started to pay attention to his legacy. And he wanted to do some things that people would remember him with fondness. Still, he didn't want memorials. He rejected offers from authors who wanted to write his biography and joked when approached about the idea of having a star on the Hollywood Walk of Fame. "I don't like the idea of people walking over me all day long," laughed Fess. He had responded to a similar inquiry in the January 1977 issue of *Biography* when he pointed out, "Our greatest heroes in life end up as pigeon roosts, as statues in the park. Fame is a very transient thing."

Fess wrote a letter to the Daughters of the Republic of Texas, the custodians of the Alamo and offered to donate the flintlock rifle that was presented to him by in 1955. "This rifle has been my most prized possession for almost fifty years," wrote Fess. "I don't wish to be presumptuous in suggesting that it be placed in the Alamo museum. There have been many reenactments and many actors who've played the part and there will be many more. But I would be honored if you would consider it, if this is of any interest to you, and if so perhaps it could be helpful as another way to publicize the Alamo and the wonderful work that the Daughters of the Republic of Texas have done over the years and thus inspire further support."

Dave Stewart, the Alamo's business manager immediately accepted the offer.

"We would be honored to have your wonderful rifle in our collection," answered Stewart. "We also would be very pleased to set up a presentation ceremony to receive the rifle."

Prior to his visit to San Antonio, Fess was informed by the Alamo staff about one of his biggest fans, a young boy by the name of David Monse. The youngster had become enamored of Fess after viewing his grandfather's videocassette copy of *Davy Crockett, King of the Wild Frontier.* Monse was also the son of Thomas Monse, a Texas lawman who was gunned down in a 1999 ambush. Fess requested that Monse and his family attend the Alamo Hall event as his special guests. On March 4, the young boy met his hero, and at a ceremony both were inducted as Alamo Rangers. After Monse's grandmother, Janie May, pinned the badge on her grandson, Fess requested that she also pin him. May obliged. Fess appreciated the boy's enthusiasm for his Crockett characterization but wanted to put hero worshipping in proper perspective. He turned to the boy and said, "I'm very glad you made me your hero, but your dad is the real hero."

That same day Fess also provided his handprints at the Ripley's Believe It or Not Wax Museum in San Antonio for "Celebrities Giving a Hand," a charity fund-raiser. He and Ashley also had lunch with his good friends Dr. Richard Becker and Tom and Lisa Perini at the Argyle, a private dinner club.

The main rifle presentation ceremony was scheduled for March 5, 2004 in front of the Alamo Church.

"It was presented to me at Independence Hall in 1955 an at NRA function," said Fess to a group of admiring Baby Boomers who met him before the official presentation. "And it was presented to me in a way that recalled the young men of Philadelphia who gave a similar rifle to Davy Crockett. The person who actually presented the rifle to me was a Medal of Honor winner."

Fess Parker addresses a crowd at the Alamo on March 5, 2004. Fess later donated a nineteenth-century flintlock rifle to the Alamo.
AUTHOR'S COLLECTION.

He later made this entry in the Daughters of the Republic of Texas VIP book: "The day of 3/5/04 in front of the Alamo was warm and sunny," wrote Fess. "Many history buffs were present along with Disney 'Davy' fans. My daughter, Ashley Snider, came with me and [made] the trip even better. At lunch, Jaycelyn, Dave Stewart's granddaughter, sat at my right and Mr. Stewart at the left. 'Davy Crockett,' the song, was sung by Bill Chemerka, Tony Pasqua, and Frank Thompson. The rifle was delivered to the Alamo Museum."

Fess also made a surprise visit to the Alamo Society 2004 Symposium which was held at the Emily Morgan Hotel. He entered the back of the conference room at the end of the annual meeting and walked up the center aisle to the podium. The place erupted in affectionate applause. True to form, he remained at the event and signed autographs and posed for photos.

On the next night, the 168th anniversary of the Battle of Alamo, Fess delivered an impassioned patriotic address to the Alamo Defenders Descendants Association inside the Shrine of Texas Liberty.

"The opportunity that Walt Disney gave me to play Davy Crockett and to experience a re-creation of the battle of the Alamo is one of the most memorable times of my life," said Fess. "From the beginning of film history, over the course of about one hundred years, almost every generation has had a retelling of the story. I feel that I speak for all the other actors who participated in those versions in saying how powerful is the impact of this hallowed ground and the sacrifices that were made by the men who defended the Alamo. It's certainly a symbol for all time and I will talk more about symbols later on."

Fess shifted gears as the speech developed. He went beyond a typical speech about coonskin caps and nostalgic childhood moments. Instead, Fess discussed the September 11, 2001 attacks, the war in Iraq, the media, and the Department of Homeland Security. "There is a connection between then and now in the eternal struggle to retain our democracy," he said. "So, you and I are meeting here this evening at a major crossroad in how we view our history and its impact for our future."

He reminded the audience that America had faced tremendous challenges before, especially when the nation was divided in Civil War. And then he stressed the importance of national symbols.

"There are many other symbols that [provide] evidence [of] who we are: the statements on our currency, 'In God We Trust;' slogans over libraries and public buildings; our U.S. flag and the symbol of our President are included among these," stated Fess. "Disrespect for or failure to preserve our valued symbols weakens us as a nation. Not promoting these symbols to our children weakens our future."

Fess went on to warn the audience that the war against terrorism was merely one conflict that the United States was involved in.

"Finally, I would like to conclude by saying that we are in another war, not the one I have been talking about but one that may be much more dangerous than anything that can come to us from overseas," said Fess in a tone that recalled the passion of his speech against the Indian Removal Bill in "Davy Crockett Goes to Congress" nearly fifty years earlier. "That is the fact that our core values are at risk. Who is not disturbed by the culture of today? How do we restore our nation to the basic values that seem cast to the wind in all stratus of our lives? We must [teach about] our historical values.

Or we could be divided again—or worse. Americans need to learn or rediscover our history by reading our great heritage through the values contributed by the patriots of our wars for independence and by giants in our history: Washington, Adams, Jefferson, Lincoln, and other courageous leaders throughout our history. We can meet the challenges presented to us in our time, by rekindling in our hearts and our minds that ghostly yell from our troops at San Jacinto that can still be heard through history: Remember the Alamo!"

Fess' formal speech at the Alamo was the last one he ever delivered.

But there was another program that he was invited to speak at weeks later: "Fess Parker—Celebrating an American Icon." The event, which coincided with the 50th anniversary of the first *Davy Crockett* episode and the 40th anniversary of the *Daniel Boone* show on NBC-TV, turned out to be the most important tribute that Fess ever received.

Fess and Ashley arrived in Washington D.C. on March 28, two days ahead of the scheduled event, and stayed at the Hotel Monaco.

The Smithsonian Associates' "Fess Parker—Celebrating an American Icon" event was held on March 30, 2004 at the Carmichael Auditorium at the Smithsonian Institution's Museum of American History. The $21 general admission tickets were quickly purchased and a standing-room only crowd was on hand to see Fess donate several of his *Davy Crockett* and *Daniel Boone* items to the Smithsonian. He donated a coonskin cap, a *Daniel Boone* jacket, a pair of fringed boots, and a prop rifle.

"I liked that rifle that I carried in the *Daniel Boone* series," said Fess. "As a matter of fact, it was residing in my bedroom for years. But, unfortunately, it's not an authentic rifle. It's actually a prop that I selected out of the many weapons for use in the *Daniel Boone* series. The rifles that I used in the Disney *Davy Crockett* series, however, were real."

The items were placed in a showcase that also included an issue of *TV Guide* with Fess and Buddy Ebsen on the cover, a *Daniel Boone* lunch box, sheet music covers from *Davy Crockett* and *Daniel Boone*, 45 rpm singles, and assorted photographs.

Before he entered the Carmichael Auditorium, the crowd spontaneously started to sing "The Ballad of Davy Crockett." It was

The author, Fess Parker and Debbie Chemerka at the Smithsonian Associates' "Fess Parker – Celebrating an American Icon" event, March 30, 2004.
Author's collection.

obvious that nostalgia was in the air. He was introduced by the American History Museum's cultural historian Dwight Blocker Bowers who traced Fess' career and asked him questions. Bowers then opened up the question-and-answer period to the audience.

Fess recalled the "Davy Crockett at the Alamo" episode and explained how his relationship with the Alamo had grown over the years. He told the audience of his memorable experience at the Shrine of Texas Liberty only weeks before.

"March the sixth, Bill Chemerka, my daughter and I were sitting together, and I had prepared a speech to give for the Alamo," he said. "But I didn't know until the last minute that it was going to be [given] inside the Alamo—and it was for the families who were related to the defenders. And so it was a very special occasion."

He left the auditorium and entered the museum where he officially signed over the *Crockett* and *Boone* items to the Smithsonian.

A reception—complete with Fess Parker Wines—followed. As with other events, cameras clicked away as scores of people asked for his autograph. It was a long night, but Fess kept up the pace as if he were on the 1955 cross-country *Davy Crockett* tour.

"This is the last trip dad will be taking out of state," confided Ashley. "These long trips are very tiring for him. No more after this."

In May of 2004, Fess was invited to participate at the Walt Disney Art Classics Convention which was held at Disneyland's Paradise Pier hotel. It was, after all, the 50th anniversary of the first *Davy Crockett* episode.

He entered the hotel's Pacific Ballroom and was greeted by moderator Craig Hodgkins and an audience which spontaneously broke out with an abbreviated version of "The Ballad of Davy Crockett." Sitting in a director's chair, Fess answered questions from the floor in a fashion that recalled his Smithsonian appearance a few months earlier. At the conclusion of the question-and-answer session he reminded the audience that in order to restore some of the nation's core values it was necessary to study the historical figures who made our nation great.

Coinciding with the event, the Walt Disney Classics Collection added "Davy Crockett" to its roster of sculpted, porcelain-based figurines in 2004. Kent Melton was authorized to create Fess' iconic image in an exclusive production run of only 500 pieces. Accompanying each hand-painted figurine was a numbered Certificate of Authenticity which featured Fess' printed endorsement and autograph. "Portraying Davy Crockett was one of the highlights of my career as an actor," stated Fess. "It was an amazing start to my long association with Walt Disney, which resulted in not only the landmark TV series but also six feature films including the Disney classic, *Old Yeller*. [Two thousand-four] marks the 50th anniversary of the Davy Crockett TV series and the first time I donned Davy's famous coonskin cap. Now a California vintner and innkeeper my days as Davy Crockett are far behind me, but he still retains a special place in my heart as a great film role and a hero to a generation of children and grown-ups alike."

In July, Fess returned the Hollywood Bowl, the scene of his memorable 1955 appearance with Buddy Ebsen. "I was proud to have been asked back and had a lot of fun doing a Lincoln reading and a reprise of 'The Ballad of Davy Crockett,'" noted Fess. "Jon Mauceri conducted the Hollywood Bowl Orchestra with the Cal State Fullerton Choir. It was wonderful to have Marcy and the grandchildren there, but I sure wish Buddy had been there too."

The next month, Fess celebrated his eightieth birthday party in grand style at the winery. Texas friends and Hollywood personalities like Ron Ely, Cheryl Ladd, and Peter Ellenshaw showed up with best wishes. Once again the Perini Steakhouse in Buffalo Gap, Texas provided the food. Les Brown Jr. and his Band of Renown supplied the music. And Cheryl Ladd and Chuck Bargiel provided the night's most memorable entertainment.

Ladd recited an obscure farm joke about Carnation Evaporated Milk. At the microphone, Ladd described the story of a rural woman who entered a money-prize contest in which the winner had to complete a jingle that followed the statement, "I like Carnation best of all."

Fess and the entire crowd sat and listened intently as Ladd continued her story. She said company representatives arrived at the woman's home and presented her the winnings but confessed that they could not use her jingle because of the language. And then Ladd delivered the woman's winning phrase: "I like Carnation best of all, no tits to pull, no shit to haul. No barns to clean, no hay to pitch—just punch a hole in the son of a bitch."

Everyone erupted in laughter.

Later, Bargiel, wearing a coonskin cap, made a formal presentation of a second framed photo of himself to Fess. Bargiel admitted that an earlier photo gift had been delegated to one of the Parker house's bathrooms but expressed hope that the new one would be more appropriately placed. Fess laughed at the gift and hung it in the men's room over the urinal in the Wine Country Inn for a while. But he appreciated Bargiel's generous comments about their friendship.

"Hello, husband!" toasted Marcy. "Here's to another fifty!" Marcy sang several songs as Bill Powell accompanied her on the piano. The couple then danced to "The Shadow of Your Smile."

Fess stepped up to the microphone and thanked everyone.

"Could anybody have a better birthday?" he grinned. And then he alerted the crowd about his next big birthday party: "2024!"

But another big anniversary event was on the calendar.

On December 15, 2004, the 50th anniversary of "Davy Crockett, Indian Fighter," Fess attended a special event at Disneyland where he was presented a personalized window, the park's highest honor. The large window outside the Pioneer Mercantile store states: "Davy

Crockett Coonskin Cap Co.—Fess Parker, Proprietor." The colorful window was embellished with a flintlock rifle, a powder horn, and, of course, a coonskin cap. A smaller, framed version of the window was presented to Fess. The special windows have been a traditional way of honoring people who made unique contributions to Walt Disney. They originally began as windows on Main Street U.S.A. in Disneyland and later expanded to Disney parks worldwide. But for the first time in the history of the Disneyland windows, Fess' window involved the restructuring of the building's façade. The new exterior featured large painted lettering which proclaimed "Crockett & Russel Hat Co.," an acknowledgement also to the late Buddy Ebsen who played George Russel.

CHAPTER 21
THE CHUMASH CONTROVERSY

Fess had another real estate idea. And it was a big one.

But this one seemed to borrow a page out of "Davy Crockett Goes to Congress," the episode where Crockett stands up for the land rights of Native Americans. In the 1830s, Crockett boldly took up a minority view by defending the Indians against established government interests, but lost his legislative fight. History was about to repeat itself.

The Chumash, previously known as the Santa Ynez Band of Mission Indians, were one of 107 federally-acknowledged tribes based in California. The Chumash, like some other tribes, had benefited from the New Deal's Indian Reorganization Act of 1934, which compensated Indians for the loss of land that had been previously acquired by the federal government through treaties. The lands were subsequently placed in trust and managed by the Bureau of Indian Affairs, which allowed Native Americans to freely develop the properties. The designated lands would not be subject to taxation, local zoning ordinances, building restrictions or environmental rules.

The Chumash took advantage of the economic opportunities that federally-designated trust land provided and built the Chumash Casino Resort in Santa Ynez, a round-the-clock gambling complex in 2003. The facility quickly expanded with the addition of a luxury hotel with 106 rooms and seventeen luxury suites, a 1,400-seat Samala Showroom concert and sports facility, and several restaurants. The tribe of some 150 members had improved its financial status to such an extent that per capita income topped $300,000 annually.

Fess' plan involved a joint venture with the Chumash Indians that would result in the development of 745 acres of Santa Barbara County land into a resort hotel, a pair of golf courses, and upwards of 500 luxury homes. The Chumash reservation consisted of 138 acres, twenty-five of them acquired through purchase since 2000.

Fess purchased a 1,428 acre parcel of land, commonly known as "Camp Four," for $6 million in 1998. He originally hoped to develop the land beyond the five housing sites that the local and state zoning laws allowed but was thwarted at every turn. He realized that he could not change the local laws so he proposed to sell 745 acres to the Chumash for $12 million. Upon gaining federal trust status, Fess would help develop the real estate.

"I hope it goes without saying that the final project will be of the highest quality and of a scale and style that is worthy of the beautiful area that we live in," explained Fess. "I am honored to work with the Chumash Tribe to create an environment that they will be proud to call their own, because after all, it was theirs to begin with."

The Chumash tribe approved of the partnership by a vote of 72-37 in March 2004, and expected that Fess' name and real estate experience would carry the development project to fruition. The Chumash were eager to build over a hundred new homes on the property and a new 300-room hotel.

"This is an opportunity as a business to expand and diversify," said Chumash Chairman Vincent Armenta in a *Los Angeles Times* story of March 16, 2004. "We need to look at things other than gaming that will benefit our tribe and ensure a healthy financial future for our people."

The tentative agreement provided a 51% ownership of the property to the Chumash and a 49% share to Fespar LLC. The Parker company would also have primary control over the planning and development of the proposed $250 million project.

"We are honored to be associated with Mr. Parker," stated Armenta.

"If we implement our plans, we'd like to do what we can to preserve the beauty of the area," said Fess. "We're not out to destroy anything."

Once the sale was completed, the Chumash planned to seek approval from the Department of Interior to place the newly-acquired real estate into federal trust status. Of course, all subsequent capital improvements would be free from local, state and federal taxes.

But local citizenry who wanted the land preserved as open space lined up to oppose the plan. To some of them, the Santa Ynez Valley was developed enough. The Women's Environmental Watch of Santa Ynez and the Santa Ynez Valley Concerned Citizens Inc. were joined by such well-known area residents as singer-songwriter David Crosby and Bernie Taupin, who penned many of Elton John's songs.

Actor John Forsythe—the star of TV's *Batchelor Father* series from 1957 to 1962, and the unseen title character on TV's *Charlie's Angels* from 1976 to 1981—was particularly upset with Fess' plan.

"We love and respect you, Fess, yet we are deeply, deeply saddened, shocked, and unable to grasp why you are involved with the Chumash development deal that will forever change what we all cherish about our beloved Valley," wrote Forsythe and his wife, Nicole, in a letter which was quoted in the May 17, 2004 edition of the *Los Angeles Times*. "What is particularly distressing is how people are now talking about you, our good friend, the revenge they will take if you do go through with this and the betrayal everyone feels."

Cheryl Ladd, who worked with Forsythe on *Charlie's Angels*, recalled the animosity.

"The whole issue was very divisive," stated Ladd. "The community was really split over it and some people wrote and said things too quickly without pausing to think. Through it all, Fess was my friend and that never changed."

Despite the growing criticism, Fess stayed the course. He remained firm that he was doing the right thing for the Chumash. However, his opponents wrote letters and took out ads in area newspapers, boycotted Fess' wines and the Fess Parker Wine Country Inn & Spa in Los Olivos, and augmented street corner stop signs with "Fess" stickers.

Ashley tried to be as diplomatic as possible in an effort to calm the critics and yet be supportive of her father's plan. "Personally, I would not want to see a really dense housing project out there," Ashley told the *Los Angeles Times*. "I do hope and pray that Fess gets the control that he needs in this partnership with the Chumash to put together something that is appropriate for the valley."

However, Ashley acknowledged that she was not immune to the criticism. "People have said some very hurtful things," she said. "I am reluctant to frequent stores or restaurants in the valley at this point."

Although community criticism continued, the deal collapsed when Fess and the Chumash couldn't agree on the value of the land and the size of the new hotel, among other items. "My impression is that they liked the idea of acquiring the land, they liked the idea of acquiring taking it into their trust but they didn't like the idea that Fess would control the development after they owned it," said Osterbauer. The animosity directed at Fess began to wane and the boycotts ended.

"The Chumash remain my friends but we have no plans to work together as of now," explained Fess. "As far as the land, it will stay in the family and perhaps be used for cattle or planting."

With the Chumash experience behind him, Fess devoted more time to his other enterprises. In 2005, Eli elevated associate winemaker Blair Fox, a 1999 graduate from the University of California at Davis who had earned a combined degree in viticulture and enology, as the head winemaker. Fess enjoyed encouraging younger members of his staff to accomplish more, not only for the commercial benefits of his business operations but for their own personal growth. He had high expectations for Fox and the winemaker would not disappoint his boss and mentor.

Fess was always busy but always took time out for fans and for employees—and no one knew that better than Leslie A. Wilson, who began her employment as a part-time worker in Fess' accounting department in September 2005.

"I remember my first day of work," recalled Wilson. "The person training me had not shown up yet and I was sitting downstairs waiting. Fess came downstairs for something and asked who I was. He sat next to me at the table and said, 'No one should sit alone on their first day of work.' He had Bill Osterbauer and his assistant telling him he was going to be late for a meeting in Santa Barbara but he still waited until someone came in to train me."

Wilson later worked full time in the position before being promoted as Fess' Personal Assistant and Director of Human Resources in July 2006. She was amazed at his fan base and how he responded to them.

"When I first started working for Fess Parker he told me how important the fans were and how much he still appreciated the e-mails and letters," said Wilson. "When he was at the office, or at home, he would read each one and always told me that every fan would receive a response from him or his office. Even if a fan was requesting something he couldn't provide, everyone got a response back thanking them for their kind words. I made sure that I carried on his request and answered each and every e-mail that came in over those days. It was truly amazing reading every one and seeing the effect he had on so many people all over the country. As I was reading e-mails from fans that never met him—but nonetheless they thought the world of him—I remember thinking they are in love with this great actor and what a privilege for me that I got to know this great man on a personal level. He was professional, but so very kind and down to earth; you would never know that he was Hollywood Royalty."

Another employee, Tara-Mae Ross, the winery's Merchandising Manager, acknowledged Fess' appreciation of his community and his employees.

"Fess was very passionate as a local in regards to the beautiful surrounding landscapes out here in wine country," said Ross. "He use to always come in to the winery wearing his cowboy boots and would tell me stories about the area. He was always recommending fun and scenic places to go check out! To me, this was very personable and helpful. Since I was not a local living resident here in the Santa Ynez Valley he made me feel right at home as an employee! Fess was a very knowledgeable, generous and down-to-earth man."

Bob Andrews, who worked with Chuck Bargiel at Mullen and Henzell, was impressed by Fess' appreciation of his fans.

"No matter how busy we were, how important the meeting or meetings we may have been rushing off to were, or how late we may have been, he would always stop, be flattered at the request, take time to ask the name of and a thing or two about whoever it was who had stopped him, and then graciously signed his autograph as I stood to the side and watched," explained Andrews, who was extensively involved in Fess' business activities. "It was always about them, never about him."

The 50th anniversary of the *Davy Crockett, King of the Wild Frontier* caused Fess to rethink his 10 percent merchandising deal with Disney. He started collecting information about the various products that were marketed with his name and image and hired celebrated attorney Bert Fields to assist him. "Also, a friend at the *Wall Street Journal* is looking up old financial records," noted Fess. "Don't know if we will be able to find the correct data."

By early 2006, Fess was in contact with Disney.

"There have been several letters exchanged and our man Bertram Fields has put it to them to 'share the records' so that the issue could be resolved," stated Fess. "All I want is a look at the documents." But a satisfactory resolution didn't result. Detailed records could not be located and Disney believed that Fess had reaped an appropriate financial return from *Davy Crockett* merchandise. "He probably made about $200,000 from the merchandising," explained Bargiel. "But he could have been eligible for more."

Fess was disappointed but soon devoted all his energies back to the winery and his real estate projects. He found pleasure working—and working alongside his family. He relaxed with his family, friends, and visitors at the winery. And he enjoyed the four-legged members of the Parker Family.

"I've had dogs throughout my life," said Fess.

"The first dog we had was Ralph Von Pepper, a Weimaraner," said Marcy. "Fess gave him to me." Pepe entered their home next, followed by Charlie and Ginger, a pair of German Shepherds. On March 29, 1973, Marvin L. Martin, a truck driver making a bread delivery at the Parker home, claimed that the dogs bit him. He said his leg required thirteen stitches and promptly sued Fess for $50,000. "But I can't recall whatever happened after that," said Marcy.

Later, Tex, a Doberman Pinscher, became a member of the family. Tuxedo, a loveable black Poodle, was next in line.

"Fess and Marcy loved dogs and they loved that dog," said Ladd. "They even threw a birthday party for Tuxedo one year, and I went with my black Poodle, Marley."

Tuxedo was frequently seen at the winery.

"Tuxedo was by our side when we first opened the winery and tasting room and probably shook as many hands as we did over the years," wrote Fess in his winery's spring 2006 newsletter, which featured a photo of the dog on the canine's tenth birthday. However, Tuxedo passed away on September 27, 2005. "He was a wonderful companion to both Marcy and me, and we are grateful to have been his family. He was thirteen years old when he died but he remained debonair to the end."

A Tuxedo offspring, Picasso, joined the family and later Jake and Lucy, brother and sister Poodles, were frolicking in Los Olivos.

In 2005, Fess had another idea: he wanted to create a cultural marriage between his wines and the Texas cuisine that he loved. He contacted Tom Perini at his steakhouse in Buffalo Gap, Texas and Dr. Richard Becker of Becker Vineyards, the Texas Hill Country-based winery, about forming a non-profit organization that would promote the appreciation of fine wine and food. As a result of their efforts, the Buffalo Gap Wine and Food Summit debuted as a three-day event in April of 2005.

"Fess came up with the initial idea for the summit during a conversation we had at the Bob Bullock Museum in Austin, where the Davy Crockett exhibit had been a few years earlier," said Perini. "Well, we've had them ever since and they've been quite a success."

That same year, a number of craftsmen in the Contemporary Longrifle Association (CLA) acknowledged that they became flintlock gunsmiths due to Fess' characterization of *Davy Crockett.* The organization presented Fess with a custom-made powder horn. The horn's inscription, written by Dr. Paul Hutton, a professor of history at the University of New Mexico, read:

To Fess Parker
Who inspired a nation
By bringing its frontier past
To life... Go Ahead!

The amber-tipped cow horn, made by CLA member Mark E. Thomas, was dyed with such natural dyes as osage orange, butternut hulls and walnut hulls. "The grain was then highlighted using another dye to enhance the wonderful grain or growth rings of the horn," said Thomas. "The horn has been polished by hand without the use of sandpaper." The horn also features a walnut base plug and a sterling silver inlay.

"It's a beautiful powder horn," said Robert Weil, a CLA member who appeared as George Russel in the David Zucker comedy *Naked*

Gun 2 ½ : The Smell of Fear. "And it's certainly well deserved. Fess truly inspired a nation. It's so true: there are so many men today involved in flintlock gunmaking, powderhorn work, and other period skills who trace their initial interest back to Fess Parker as Davy Crockett."

And Fess continued to remember the Alamo.

He sent a special message to the Alamo Society which was celebrating its 20th anniversary in 2006 with a symposium in San Antonio.

"Through the Alamo Society I have met a number of international professional and amateur historians, Alamo buffs, and researchers," proclaimed Fess. "I've always been pleased that many of them had fond recollections of Walt Disney's *Davy Crockett.* I would like to recognize the Alamo Society's 20th anniversary and to salute all of those who have been rewarded your fidelity in honoring history. I will hold the hope that the Alamo Society will exist indefinitely into the future. We need to continually be reminded of the price paid for our liberty and independence."

Fess' *Daniel Boone* legacy was about to have a renaissance all its own.

In 2006, the first two seasons of *Daniel Boone* were released on DVD; as a matter of fact, the items were released, thanks in part, due to the efforts of Fess' fans.

"*Daniel Boone* has always been my favorite television show," said danielboonetv.com's Karen Dusik. "Through the internet I met many other people from around the world who felt the same way. We were swapping third and fourth-generation copies of episodes videotaped from broadcasts in the eighties and nineties, and even those tapes were being worn out with playing and copying. There was a finite amount of time left before 'our' show would be only a distant memory. The website led to contact with Twentieth Century Fox and to Fess himself and his attorney who was instrumental in making certain that fans were kept informed and represented in the push to get *Daniel Boone* back on our TV screens. Having it released to DVD—especially after a half-hearted VHS effort in 2000—not only meant that 'we' got to see crisp, clean copies of *Daniel Boone*, but it also meant that it was out there for another generation to watch and fall in love with. And they have!"

Fess Parker, Veronica Cartwright, Darby Hinton, and Ed Ames sing at the Fess Parker Wine Country Inn & Spa.
Photo courtesy of Darby Hinton.

On June 14, Dusik was invited to join Fess, Ed Ames, and Darby Hinton at the Fess Parker Doubletree Resort for a reception celebrating the DVD's release. The next evening, the group was joined by Veronica Cartwright at the Fess Parker Wine Country Inn & Spa for a sing-a-long celebration.

The popular cable program *TV Land* aired a *Daniel Boone* marathon during the August 26–27, 2006 weekend. "I was surprised it was on TV for the day," stated Fess, who noted that the broadcast helped boost sales of the DVDs. "It is really nice to have this kind of response. The DVDs did very well on Amazon.com. I understand they reached #26 on the daily sales list, maybe higher."

On Fess' 82nd birthday, Governor Ernie Fletcher of Kentucky issued a proclamation which recognized that for "the first time, *Daniel Boone*, an historical television show DVD will be released on September 26, 2006, to honor Daniel Boone, a man of unsurpassed courage and to whom the Commonwealth owes a debt of gratitude." The release date coincided with the 186th anniversary of Boone's death.

Twentieth Century Fox was initially interested in digitizing the *Daniel Boone* series but it would have cost at least $1 million. The studio hesitated lending its financial support.

"Fess suggested that I talk to Liberation Entertainment," explained Bargiel. "They were willing to advance the money but they wanted the distribution rights." Twentieth Century Fox was reluctant but a seven-year agreement was worked out and the entire series was eventually released."

The excitement of the *Daniel Boone* releases was tempered by the death of Peter Ellenshaw on February 2, 2007. The talented Disney matte artist had been a friend of Fess' since 1954, and was the last of the original group of *Davy Crockett* friends which included Buddy Ebsen, Bill Walsh, and William Bakewell. "He was a dear friend," said Fess.

The third season of *Daniel Boone* was released on DVD on May 8, 2007; the fourth season was released on June 19, 2007. On August 7, 2007, the fifth season was released on DVD. The fifth season's Special Features section includes a restored five-minute scene from the first season's "My Brother's Keeper." The scene, which features a revealing conversation between Boone and Mingo, had been unavailable in satisfactory quality during the production of the first season's DVD. Interestingly, Paul King's wonderful teleplay includes a line delivered by Mingo to Boone that essentially described Fess' real-life personality: "Daniel, you're like a great granite boulder, rolling down a mountain. Nothing can stop you. Not even the mountain itself."

Also at that time, the leadership roles at the winery changed. Fess remained the person most associated with the winery, but his son and son-in-law took up new titles.

"Around 2007, I stepped down as president of the winery and Tim moved into that role," said Eli. "Dad stepped down as Chairman and I moved into that position and assumed other responsibilities within the family enterprises."

The 2007 summer in California and been particularly hot and dry, and the unseasonable weather continued into the autumn. Brush fires soon broke out in clusters and high winds spread them around. A state of emergency was declared in Southern California. By the third week of October, flames were approaching Los Olivos, but the winds eased and firefighters managed to contain most of the fires. "They burned yesterday," explained Marcy on October 23. "They were about eight miles east of our home. That's close enough. But we're not out of the woods yet."

The Parkers and the other residents of Los Olivos were worried when they heard the news about the many homes that had been consumed by the spreading fires. "I'm telling you that this is a terrible tragedy," explained Fess. "But we've been lucky so far."

Fortunately, the fires were eventually extinguished and Fess redirected his concerns back to his businesses and the release of *Daniel Boone* on DVD. The final season was made available to the public on November 18, 2008. Two supplemental DVDs, *Fess' Favorites* and *The Best of Mingo*, were released on November 24, 2009.

"It will be great to see some old friends and terrific actors who guest starred on the show, and I especially look forward to watching it again with the grandkids," said Fess. "I remember when Kristopher was ten or eleven he noticed that Fess Parker had the same name as his grandfather!"

Fess and Hinton appear in a "Special Features" round-table interview session on the sixth season DVD in which Dusik and another fan, Mike Almeida, appear.

"The principal goal was to save the series, not to make money," said Bargiel. "Seasons one and two were deteriorating to such an extent that in the matter of a year or two they would be unusable. Fess was extremely grateful that we were able to accomplish that and save that series for his family, his fans and posterity."

CHAPTER 22
"BE SURE YOU'RE RIGHT, THEN GO AHEAD"

Fess and Marcy included messages about wine, real estate and family in their 2007 Christmas card.

"Our wines did very well this year with the critics: The Wine Enthusiast graciously awarded 96 points to our 2005 Clone 115 Pinot Noir and 94 points to our Ashley's Vineyard Pinot Noir, outstanding ratings from one of the top wine publications in the world," wrote Fess and Marcy. "The San Francisco International Wine Competition also recognized two of our family wines, giving Double Gold distinctions to both the 2004 Fess Parker Rodney's Syrah and to Eli Parker's 2004 Epiphany Revelation."

The family news in the Christmas card was significant.

"We are also happy to announce the birth of our first Great-Grandchild this year, Braeden Elisha Parker, the son of Kris and Michellene Parker," noted Fess and Marcy. "He was born on August 30, and weighed 7 pounds, 14 ounces. The Parker Family continues to grow and prosper in Santa Barbara." Four generations of Parker males graced the cover of the *Fess Parker Winery & Vineyard* winter newsletter of 2008.

But the card's real estate message was premature: "Also, after fourteen years of excruciating bureaucracy, we finally broke ground on our new hotel on Santa Barbara's waterfront. It should be complete in the latter part of 2009."

Fess had wanted another hotel, a classier facility, a five-star establishment. His initial plans for a 150-room hotel on a 3.4-acre parcel of land near his first hotel was approved by all the relevant government boards and agencies but when he wanted to add 50 more rooms some community groups, like the Citizens Planning Association, rose up in opposition.

According to the *Santa Barbara Independent,* the City Council agreed to review the "supplemental environmental analysis" that the Citizens Planning Association proposed. He removed his plan from the City Council and appealed to the citizens via an initiative but failed to secure enough popular support. "I've learned a thing or two from Davy Crockett," said Fess. "I don't give up."

And he didn't.

"Eventually, Parker would come back, go through environmental review, and secure the permits needed to build his five-star hotel," stated the *Santa Barbara Independent* on March 2010. "For a host of reasons, known and inexplicable, Parker never managed to get beyond the excavation site now in the ground."

Eli chalked it up to the economy.

"It's been in a holding pattern," he pointed out. "We did break ground and made progress for about three or four months but one of the banks that was originally involved in the financing backed out."

Fess had been remodeling his office in Los Olivos in 2008, and he displayed a few items from some of his important acting roles. For example, a large framed painting of the actor as Davy Crockett hung from a back office room wall, and a large-scale model of the *General* was enclosed in a large showcase in the main office. The *General,* of course, was the name of the locomotive that James Andrews and a small Union force hijacked in 1862, and Fess portrayed the daring Andrews in Disney's *The Great Locomotive Chase* in 1956.

As a result of Fess' portrayal of Crockett and Andrews, he was presented with a special Lifetime Achievement award in 2007 that was also displayed in his office.

The award plaque reads:

Walter E. Disney
Lifetime Achievement award
Presented to Fess Parker

With grateful appreciation for decades of activities that reflect the ideals of Walt Disney and his lifelong passion for quality, the Carolwood Pacific Historical Society is honored to present you with this citation named in memory of Walter Elias Disney, who established high standards for family entertainment with the conviction that anyone can achieve their dreams if they have curiosity, confidence, courage and consistency. Your portrayal of American heroes such as Davy Crockett, "King of the Wild Frontier," and James Andrews in "The Great Locomotive Chase" and your numerous successful business enterprises, have resulted in a durable legacy that has benefited generations of admirers and will continue to inspire others to pursue their dreams.

In witness thereof the Governors of Carolwood Pacific Historical Society hereby authorize the representative to sign and present this citation on its behalf.

March 4, 2007
Santa Barbara, California

Michael Broggie
Founding Chairman
Carolwood Historical Society

The award provided Fess with yet another opportunity to explain his relationship with *Davy Crockett.*

"I don't know why the series had so much success," admitted Fess. "Perhaps, though, it was a combination of several factors: the Walt Disney magic, a sense of believability, and the casting. But as for the way feel, I tell you what: it's like that song from Mr. Disney's *Song of the South*, 'Zip-a-Dee-Doo-Dah.' It is a special feeling that I have about the series and I feel very good about having done the production. I've maintained a number of friendships as a result of it. Sincerely, though, after all these years I am still surprised that so many people were positively affected by Mr. Disney's series. I've spoken to many people over the years who have said that they enjoyed the show and still remember it fondly."

Fess had certainly come a long way from those early days in Texas and the not-so-successful Hollywood days in the early 1950s. Nearly one hundred employees worked for him at his winery, the Inn and at Fespar. And he was pleased that his children worked with him, too. He was particularly pleased with his status as a grandfather and great-grandfather—and devoted husband.

"Dad had nine biological grandchildren: Eli's Kristopher, Katie, Amanda, Olivia, Clayton, and Jack," said Ashley. "And my three: Spencer, Greer, and Henry. Plus Tessa and Tara, Laureen's daughters from her first marriage. And, of course, one great-grandson: Braedon, Kristopher's son."

Marcy celebrated her 80th birthday on March 18, 2008.

"She was so appreciative of the many beautiful bouquets of her favorite roses that were sent by family and friends," said Fess. "The house looked like a first-class florist shop for weeks!" Marcy, though, was dealing with her own health issues, especially arthritis.

Still, some good news was on the way.

Blair Fox was named Andre Tchelistcheff Winemaker of the Year at the 2008 San Francisco International Wine Competition. It was the same prestigious award that Eli had received two years earlier. At the competition, Fess Parker and Epiphany Cellars Wines received eight significant awards, including a Best of Show, White for Eli's 2007 Grenache Blanc.

Fess was pleased with the favorable attention that his wines were receiving.

"We're keeping up doing what we can, putting our brand out there," remarked Fess. "There are so many people making wine these days." Furthermore, Robert M. Parker had given impressive scores of 93 to a number of Fess' wines, including several Syrahs from Rodney's Vineyard.

Fess' *Daniel Boone* portrayal received more attention when Ron Barzo of Barzo Playsets, an Illinois-based plastic toy manufacturer, released an Officially Licensed Fess Parker Daniel Boone Playset in September of 2008. The playset featured detailed characters, buildings, and an autographed photo of Fess as the trail-blazing frontiersman. Chuck Bargiel, who drafted the deal with Barzo, Twentieth Century

Fox, and Fess, was rewarded in a unique way. "I became 'CB Captain of the Stockade,'" said Bargiel. Fess wanted Bargiel to be featured as one of the playset figures and Barzo obliged.

"My wife and I visited Fess in December after the playsets were released," said Barzo. "We had a three-hour breakfast meeting and I remember his son, Eli, stopping by, looking at one of the playset cabins and saying, 'I remember running in and out of that building.' His comment made me feel good. We were going to rent a room in Santa Barbara but when he found out he insisted that we be his guests at his Inn. When we checked in, we discovered Fess had placed us in the Presidential Suite! He couldn't have been nicer to us." The Daniel Boone playset became Barzo's all-time best-selling set.

Businesswise, it was a very good year.

But Fess was getting weaker.

The treatments and surgery had eliminated Fess' prostate and kidney cancers. "However, the bladder cancers recurred two or three times," said Dr. Rhodes. "But after the BCG, they never came back."

Yet another cancer emerged.

"He developed anal carcinoma; that's what finally got him," said Rhodes. "I wish he had gone through the prostate surgery rather than the radiation. The radiation cured the prostate cancer but it may have proved to be a fatal cure."

Kristopher recalled the impact of the chemo and radiation treatments on his grandfather.

"They began in the summer of 2008 after his diagnosis was confirmed," explained Kristopher. "It was difficult for him but he never complained. It was incredibly revelatory to see how strong and polite he was at that time. He even joked around during his treatments. I remember him one time wearing his hospital gown—with the back wide open—and hearing him hum 'Moon River' to the nurses. But during his last six months, the radiation and chemo treatments really knocked him out."

Fess put an optimistic spin on his condition. "I can assure you that I am in no great danger; in fact, I haven't felt as good as I do today in quite some time," announced Fess on his winery's website. "As a bonafide octogenarian I can tell you that with each passing day your family will become more and more important to you. Work at those relationships and make the time to spend time with those you love. I can assure you that you won't be sorry."

As his pain increased, Fess remained as stoic as ever.

"He was a big man in so many ways," said Rhodes. "You could tell as time went on he was in pain—and he did not like that. He lost that optimism that he always held and his face seemed to say, 'I'm losing this battle; I've had enough of all this.'"

But Fess never stopped caring for Marcy.

"During all of this he always kept reminding all of us to watch out for grandma, to look out for grandma," said Kristopher. "He wanted to make sure that she was comfortable."

Fess spent some time in rehabilitation, but he believed that while he was in that situation he should still have some fun. He promptly placed a beer order with his son-in-law.

"Fess and I shared a fondness for good, sturdy beer," said Snider. "Fess' favorite was Chimay and I enjoyed fuller-bodied styles. It started when he was recovering in the Rehabilitation Institute in Santa Barbara during the late summer or early fall of 2008. I would smuggle in two beers—one for him and one for me. We watch sporting events, usually football, on TV for a while. I certainly remember watching the Texas-Texas A&M game on Thanksgiving, which Texas won 49-9. This was before he basically became bed-ridden."

The song-filled Thursday nights at the Inn became just another night.

"The music stopped in March of 2009 due to health issues affecting both Fess and Marcy," said Powell. "The piano found a new home."

CHAPTER 23
"Mackie Raised Him Right"

"I watched him become ill," said Ames. "I know that he made a conscious decision as to how to handle the cancer and the illness. Obviously, it didn't work out the way we wanted it to. But I never saw a person who was more gentle, who never complained. If he started coughing and you got a little frightened, he would pass it off. He was probably the best patient whoever was. He was very brave accepting of the condition. He was so wonderful to be with even in his illness, heartbreaking as it was to see him get frail. But his spirit was the same. I hope I have the same kind of courage that he had when my time comes."

In June 2009, a library was named in his honor in Sidoarjo, Indonesia, on behalf of The World is Just a Book Away, a non-profit group that builds schools and libraries in developing countries. Sidoarjo had been the scene of an ongoing mudslide since 2006.

"My college friend, Jim Owens, spearheaded The World is Just a Book Away project and dad was one of the original people he interviewed," explained Ashley. Fess was one of a number of individuals who made financial contributions to the organization.

Although he endured pain, he never shared his suffering with anyone. "He didn't complain, even to me," said Marcy. "How he handled himself was absolutely amazing to me."

Despite his illness and the pain, he kept participating in telephone interviews for *The Crockett Chronicle* and other media. On July 2, 2009, a PBS crew visited him at his home in Los Olivos for a documentary about TV Westerns for *The Pioneers of Television* series. Sporting a grayish-white beard, Fess looked noticeably thinner. And his voice lacked the strong richness that had characterized his speech for nearly all of his adult life. Still, he participated as if everything was fine. He particularly enjoyed Darby Hinton's contributions to the program. "Hard to believe he's fifty years old now," said Fess. "Then again it's hard to believe than I'm eighty-five!"

The accomplished octogenarian was ailing but he thrived on the love and attention he received from his family. Fess invited guests to visit the winery on July 24th because he was going to screen *Davy Crockett, King of the Wild Frontier*. "It was the kids' idea, mostly, I think," explained Fess. "They all pitched in with a lot of enthusiasm. I haven't watched the film in a long while and I can't imagine a more unique setting for doing so. Save me some popcorn!" Proceeds from the event would benefit the Rehabilitation Hospital Foundation in Santa Barbara.

"It was the last time he was ever at the winery in any sort of public way," recalled Ashley. "We had a great crowd of about 250-plus out on the lawn and it was a beautiful evening. It was really festive and beautiful. I picked dad up from the house in his black, gangster ca Mercedes. We stopped at R. Country Market in Los Olivos fo some cold beers and then drove out to the winery. We drove up o to the tent pad above where the big screen was all set up and th crowd was seated. We sat in the car for a bit and the grandkid came up one by one to say hi. They had been selling food and tri-ti sandwiches and handing out free candy and popcorn. It was th ultimate all-hands-on- deck kind of family event that dad loved."

Fess told Ashley, "Well, I should go out there and say hello."

But he couldn't walk on his own.

"Keep in mind that at this point he probably weighed 170 pound and was weak as a kitten," said Ashley. "He was wearing jeans, sport coat, and his Crow Bar Ranch baseball cap and he looked s cute. Eli and Tim got him out of the car and into his wheelchai and rolled him backward down the lawn into the front row of th audience."

Ashley awaited the usual rush of the crowd but it didn't happe

"In all of the years of being at events with dad, people we especially kind," said Ashley. "They didn't mob him or ask him t sign anything. They just came up and said how nice it was t see him, introduced their grandkids to him, that kind of thin Several grandparents told dad that they were so excited for the grandchildren to see the movie with them. Dad, of course, was awesome as usual."

Before the movie started Ashley's daughter, Greer, sat next to Fess who was covered with several lap robes. The film's opening credits rolled as "The Ballad of Davy Crockett" played in the background. Fess was back on a movie screen and the crowd was loving every minute of it.

"He got about halfway through the movie when he told Greer that he was really cold and thought it would be best if he went home," said Ashley. "We had repositioned the car down at the loading dock so the quickest route back to the car was to wheel him across the front row. Eli and Tim were pushing and pulling him, and when people realized that he was leaving they stood up and started clapping for him. Tim said, 'Fess, look over there, everyone is clapping for you.' Dad said, 'Oh,' and then he doffed his cap—coincidentally right as he moved in front of the projector so that silhouette of him moved across the screen. I was standing at the back of the audience and absolutely lost it. He nailed his exit perfectly without even trying. We cranked the heat but good up on the drive home, and he was really pleased that it was such a good event."

Weeks later, Fess recalled the event.

"It went very well," noted Fess. "I was really pleased. We had over one hundred people. They seemed to enjoy it. The weather was normal, a bit cool in the evening. But folks brought their coats with them. The event went so well that we'll probably do it next year."

Phil Kendrick saw Fess on August 16, 2009, his friend's 85th birthday.

"He was in a wheelchair and it was quite shocking," said Kendrick. "I spent about four hours with him that day and they were the best four hours we ever spent together. But that was the last time I saw him."

Kendrick later wrote Fess a four-page letter which chronicled their 68-year friendship.

"It doesn't seem to long ago I remember meeting you as we both sat on the curb in front of the Clinic Pharmacy and Drug Store," wrote Kendrick, who also vividly described their years as members of Pi Kappa Alpha at the University of Texas and the infamous 1954 drive from California to Texas.

But Kendrick devoted most of the letter to his friend's baptism in 1954.

"Fess, I know you were sincere when you publicly expressed your belief and I know you still believe, and that means more to me than any of the great times we've had," wrote Kendrick. "I know that your life has been influenced by the gift of the Holy Spirit as God promised. It's reassuring to know that we are blessed by God's love and grace and forgiveness."

Cognizant of Fess' condition, Kendrick concluded his letter with a sense of optimism and understanding.

"You're the best friend I ever had and here's wishing your medical problems will continue to improve, and we will have a good long visit soon," wrote Kendrick. "I'm also glad we're brothers in Jesus Christ."

Ron Ely remembered Fess' suffering.

"Fess' final battle was prolonged and painful," said Ely. "Fess made the decision to combat his disease in a way that he believed would give him the best chance of surviving it without losing himself to it. I believe the opposite happened. Initially, it appeared that Fess was having success with his treatments. But the treatments were so harsh on his system that it took a tremendous toll on him. His weight began to drop and he endured a great amount of pain. He took it so well that most people might not have known what he was going through. He did not share the pain and gradual loss of inner contentment with many people. I think only those closest to him really knew what he was enduring, as he made a great effort to keep up a positive front. As brave as he was—and he was incredibly brave—it was impossible to hide the ravages of his physical decline. All that being said, he was always cheerful to those who visited him and tried to make them feel at ease. On his last day, his eyes were bright and interested, and his smile was still there. A lesser man would have exposed his pain to others and packed it in a year earlier. This was just not in Fess' character."

In the autumn of 2009, Fess received a phone call from Max Evans, the author of *The Rounders* who had a falling out with him over the failed movie deal decades earlier.

"We spoke for about forty-five minutes the first time," said Evans. "Fess told me that he had experienced four cancers. And then after a while he told me, 'Well, Burt Kennedy did a good job for you, Max.' That was nice of him to say that. I appreciated hearing that from him after all those years."

Bargiel, who had visited Fess every week when he was in the hospital and the rehabilitation facility, remembered his friend's courage.

"He remained as charming, as gracious, as brave, as good an example in the last months and weeks of his life as he had been throughout his life to me and millions of others," said Bargiel. "What a dream it was—a dream come true—to meet and know him, and then to become his lawyer. I was his sidekick on a few matters, and he always seemed to have a sidekick whether he was Davy Crockett or Daniel Boone. I'll always consider him to be one of the great blessings in my life."

Fess received news that a good friend had passed away.

"On Monday, March 15, dad's longtime friend and business partner, Fred Rice died," said Ashley. "Fred's son, Fred, Jr., called me that morning to give me the news and asked if he could go to the house and let mom and dad know in person that Uncle Fred, as we called him, had finally succumbed to Alzheimer's disease. Fred had been in a nursing home in the valley for at least five years. He didn't know anybody anymore and I know that pained dad a lot more than he let on. Dad and Fred had developed and built three mobile home parks together in Santa Barbara County. They were also boating buddies from way back. In the mid 1950s, they all used to sail out of the Newport Harbor before mom and dad even got married. Anyhow, I was a little worried about how they would take the news so I told Fred Jr. that I would meet him up there. Fred Jr. told Marcy first as they visited in the kitchen, then I took him back to dad's bedroom. Dad seemingly took it pretty well and even in his tremendously weakened state he said all the right things to Fred Jr.—or Tad, as we called him, for Tadpole. After Fred Jr. left, I sat with dad and we reminisced about how funny Fred was and what a good friend he had been. After a bit of silence he looked at me and said, 'You know it's too bad about 'ol Freddy, but I can see him wanting to get out of that place.' I agreed with him and we visited for a while longer and then I headed out to the winery. There is no doubt in my mind that dad decided to 'let go' right then and there. I think he had just had enough of lying in bed day after day."

Monday was a significant day for Ashley.

"Monday the fifteenth was the last time I saw him alive," said Ashley. "We didn't say 'goodbye,' but I had such thoughts many times over the last few years when he was in really bad shape due to sepsis or whatever else was plaguing him. His condition on this day was actually pretty good, though all things considered. Sometimes his blood pressure was so low it was hard to understand how he was even conscious, and he had no appetite at all anymore. I could never get used to that because food had always been such a huge part of his life and personality. He's the only person I've ever known who would ask you what the plans were for dinner while he was eating lunch."

Ashley was constantly updated about her father's deteriorating condition.

"Hilary Murphy, dad's wonderful nurse had indicated to us that maybe dad was getting weaker," said Ashley. Of course, he had been weak for quite some time but Ashley detected something more ominous in the tone of the care-giver's voice.

The strong tall Texan was failing.

On March 17, Tim Snider visited his father-in-law.

"It was St. Patrick's Day and, of course, I thought Fess might enjoy a cold Guinness to commemorate the holiday," recalled Snider. "I stopped by in the evening after leaving the winery. Fess was dozing a bit when I got there because he had been busy with several other friends who had visited him earlier that day. I stayed for a while talking to one of the nurses. Fess woke up a little startled, but then recognized me and smiled. I told him I brought him one of Ireland's finest for the holiday and he again flashed his big smile."

Snider appreciated Fess' inviting smile but realized that he should leave.

"I said that I was going to get out of his hair and let him sleep, but before I left he reached up and grabbed my hand," said Snider. "I remember he looked up at me clearly and said in his then weakened voice something to the effect of, 'Thanks' and 'I'll see you around, my friend.' He was smiling and really seemed very peaceful. We'd shake hands occasionally at the end of visits but not every time and this just seemed different. It sort of struck me that it may be the last time I'd see him. I had felt that way once or twice before but more because he was really struggling or in pain. This time was different: he was peaceful and smiling but it was strange aura. When I left his room I spoke with the nurse who said she thought he was close to the end—but on his terms."

Fess went to sleep.

March 18, 2010 was a gorgeous day in Los Olivos.

"It was beautiful, sunny and bright with a blue sky," stated Eli. "Not a cloud in the sky. I arrived at the office about eight in the morning. I was sitting with Bill Osterbauer and my son, Kris, when I received a phone call from Hilary. She told me that dad was not doing well."

Eli and Kris rushed up to Fess' house.

"It was me, Kris, Mom, Hilary and Maria Ibarra, a long-time employee and family helper, in dad's room," said Eli. "I called the rest of the family—the kids and the grandkids."

"When dad and I arrived he was in the process of going," explained Kristopher. "His breathing was short and strained. I just wanted to be there for him and hold his hand."

Ashley was home in Santa Barbara when she received her brother's phone call.

"Eli called me on Thursday morning and said, 'Ash, you had better get up here now,' said Ashley. "I knew that he was getting close. I left my house in Santa Barbara and as I was on the San Marcos Pass, a road that dad loved to drive and Marcy forbade any of us to be on, I came to this long straightaway with huge fields on each side. It was about the midway point of the forty-minute trip. I was thinking and praying and all of a sudden I said, 'It's okay, dad, you can let go,' and I just felt right then that he had died."

Ashley didn't pull over and stop; she kept driving.

"I'm not a big one for mystical moments but I know that's exactly when he left me," said Ashley. "He was so darn polite to the end, he was probably trying to hang on."

Marcy was at his Fess' bedside when he turned and looked at her. "He said, 'Marcy, kiss me,'" she noted. "And I did. In essence, those were the last words he ever spoke."

Ashley approached the house.

"When I pulled in the gate at the house I saw Eli and Kristopher outside and could tell that they had both been crying," she recalled.

"We had a group hug and then I went inside to see him. Maybe on some level he knew that we would all be gathering for Marcy's birthday that day so he knew she would have us all there. I don't know if you have ever experienced how much a person changes when their soul leaves their body but it should make a believer out of everyone. He looked so different."

Kristopher believed that his grandfather didn't want to die until Marcy's birthday.

"Grandpa had the ability to plan everything," stated Kristopher. "I think he wanted to make it to that day—grandma's birthday—so that all the birthday wishes she would receive throughout the day would help soften the blow for her."

Fess' pain had ended.

"It was around nine-thirty or so in the morning," said Eli. "His treatments were so brutal, the chemo, and the radiation. He was so weak; he couldn't beat that."

Eli and Ashley thought it best to have their father look like the Texan that he was.

Katie, Eli's oldest daughter, was quick to lend a hand.

"Katie and the girls helped Hilary get him dressed in his jeans and they decided which boots to put on him," said Ashley. "It was bittersweet because it was good to see him in his 'uniform' again."

"Katie made sure that dad left the house with his boots on," said Eli.

Ashley recalled a conversation she had with her father about heaven.

"I think dad was at peace when he went, unlike a few years earlier when he had spent most of the summer in Santa Barbara at Cottage Hospital," said Ashley. "He had been very ill and was coming to terms with the fact that the course of treatment he had chosen was beating him up very badly. He asked me if I believed in heaven and if I thought you had to be a churchgoer to get in. It wasn't as straightforward as that but that was the gist of his question. I told him that I didn't know exactly what came after but that I believed there had to be more. I also told him that I didn't think church had anything to do with it. I told him, and I believe that you will be judged on the sum total of your life's work. I likened it to a scale, and if the good you did during your lifetime outweighed the bad you were in good shape. He seemed to like that. I told him that I thought he was in home free because he literally had millions of people all over the world who loved him and looked up to him."

Before his death was reported to the media, Ashley, Eli and Marcy made a number of phone calls to relatives and close friends.

"Marcy phoned me and said, 'He's gone,'" said Fishman. "We didn't talk for long. It was sad but I acknowledged that his pain and suffering had ended."

Robert Loggia received a phone call, too. Loggia found it difficult to explain his emotions when he heard the news. He paused and then said, "He was the American dream."

"He was such a darling man," said Audrey Loggia.

When Bill Powell heard the news he immediately thought of Marcy.

"So sad that Fess would give Marcy a lasting memory of his passing on her 82nd birthday," remarked Powell. "He loved Marcy and loved his family. You could feel and see the love. They were a dynamic pair. I have been truly blessed in having the opportunity to know these fine people and call them friends."

Ashley informed Sao Anash, the Parker Family's spokesperson about her dad's death. "I was at breakfast when Ashley called to give me the news," recalled Anash, who issued the news of Fess' death to the media. "I then received calls and inquiries all day, and into the coming weeks, from every major news outlet in the country. There were television crews parked outside, even in front of my house, wanting a comment from the family spokesperson. It was a sad day, but at the same time very moving as I couldn't have conceived of how many people reached out with condolences. There were e-mails from Vietnam vets who had been visited by Fess when they were much younger and on their tours of duty. They were frightened, they told me, but when Fess landed in a helicopter and got out and gave them each a hug, they felt empowered to fight another day. They said he even stuck around and had beers with them later when they returned from battle."

The national media quickly filed reports about Fess' death.

"When he passed away there was suddenly world-wide coverage blossoming about a man who wasn't in the public eye for a long, long time," said Ames. "But he had spread the seed of his personality.

It was very pleasing to me to see the coverage he received and all the wonderful eulogies."

NBC's KSBY-TV anchor Jeanette Trompeter told her California audience: "We lost an American icon today."

Lee Cowan of NBC-TV's *Nightly News* said on March 18, "If you were a kid in the nineteen-fifties and sixties, chances are your history of the American frontier was framed, in part, by Fess Parker." During the report, film historian Leonard Maltin stated: "Think of Elvis, think of Beatlemania. Think bigger. That was Davy Crockett." Cowan concluded the thoughtful segment by saying, "The man who played legends is being remembered tonight as one himself—from the Golden Age of Television to his own golden years."

Entertainment reporter George Pennacchio of Chicago's ABC affiliate WLS-TV delivered a splendid tribute complete with numerous clips from *Davy Crockett.*

A *USA Today* headline read: "Fess Parker, forever a frontiersman." The *Los Angeles Times* proclaimed: "Fess Parker, TV's frontier hero." Great Britain's *The Guardian* called him "A quintessential westerner."

Mark Streeter, the editorial cartoonist for the *Savannah Morning News*, drew a very touching illustration that depicted a halo with a raccoon tail hanging from it. "Fess Parker's Halo" also featured a youngster—Streeter himself—who toasted the King of the Wild Frontier with a cup of ink.

"Being an editorial cartoonist of a certain age, I have unique opportunity, from time to time, to pay tribute or say farewell to personalities that have impacted me in a positive or personal way," explained Streeter. "Often times, these larger-than-life personalities will have had that same impact on much of my Baby Boomer generation. Fess Parker and his coon-skinned portrayals of Davy Crockett and Daniel Boone was just such a personality. The 'obit' cartoon is often my only chance, on behalf of the little kid in me and, perhaps, my generation's self, to simply say, 'Thank you.'"

Brad Thompson, his childhood friend, heard about Fess' passing on the national news. "I was astonished when I heard about it, I really was," remarked Thompson. "It was sad to hear. I will always remember that I enjoyed his company."

SAVANNAHNOW.COM
TO THE KING OF THE WILD FRONTIER!
FESS PARKER'S HALO
INK
MSTREETER SAVANNAH MORNING NEWS © 3·18 10

"Fess Parker's Halo."
Courtesy Mark Streeter/*Savannah Morning News*.

Verlyn Klinkenborg noted in his *New York Times* column: "In my memory, he embodies an inexplicable authenticity. This was not just the naïveté of a child viewer, unaware of how TV shows were made or coonskin caps sold. It was something inherent in Mr. Parker."

The front page of the *Los Angeles Times'* Late Extra edition featured "King of the Wild Frontier," an extensive article on Fess' life. The *Santa Barbara News-Express* also printed a front page story about his passing and included a number of statements by friends and associates. Cheryl Ladd's comments were particularly poignant.

"He was a dear, dear, dear friend of ours," said Ladd. "The kindest, gentlest, fun, generous man I have ever met. I can go on and on. We have so many cherished memories of him and Marcy. The world is a sadder place without him. He was so intelligent, quiet, never bragged, he would put you at ease, always kind and generous beyond belief. What I admired most about Fess was his determination. He had conviction. He never gave up. I admired him so much as a child and having met so many celebrities in Hollywood, Fess was more... uniquely himself, authentic. Fess was better than I could have imagined."

The *Montecito Journal's* front page said, "So long, Fess." The weekly publication featured a touching story by Erin Graffy de Garcia, whose father had been one of Fess' pilots during the *Daniel Boone* years. The writer noted that her father said that "Fess was very easy to deal with. Soft spoken. Polite. He was a genuinely honest personality."

Walt Disney President and CEO Robert A. Iger issued a statement: "Like many kids growing up in the 50s, Davy Crockett was my first hero, and I had the coonskin cap to prove it...Fess is truly a Disney Legend, as is the character he portrayed, and while he will certainly be missed, he will never be forgotten."

California Governor Arnold Schwarzenegger called Fess a "true Hollywood legend" and an "inspirational Californian whose contributions to our state will be remembered forever."

Phil Kendrick made a number of phone calls to some of Fess' friends from the early years.

"Phil called me and told me about Fess," said Carolyn Wright. "He was a lovely man."

Phone calls and e-mail messages were sent to the various Parker enterprises.

"I received a total of 411 e-mails of condolence and great sadness," explained Leslie A. Wilson, Fess' Executive Assistant. "That, of course, is not including the number sent directly to the family, the Inn or the Winery. On March 18, we got 151 e-mails from the time it was announced until midnight. The e-mails continued throughout the night into the morning hours. I actually lay in bed listening to them all come in during the middle of the night on my Blackberry. The phone calls were amazing, not so much my line because it was a private number, but from what the Inn and Winery told me, it was one call after another the first few days."

Wilson pointed out that a large amount of flowers and gift baskets were received.

"It was announced that in lieu of flowers, people could donate to Direct Relief International, an organization Mr. Parker and Ashley were both involved in," said Wilson. "From what I understand, they received a huge response."

The Alamo responded quickly to the news of Fess' death.

"We wanted to publicly acknowledge the important cultural connection between the Alamo and Fess Parker," said Dr. Bruce Winders, the Alamo's Historian and Curator. We also wanted to give visitors a way to express their feelings. We decided on a memory book for his family."

The book and a photograph of Fess were placed on a flower-filled table that was placed on Alamo grounds. "We had many visitors thank us for doing it," said Winders. "Some of the comments about him were great. Some remembered him for his role as Davy Crockett, some for Daniel Boone."

The book was subsequently sent to the Parker Family in Los Olivos.

A private graveside service was held at the Santa Barbara Cemetery on March 22 at 1 p.m. Father John Love officiated. Besides Fess' family the attendees included Ed and Jeanne Ames; Cheryl Ladd and her husband, Brian Russell; Nolie Fishman and her son, David; Tom and Lisa Perini; long time friends Morgan Woodward and Jimmy Tittle; and various other friends and employees.

"The ceremony was simple and straight forward, just the way he would have wanted," said Tittle. "It reflected who he was."

"Ed Ames sang 'Amazing Grace,'" said Tom Perini. "And with the backdrop of the Pacific Ocean, it was quite something. Fess was a gentle man and a gentleman."

Lisa Perini concurred with her husband but started to cry. "He was a gentleman," she said.

Chuck Bargiel delivered the eulogy. He noted that Fess "was the champion of plain people—kids and grownups alike—achieving that renown, in part, by portraying frontier heroes," and that he had "blazed a trail marked by gentility, unpretentiousness, simple manners, genuine modesty, plain courtesy, and good example."

Bargiel explained that "the world learned something more profound about Fess than about those he portrayed. It wasn't, after all, just a role he played; it was Fess, himself, who was the hero."

In his conclusion, Bargiel noted, "Even on this saddest day of all: By the example of his great life he tells us today that although grief has its place in life, it is not a place we should 'make camp' or 'hold up' or 'lay low' for very long. And so, as we trudge along without him, remembering the blessings of life as he taught them, we bear witness today to a truth known to the world over: So long as men walk upon the earth, the likes of Fess Elisha Parker, Jr. shall never be seen again."

Fess had been placed in the "simple pine box" that he had requested. And the left leg of his jeans was placed inside his boot. "His left pant leg always ended up in his boot for some reason," said Ashley. "It was a source of chuckles over the years."

And a bottle of Syrah, his favorite wine, was placed in the coffin.

Wilson remembered the melancholy atmosphere that pervaded the Parker businesses the days after Fess' death.

"From the Thursday he passed away until the following Friday Memorial, it was just an extremely sad week," said Wilson. "My heart was breaking for Marcy, Eli, and Ashley. Working in the position I do, and even before at the winery, we were on a personal level as well and I knew how much they loved and adored him."

The memorial service was held in the rotunda at the Fess Parker Doubletree Resort on March 26. Although a mournful gathering, Fess' children wanted the event to be celebratory. And it was. The hundreds who attended the event were greeted by Eli, who said, "Dad would have gotten a kick out of seeing this turnout today." Ashley compared her father to his favorite wine, "Imposing and impressive, but at the same time, approachable and friendly."

The invited speakers at the service were Ron Ely, Darby Hinton, Jed Steele, Dave Davis, and Rick Fogg. Each man mixed lighthearted anecdotes with carefully worded sentiments of affection and respect.

Ely spoke first and told the audience about their decades-long friendship and the consistency of the relationship. "He was a friendly, nice, generous, warm human being from the day I met him until the end," said Ely, who amusingly pointed out that Fess liked everyone in the entertainment business—even Hollywood agents.

Darby Hinton followed with the humorous story of his *Daniel Boone* audition and how Fess became his surrogate father. He also spoke about Fess' love for Marcy, Eli, Ashley, and the rest of the family. "What he was most proud of—his family," stated Hinton. "He lived for you."

After explaining how he been had recruited as a wine consultant, Steele explained the kindnesses that Fess had demonstrated to others, including his own children and the bedridden father of wine critic Robert Parker. He became emotional when he concluded with something that an Algerian-born taxi driver said to him during the drive from the airport. The driver said he had met Fess twice and told Steele, "He was very humble. He seemed to be a good man."

Davis recalled his numerous struggles over the development of the hotel and noted Fess' determination to constantly go ahead. "Idea, idea," said Davis with a smile about Fess' behavior. "Move this here, move that there. Here's an architect, there's an architect." In his conclusion, Davis acknowledged Fess for improving the waterfront site and providing land for Chase Palm Park.

Fogg stated that Fess "genuinely wanted others—all the rest of us who briefly came into his world—to experience the same kind of enjoyment from life that he himself derived." And he read a number of Fess-isms, assorted statements which Fess made about life, relationships, food, and drink. including "Be the only one at a business meeting with no business card, no papers, and no anxiety," "Eat spicy foods," "Drink good coffee," and "Be genuinely interested in what other people are saying about you."

Ashley and Eli concluded the ceremony with a reading from *Desiderata*, Max Ehrmann's classic poem that Fess made his children memorize when they were young. More importantly, much of the poem reflected Fess Parker's character: he spoke his "truth quietly and clearly," he embraced "the counsel of the years," and he remained "cheerful."

Months later, Fogg explained his role in the service.

"Eli and Ashley asked me to consider speaking at Mr. Parker's memorial service," said Fogg. "I remember Ashley saying something like she felt that I really 'got' her father and that I might be a good candidate to wrap up the remembrances of friends. This was a tremendous honor. It was also a particularly hectic moment for the family, not only for the obvious reason of Mr. Parker's passing, but also to do with some pressing business matters. I remember those days now as a blur of feelings, stress and emotion. But I also remember the clarity of the time actually delivering my comments. Here were hundreds of friends, family, acquaintances, and fans from near and far: those who knew Fess from Hollywood; those who knew him socially; those who knew him from business dealings; those who had known him for sixty years; and those who met him merely a few years before. It was a tremendous privilege to share just a bit of my reflections about this man who will forever be a larger-than-life character to me, and to all who knew him. As I said there, there will never again be a man like Fess Parker."

Ely considered Fess more than a friend.

"In the last few years, we considered each other to be the brothers we were not born with," explained Ely later. "I often referred to Fess as my brother and he did likewise. My comments about Fess at his memorial were entirely extemporaneous. It was important for me to speak simply and from the heart without the words coming from a scripted and carefully-planned speech that would run counter to what Fess was. My greatest chore in speaking that day was in keeping the emotions to myself. It was very difficult to say goodbye to my friend and brother in such a manner, but it was the way Fess would have wanted it."

Jed Steele accepted the invitation but confessed that it "was tough duty."

"But I did it," said Steele. "Fess was a great guy. I became fond of him as a human being."

Family spokesperson Sao Anash stated that she was "a better person for having known Fess." She recalled Fess' priorities. "Fess had a very clear idea of what truly matter in his life: family, fun, and friends," said Anash. "He considered being successful in business a fun enterprise, so he even had fun while conducting business. What I learned most from Fess was gratitude. He was very thankful for every blessing he had received. He never took anything for granted. I think that's what kept him young at heart for so long. I miss seeing him around town, having him tip his cowboy hat to me when I ran into him, and calling me 'little lady.' He was a true gentleman."

Ashley also reflected on her dad's passing.

"From the time I was a little girl I think on some level I always knew that dad was special because of the way people treated him," she said. "People always seemed very happy to see him and couldn't have been nicer. There was never any expectation of special treatment on dad's part, and he was never anything but a gentleman. I wasn't born until '64, so 'Dad as Daniel' is my strongest memory of his acting days. I remember him occasionally coming home in costume and occasionally being on the set. He also did the rodeo circuit during the Boone days so those memories are pretty fresh for this horse-loving girl. When people referred to him as Davy Crockett, it confused me a little bit because in my mind he played Daniel Boone. It was in my teens that I realized that there was an entirely different generation that knew him as Davy Crockett. Through my adult years, Davy Crockett definitely took center stage over Daniel Boone; it just seemed to cut a wider cultural path."

She also noticed a difference in his fan base.

"I think that there was a distinct difference between a Davy and Daniel fan," said Ashley. "Age was the first difference. Daniel Boone fans were close to my age and there also seemed to be more of a Christian, home-schooled, way right-of-center aspect to the Boone fans that I never really picked up on with the Crockett fans."

Ely explained his friend's uniqueness.

"To say that Fess was a nice man or a good guy would be telling it straight but greatly understating what he was," noted Ely. "He somehow made everyone feel important. He showed genuine interest in other people's lives. He managed that difficult chore of keeping contact with his friends—and he had a multitude of them. He was easy to be with and fun, but more than anything else about him was his obvious honesty. I have always taught my children that people attract what they project. A person's quality as a human being is reflected in the people he chooses as friends. The simplest form of this statement is the old adage that a man is judged by the company he keeps. With that in mind, I can best summarize Fess and Marcy with a comment I made in offering a toast to them on one of their anniversaries. At that time I said, 'I have never met a person introduced to me by Fess or Marcy as their friend that I did not like.' That holds true to this day."

Ed Ames concurred.

"One by one he would deal with each person and give them his full attention," said Ames. "There was something Lincolnesque about Fess. That's why he remembered people and remembered names: he was genuinely interested when he met and spoke with them. And people should also know that he did a lot of charity events, sometimes incognito, sometimes public and sometimes at his winery. He even hosted a Shakespeare festival at the winery, outside on the property. And he always did them out of the kindness of his heart."

Fess was also involved in Direct Relief International, a Santa Barbara-based organization that "provides medical assistance to improve the quality of life for people victimized by poverty, disaster and civil unrest at home and throughout the world."

Bargiel pointed out that Fess added something to a conversation with a fan, acquaintance or friend.

"You could tell every time that the person or persons who left the conversation left feeling like they were the more important part of the exchange," said Bargiel. "It was genuine and sincere. When he went out horse trading, however, he left his compassion at home. He was tough with a country kind of logic and plain and simple talk. He was a remarkable person to watch in a negotiation. He had the art of listening and he was also gifted with silence, he would bring adversaries out by just kind of quietly sitting there and looking unconcerned about things. And somehow they'd wind up making the deal a little bit better and a little bit better until he finally had the deal made—shaped pretty much the way he wanted it. But always with that gentlemanly skill."

Andrews recalled Fess as "a visionary of the first order" and a devoted family man who he characterized as "honest, tough, strategic, determined, gentle, caring, and kind."

"Fess could accomplish things no one else could due in part to his celebrity but due also in part to many of those characteristics," explained Andrews. "At the same time he was stubborn, ornery, and very willing—and able—to ignore conventional wisdom and advice. He was occasionally emotional. He was unyielding in his political views and convictions and in his sense of right and wrong—politically, ethically, and strategically. His demeanor, height, and overall 'presence' combined to 'take the oxygen out of the air' whenever he entered a room."

Jeanne Ames remembered Fess as a gentleman.

"He was the embodiment of what an American gentleman should be," she said. "He made you feel like a million bucks. He listened to the most minute thing you wanted to say and he was interested. He was truly interested. I never met anyone so interested in what everybody had to say. He met a girlfriend of mine. She told him about her son who was an ardent fan. He met her at another time and immediately asked her, 'How's David?' Of all the things he had to do that day, he remembered meeting her for a second time and asking how her son was. And that's just a small example of how he was in the entire universe."

Andrews explained that Fess "had an uncanny ability to remember people and their names" which he "he used to endear himself to others."

"I do not remember when or under what circumstance I first met Fess, but he did," said Andrews. "He told me that we first met when I was Student Body President at the University of California Santa Barbara. That was during the 1963–64 academic year. To put that in perspective, it was about the time of the assassination of President Kennedy, so I guess I can say I knew Fess for about forty-six years."

Ames said that he still feels the pain of losing his good friend.

"Something will remind me of Fess and it would hit like a hammer—the sense of loss, a great, great loss," said Ames. "I miss him terribly and I'm not ashamed to admit that."

Dr. Rhodes remembered Fess, too. "He was a kind, gentle giant of a man," stated Rhodes. "I've never met a man with his loyalty to his friends, family and his physicians. He never forgot a face in my office, often remembering a nurse or a receptionist several months after one meeting for an appointment."

Morgan Woodward received a clipping from an unidentified newspaper that included a letter written by John Syphrit of North Richland Hills, Texas.

The letter read:

"I was in Vietnam in the late '60s when Fess Parker came for a visit. He was doing the celebrity thing and shaking as many of the guys hands as he could. As the time went on, we presented him with a coin that had our unit insignia on it. He told us that he would keep it with him as long as he lived. Never thought that much about it until…fast-forward 30-something years. I was a wine buyer for a chain here in Texas when I went on a trip to Los Olivos, the location for Parker's winery. A friend who was a friend of Parker's met me there. I was invited to lunch with him and Fess. At lunch I finally got the nerve to ask Fess about the coin. He looked at me and stared for at least a minute. I thought I had embarrassed him and was getting ready to change the subject when he said, 'Ummm.' He reached into his pocket. 'You mean this coin? I told you I would keep it for as long as I lived.' I will never forget that day. Cheers to you, Fess, for that day."

Kristopher never knew Fess as a celebrity—only as his grandfather.

"I remember being in fourth grade on a rainy day when a movie was shown: *The Great Locomotive Chase*," remarked Kristopher. "I knew that he wasn't like other grandfathers. But the celebrity component for me was a manifestation of what made him special—how he remembered everyone's name, how he treated people, his life lessons. He carried himself with a dignity that was mind boggling. It was something special for me to work for him and with him since 2005."

Ashley pointed out that her father was uniquely consistent in his social relationships with everyone.

"I think that dad's manner with friends and fans alike was rooted in his upbringing," said Ashley. "I always used to joke that 'Mackie raised him right.' I'm certain that his dad, F. E., had just as much to do with that but I don't really remember him as he died when I was a baby. As I said at dad's memorial, he just enjoyed visiting with people. I think that is a very Texan thing. I always remember him being very patient with people—I was often alternately awed and annoyed by his patience—and I think it was rooted in his knowledge that he was just so darn lucky to have been chosen for this particular 'ride.' He knew he had been given the opportunity of a lifetime and felt a responsibility to live up to that. He really seemed to connect with people and his ability to remember names was *amazing*! He had amazing stamina. Even into his eighties, he would sit and sign wine bottles, hats, everything, for hours. It was incredibly hard work, but he never complained. He almost seemed re-charged by it. He certainly had a gift."

Indeed he did.

AFTERWORD
"TALKIN' WITH FESS"

It began with a 1987 interview ended with the death of a friend.

For twenty-three years, Fess Parker was someone who I could count on as I published *The Alamo Journal* and *The Crockett Chronicle.* His interviews provided readers with interesting insights to his career as both an actor and as a businessman. For me, it was just plain fun. Occasionally, some folks asked me to contact Fess regarding questions about the *Davy Crockett* series, autographs, photos, invitations, and related matters. Depending on the nature of the request I either contacted him directly or passed on the request to his administrative assistant. On one occasion in the 1990s, Fess was asked to write the introduction to a book. He asked for my assistance and I gladly obliged.

Fess turned sixty-five in 1989, and I thought it would be a good idea to host a birthday party for him. It was understood that he was not going to travel 3,000 miles to New Jersey to consume birthday cake, but my wife, Debbie, and I held the party for him anyway—*in absentia*—in August of 1990. Since Fess was born on August 16 and the real Davy Crockett on August 17, it seemed to be an ideal event. The next year, we hosted another one. And once Fess Parker Wines were available, they became an essential part of the celebration. The Fess Parker-Davy Crockett Birthday Party became an annual event and grew in size. The 1995 party was represented by Fess and Crockett fans from six states; as a matter of fact, the event even received newspaper coverage. "Thank you for the birthday wishes," wrote Fess on August 18, 1998, a day after his seventy-fourth birthday. "It's awfully kind of you to throw a birthday party for me and toast with our wines! What a treat. Thank you."

The most important aspect of Fess' portrayal of Davy Crockett was its influence on a generation of youngsters. The Crockett Craze was more than just a fad—hula hoops were a fad. As a result of the coonskin-cap mania many of those kids, like me, developed a life-time interest in history and continued to enjoy learning more about other famous Americans who helped shaped the nation. Davy Crockett and Daniel Boone were real people who school-age kids could read more about. And as we read, we became associated with other names from the past like Wild Bill Hickok, Annie Oakley, Wyatt Earp, Sitting Bull, and many more. Ah, the good old days. One can only speculate about future generational manifestations which originated with the likes of Teenage Mutant Ninja Turtles, Power Rangers, Transformers, and Harry Potter. Yikes!

Many of Fess' young fans became teenagers when President John F. Kennedy launched his New Frontier. I always thought Kennedy's domestic policy name owed at least something to Disney's *Davy Crockett, King of the Wild Frontier*. Many of those young adults grew up to become teachers, historians, writers, artists, diorama creators, historical interpreters, and history buffs. And some became veterans who gave all.

Unlike any other actor who ever portrayed Davy Crockett or Daniel Boone, Fess maintained a strong bond with his character years after his performances. His appearances at the reconstructed Davy Crockett Cabin-Museum in Tennessee and the Alamo in the 1990s and 2000s were important to him and many appreciated his sincere efforts.

When Fess renewed his effort to get *After Sundown* made he offered me a part in the film as either the character Bob Hayes or Amos Jennings. The part was a small one, to be sure, but the idea of working with my childhood hero in a movie was beyond description. However, the film was never made.

When Fess arrived at David Zucker's 1991 flintlock rifle frolic in Ojai, California, we had a long conversation before joining the others on the make-shift rifle range. As always, Fess was interested in my teaching—what I was teaching, how I was teaching it, and how the kids were responding. He told me that successful teachers should go beyond the classroom in order to make an additional positive impact on society. When I questioned him about how one could make such an impact he suggested that I run for public office! Public office? I felt like Fess in "Davy Crockett Goes to Congress" when Andrew Jackson suggested that he run for Congress. Fess had the "wrong bear up a tree" with me. Of course, while this conversation is going on he's wearing his *Daniel Boone* jacket and clutching a coonskin cap. It was surreal.

Although the theatrical film *Davy Crockett, King of the Wild Frontier* had been out for years on videocassette, the original three hour-long episodes had never been commercially released. I contacted Buena Vista Home Video and requested that the complete episodes be made available to the public. Of course, I had a number of enthusiastic Alamo Society members join me in the effort. We wrote lots of letters and patiently waited for a reply. Finally, on October 6, 1993, I received a letter from Ronald Fulton from Buena Vista Home Video's Consumer Relations department: "The three-hour television program has never been released on videocassette or laserdisc," wrote Fulton. "We have begun the process of its restoration, but it will take approximately one or two years to complete." But it took eight years for the original episodes to be released. Still, the original episodes in the Disney Treasures series were wonderful to have and worth waiting for. Fans of *Daniel Boone*, though, would have to wait even longer.

After reading the "Talkin' With Fess" column in *The Alamo Journal* for years, members of the Alamo Society, many of whom were fans of Walt Disney's *Davy Crockett* and *Daniel Boone*, wanted to see the frontier hero in person. Fess had an open invitation from me to attend the organization's annual symposium but he was always too busy. However, he finally accepted to be the guest of honor at the 1994 Alamo Society Symposium in San Antonio. I was thrilled but quickly realized that anything could happen and he might not be able to show. I explained to my fellow Alamo Society members that Fess was a busy man and there was always the possibility that he would have to cancel at the last minute. They wouldn't hear it.

March 6, 1994 arrived and Alamo Society members waited for Fess to appear at the Emily Morgan Hotel, the site of the symposium. And they waited. I started to get nervous. I delayed the opening of the symposium as long as I could but since he didn't appear, I had to begin. But then I had no idea what I was going to do next, and

The author and Fess Parker in front of the Alamo, March 6, 1994.
AUTHOR'S COLLECTION.

I wondered what the members of the Alamo Society were going to do to me if he didn't show up. Fortunately, I saw Fess enter a side room where he promptly put on his coonskin cap and his *Daniel Boone* jacket.

I exhaled.

Moments later, I started to introduce him as the musical introduction from *Davy Crockett, King of the Wild Frontier* was strategically piped through the room's audio system.

But he didn't come in on cue.

He deliberately stopped at the entrance to the room and delivered a squinty-eyed grin in my direction. It was one of his pranks and the joke was on me. Meanwhile, everyone at the symposium was squirming in their seats. It seemed like an eternity. Finally, with a big smile, he entered the room. And as all the adults turned into nine-year olds, I finally relaxed.

He introduced himself as Davy Crockett, to the delight of the crowd, and then spoke sincerely about the unsatisfactory commercial environment that surrounded the Alamo. Upon completion of his presentation he patiently signed countless autographs and posed for photos. After the symposium we had our photos taken in front of the Alamo and then went to lunch at Mi Tierra, a popular restaurant located in El Mercado, San Antonio's historic market square. He enjoyed Mexican food; in fact, he enjoyed food period. More than that, he enjoyed the conviviality of dining with others. To Fess, there was something special about sitting down at a bountiful table with family, friends, and acquaintances.

Fess contributed to my *Alamo Almanac & Book of Lists* book in 1997. He provided "Fess Parker's Most Memorable Scenes from 'Davy Crockett at the Alamo.'" Three years later he contributed "Fess Parker's Top Ten Most Memorable Scenes from *Davy Crockett, King of the Wild Frontier* to *The Davy Crockett Almanac and Book of Lists.* And I dedicated the book to him.

"Thank you for sending me a copy of your wonderful book," wrote Fess in a letter dated April 4, 2000. "I was touched by your dedication and I am honored that you found my portrayal of Davy Crockett 'absolutely unique' and 'the most memorable of all' from Crockett and Alamo films. I congratulate you on this publication and all of your achievements in teaching and I wish you much success in your future projects."

My childhood hero was still encouraging me and I appreciated that.

When we later crossed paths, he signed a copy of *The Davy Crockett Almanac and Book of Lists*: "For my friend, Wm. R. Chemerka, Continued Success in History and Life!"

Nice.

During my last year as a high school history teacher, I was pleasantly surprised to be the only educator in my state to receive the Award of Recognition from the New Jersey Historical Commission. When Fess found out, he sent a letter to Marc Mappen, Executive Director of the organization. "I have known Mr. Chemerka for a number of years and have never met anyone more dedicated to our past and to honoring the accomplishments and celebrating the annals of courage in our history," wrote Fess. "I congratulate you and Mr. Chemerka and hope that you will continue to provide teachers with the necessary support to talk about our American history in a way that is a living testament to our good fortune."

I kept pinching myself. Here was the guy who got me excited about early American history, the man who inspired me to become a teacher of history. And decades later, he's writing generous words about me.

In the summer of 2003, I created *The Crockett Chronicle*, a quarterly journal dedicated to the life and legend of David Crockett, as a companion to *The Alamo Journal*. The "Talkin' With Fess" column would be the publication's regular feature, a way in which television's frontier hero could stay in touch with his appreciative fans. But when some readers asked about his health, I carefully avoided answering the questions. Fess told me to keep that information to myself. And I did.

When my wife and I moved into our new home in 2003, a floral centerpiece was delivered to us just before Thanksgiving—well wishes from Fess and Marcy. Typical. And we regularly exchanged birthday and Christmas cards.

In January of 2004, I received a request from a fellow Alamo Society member, Tom Feely, a Vietnam vet and a gifted diorama and miniature figure artist. Feely had just finished a four-year project: a huge Battle of the Alamo diorama that included over 2,000 54mm detailed figures on a massive 336 square-foot base. But he wanted to include one more figure: Fess as Crockett. He requested Fess' permission, even though it wasn't necessary. When I informed Fess about Feely's military service and his creative project, he quickly approved. Feely was delighted.

Fess and I returned to San Antonio in March of 2004. I assisted Dave Stewart, then Director at the Alamo, in organizing a program in which Fess would present a flintlock rifle to the Alamo that had been given to him in 1955 by the National Rifle Association. Medal of Honor recipient Merritt Austin Edson was at the presentation, a soldier Fess held in the highest regard. "I want to be helpful to the Alamo," said Fess, who later donated the rifle during an official ceremony at the Alamo. He also approved an entertainment idea of mine: a performance of "The Ballad of Davy Crockett." Fellow Alamo Society members Tony Pasqua and Frank Thompson joined me in the sing-a-long in front of the Alamo Church. We later joined Fess for lunch. What a great day!

Fess, Ashley, and I had stayed at the Riverwalk Vista a few blocks from the Alamo. Fess showed up for breakfast on March 5, 2004, and started to drink some coffee. Then he paused and said, "You know what I just realized after all these years?" Ashley and I waited for his reply. "When I auditioned for Walt Disney and sang 'Lonely,' I never realized that he was the world's biggest train buff. It wasn't that I sang just a song for him with my guitar; it's that the song was about a *train*. That's why I got the part of Davy Crockett."

The next morning, Fess made a "surprise" visit to the Alamo Society Symposium at the Crockett Hotel. Fess and I pre-arranged that he would slip in the back of the room near the end of the symposium. During my concluding remarks from the podium, I "noticed" that someone entered the meeting without paying the $5 admission charge. I criticized the individual and asked him to step forward and pay. Some in the audience became uncomfortable with the atmosphere that had developed between me and the stranger in the back of the room. Then the individual walked down the center aisle towards the podium. As he walked by, each row of attendees noticed that it was Fess. A standing ovation greeted him by the time he joined me at the podium. Fess remained to sign autographs and have his photo taken. And he signed an I.O.U. to me for $5!

At the "Fess Parker—Celebrating an American Icon" event, which was held on March 30, 2004 at the Carmichael Auditorium at the Smithsonian Institution's Museum of American History, he told the crowd: "Bill Chemerka. I hope some of you will introduce yourself to Bill. He's sitting right over here on the corner. He knows more about Disney and all of this than I do."

I was floored.

After he answered the last question from the audience he paused on stage and looked my way again.

"I'd just like to say one other thing about my friend, Bill Chemerka, who brought his wife, Debbie, with him tonight," explained Fess. "Bill has told me a long time ago that because of his interest in American history—partly generated by Davy Crockett—he became the number one history teacher in New Jersey and upon his retirement the number one teacher in the state of New Jersey."

I was floored again. My 1986 Outstanding Teacher of American History Award and my 2001 Award of Recognition by the New Jersey Historical Commission had been elevated to an unimaginable level, courtesy of my childhood hero. Then he said, "Bill, would you stand up and let everybody…" The generous applause shrouded his last words. That was a wonderful moment.

Fess and Ashley traveled to Manhattan a few days after the Smithsonian event in order to participate in a few more wine promotion events and media interviews. On April 4, we had lunch at Charlie Palmer's Métrazur and later returned to the Iroquois Hotel to participate in another round of questions and answers. At the end of the interview, Fess told me that his visit to the East Coast was "probably going to be my last." On April 7, Fess and Ashley flew back to California.

Weeks later, in the May 2–8, 2004 issue of *TV Guide*, he was the focal point of an article that asked, "Whatever Happened to Fess Parker?" Fess was always amused by nostalgic articles that essentially questioned his status on the planet. "I'm still here," laughed Fess.

Later in the year, a 2004 trip to Fess' home was particularly memorable.

One of the original nineteenth-century flintlock rifles used in the "Davy Crockett Goes to Congress" episode was purchased at auction a year earlier by veteran motion picture production and story-board illustrator Joseph Musso, who has worked on over one hundred motion pictures and television programs. Musso and I had been friends and fellow Alamo Society members since 1986. He asked me if I could arrange a trip to see Fess so that he could sign the rifle. I complied. Accompanied by Dan Gagliasso, a co-writer of *Boone and Crockett: The Hunter Hero*, we met Fess at his Wine Country Inn & Spa on June 30, 2004. Fess treated us to a pleasant private wine and hors d'oeuvre luncheon on the back patio of the Inn. Afterwards, our gracious host signed the rifle stock in gold pen: *Fess Parker "Davy Crockett."* Musso was extremely happy and Gagliasso was enjoying himself, too. We could have departed for Los Angeles with a great memory, but the day was young. "How'd you like to see the property?" asked Fess. "Yes!" exclaimed the three of us in child-like unison. Fess took us on a thrilling three-hour Hummer tour of his property, and I sat in the front seat like a George Russel-like motor-vehicle sidekick. Fess enjoyed the ride as much as we did. He enthusiastically described numerous details about his vineyards, the undeveloped land, and his distant "next door" neighbor, Michael

The author with Fess Parker, who is holding Joseph Musso's *Davy Crockett* rifle in Los Olivos, California, June 30, 2004.
AUTHOR'S COLLECTION.

Jackson. We ended the day with Fess and Marcy at a special dinner at the Inn.

Always aware of anniversary dates, I made it a point to phone him on December 15, 2004; January 26, 2005; and February 23, 2005, the fifty-year anniversary dates of the first three *Davy Crockett* episodes. He was amused and appreciative.

The 60th anniversary of the end of World War II was in 2005, and I thought it would be appropriate to send Fess a Veterans Day greeting. "Bill: thanks for the Veterans Day thought," he wrote on November 16, 2005. "Six weeks short of three years in the Navy and little to show for my room and board."

Although Fess didn't want a biography there was nothing to stop me writing about his experience as Walt Disney's *Davy Crockett, King of the Wild Frontier.* It seemed to be a great idea for a book. I traveled to the various locations where *Davy Crockett* was filmed—from Cherokee, North Carolina and Nashville, Tennessee to Thousand Oaks, California and Sound Stage #3 at the Walt Disney Studios in Burbank. After conducting research and some interviews, I promptly contacted Wendy Lefkon, Editorial Director of Disney Editions/ Disney Press about the book proposal. She politely responded on October 12, 2006. "Unfortunately, I've discussed this with our sales team and at this time they are not confident that we could place and sell enough copies of a Davy Crockett book to make the numbers work," wrote Lefkon. "I met Fess some years ago and I am a fan myself, but I'm afraid it won't fit into our publishing plans in the near future."

Disney not interested in *Davy Crockett*? It couldn't be true.

I responded to her e-mail message and reminded her of the many unique retail possibilities which included the Alamo Gift Museum and Walt Disney theme park stores. Lefkon replied on October 18, 2006. "Thanks again for your note," she wrote. "I had a chance to speak to the sales team again and I'm afraid they just don't think there is enough of a market in traditional book channels for us to make a go of this. I also spoke to our book sales person at Walt Disney World and she feels the market at Walt Disney World would be minimal at best so I'm afraid we just aren't going to make this happen."

Despite the rejection, I was determined to one day acknowledge Fess' iconic portrayal in book form.

Fess' controversial land deal with the Chumash had generated some negative responses from members of the community. Nothing was more obvious than the "Fess" stickers that were affixed to stop signs in the Santa Ynez Valley. As a counter to that, I sent to him, as a birthday gift, a custom "Don't Mess With Fess" T-shirt, which was inspired by the Lone Star State's anti-litter slogan, "Don't Mess With Texas." He thanked me for the shirt and told me the gift was "great," but I doubt that he ever wore it while walking the streets of Los Olivos. Fess Parker Enterprises finally sold the 1,390-acre property to the Chumash in April 2010.

Over the years, a number of businessmen and entrepreneurs approached me with projects that involved Fess, and a few of their endeavors were produced. The "Fess Parker Daniel Boone Playset," manufactured by Barzo Playsets, immediately comes to mind as the best item I was associated with. Ron Barzo, who was inspired by the wonderful toy playsets of the 1950s and 60s, took special care in making his "Daniel Boone" offering. It featured a number of plastic buildings, figures, accessories, and a 5-inch by seven-inch autographed photo of Fess. Since it involved Twentieth Century Fox and royalties on each set that was sold, Fess' attorney, Chuck Bargiel, was brought in on the negotiations. The deal was settled and the excellent sets were manufactured.

In 2006, the Alamo Society celebrated its 20th anniversary and Fess was kind enough to send a special letter of acknowledgment to the group. In the letter he generously noted my accomplishments and I was very appreciative. However, in a follow-up phone call, he discussed his on-going health problems. He described them as just another situation that one must deal with in life. Talk about optimism and bravery.

At lunch one year in Los Olivos, Marcy thanked me for "helping Fess." What had I done? She told me she was pleased that I had maintained an ongoing dialogue between her husband and his many fans through *The Alamo Journal, The Crockett Chronicle*, and various Alamo Society symposiums. I was too choked up to say, "You're welcome." But she could see it in my eyes.

Months later, I arranged for Fess to be interviewed for *Playset Magazine's At the Alamo* DVD (Atomic Home Video). The magazine wanted Fess to appear with one of the Marx Alamo playsets which had originally been issued during the Crockett Craze. I emphasized that a simple photo session of Fess with the playset would be better than a video-taped session since he was eighty-two years old at the time and not in the best of health. Nevertheless, Fess agreed to the video-taped interview. The completed DVD featured Fess awkwardly attempting to organize pieces of the playset while being asked questions about the "Davy Crockett at the Alamo" episode. It was somewhat uncomfortable to watch.

In 2007, Fess sought names for his new hotel and asked me for some ideas. My offerings included the Fess Parker En Calma Resort, the Fess Parker Marea Resort, the Fess Parker Fuego del Holgar Resort, and a few others. He rejected them all! In a July 14, 2007 e-mail he instructed me that I needed a "romantic element" to my proposed title. He instructed to keep in mind such elements as "Bel air" and "shutters." He ordered me to "keep thinking" and I offered such choices as Seascape Vista, Four Winds, Ocean Garden, Pacific Terrace, and El Pacifico Terraza. He wasn't impressed. Fess responded with, "Thanks, Bill. Looking for a single name such as 'Bahia.'"

Oh well, I tried.

Fess appreciated a bound set of *Crockett Chronicles* I sent him in 2008. "I've been glancing through the research you did on Davy Crockett and it's quite impressive," stated Fess. "It's quite a resource document."

I had worked extensively with Fess in his effort to reclaim what he perceived as his proper percentage of *Davy Crockett* merchandising sales. I compiled a complete list of the Disney merchandise from my collection and other privately-held collections, and attempted to track down legal documents in Maryland where a copyright on Crockett was allegedly held. Fess asked me to keep the concern private until it could be resolved. However, it never was.

I was working on *What Went Down: The Alamo*, another History Channel series in 2008. The main action segments of the documentary were filmed in San Antonio and Dripping Springs, Texas, the site of the 2004 film, *The Alamo*. The director and his production team needed additional interview footage of me at their Los Angeles studio so I was flown out; Debbie, accompanied me. During the interview sessions, a few photos of Fess and me were edited into the production. I appreciated that Fess and I were on the screen together for a few moments. Once taping was completed Debbie and I planned to visit Disneyland for several days.

Adhering to Fess' "open invitation" rule, I gladly informed him about our forthcoming California visit. He was pleased and immediately scheduled a day for our visit. Upon our arrival, we

The author, Debbie Chemerka, and Fess Parker standing in front of a Buddy Ebsen painting at the Fess Parker Wine Country Inn & Spa, June 2008.
AUTHOR'S COLLECTION.

phoned him and he told us to wait for him in the lobby of his Wine Country Inn since it was too hot to stay outside. "Look for me at the front door and we'll have lunch," instructed Fess.

We waited patiently.

Suddenly, a baseball cap flew through the lobby like a tomahawk!

"Howdy!" said Fess who had entered through another doorway. He was wearing a cowboy hat and one of his patented squinty-eyed grins. "Mr. Chemerka and Mrs. Chemerka," proclaimed Fess. "Welcome. Let's have some lunch."

He later introduced us to his new car, a previously-owned, black 2004 Mercedes Benz S600. "Everybody needs to drive one of these one day," beamed Fess. "It's a used one, but I love it." Fess drove us to his office where we sat in a conference call in which the new hotel was discussed. Afterwards, he drove us back to the Inn where we had parked, and we said goodbye in his air-conditioned car. As I got out of the car, my cell phone fell out of my pocket and into a nearby storm drain. It was lost—at least that's what I assumed. Fess said, "I'll take care of that." He got on his cell phone and within minutes two of his employees arrived with tools and a ladder. They removed the storm drain cover and one of them climbed down to retrieve my cell phone from the dry storm drain floor. Cool. I thanked Fess and he drove off. He turned around at the corner and waved to us as he headed back to the office. That's the last time I saw him.

Fess was kind enough to write the wonderful Foreword to *Music of the Alamo: From 19th Century Ballads to Big-Screen Soundtracks*, the book Allen Wiener and I wrote in 2008. Fess was raised on Texas music and enjoyed sharing the information in the book.

Whenever I was at Walt Disney World, I would always keep an eye out to make sure that Fess and Davy Crockett were correctly represented. Call it my personal Coonskin Crusade. Although Disneyland had more of a history with Fess, the Lake Buena Vista, Florida-based theme park still had a Frontierland and such attractions as the Davy Crockett Explorer Canoes and the Mike Fink Keelboats. And coonskin caps and toy Old Betsy rifles were available for purchase. But in 1994, the Davy Crockett Explorer Canoes attraction closed and three years later the Mike Fink Keelboats were dry-docked. The imitation coonskin caps were replaced by another faux-fur creation which didn't even mention Davy Crockett on the label. Finally, the Old Betsy rifles were replaced by colorful pirate guns.

During one visit, I noticed that the Grand Floridian Café dinner menu made a reference to Fess Parker Wines and mentioned that Fess portrayed Daniel Boone. There was no mention of Fess' role as Walt Disney's *Davy Crockett.* I politely complained and the menu was corrected. And I was constantly reminding the Crockett Tavern staff at the Fort Wilderness Campground to properly showcase Davy Crockett. Finally, a new exhibit debuted there in 2009, and I wrote about it in a *Celebrations* magazine article, "Davy Crockett: King of the Wild Frontier(land)" the following year. Unfortunately, the few *Davy Crockett* collectibles that shared a showcase in One Man's Dream at Walt Disney World's Hollywood Studios were removed during the attraction's 2010-2011 refurbishment.

We continued to conduct the "Talkin' With Fess" interviews for *The Crockett Chronicle* but by 2009 he started to lose the rich strength that I had been accustomed to listening to. As he battled his illness and the treatments, Fess always maintained an optimistic posture. He had a great deal of courage. But then again, he was a World War II veteran. And that speaks volumes.

In the autumn of 2009, Lou Mongello of WDW Radio conducted an interview with me at Walt Disney World's Frontierland about Fess and *Davy Crockett.* It was an ideal setting and fun to do. Mongello, a knowledgeable and gracious host, archived the interview [Show #145; November 15, 2009, at www.wdwradio.com]. I phoned Fess about the interview and he was pleased. But he didn't sound well.

During a stay at Walt Disney World on December, 20, 2009, I phoned Fess from the Prime Time Café at Hollywood Studios. The restaurant served Fess Parker Chardonnay, and Debbie and I always made it a point to go there and salute Fess with a toast. I told him that we were drinking his wine and he replied, "That's great!" But his voice sounded even weaker than it did during our previous phone call. I didn't want to tax him any further and politely wished him well and ended the phone call.

I realized that at some point our regular conversations were going to end. I returned from San Antonio during the second week of March and planned to start work on issue #28 of *The Crockett Chronicle.* But because of his illness there was no reason for me to phone him about the "Talkin' With Fess" column.

My phone rang on March 18. It was Ashley. She informed me that her father had died hours earlier. He was gone, and I felt the loss immediately. It wasn't a complete surprise but it was still a shock. And then images of Fess flew across my mind—as *Davy Crockett*, as the man I met at the San Antonio airport in 1987, as the host of wonderful meals at his Inn. Debbie and I promptly sent flowers and a sympathy card to Marcy, Ashley, and Eli. The lives of Fess, Davy Crockett, and Daniel Boone had come full circle. Fess and Crockett were both born in August and both died in March; Fess and Boone both died at age 85.

Debbie and I were invited to the special memorial for Fess a week later but we were already on the road—to Walt Disney World, of all places. On the day of the memorial, we went to the place in Hollywood Studios where Fess had placed his handprints and

Remembering Fess Parker.
Author's collection.

autograph back in 1992. I reached down and placed my hands in his prints. The morning had been much cooler than normal but it seemed as if the Florida sun had warmed the concrete. It had to be the sun.

Upon our return home, Ashley phoned me again. "I felt awful about calling you but knowing that the press release was going out shortly I couldn't imagine you hearing it on the news," she said.

And that's when his death really hit me. The man of great dignity and courage, the man of personal responsibility and determination, the man of honor and integrity, the man with the squinty-eyed grin who enjoyed practical jokes, the man who was a role model on and off the screen was gone.

Months later Ashley informed me that her father's headstone was completed and in place. She said that it wasn't going to be elaborate because that was not her dad's style; it was simply going to reflect who he was and how his family felt about him.

In Loving Memory
Fess E. Parker Jr.
1924 – 2010

And placed between the years on the headstone was a coonskin cap.

As I was putting finishing touches on this manuscript Ashley contacted me and said that he had forgotten to tell me something that "might be appropriate for the book." She said that on August 7, 2010, the winery held an outdoor film screening of *Davy Crockett and the River Pirates*. Like the previous year's showing of *Davy Crockett, King of the Wild Frontier*, guests sat in lawn chairs and on blankets and waited for darkness. Once the sunset faded over the Pacific Ocean the film began.

But the heavens were about to upstage the event.

"Just a few minutes after the film started, a shooting star went across the sky off to the east, directly above the screen," said Ashley. "I swear it was him stopping by to say, 'Howdy.'"

APPENDIX A

REMARKS UPON THE BURIAL OF FESS E. PARKER, JR. ON MONDAY, MARCH 20, 2010
WRITTEN AND DELIVERED BY CHARLES S. BARGIEL

His life began on August 16, 1924.

It was a Saturday early evening in Fort Worth, Texas.

He was the only child of F. E. Parker and Ricksy McKnight McFarland Allen.

He honored his father and his mother during their lives.

He honored his father and mother throughout all of his own.

During the 31,260 days of his remarkable life upon this earth, he blazed a trail marked by gentility, unpretentiousness, simple manners, natural kindness, genuine modesty, plain courtesy and good example.

That lifelong trail blazed right into the minds and hearts of the whole world.

It blazed into the heart of his bride of 50 years and best friend of 57 years, Marcella Rinehart Parker.

It blazed into the hearts of his family, friends and acquaintances, those who knew him personally.

And it blazed into the hearts of hundreds of millions of fans and admirers across the globe who only knew *of* him, but never had the joy of so much as shaking his hand.

He was the champion of plain people—kids and grownups alike—achieving that renown, in part, by portraying frontier heroes.

Before Fess, few in America knew much about those frontier heroes.

Before Fess, hardly anyone elsewhere in the world knew anything about them.

So he filled the void and taught America and the world that they were tall, handsome, strong, brave, steadfast American patriots, loving family men, good neighbors, community leaders, plain men with a sense of humor who always lent a helping hand to the little guy or anyone in need, who knew the simple difference between right and wrong, who always did right—no matter how high the cost or how great the odds, who proved you could overcome great odds and still do the right thing.

But as he blazed that trail the world learned something more profound about Fess than about those he portrayed: It wasn't, after all, just a role he played.

It was Fess, himself, who was the hero.

It was, in truth, the shining inner goodness of his nature that shone through to us and to all the world.

And because of it, he uniquely was beloved as no other man.

And now we few are honored to be here on this sad day and at this sad moment to say so long.

Thusly honored, we here are duty bound by the honesty he would expect of us.

To remind ourselves of what he so often would say: "The best is yet to come."

In our deep grief, those are unwelcome words today.

We are now without him, yet we still are blessed with the gift of life.

Nonetheless, we are obliged to remember what he said,

To honor him,

To help ourselves and especially for his children, grandchildren, great grandchildren and great, great grand-children.

His words were meant to instruct us today that:

There are horses and mules to ride,
There are airplanes to fly,
There are boats to sail,
There are dreams to dream,
And there are still mountains to climb.
There are trails to be blazed,
And frontier values to be lived,
There are mobile home parks to be built,
Theme parks to be built,
Motels to be built,
Hotels to be built,

There are ranches and livestock to be tended to,
Vineyards to plant,
Grapes to be harvested,
Wine to be made.
There are songs and screenplays to be written.

There are doors to be knocked on, doors to be opened and sometimes doors to be knocked down.

There is hospitality to be bestowed upon family, friends, neighbors, acquaintances and strangers, too.

The bounty at our table is to be shared with others.

There is good food, good wine and good conversation to be enjoyed.

And when meals are over, there are songs to be sung until another day of life is done.

By the example of his life these lessons forever remain among us here and all he touched.

And yet, our deep grief compels us to admit that Thursday last, in the early morning of a new day, a deep and abiding hole was opened in all our hearts.

There persists an unyielding emptiness in our hearts that will never completely heal.

Fess is gone.
This profound loss will not withdraw easily or soon.
Here, too, he is of help to us,
Even on this saddest day of all:

By the example of his great life he tells us today that although grief has its place in life, it is not a place we should "make camp" or "hold up" or "lay low" for very long.

And so, as we trudge along without him, remembering the blessings of life as he taught them, we bear witness today to a truth know the world over: So long as men walk upon the earth, the likes of Fess Elisha Parker, Jr. shall never be seen again.

APPENDIX B

FESS-ISMS

(HOW TO LIVE LIKE FESS PARKER)
FROM COMMENTS DELIVERED BY RICK FOGG AT
FESS PARKER'S MEMORIAL, MARCH 26, 2010

Sing more…and wouldn't you enjoy taking voice lessons, because to sing well would make it so much more enjoyable.

If you ever have the chance, you ought to buy an early 1990s Mercedes two-door coupe, which is the perfect car.

Stand up tall and straight.

When you're in Los Olivos, you're gonna have to learn how to *saunter*.

When you are sick, you ought to "knock it out" with a hot toddy, which—if you do not know—involves a hot towel and a stiff drink.

You ought to be suspicious of corporate vice presidents, who are not to be trusted.

Likewise you ought to be suspicious of excessive involvement by lawyers in business dealings.

You ought to weigh yourself each morning, exercise, and eat more tomatoes to maximize health.

You ought to never consider retiring from work, because remaining engaged in some creative occupation makes life so much more full.

Enjoy the warm company of family and friends, as much as possible around a table with good food, drink, stories, and song.

Doggedly pursue a business challenge—while always on the lookout for a new one.

At all times conduct oneself as a gentleman, particularly in a man's love and devotion to his wife.

Don't back down from a challenge or opposition if you really believe in your cause.

A day's success is defined not by how much money was made or how much work was completed, but rather as a day that held at least one occurrence that was truly fun, creative or surprising.

Help others in need—whenever possible, outside of anyone else's view.

Keep your word.

Don't overcomplicate simple things.

Devote yourself to friendship.

Never be too busy, famous or important to have time for strangers who want to talk to you (or sing to you).

When in a negotiation or horse trade, never shy from asking for everything you want.

Develop a sacred connection with your land.

Let your vision for a real estate project be restrained by good taste, the habits of a good neighbor and practicality over rules.

Tell good stories—particularly if they are sure to get a laugh.

Speak softly.

Be the only one at a business meeting with no business card, no papers, and no anxiety.

Sing old songs, particularly when others least expect it.

Drink good beer at lunch (Chimay if possible) and great wine with dinner (preferably Fess Parker).

Eat spicy foods.

Eat leisurely breakfasts (ideally huevos rancheros with toast burnt and blackened beyond recognition as bread).

Eat ice cream.

Eat doughnuts and cookies.

Drink good coffee.

Be genuinely interested in what other people are saying to you.

Always see things creatively, with vision, and look for untapped opportunity where others may see only problems.

And—perhaps most urgently of all—shouldn't you think of moving your family to the Santa Ynez Valley; after all, what other place could be so beautiful?

FILMOGRAPHY

THE FILMS OF FESS PARKER
(TITLE, YEAR OF RELEASE, AND NAME OF CHARACTER)

Climb and Angry Mountain (1972): Sheriff Elisha Cooper
Smoky (1966): Clint Barkley
Hell Is for Heroes (1962): Sgt. Pike
The Jayhawkers (1959): Cam Bleeker
Alias Jesse James (1959): Davy Crockett [uncredited]
The Hangman (1959): Sheriff Buck Weston
The Light in the Forest (1958): Del Hardy
Old Yeller (1957): Jim Coates
Westward Ho the Wagons! (1956): John "Doc" Grayson
Davy Crockett and the River Pirates (1956): Davy Crockett
The Great Locomotive Chase (1956): James J. Andrews
Davy Crocket, King of the Wild Frontier (1955): Davy Crockett
Battle Cry (1955): Pvt. Speedy
Them! (1954): Alan Crotty
Dragonfly Squadron (1954): Texas lieutenant
The Bounty Hunter (1954): cowboy [uncredited]
Combat Psychiatry: The Division Psychiatrist (1954): U.S. Marine [uncredited]
Thunder Over the Plains (1953): Kirby
Island in the Sky (1953): Fitch's Co-pilot [uncredited]
The Kid From Left Field (1953): McDougal
Take Me to Town (1953): Long John [uncredited]
Springfield Rifle (1952): Jim Randolph [uncredited]
Untamed Frontier (1952): Clem McCloud
No Room for the Groom (1952): Cousin Ben [uncredited]
Harvey (1950) Leslie the chauffeur [uncredited voice-over]

Fess Parker on National Television, Select Appearances

CBS News Sunday Morning (2/27/05)
Hollywood's Talking (3/26/73)
The Andy Williams Show (3/17/71)
The Red Skelton Hour (3/17/70)
The Dean Martin Show (10/9/69; 3/17/72)
The Beautiful Phyllis Diller Show (10/27/68)
The Jonathan Winters Show (1/24/68)
The London Palladium Show (11/6/66)
The Danny Kaye Show (10/6/65)
What's This Song? (12/28/64)
Daniel Boone (9/24/64 – 5/7/70)
Today (9/14/64; 8/25/69)
The Tonight Show Starring Johnny Carson (9/14/64)
Burke's Law (4/3/64)
Destry (2/21/64)
The Alfred Hitchcock Hour (11/8/63)
Mr. Smith Goes to Washington (9/29/62–3/30/63)
G. E. True Theater (4/17/60)
Startime (11/24/59)
Schlitz Playhouse (10/10/58)
Playhouse 90 (4/3/58)
The Ed Sullivan Show (3/4/56; 1/20/57)
City Detective (3/15/55)
Disneyland/Walt Disney's Wonderful World of Color (numerous, beginning10/27/54)
My Little Margie (9/8/54)
Annie Oakley (5/1/54; 5/8/54)
Death Valley Days (4/10/54; 1/26/62)
Stories of the Century (3/18/54)
Dragnet (3/4/54)

DAVY CROCKETT

Initial broadcast dates of the original *Disneyland* episodes and the national theatrical release of the feature film.

1. "Davy Crockett, Indian Fighter" (12/15/54)
2. "Davy Crockett Goes to Congress" (1/26/55)
3. "Davy Crockett at the Alamo" (2/23/55)
4. "Davy Crockett's Keelboat Race" (11/16/55)
5. "Davy Crockett and the River Pirates" (12/14/55)
6. *Davy Crockett, King of the Wild Frontier* (5/25/55)

DANIEL BOONE

TV season and date of initial broadcast; FP = Directed by Fess Parker; * = One of Fess Parker's favorite episodes. ** = Favorite episode of the season as selected by the fans of the Daniel Boone TV Fan Club [www.danielboonetv.com]

SEASON 1:1964–1965

1. "Ken-Tuck-E" (9/24/64) *
2. "Tekawitha McLeod" (10/1/64)
3. "My Brother's Keeper" (10/8/64) **
4. "The Family Fluellen" (10/15/64)
5. "The Choosing" (10/29/64)
6. "Lac Duquesne" (11/5/64)
7. "The Sound of Wings" (11/12/64)
8. "A Short Walk to Salem" (11/19/64)
9. "The Sisters of O'Hannrahan" (12/3/64)
10. "Pompey" (12/10/64)
11. "Mountain of the Dead" (12/17/64)
12. "Not in Our Stars" (12/31/64)
13. "The Hostages" (1/7/65)
14. "The Returning" (1/14/65)
15. "The Prophet" (1/21/65)
16. "The First Stone" (1/28/65)
17. "A Place of 1,000 Spirits" (2/4/65)

18. "The Sound of Fear" (2/11/65)
19. "The Price of Friendship" (2/18/65)
20. "The Quietists" (2/25/65)
21. "The Devil's Four" (3/4/65)
22. "The Reunion" (3/11/65)
23. "The Ben Franklin Encounter" (3/18/65)
24. "Four-Leaf Clover" (3/25/65)
25. "Cain's Birthday, Part 1" (4/1/65)
26. "Cain's Birthday, Parr 2" (4/8/65)
27. "Daughter of the Devil" (4/15/65)
28. "Doll of Sorrow" (4/22/65)
29. "The Courtship of Jericho Jones" (4/29/65)

Season 2: 1965–1966

30. "Empire of the Lost" (9/16/65) *
31. "The Tortoise and the Hare" (9/23/65)
32. "The Mound Builders" (9/30/65)
33. "My Name is Rawls" (10/7/65)
34. "The Old Man and the Cave" (10/14/65)
35. "The Trek" (10/21/65)
36. "The Aaron Burr Story" (10/28/65)
37. "The Cry of Gold" (11/4/65)
38. "The Peace Tree" (11/11/65)
39. "The Thanksgiving Story" (11/25/65)
40. "A Rope for Mingo" (12/2/65) **
41. "The First Beau" (12/9/65)
42. "Perilous Journey" (12/16/65)
43. "The Christmas Story" (12/23/65) *
44. "The Tamarack Massacre Affair" (12/30/65)
45. "Gabriel" (1/6/66)
46. "Seminole Territory" (1/13/66)
47. "The Deserter" (1/20/66)
48. "Crisis of Fire" (1/27/66)
49. "The Gun" (2/3/66)
50. "The Prisoners" (2/10/66)
51. "The Fifth Man" (2/17/66)

52. "Gun-Barrel Highway" (2/24/66)
53. "The Search" (3/3/66)
54. "Fifty Rifles" (3/10/66)
55. "The Trap" (3/17/66)
56. "The Accused" (3/24/66)
57. "Cibola" (3/31/66)
58. "The High Cumberland, Part 1" (4/14/66)
59. "The High Cumberland, Part 2" (4/21/66)

SEASON 3: 1966–1967

60. "Dan'l Boone Shot a B'ar" (9/15/66)
61. "The Allegiances" (9/22/66)
62. "Goliath" (9/29/66)
63. "Grizzly" (10/6/66)
64. "First in War, First in Peace" (10/13/66)
65. "Run a Crooked Mile" (10/20/66)
66. "The Matchmaker" (10/27/66)
67. "Onatha" (11/3/66)
68. "The Loser's Race" (11/10/66)
69. "The Enchanted Gun" (11/17/66)
70. "Requiem for Craw Green" (12/1/66) **
71. "The Lost Colony" (12/8/66)
72. "River Passage" (12/15/66)
73. "When a King is a Pawn" (12/22/66)
74. "The Symbol" (12/29/66)
75. "The Williamsburg Cannon, Part 1" (1/12/67) *
76. "The Williamsburg Cannon, Part 2 (1/19/67) *
77. "The Wolf Man" (1/26/67)
78. "The Jasper Ledbedder Story" (2/2/67)
79. "When I Became a Man, I Put Away Childish Things" (2/9/67)
80. "The Long Way Home" (2/16/67)
81. "The Young Ones" (2/23/67)
82. "Delo Jones" (3/2/67)
83. "The Necklace" (3/9/67)
84. "Fort West Point" (3/23/67) *

85. "Bitter Mission" (3/30/67)
86. "Take the Southbound Stage" (4/6/67)
87. "The Fallow Land" (4/13/67)

SEASON 4: 1967–1968

88. "The Ballad of Sidewinder and Cherokee" (9/14/67) **
89. "The Ordeal of Israel Boone" (9/21/67)
90. "The Renegade" (9/28/67)
91. "Tanner" (10/15/67)
92. "Beaumarchais" (10/12/67)
93. "The King's Shilling" (10/19/67)
94. "The Inheritance" (10/26/67)
95. "The Traitor" (11/2/67)
96. "The Value of a King" (11/9/67)
97. "The Desperate Raid" (11/16/67)
98. "The Spanish Horse" (11/23/67)
99. "Chief Mingo" (12/7/67)
100. "The Secret Code" (12/14/67)
101. "A Matter of Blood" (12/28/67)
102. "The Scrimshaw Ivory Chart" (1/4/68)
103. "The Imposter" (1/18/68)
104. "The Witnesses" (1/25/68)
105. "The Flaming Rocks" (2/168)
106. "Then Who Will They Hang From the Yardarm If Willy Gets Away?" (2/8/68) FP
107. "The Spanish Fort" (2/15/68); also known as "Fort New Madrid"
108. "Hero's Welcome" (2/22/68)
109. "Orlando, the Prophet" (2/29/68)
110. "The Far Side of Fury" (3/7/68)
111. "Nightmare" (3/14/68)
112. "Thirty Pieces of Silver" (3/28/68)
113. "Faith's Way" (4/4/68)

SEASON 5: 1968–1969

114. "Be Thankful for the Fickleness of Women" (9/19/68)
115. "The Blackbirder" (10/3/68)
116. "The Dandy" (10/10/68)
117. "The Fleeing Nuns" (10/24/68)
118. "The Plague That Came to Ford's Run" (10/31/68) FP
119. "The Bait" (11/7/68)
120. "Big, Black and Out There" (11/14/68)
121. "A Flag of Truce" (11/21/68)
122. "The Valley of the Sun" (11/28/68)
123. "The Patriot" (12/5/68) FP **
124. "The Return of the Sidewinder" (12/12/68)
125. "Minnow for a Shark" (1/2/69)
126. 'To Slay a Giant" (1/9/69)
127. "A Tall Tale of Prater Beasely" (1/16/69)
128. "Copperhead Izzy" (1/30/69)
129. "Three Score and Ten" (2/6/69)
130. "Jonah" (2/13/69)
131. "Bickford's Bridge" (2/20/69)
132. "A Touch of Charity" (2/27/69)
133. "For Want of a Hero" (3/6/69)
134. "Love and Equity" (3/1/3/69)
135. "The Allies" (3/27/69)
136. "A Man before His Time" (4/3/69)
137. "For a Few Rifles" (4/101/69)
138. "Sweet Molly Malone" (4/17/69)
139. "A Pinch of Salt" (5/1/69)

SEASON 6: 1969–1970

140. "A Very Small Rifle" (9/18/69)
141. "The Road to Freedom" (10/2/69)
142. "Benvenuto…Who?" (10/9/69)
143. "The Man" (10/16/69)
144. "The Printing Press" (10/23/69)
145. "The Traitor" (10/30/69)

146. "The Grand Alliance" (11/13/69)
147. "Target Boone" (11/20/69)
148. "A Bearskin for Jamie Blue" (11/27/69)
149. "The Cache" (12/4/69)
150. "The Terrible Tarbots" (12/11/69)
151. "Hannah Comes Home" (12/25/69) FP *
152. "An Angel Cried" (1/8/70) FP
153. "Perilous Passage" (1/15/70)
154. "The Sunshine Patriots" (1/22/70)
155. "Mama Cooper" (2/5/70) * **
156. "Before the Tall Man" (2/12/70)
157. "Run for the Money" (2/19/70)
158. "A Matter of Vengeance" (2/26/70)
159. "The Landlords" (3/5/70)
160. "Readin', Ritin', and Revolt" (3/12/70)
161. "Noblesse Oblige" (3/26/70)
162. "The Homecoming" (4/9/70)
163. "Bringing Up Josh" (4/16/70)
164. "How to Become a Goddess" (4/30/70)
165. "Israel and Love" (5/7/70)

Mr. Smith Goes to Washington

1. "Washington Hostess" (9/29/62)
2. "Bad Day at Cuttin' Corners" (10/6/62)
3. "...But What Are You Doing For Your Country?" (10/13/62)
4. "The Musicale" (10/20/62)
5. "The Country Sculptor" (10/27/62)
6. "The Senator and the Pageboy" (11/3/62)
7. "The Fork in the Road" (11/10/62)
8. "First Class Citizen" 11/17/62)
9. "The Senator Baits a Hook" (11/24/62)
10. "For Richer or Poorer" (12/1/62)
11. "Man's Best Friend" (12/8/62)
12. "The Sleeping Sentry" (12/22/62)
13. "Without a Song" (12/29/62)

14. "That's Show Business" (1/5/63)
15. "Miss Ida's Star (1/12/63)
16. "Think Mink" (1/19/63)
17. "The Resurrection of Winesap Corners" (1/26/63)
18. "Oh, Pioneers" (2/2/63)
19. "Grand Ol' Opry" (2/9/63)
20. "And Still the Champ" (2/16/63)
21. "Citizen Bellows" (2/23/63)
22. "Kid From Brooklyn" (3/2/63)
23. "To Be or Not to Be" (3/9/63)
24. "High Society" (3/16/63)
25. "The Lobbyist" (3/23/63)
26. "Cloak and Dagger" (3/30/63)

The episodes of *Mr. Smith Goes to Washington* are available in black and white 16mm film for on-site viewing at UCLA's Television Collection. "The Resurrection of Winesap Corners" episode is listed in the UCLA collection as "The Resurrection of Winesat Corners."

FESS PARKER
Recordings on the *Billboard* Charts

Billboard magazine expanded its "Best Sellers in Stores" chart of 25 recordings to "The Top 100" chart on November 12, 1955. The expanded chart incorporated several charts including the "Best Sellers in Stores," "Most Played in Juke Boxes," and "Most Played by Jockeys" rosters. Thus, the Weeks on Chart length for "The Ballad of Davy Crockett" reflects a 25-position chart, while the duration for "Wringle Wrangle" represents a 100-position chart. However, "Wringle Wrangle" reached the #12 position on the "Best Sellers in Stores" chart on February 23, 1957.

Song Title	Chart Debut	Highest Position	Weeks on Chart
"The Ballad of Davy Crockett"	3/12/55	#5	17
"Wringle Wrangle"	1/26/57	#21	10

BIBLIOGRAPHY

Abbott, John S. C. *David Crockett: Hs Life and Adventures.* New York: Dodd, Mead & Company, 1874.

Chemerka, William R. *Alamo Almanac & Book of Lists.* Austin, TX: Eakin Press, 1997.

Chemerka, William R. *The Davy Crockett Almanac and Book of Lists.* Austin, TX: Eakin Press, 2000.

Chemerka, William R. and Allen J. Wiener. *Music of the Alamo: From 19th Century Ballads to Big-Screen Soundtracks.* Houston, TX: Bright Sky Press, 2008.

Cobia, Manley. *Journey into the Land of Trials: The Story of Davy Crockett's Expedition to the Alamo.* Franklin, TN: Hillsboro Press, 2003.

Craddock, Jim, editor. *Videohound's Golden Movie Retriever.* Farmington Hills, MI: Gale Cengage Learning, 2010.

Crockett, David. *A Narrative of the Life of David Crockett of the State of Tennessee.* Philadelphia: E. L. Carey and A. Hart, 24th edition, 1837.

Draper, Lyman C. *The Life of Daniel Boone.* Ted Franklin Belue, editor. Mechanicsburg, PA: Stackpole Books, 1998.

Ebsen, Buddy. *The Other Side of Oz*. Newport Beach, CA: Donovan Publishing, 1993.

Ellenshaw, Peter. *Ellenshaw Under Glass—Going to the Matte for Disney*. Santa Clarita, CA: Camphor Tree Publishers, 2003.

Finch, Christopher. *Art of Walt Disney: From Mickey Mouse to the Magic Kingdoms*. New York: Harry N. Abrams, 1973.

Glut, Donald F., and Jim Harmon. *The Great Television Heroes.* New York: Doubleday & Company, 1975.

Grabman, Sandra. *Spotlights & Shadows: The Albert Salmi Story.* Albany, GA: BearManor Media, 2003.

Groneman, William III. *David Crockett: Hero of the Common Man*. New York: Tom Doherty Associates Book, 2005.

Hauck, Richard Boyd. *Crockett: A Bio-Bibliography*. Westport, CT: Greenwood Press, 1982.

Lackman, Ron. *The Encyclopedia of 20th Century Television*. New York: Checkmark Books, 2003.

Smith, Dave. *Disney A to Z: The Updated Official Encyclopedia.* New York: Hyperion, 1998.

Todish, Tim J. and Terry S. *Alamo Sourcebook 1836: A Comprehensive Guide to the Alamo and the Texas Revolution.* Austin, TX: Eakin Press, 1998.

Walt Disney's Davy Crockett, King of the Wild Frontier Exhibitors Campaign Book. Buena Vista Film Distribution Company, Inc., 1955.

Whitburn, Joel. *Joel Whitburn Presents the Billboard Pop Charts: 1955-1959.* Menomonee Falls, WI, Record Research, Inc., 1992.

INDEX

95300569R00232

Made in the USA
Middletown, DE
25 October 2018